Thomas Kruessmann (Ed.)

Moving beyond the "Kosovo Precedent"

Grazer Beiträge zum Recht der Länder Südosteuropas und der Europäischen Integration

herausgegeben von

Prof. Dr. Dr. h.c. Wolfgang Benedek
Prof. Dr. Tomislav Borić
Prof. Dr. Hubert Isak
Prof. Dr. Joseph Marko
Prof. Dr. Dr. h.c. Willibald Posch

Band 4

LIT

Moving beyond the "Kosovo Precedent"

EU-Integration for Moldova and the South Caucasus

edited by

Thomas Kruessmann

LIT

Printed with support of the Government of Styria
and the University of Graz

Das Land Steiermark
→ Wissenschaft und Forschung

UNI GRAZ

Bibliographic information published by the Deutsche Nationalbibliothek
The Deutsche Nationalbibliothek lists this publication in the Deutsche Nationalbibliografie; detailed bibliographic data are available in the Internet at http://dnb.d-nb.de.

ISBN 978-3-643-90599-4

A catalogue record for this book is available from the British Library

Klosbachstr. 107
CH-8032 Zürich
Tel. +41 (0) 44-251 75 05 Fax +41 (0) 44-251 75 06
E-Mail: zuerich@lit-verlag.ch http://www.lit-verlag.ch

Distribution:

In the UK: Global Book Marketing, e-mail: mo@centralbooks.com
In North America: International Specialized Book Services, e-mail: orders@isbs.com
In Germany: LIT Verlag Fresnostr. 2, D-48159 Münster
Tel. +49 (0) 2 51-620 32 22, Fax +49 (0) 2 51-922 60 99, E-mail: vertrieb@lit-verlag.de

In Austria: Medienlogistik Pichler-ÖBZ, e-mail: mlo@medien-logistik.at
e-books are available at www.litwebshop.de

ACKNOWLEDGEMENTS

The young scholars who participated in this project had the privilege of meeting a number of outstanding practitioners from among the EU institutions and the foreign policy community in Brussels. The initial conversations held with them in the course of a three-day study trip in September 2011 provided much inspiration and helped sharpen the understanding of the complex policy dimensions that are inherent in the EU's proclaimed goal of establishing a "ring of friends" in its neighbourhood towards the East. Further thanks needs to be extended to the Centre for European Studies at the State University of Tbilisi which hosted a dissemination conference in March 2012. In the course of this conference participants managed to refine a number of arguments. More importantly, the presentation gained additional "transformation flavour", as participants were able to see the effects of EU integration of at least one country of the South Caucasus with their own eyes.

For the study trip to Brussels in September 2011, special thank goes to the following persons who shared their time generously and offered invaluable insight into their work:

Members of the European Parliament

- Elmar Brok
- Knut Fleckenstein
- Ulrike Lunacek
- Monica Macovei
- Werner Schulz

Representatives of other EU institutions

- Rainer Emschermann (DG Enlargement)
- Katerina Lopo and Remi Duflo (EEAS Desk Officers)
- Isabelle Combes and Pier Luca Lepri (DEVCO – Geographical Coordination Neighbourhood East)
- Laurent Muschel (Deputy Head of Cabinet, Commissioner Malmström)

Permanent Representatives to the EU[1]

- H.E. Ambassador Selim Küneralp, Permanent Delegate of the Republic of Turkey to the EU

[1] For reasons of time it was impossible to meet with more diplomatic representatives, although an effort was made to address all relevant missions.

- H.E. Ambassador Avet Adonts, Head of the Mission of the Republic of Armenia to the EU
- Minister Plenipotentiary David Solomonia, Deputy Head of the Mission of the Republic of Georgia to the EU

Finally, special thanks needs to be extended to the head of the EU Delegation to Georgia, H.E. Ambassador Philip Dimitrov and his entire team who proved to be helpful on many occasions.

PREFACE

STYRIA – REGION UNLIMITED

In times of an ever-growing global planet, regional co-operation is a critical success factor. The main aim is to cross borders through common projects – for example in the fields of economics, science, culture and sports – and to broaden one's horizon, to exchange innovative ideas and to profit from one another in order to enhance the quality of life of people living in a region. Styria has been transcending borders in various fields for many years.

In the field of economics Styrian enterprises have been constantly developing new products, services and technologies to enter new markets. In order to achieve this goal, they transgress geographical borders and established thought concepts and patterns of action. Due to this orientation on innovation, Styria is the most innovative region in Austria, having a research and development quota of 4.6 percent and is, moreover, ranked among the top innovation regions in Europe. Styria has thus been granted the award "European Entrepreneurial Region 2013" by the EU.

The regional government's department for Europe also aims to transgress borders. Intensifiying relations with our neighbouring regions is thus a main focus in Styria's European strategy. With its Centre for Russian, East European & Eurasian Studies, the University of Graz has been an important partner in helping to overcome existing boundaries between Styria and Russia and the Black Sea region, respectively.

This book, renders the experiences of South-Eastern European countries on their way to integrate into a common Europe accessible for the Black Sea region.

I hope you will enjoy reading this book and it will stimulate your desire to transgress and overcome many boundaries in your future life.

Dr. Christian Buchmann
Regional Minister for Economic Affairs, Europe and Culture
Styria, Austria

TABLE OF CONTENTS

AA	Association Agreement
AP	Action Plan
BiH	Bosnia and Herzegovina
BSEC	Black Sea Economic Co-operation
BSS	Black Sea Synergy
CEI	Central European Initiative
CEFTA	Central European Free Trade Agreement
CFSP	Common Foreign and Security Policy
CIS	Commonwealth of Independent States
CoE	Council of Europe
CSF	Civil Society Forum
CSDP	Common Security and Defence Policy
CSES	Common Space on External Security
CSTO	Collective Security Treaty Organization
DCFTA	Deep and Comprehensive Free Trade Agreement
EA	Europe Agreement
EAEC	Eurasian Economic Community
EaP	Eastern Partnership
EC	European Community/ies
ECHR	European Convention on Human Rights
ECtHR	European Court of Human Rights
ECJ	Europen Court of Justice
ed/s	editor/s
EEC	European Economic Community
EEAS	European External Action Service
ENP	European Neighbourhood Policy
ENPI	European Neighbourhood and Partnership Instrument
EP	European Parliament
EU	European Union
EUBAM	EU Border Assistance Mission to Moldova and Ukraine
EUMM	EU Monitoring Mission in Georgia
EURATOM	European Atomic Energy Community
EURONEST	EU-Neighbourhood East Parliamentary Assembly
GBER	General Block Exemption Regulation
ICC	International Criminal Court
ICCPR	International Covenant on Civil and Political Rights
ICESCR	International Covenant on Economic, Social and Cultural Rights
ICJ	International Court of Justice
ICTY	International Criminal Tribunal for the former Yugoslavia
IDP	internally displaced person(s)
MEP	Member of the European Parliament
NATO	North Atlantic Treaty Organization
NSD	New Strategic Direction
OHR	Office of the High Representative
OSCE	Organization for Security and Co-operation in Europe
PCA	Partnership and Co-operation Agreement
SAA	Stabilisation and Association Agreement

SECI	Southeast European Cooperative Initiative
SEE	South Eastern Europe
SELEC	Southeast European Law Enforcement Center
SGC	Southern Gas Corridor
TANAP	Trans-Anatolian Pipeline
TAP	Trans-Adriatic Pipeline
TFEU	Treaty on the Functioning of the European Union
UN	United Nations
UNHCR	United Nations High Commissioner on Refugees
WTO	World Trade Organisation

Beqiri, Romina

is a PhD candidate in International Law at the European University of Tirana in Albania and graduated from Lund University in Sweden with an LL.M in International Human Rights Law. She works in the fields of International Criminal Law, Human Rights and Public International Law. Currently she is performing a legal internship at the Organisation for the Prohibition of Chemical Weapons (OPCW). Previous positions include legal intern at International Criminal Court (ICC), trainee at EU Delegation to Albania, research assistant in Raoul Wallenberg Institute of Human Rights and Humanitarian Law (Lund Sweden), lecturer in "Minority Rights" and "Albanian Political and Judicial Thought".

Davitashvili, Gvantsa

holds a Bachelor of Jurisprudence Degree from Georgian Technical University and an LL.M (Master in Southeast European Law & European Integration) from the University of Graz. Currently, she is a Ph.D. researcher at the University of the Basque Country at the Faculty of International Relations. She was an invited lecturer at Georgian Technical University and Batumi State University. At different times she has been also working for an American Bar Association project and for the Transparency International Georgia. She is the author of several publications in Georgia.

Devidze, Aleqsandre

holds a B.A. degree in Law from Technical University of Georgia and an LL.M. degree (Master in Southeast European Law & European Integration) from the University of Graz. Currently he is head of Legal Department at United Water Supply Company of Georgia - Ministry of Regional Development and Infrastructure of Georgia.

Dias, Vanda Amaro

is a Ph.D. candidate in International Politics and Conflict Resolution at the School of Economics, University of Coimbra. She has worked at the Institute of International Law and International Relations, University of Graz, as a Marie Curie fellow. She received her M.A. in Political Science and International Relations from the Nova University of Lisbon and her B.A from the same institution. Her research interests include EU Foreign and Neighbouring Policies, European Security, Russia and the former Soviet Space. She has participated as a speaker in several international conferences and her research has been published in peer-review journals such as European Security and Perspectives on European Society and Politics.

Ergen Breitegger, Sezen

is regional manager / legal counsel at the Turkish Desk of Lansky, Ganzger + partner Vienna. In 2009 she graduated from the Law Faculty of Galatasaray University and also studied at Vrije University of Amsterdam during a semester abroad. Thereafter she worked at a prominent law firm as a legal trainee and became a registered attorney in 2011 at the Bar Association of Istanbul. She acquired her LL.M Degree of International and European Business Law with distinction at the University of Vienna as a Jean Monnet scholar and is currently pursuing another title (LLM private law) at Galatasaray University.

Harutyunyan, Ani

holds a Master's degree in International Relations and International Law from Yerevan State University, Armenia. She is also a graduate of the Diplomatic Academy of Armenia. She has several publications on the topics of the law of armed conflict. After gaining experience in the Ministry of Foreign Affairs and the Government of Armenia, as well as in different international organisations such as OSCE, ICC, Russian UNEPCOM, she is currently an assistant professor at the Russian, East-European & Eurasian Studies Centre of the University of Graz.

Harzl, Benedikt

graduated in Law from the University of Graz and holds an MA degree in East European Studies from the Free University of Berlin. After international work and research experience gained at the Institute for German Studies in Minsk, the German Council on Foreign Relations in Berlin and the European Academy of Bolzano / Bozen, he is now assistant professor at the Russian, East European & Eurasian Studies Center at the University of Graz. His research concentrates on legal accommodation of diversity in post-Soviet states and EU foreign policy. He is currently writing his PhD at the University of Frankfurt in this particular field.

Lapiashvili, Nino

is Director of the Institute for European Studies of the Tbilisi State University and Visiting Professor at Law Faculty of Tbilisi State University since 2009. She is teaching Theory of Law and The Law of EU External Relations. She was awarded a Master of Science in Policy Studies from the University of Edinburgh in 2008. In 2006 she obtained an LLM degree in Human Rights after successful completion of Central European University, Faculty of Law Program in Human Rights in Budapest, Hungary. Earlier she has graduated from Tbilisi State University (LLB and MA degrees in 2005)., During 2006-2009 she was heading the Unit of Integration of Georgia in European and Euro-Atlantic Structures of the International Relations Department of the Ministry of Internal Affairs of Georgia where she, *inter alia*, was responsible for the elaboration and implementation of the human rights protection related national action plans (NAPs) including the NAP on Anti-Trafficking in Persons. In 2004-2006 she was working as the Legal Advisor at the Ministry of Justice of Georgia.

Midorović, Sloboda

graduated in law from Novi Sad University in Serbia and earned her LL.M. degree (Master in Southeast European Law & European Integration) from the University of Graz. She was a member of the Vojvodina Bar Association from 2010 until 2013. Since 2012 she was also affiliated with the Faculty for Legal and Business Studies in Novi Sad as an external associate (corporate and commercial law). Currently she is employed at the Development Fund of the Autonomous Province of Vojvodina as a senior associate for legal affairs.

Mocanu, Eugenia

holds the degree of Licentiate in Law with a focus on Constitutional and Administrative Law from Moldova State University and an LL.M (Master in Southeast European Law & European Integration) degree from the University of Graz. She was a visiting student at EuroCollege, University of Tartu. At different times she has been working for Election Observation Missions to Moldova, United Nations Office in Vienna and other international organisations. She is an arbitrator at Willem C. Vis International Commercial Arbitration Moot. She is a Member of the Association of Certified Fraud Examiners.

Orhei, Aelita

works as an attorney-at-law and as CEDR (Centre for Effective Dispute Resolution)-certified mediator. She is with Gladei & Partners law firm since 2008 and holds the position of Senior Associate since 2010. The legal practice of the firm has a strong focus on corporate and commercial law. Aelita has participated in most of the firm's assignments for different clients and has expertise in general business law, commercial litigation, competition law, corporate law, labour law, tax law, IP, and regulatory issues. Aelita received her LL.M degree from the University of Graz (Master in Southeast European Law & European Integration) and her bachelor degree in Economic Law from Moldova State University. Aelita is a contributor for World Bank Doing Business Surveys "Getting Credit - Legal Rights – Moldova", "Enforcing Contracts – Moldova" (2008-2014); Contributor for the Investing Across Borders (IAB) indicators (Investing across sectors, Starting a foreign business and Accessing land) project, implemented by the International Finance Corporation (IFC) and the World Bank (2009-2010); Co-author of "Securities and Banking" and "Insurance" COMPLINET articles, jurisdiction overview: Moldova (2009 - 2013) and author of numerous articles on legal subjects in a local weekly newspaper "Economist".

Samoilova, Elizaveta

is a PhD candidate in European Law at the University of Graz. She received her master's degree and worked as an assistant professor at the Department of European Law of the University of Graz as well as the Russian, East European & Eurasian Studies Centre at the same institution. Her fields of research concern the External Relations of the EU and the EU's policy towards its Eastern Neighbours. In 2014, she was a trainee at the Austrian Constitutional Court as well as a visiting researcher at the European University Institute in Florence.

Šaranović, Aleksandra

holds a Bachelor's Degree in Law from the University of Montegro and is currently enrolled in the LL.M. Programme "Master in Southeast European Law & European Integration" of the University of Graz.

Surmava, Lita

graduated in 2002 from Ivane Javakhisvhili Tbilisi State University, Faculty of International Law and International Relations, majoring in International Law, with honours. In 2005 she was awarded an LLM in EU Law from Stockholm University (Sweden) and in 2013 a PhD degree in Law from Tbilisi State University. She is a holder of various international scholarships, amongst them from Swedish Institute and the University of Lodz. She is an alumna of the Fund for Development and Reforms under the President of Georgia. From 2006 she works as assistant professor at Tbilisi State University, by 2013 she additionally became associate professor at New Vision University (Georgia) and also invited professor at the American University of Humanities, Tbilisi Campus. Currently she is Head of International Relations Division at the Ministry of Agriculture of the Republic of Georgia. Her research fields are EU institutional law, competition law, legal approximation and harmonisation.

Wagner, Lorin-Johannes

studied Law at the University of Graz and the University of Helsinki. He received his doctoral degree from the University of Graz. He was Assistant Professor at the Department of European Law at the University of Graz and is now working at the Institute of Minority Rights at the European Academy in Bolzano. His research interests include European Data Protection Law, the legal status of Union citizenship and European fundamental rights.

Part 1:

Introduction by the Editor

Thomas Kruessmann

INTRODUCTION BY THE EDITOR

"Four years ago we had political declarations, recommendations and programmes to address reforms in this part of eastern Europe but if we are able to sign one of those Association Agreements and initial others, for the first time we will make a quantum leap towards the real transformation in that post soviet space and I do not know whether you would agree or not that this is a game changer."

Štefan Füle[1]

1. SOME GENERAL REMARKS

"Moving Beyond 'the Kosovo Precedent'" is the short title of a research project that set out to study the lessons learned in the EU integration of South Eastern Europe, in particular the Western Balkan countries, and study their usefulness for Moldova and the South Caucasus. The shorthand "Kosovo" used to be seen as a synonym for "frozen conflicts"; later on the question whether the declaration of independence of Kosovo from Serbia was legal and legitimate[2] became one of the central bones of contention not only in dealing with the breakaway territories of Moldova, Georgia and the dispute around Nagorno-Karabakh. Its supposed illegality under international law has also become a central doctrine of Russia's foreign policy *vis-à-vis* its "near abroad", and it is used to create a powerful precedent in supporting self-determination of Russian-speaking populations in Ukraine and beyond.

In looking "beyond the 'Kosovo precedent'" this research will not only cover post-conflict resolution in ex-Yugoslavia from a security point of view, but the EU integration of South Eastern Europe[3] in a comprehensive and holistic fashion. The reason for doing so is that South Eastern Europe has become a fascinating laboratory of EU integration, and possible "lessons learned" must be assessed in their use-

---

1 Manuscript of the speech of EU Commissioner for Enlargement and Neighbourhood Policy *Štefan Füle* (to be checked against delivery), addressing the Third Ordinary Session of the EURONEST Parliamentary Assembly, Brussels, on 28 May 2013, available at <http://europa.eu/rapid/press-release_SPEECH-13-477_en.htm>.

2 See on this issue the ICJ's Advisory Opinion of 22 July 2010, available at <www.icj-cij.org/docket/index.php?p1=3&p2=4&case=141&p3=4>.

3 Arguably, the Republic of Moldova due to its intimate relationship with Romania is very often considered as a part of South Eastern Europe already. However, in the current political process Moldova shares a greater commonality with the countries of the South Caucasus than with Romania.

fulness for the challenges facing the Republic of Moldova and the countries of the South Caucasus. Still, what was originally conceived of as an academic project has now also become a critical companion on the entire Eastern Partnership (EaP) process. Writing this introduction at a time when not only Ukraine is in crisis, but the entire EaP at the crossroads and the signing of the AAs with Georgia, Moldova and Ukraine perceived by Russia as the next blow to its economic and security interests, there should not be a second of triumphalism. Indeed, the EaP has run into rough waters, and it is not for the "Russian factor" alone, but also for the technocratic approach that so far has prevailed in the EU's external relations with its post-Soviet neighbourhood.

The introductory quote by Commissioner *Füle* when read against the background of the Russian annexation of Crimea, and also against calls for "re-unification" with Russia in Eastern Ukraine and unrest in the breakaway territories of Moldova and Georgia, lends a whole new meaning to the term "game changer". Indeed, the "game" has been changed, its rules re-written in a way that nobody deemed possible in the 21st century. It would of course be unfair to blame the EU alone in this process. But the abovementioned quote transmits the sense of urgency that many of the EU key decision makers felt in the run-up to the Vilnius EaP summit in November 2013. A benevolent reading would suggest that the EU's impatience with breaking the deadlock of post-Soviet economies and creating welfare for everyone in a joint neighbourhood is an entirely good thing. A more critical reading would suggest that the EaP for one reason or the other has become an arena in which the EU is seeking quick successes, perhaps even over frustration about accession delays in the Western Balkans, or, as critics might claim, for geo-strategic reasons and / or to conquer new markets for EU businesses. One way or the other, it was two months before the Vilnius summit when *Putin*, speaking at the Valday International Discussion Club in September 2013, made it unequivocally clear: "Eurasian integration is the chance for the entire post-Soviet space to become an independent centre of global development, and not a periphery for Europe or Asia."[4] Statements like these were no singular incidents, and they should have served as writing on the wall for the entire political class in the West.

The scholars who participated in this project share an affiliation with the University of Graz. Most of them are graduates of the LL.M. programme "Master in South East European Law & European Integration" which is the flagship programme of the University's Law Faculty. Supported by a generous grant from the Styrian government, these researchers set out to understand the critical lessons learned in the EU integration process with regard to South Eastern Europe, identify the key policy issues as seen from a Brussels perspective, and translate them into a legal analysis of developments in their home countries.

According to the EU rule book, "enlargement" and "neighbourhood" are distinct concepts, the latter being defined by the lack of a membership perspective. This fundamental dichotomy has been part of the message sent by EU Member States and the Council for the longest time, and it is a tenet that countries such as Georgia and – to a lesser extent – Moldova have never accepted. And indeed, the European

---

[4] <http://kremlin.ru/news/19243>.

Parliament (EP) in its Resolution of 17 April 2014 "On Russian pressure on Eastern Partnership countries and in particular destabilisation of eastern Ukraine" emphasized that "the AAs with Ukraine and the other EaP countries do not constitute the final goal in their relations with the EU", rather "that, pursuant to Article 49 of the TEU, Georgia, Moldova and Ukraine – like any other European state – have a European perspective and may apply to become members of the Union…". While reiterating the letter of Art 49 TEU and stipulating the usual preconditions such as adherence to the principles of democracy, respect of fundamental freedoms and human and minority rights as well as rule of law, this explicit mentioning of the membership perspective in the current crisis situation indicates a watershed in the thinking of the EP. The current AAs follow this approach by taking into account "that this Agreement shall not prejudice and leaves open the way for future progressive developments in EU-Georgia [respectively "EU-Republic of Moldova"] relations".[5]

On the ground, distinctions between "enlargement" and "neighbourhood" have always become fuzzy when broken down to a technical level. In fact, when comparing the terms "accession" and "association" the differences begin to wither, and very often the famous saying "anything but institutions" becomes the last resort for the teacher of European integration studies. So it is not just academic thinking out of the box, but indeed an approach grounded in practical politics that calls for the integration experience of South Eastern Europe to be used as a measure for discussing the (legal) dimensions of EU policies *vis-à-vis* its Eastern neighbours.

From an editor's point of view, two particular challenges stand out that are symptomatic not only for the presentation of papers in this book, but also for the state of research in the entire field:

The first challenge is the regional approach. Considered by the EU as *de rigueur* in light of the integration experience of the Western Balkans and developed into a mix of regional incentives and bilateral ("regatta principle") relationships, it nevertheless fails to embrace the true complexity of the region. Technically, EaP countries are in another "box" as Turkey which is – from a bilateral point of view - an accession candidate, but in reality a regional power in its own right with a pronounced Black Sea agenda. And again technically, the Russian Federation is not part of the EaP process while Belarus is, but in a confederation with Russia. Apart from such classifications, the real problems appear to lie in the complexities of decision-making in the EU Commission (High Commissioner for Foreign Affairs and Security Policy / EEAS versus the portfolios of the Commissioner for Enlargement and ENP and the Commissioner for Development) and the desire in the Council to informally delegate the EaP agenda to the new Member States in the East which for historic reasons have a more contentious relationship with the Russian Federation.

---

5 Recital 6 of the Association Agreement (AA) between the EU and EURATOM and their Member States, of the one part, and Georgia, of the other part, available at <http://eeas.europa.eu/georgia/pdf/eu-ge_aa-dcfta_en.pdf>. Likewise Recital 4 of the AA between the EU and EURATOM and their Member States, of the one part, and the Republic of Moldova, of the other part, available at <http://eeas.europa.eu/moldova/pdf/eu-md_aa-dcfta_en.pdf>. Both AAs were signed on 27 June 2014 and are currently in the process of ratification by the EU member states.

Adopting a holistic view to the entire region, e.g. in the current crisis by consulting not only with the Ukrainian central Government, but also Crimean Tartars, Turkey, North Caucasus Islamists and the Russian Government, appears to be possible only in moments of crisis. But in everyday work the EU pursues its policies according to the standing programmes and funding schemes.

The second challenge which is less obvious to see concerns the assumptions made about legal approximation as the day-to-day business of association. Legal approximation from the EU's point of view is seen as a technical business, requiring in essence the same kinds of legal transformations as are typically required in the context of EU Member States implementing directives. It is only in a very summary way that weak institutions and widespread corruption are acknowledged also for the EaP region. But while the little understanding that we have about the functioning of post-Soviet law in Russia[6] is very often brushed aside by "law in the books vs. law in action" talk, there is actually complete ignorance when asked about the legal cultures of the EaP region. While the EU's deep engagement with societies of South Eastern European countries has produced at best clichés of "balkanesque" situations, in the EaP region we have not come further than stating some diffuse post-Sovietism, devoid of any positive analysis. This is not to promise that this book will contribute some positive knowledge on these issues, but it is meant to indicate a trap that EU external relations specialists sometimes fall into. Having among the contributors of this volume a large number of young scholars who have obtained advanced training in the EU before going back to their home countries, sometimes now even working at State Ministries, leaves us hoping that some grounded skepticism is applied in their analysis after all.

2. DESCRIPTION OF THE VOLUME'S ORGANISATION AND OF THE INDIVIDUAL PAPERS

This book presents an example of interdisciplinary work. Starting with introductory chapters written from a political science perspective that analyse the relevant policy frameworks, followed by an analysis of the wider regional dimension, the main body of the collection comprises a variety of technical papers which are devoted to key issues of legal transformation. Contributors were encouraged to identify the policy choices as perceived by the EU (primarily the EU Commission) and reflect on them in the light of their own country experience. For educational purposes each chapter starts with a quote from the relevant AAs concluded with the Republic of Moldova and Georgia to show how the issues under consideration are framed in the newest agreements governing bilateral relations.

The first section is entitled "Black Sea and the South Caucasus: Using the Southeast European Integration Experience as a Toolbox for the European Neighbour-

---

6 See e.g. *Hendley*, Varieties of Legal Dualism: Making Sense of the Role of Law in Contemporary Russia, Wisconsin International Law Journal 2012 Vol 29 No 2, 233-262.

hood Policy". It contains a peculiar juxtaposition of two policy-oriented papers and one trying to gauge the legal content of the new and very critical Art 8 TEU for integration in the neighbourhood. The first chapter by *Harzl* is a sweeping analysis of the ENP as the overall policy framework, the second by *Dias* continues by focusing on the EaP and Black Sea Synergy (BSS) in particular. While by today's standards the BSS has not seen many public successes, the EaP is so much at the centre of attention that one may even forget that it is only an ancillary policy of the ENP. Indeed, some of the points that *Harzl* identifies as weaknesses of the ENP have actually now come into the open in the EaP framework while other criticisms have effectively been addressed and accommodated. Among the group of problems is the EU's preoccupation with regional approaches. Clearly a legacy of policies in Southeastern Europe, the EU believes in regions where the countries concerned have not even developed a regional identity. This can be safely said both for the Black Sea and for the South Caucasus. At the same time the EU closes its eyes on the true regional players, i.e. Turkey and Russia, and in particular to the Eurasian integration dimension that appears as some kind of iceberg in the mist towards which the EU is heading.

Interestingly, compared to the foregoing analysis *Dias* arrives at a diametrically opposed position. She presents BSS and EaP as twin programmes, not only simultaneously launched, but also interlinked and even overlapping in agendas and policy priorities. She sees the EU taking account of the interests and *modi operandi* of the two players Russia and Turkey while at the same time adopting a pragmatic and cautious approach to the South Caucasus. In any case, both authors agree that the impact of the ENP and its related policies has been rather limited.

One ongoing theme is whether the promises of market access and mobility (people-to-people contacts) will be enough of a "soft pull" to convince the governments of the Republic of Moldova and the South Caucasus to adopt the kind of structural reforms that will effectively break the vicious circle of autocratic rulership, oligarchic networks, lack of transparency and accountability, corruption and manipulation. It is at this point that *Davitashvili* with her technical analysis of Art 8 TEU contributes to the discussion initiated between the first two papers. If it is true that people in the Republic of Moldova and the South Caucasus (albeit to varying degrees) see themselves as Europeans, it will be safe to say that they will not just care for access to Western consumer goods or travel opportunities, but for what Euromaidan showed in the clearest of ways: the desire to belong to the Western world.

Against this background Art 8 TEU creates a fundamental puzzle: assuming that the EU is a community built on law and that the "founding fathers and mothers" of the Treaty of Lisbon, short of adopting a Constitution, agreed to enshrine a specific competence to conclude neighbourhood agreements, how can the ENP as a mere policy framework override this commitment and deny a membership perspective? The issue of membership is the single-most wanted prize, and by opening the door to membership or even integration short of membership the EU created a publicity stunt that nobody in the Commission would have dared to imagine. As *Davitashvili* shows, there is much technical debate on the interpretation of Art 8 TEU, but fundamentally the mere existence of this provision presents a promise that citizens of Georgia, Ukraine and Moldova will hold on to. And, as the case of Ukraine shows, it will put EU politicians into a very difficult situation between the legitimate aspirations of “neo-Europeans” (who are actually among the oldest Europeans) and domestic constituencies concerned about their own well-being.

The second section is entitled “Regional Powers and their Interplay with the EU’s Strategy in the Black Sea and the South Caucasus Region”. Adding the Black Sea concept as another regional concept is not an invention of this research project, of course. Instead, it is something that the EU brought up to recognize the importance of Turkey beyond the bilateral perspective of an accession candidate. Turkey is next to Russia the second Eurasian power in the region, and despite its obvious connection to the Black Sea it maintains bilateral relationships with all three South Caucasus countries. However, those bilateral relationships are not independent of each other. In particularly Azerbaijan keeps a very keen eye on any Turkish-Armenian rapprochement. And although relationships between Turkey and Russia are traditionally good and constructive, the various roles played by the two countries in the South Caucasus conflicts, especially the Russian-Georgian war of 2008, puts them often in an uncomfortable situation *vis-à-vis* each other.[7] Interestingly, very little is known on the position of Turkey *vis-à-vis* the Republic of Moldova.

In the paper on Russia[8] *Samoilova* chronicles the history of a difficult relationship. The same impression of a multi-dimensional and not always straightforward relationship appears in the analysis of *Ergen-Breitegger and Harutyunya*n when looking at the EU-Turkey dimension. But when taking the two analyses and putting them side by side, a number of important differences emerge. It appears that from the days when the Soviet Union collapsed Russia was always seen as “special” by the EU, - an entity that by its sheer geographical size and magnitude of its potential could never be placed into one basket with ordinary accession candidates. Turkey, on the other hand, was considered by the EU for the longest time a hapless accession candidate which reached economic integration fairly early on, but never delivered on the kind of Western reforms that Europeans expected. So while on the one hand EU policies showed a lot of respect to Russia, they very often carried an air of impatience and indignation at the unwillingness of (predominantly Muslim) Turkey to become “fully Western”. It is safe to say that this traditional attitude has changed within the last couple of years. Both Russia and Turkey showed extraordinary economic successes (although many Europeans tend to dismiss these achievements as windfalls without structural merit) that bolstered regional and even global ambitions; on the other hand the USA under *Obama* are not as vigorously defending their geostrategic interests as in the past. This new world order creates a lot of uncertainties for the EU especially when dealing with the Republic of Moldova and the South Caucasus. It appears that the EU is preferring bilateral relations (where it is always stronger) or multilateralism among “friends” (which individually can be brought to heel, if they do not follow), but is unable to formulate its policies in an inclusive way that would take account of the interests of the two regional powers Russia and Turkey. This lack of coherence is undesirable when it comes to creating the kind of “game-changing” agreements that Commissioner *Füle* mentioned. But it

[7] For more details see <http://m.ceip.org/publications/?fa=55945>.
[8] „Russia“ is being used here as shorthand for the Russian Federation.

is outright disastrous when considering that the EU's first goal was to create energy security not only for itself, but also for the countries in its neighbourhood.

The third section is entitled "Signature Issues in the EU Integration of South Eastern Europe and their Relevance for the Black Sea and South Caucasus Regions". It starts with two papers by *Wagner* and *Mocanu* which should be read in conjunction. While *Wagner* presents a nuanced answer to the question whether and to which extent an EU member state is limited by EU law in pursuing an expansive citizenship policy, *Mocanu* examines the case of Romania and Moldova where it has been claimed that Romania, by generously granting Romanian and thus EU citizenship to Moldovan citizens, is actually undermining the EU's common immigration policy approach and the instrument of visa liberalisation.

The following paper by *Devidze* is a broad comparative analysis in the field of rule of law. He argues that the European spirit in applying human rights laws in a country's judiciary is best served when constitutional courts become judicially active. Drawing on a wide array of case law from various Central, East and Southeast European Constitutional Courts he manages to show that constitutional courts are far more than guardians of national constitutions, but actors in the European integration process of their countries.

Beqiri and *Midorović* present a joint analysis that addresses one of the most visible "lessons learned" from the conflicts in the Western Balkans, but perhaps also one of the most difficult. In the Republic of Moldova (Transnistria) and the South Caucasus the level of atrocities may not have been as high as in the Balkans, but the military conflicts that erupted in and around the breakaway territories of Georgia and in Nagorno-Karabakh have been no less vicious and led to numerous suffering and losses. While "hot" conflicts lasted only for a short time, the ensuing "frozen conflict" period means that governments involved have a vested interest in delaying investigations and using the fate of those who suffered as bargaining chips in the continuation of conflict. In the research, the examination of the ICTY experience and co-operation in the Western Balkans makes it possible to draw a parallel between South Caucasus-ICC-EU and the Western Balkans-ICTY-EU strategy for integration.

A part of the international crimes committed during the conflicts in the South Caucasus concerns the question of property rights, especially property in land and housing. It is in this field that *Šaranović* presents a fascinating analysis of the practice of return and restitution developed by the international community in Bosnia-Herzegovina (BiH) which is now gradually taken over by local authorities. This study contains a large number of best-practice examples, but it also shows how ill-conceived policies can be used to undermine the process.

Lapiashvili traces in her paper the connection between high levels of crime in Georgia's breakaway territories and the isolation of local populations. Drawing on the lessons learned from the Kosovo, but also on the Kaliningrad compromise with Russia, she does see a role for "soft conditionality" by the EU even in the absence of a clear membership perspective for Georgia. In her opinion, enhanced travel possibilities will empower local populations and help them to refuse to be taken hostage by *de facto* bureaucracies and governments.

The chapter on state aid by *Orhei and Surmava* is a fascinating comparative analysis between the Republic of Moldova and Georgia in one of the most crucial and painful areas of legal approximation. While both countries are best-known for their agricultural products, Moldova's economy (including Transnistria) underwent an explicit industrialisation and integration into the larger COMECON production schemes. This industrialisation followed not so much an economic, but a political logic, and it went hand in hand with the influx of large Russian-speaking populations to keep this part of the Soviet empire under control. Georgia, on the other hand, did not experience an outright russification. It was always among the richest republics of the Soviet Union, but its wealth was not attributable to large industrial production capacities. Experience from the equally fragmented post-Yugoslav space showed that the difficulty in introducing state-aid rules is not so much correlated to the amount of "old" industries, but to the problem of changing culture. For this reason *Aelita and Surmava* go beyond the technical details of state-aid rules and emphasize the importance of building a constituency for change by explaining what amount of flexibility is built into state-aid rules.

3. CONCLUSION / OBSERVATIONS

It is now clear that the idea of raising the amount of engagement with the EaP countries and bringing the EU (and possibly NATO, as is feared in Russia) closer to the Russian neighbourhood turned out to be a "game changer", but in quite a different way than Commissioner *Füle* expected. In fact, the "road to Vilnius" and beyond, if seen through the official statements of the EU, is one of over-ambitiousness and neglect of sensibilities. While the prospect of visa liberalisation was handed out as a carrot to post-Soviet populations eager to adopt a European life style, the idea of DCFTA's remained removed from people. Instead, it was brought to the attention of elites who did not see trade liberalisation as an instrument of bringing welfare to the people, but one of bolstering their own positions of economic and political power. The current Russian administration understood this currency of power far better than EU diplomats and technocrats, and so the oligarchs – as can be seen in Ukraine and Transnistria – are becoming increasingly the linchpins of the EU's external action.

It is now only Georgia that has gone through the ordeal of defending its position versus Russia and will remain a staunch ally of the EU (and NATO) in the foreseeable future. Moldova, even though it is being heralded as a showcase of legal approximation and especially visa liberalisation, is utterly vulnerable due to the fact that it cannot isolate itself from Russian-inspired developments in Gagauzia and Transnistria. In fact, the Moldovan parliamentary elections scheduled for 30 November 2014 will offer Russia a welcome possibility to help communists return to power by threatening to destabilise Moldova. Armenia pulled back from signing its AA with the EU in the last minute, causing utter consternation among the EU political elites. And Ukraine is now even beyond the brink of economic, if not political disaster. This leaves two more countries: Azerbaijan, keeping aloof and carefully balancing its interests, and Belarus firmly tied to the Russian Federation and without any leeway to negotiate an independent position *vis-à-vis* the EU.

Back in May 2013 when addressing the EURONEST Parliamentary Assembly *Füle* acknowledged: "The more we cooperate with our partners the more we feel the need to strengthen and widen the exchange of views with Russia." This is surely the correct approach. But it will be very difficult to convince the Russian counterparts of the EU's good intentions, when the dominating perception of "the West's" behaviour (thus putting the EU with NATO and the U.S. into one boat) is one of deception and double-standards.

This book offers a variety of perspectives on the EU integration experience in South Eastern Europe and how the "lessons learned" might play a role in the development of the EaP process. What this book calls for is contextualising expert knowledge, not succumbing to the logic of military violence and intimidation. It also calls for explaining values and defending them. Much of what appears to be an issue of technical legal approximation is actually about the implementation of values: from food safety to transparency, accountability and ultimately citizens' welfare. EU elites may have been high-handed and short-sighted in their approach. But the values that they represent create what is now so-often called "soft power". It is up to the people to make their choice.

Part 2:

Black Sea and the South Caucasus: Using the Southeast European Integration Experience as a Toolbox for the European Neighbourhood Policy

Benedikt Harzl

POTENTIALS AND SHORTCOMINGS FOR CONFLICT RESOLUTION IN THE CAUCASUS THE EUROPEAN NEIGHBOURHOOD POLICY

1. INTRODUCTION

The purpose of this paper is to identify and explain the difficulties the EU is encountering when formulating a coherent policy framework such as the ENP to tackle specific, mostly ethnically colored disputes in the Caucasus. The paper will therefore begin with a brief description of the region as a highly volatile and unpredictable, but highly strategic, spot and will continue with a discussion of the first EU attempts to include the region into its foreign policy realm. Section 3 will be dedicated to analyzing the policy framework of the ENP more in detail, and Section 4 will provide insight into the shortcomings and deficiencies of this policy in general. As single case study, Azerbaijan will be highlighted in the view of the ENP in Section 5, and the conclusion will again sum up the main arguments of the paper. Additionally, the article contains many direct references to "frozen conflicts" and how they are included in the ENP and which measures should be undertaken to improve EU-led conflict resolution on the ground.

2. A BRIEF GLANCE AT THE STRATEGIC IMPORTANCE OF THE CAUCASUS

How can we categorize and explain the importance that is ascribed to this subregion? The Caucasus, a picturesque mountainous region, conveniently located between the Black and the Caspian Seas and of strategic importance for the transport of energy resources to Europe, nowadays represents the biggest security risk in Eurasia. The whole region, which is marked by ethnic, linguistic and cultural diversity, has been afflicted by armed conflicts, terrorist attacks and impoverishment during the past 20 years. The northern Caucasus subregion alone, including seven Russian federal subjects, is one of the most ethnically complex and at the same time conflict-ridden regions in the world. For instance, the Republic of Dagestan, with a population of about two million, contains more than 30 distinct ethno-linguistic groups.[1] After the collapse of the Soviet Union, the whole region managed to gain some degree of visibility in Europe and the rest of the world and not merely because of the ongoing conflicts. It was the strategic importance of the Caucasus as a geographic concept that led to an increasing awareness of the region in Brussels and Washington. However, in consideration of the divisions in the region, generated by ethnically motivated tensions, wars, blockades and trade restrictions, it seems like a curse that the region as such does not have a unique structure to allow Georgia, Armenia, Azerbaijan and Russia to discuss questions that affect the region as a whole on one platform.[2] The August 2008 war in Georgia especially shows the lie of the denomination of "frozen conflicts". The only "frozen" element turned out to be the peace and settlement process.

The strategic weight of the region rests on three main factors. First, a very important and increasingly dominant factor is Islamic radicalism: it is the irony of history that the Chechens and Ingush were brutally displaced to Kazakhstan under Stalin's iron rule because of their supposed collaboration with the advancing German Wehrmacht. They maintained their strict Sufi fraternity[3] in the steppes of Altai and even revived the beliefs of Kazakh Islam, which was already regarded as a folkloristic aspect of the past.[4] It was the former Soviet Air Force General Dzhokhar Dudayev who declared the sovereignty of Chechnya in 1991 by swearing on the Quran, yelling, "Allah Akbar",[5] and thereby setting the stage for what would become two full-scale wars with atrocities on both sides and thousands of refugees. The major massacre of about 400 people, mostly children, in Beslan in September 2004 seems to underline how radical Islam and claims for secession in the region are interrelated. Additionally, because this attack was staged out of Ingushetia against a city in northern Ossetia, it appeared to be a blatant attempt to expand the Chechen conflict throughout the Caucasus.[6] This is also compounded by inter-land claims within the Russian Federation, which demonstrates that regional conflicts cannot simply be downsized to episodes of war between one state and one sub-state actor. For instance, Ingushetia and Northern Ossetia, both federal entities of Russia, have been for quite some time now involved in a long-standing and continuing conflict over the Prigorodny District,[7] a dispute that escalated in 1992 to violence and

---

1 *Nation,* "Russia, the United States, and the Caucasus" (Strategic Studies Institute, Carlisle, 2007), 1.

2 *Lynch*, A Regional Insecurity Dynamic, in *Baev et al.* (eds), The South Caucasus: A Challenge for the EU (Chaillot Papers, Institute for Security Studies, Paris, 2003), at 9.

3 Sufism is also known as the mystical dimension of Islam. Although all Muslims believe that they are on the pathway to God only after death and the final judgment, those who affiliate with Sufism think that God can be experienced while one is still alive. See <http://www.uga.edu/islam/Sufism.html>.

4 *Scholl-Latour*, Den Gottlosen die Hölle – Der Islam im zerfallenden Sowjetreich (1994), at 15.

5 Ibid. 14. This is the common Arabic expression for "God is great".

6 *Nation*, op. cit. note 1, 6.

7 Whereas Chechen representatives are advocating the re-combining of Chechnya and Ingushetia into one single Russian federal subject, Ingushetia makes claims to the Prigorodny Raion and causes permanent tensions with Northern Ossetia. See *Fuller*, Chechnya Seeks to Subsume, 'Stabilize' Ingushetia, Radio Free Europe, 13 June 2006, at <http://www.rferl.org/featuresarticle/2006/06/7A1789A0-9158-48EE-BEDE-1ED4AACD9525.html>.

resulted in some 60,000 refugees and 600 deaths[8] and which was additionally heated up by the arrival of thousands of refugees during the intra-Georgian war over South Ossetia. Therefore, the denomination of *South* Caucasus often reflects a European preference to see all these enormous tasks embedded in one well and clearly arranged region. But it would be wrong to explain this complexity by civilizational-ethnographic romanticism, whose alleged essence lies in the clash of civilizations. The manifestations of Islamic radicalism—which are actually by and large not common in the moderate and peaceful expression of Islam in this region—are to a large extent financed and planned by Saudi organisations that attempt to expand radical Wahhabism in the region by sending mercenary units.

Therefore, ethnic or religious diversity is less pronounced in the South Caucasus, but by no means less real. Hence, the second factor to which strategic importance can be accorded is regional instability, first and foremost regarding the unresolved territorial question marks, often incorrectly referred to as "frozen conflicts". These entities remain hotbeds of political instability and make the threat of a full-scale war between Armenia and Azerbaijan over the troubled entity of Nagorno-Karabakh not unlikely,[9] especially after the war between Georgia and Russia in 2008. Immediately after (in some cases even prior to) the collapse of the Soviet Union, ethnically motivated conflicts emerged, especially in the Caucasus region. Hundreds of thousands of people born in the territories of newly established states such as Russia, Georgia, Azerbaijan, etc., have found themselves with a diminished status. New national ideologies reflected the dominant groups' perception of itself as being the one and only holder of statehood, thereby, excluding from nationhood all those of other ethnicities. These conflict-generating doctrinal considerations are also legacies from the complex system of Soviet federalism, which was seen as an argument by many secessionist movements to disagree with the territorial disposition in the new state. It is exactly this nature of ethnic conflict that makes the Caucasus very well comparable with the Balkans, meaning that far-reaching decisions in the Balkans are connected to repercussions in the Caucasus. Therefore, unintended consequences of the declaration of independence in Kosovo are might be pouring fuel onto the flames on the ground. It has been repeatedly proposed by political scientists, and even published in American newspapers, that Kosovo might become exactly the kind of precedent for the Caucasus that Americans and most of the EU states denied it could be. It seems that the EU has sometimes manifested an inconsistent approach towards regions that express a desire for self-determination but are occupied by people who are perceived as 'pro-Russian' or see their security as only guaranteed by Russia.[10] Moreover, it seems clear to any observer that Tbilisi is not planning a peaceful solution; hence, "if Georgia chooses to use force, Russia is likely to respond militarily. If there is shooting between Russia and Georgia, would NATO

8 *Gadzhiev*, Geopolitika Kavkaza (Geopolitics of the Caucasus) (2002) at 50 – 51.

9 *Suzdaltsev*, Postsovetskoe Prostranstvo: Ukhodyashaya Real'nost' [The Post-Soviet Space: Outgoing Reality], in *Karaganov et al.* (eds), Mir vokrug Rossii: 2017. Kontury nedalekogo budushego [The World around Russia: 2017. Outlines of the Midterm Future] (The Council on Foreign and Defense Policy, Moscow, 2007), 122–135, at 123.

10 *Chiribka,* An Abkhaz Perspective: Abkhazia after Kosovo, Russian Analytical Digest 2008, 14 (15).

come to Georgia's defense, risking a confrontation with Russia?"[11] The answer to this question was given in August 2008 and showed the EU quite plainly how war can easily break out in its environment.

And third, the EU's and many others states' growing interest in diversification of energy supplies and, moreover, the necessity to satisfy the growing demand for petroleum and gas in the near future have pushed it towards closer co-operation with the Caucasus. The estimated energy resources of the Caspian Sea basin are approximately 200 billion barrels of petroleum and up to 500 to 600 trillion cubic feet of gas,[12] and thus constitute an important new energy source for Europe.[13] On top of this comes the fact that its convenient geographic location on the crossroads between Central Asia and Europe makes the South Caucasus attractive and even inevitably crucial in terms of trade, military and energy transportation.[14] The very same holds true for Russia: apart from Russian interests to retain the states neighbouring the Caspian basin, the Caucasus serves as a fundamental line for trade of goods out of Russia. It needs to be taken into account that the *ethnic* nature of conflict is very often debatable in the Caucasus because an international struggle over this strategic line started so that changes in local leaderships, personnel shifts and conflict situations are sometimes also an expression and a direct result of this struggle.

In other words, the interest of the EU to both bring peace to the Caucasus and to benefit strategically has clear limits given these highly problematic circumstances. But what could explain the inherent complexity of the factors mentioned above? One of the major elements in this puzzle that has explanatory value for the convoluted and obscure situation on the ground is the long-lasting presence of different external actors. Until this very day, the region has been fragmented politically and dominated by various external power centers such as the Tsarist and the Ottoman Empires as well as Persia. Hence, the Caucasus as such was never able to develop functional regional institutions or a shared political identity.[15] This is compounded by the geographic conditions of narrow valleys difficult to access, which gave as an isolating factor natural refuge to various ethnic groups so that so many different languages are still being spoken. In hardly any other region of its size in the world are there so many different ethnic groups and languages. Other regions of the world might also contain some ethnic groups, but in comparison to the Caucasus, with its nearly 60, they are nothing else but a poorly stocked ethnographical museum. However, the lack of a common political identity makes a peaceful future very hard to achieve: This assessment is redolent of the pre-war situation in former Yugoslavia, which represents the starting point for further considerations regarding ethnically motivated conflicts: "Yugoslavia was a weak state, unlikely to have the capabilities

---

11 *Simes*, The U.S. and Kosovo, Russia and Georgia, International Herald Tribune, 28 December 2007, 11.

12 *MacFarlane*, A Role for the EU in Preventing Ethnic Conflict, in *Rummel / Zullo* (eds), Rethinking European Union Relations with the Caucasus 1999, 55 (58).

13 In consideration of these figures, such capacity would make the Caspian basin the third largest oil and natural gas reserves in the world, after Saudi Arabia and Siberia.

14 *Alieva*, EU and South Caucasus, CAP Discussion Paper / Bertelsmann Group for Policy Research (2006) at 1.

15 *Nation*, op. cit. no 1, 2.

to adapt to changing international and technological circumstances".[16] And since Yugoslavia was for centuries a story of conquest and intervention by the great powers, "its international borders as well as its domestic political and economic systems, may have been constructed primarily for the convenience of outsiders",[17] and the "Great Game" (in the style of the British-Russian rivalry over Central Asia in the nineteenth century) among these outsiders triggered to a certain extent the strong desires of groups within the states for secession or revenge.

Although the South Caucasus has never constituted one entire state, one should apply the lessons learned from the Balkans to this troubled spot in order to consider the regions' relative capacities to cope with the typical dilemma of post-Soviet state engineering, that is, separatism and cultural disorientation in a region in which "outsiders" such as Russia and the United States and organizations such as NATO, Shanghai Organization of Cooperation and others try to get a foothold in this strategic region.[18] Similarly to the Balkans, the South Caucasus is an area in which the dilemma of identity and security balance remains unresolved.[19] The conflicts, among them ethnically motivated conflicts in the South Caucasus, as well as their geostrategic importance, have attracted many external actors with different and sometimes contradicting interests, objectives and perceptions, resulting in a highly complex net of international relations.[20] However, the EU took only very late notice of the region.

3. STUMBLING ON THE SOUTH CAUCASUS

What drove the EU to pay more attention to the three South Caucasian states, how did the EU try to develop a framework to deal more intensively with the region, and what have been the biggest obstacles so far? The historical enlargements of 2004 and 2007 have set in motion the EU's interest in closer cooperation with its new neighbours. Moreover, both enlargement rounds provided the hope that states that are currently located on the geographic periphery of the EU might one day become part of an intensified cooperation. But the presence of so many international actors, such as the OSCE (involved in conflict resolution in Azerbaijan and Georgia), the UN, but also states such as Russia, Turkey, the United States and Iran, has complicated the European approach towards the South Caucasian region and has left no doubt that there is little room for the EU to claim, because the lines of confrontation are not well defined: "The activities of Russia and the US, not to mention the policies of other regional actors such as Turkey and Iran, muddle rather than clarify the strategic shape of the re-

---

16 *Adams*, Structural Realism: The Consequences of Great Power Politics, in *Sterling-Folker* (ed), Making Sense of International Relations Theory 2006, 18 (19).

17 Ibid. 19.

18 *Suzdaltsev*, op. cit. no 9, 124.

19 *Nation*, op. cit. note 1, 4.

20 *Fischer*, The EU's Strategy of 'New Neighborhood' and its Impact on International Relations in the FSU, paper presented at the ISA Annual Convention, 1 – 5 March 2005, Honolulu, HI, 18.

gion".[21] And equally important, the limited possibilities of the EU are also related to disagreements within the EU itself. Apart from this, the South Caucasus as a geographic concept has had no promoter within the EU to generate a greater awareness for the region.[22]

Finland played a decisive role in the development of the Northern Dimension of the EU; France has always put the emphasis on enhanced co - operation with the states of Maghreb; Poland represents the main lobbyist for Ukraine in its membership aspirations and is very actively engaged in civil society projects in Belarus; and finally Austria regards itself as the promoter of the states of the Western Balkans. Somehow it seems that the South Caucasus has been for a long time left along the road by the EU.[23]

The first attempts to draft a new framework addressing neighbouring countries and future neighbours were unveiled in 2003, following the conclusions of the 2002 Copenhagen European Council, which confirmed "that the Union should take the opportunity offered by enlargement to enhance relations with its neighbors on the basis of shared values".[24] This process demonstrated that the EU increasingly sees itself as a full foreign policy actor that is able to act beyond the antagonism of membership/non-membership in order to pursue its interests abroad. Although the 'Wider Europe Communication' of 2003 launched a debate about its new and future neighbours, the paper did not initially include the South Caucasian states in order to "avoid drawing new dividing lines in Europe and to promote stability and prosperity within and beyond the new borders of the Union".[25] Georgia, Armenia and Azerbaijan were not among the first group of ENP countries and were only mentioned in a footnote: "Given their location, the Southern Caucasus therefore falls outside the geographical scope of this initiative for the time being".[26] Although all three states remained unmentioned in the first paper on a new neighbourhood policy, the culmination of a series of discussions and debates on the EU's policy in this fragile region resulted in the nomination of a EU Special Representative for the South Caucasus on 7 July 2003 with the task of pursuing a value-based EU policy on the ground.[27] Surprisingly, the "ENP Strategy Paper" issued by the European Commission in 2004 as a fine tuning of the first ideas of how to handle the challenge of the European neighbourhood after the enlargements, recommended, in contrast with the "Wider Europe Paper", that the South Caucasian states also be

---

21 *Lynch*, The EU: Towards a Strategy, in The South Caucasus: A Challenge for the EU (Challoit Papers, Institute for Security Studies, Paris, 2003), 171–196, at 176.

22 Ibid. 179.

23 Nevertheless, it has to be mentioned here that Lithuania and Latvia have been active in developing military ties with the three South Caucasian states, including providing training assistance at the Baltic Defense College to officers from the region. For further information, see <http://www.bdcol.ee/>.

24 Communication from the Commission to the Council and the European Parliament, "Wider Europe—Neighbourhood: A New Framework for Relations with our Eastern and Southern Neighbours", COM(2003) 104 final, 3, at <http://ec.europa.eu/world/enp/pdf/com03_104_en.pdf>.

25 Ibid. 4.

26 Ibid.

27 *Lynch*, op. cit., no 21, 172.

included in the new concept: "The Commission also recommends the inclusion of Armenia, Azerbaijan and Georgia within the scope of the ENP".[28]

Thus, within the course of only one year, the South Caucasus moved from the footnotes to within the scope of the application of the ENP. What happened? And why did the South Caucasus become so important for the EU? Was it the result of well-calculated decisions or the contrary? The strategic importance comes here into play again and explains why in retrospect, the first attempts by the EU to approach the region were anything but convincing. Moreover, they showed that Brussels is bad at differentiation: the republic of Cyprus had questioned for a long time Azerbaijani links to the Turkish Republic of North Cyprus. Only because of a single charter flight between Azerbaijan and North Cyprus, which led to a Cypriot veto, and even months before the draft ENP Action Plans (AP) were put on the table, all of the countries could not start negotiations on the ENP on time.[29] Again, the principle of differentiation and joint ownership was seriously undermined although, instead of a 'one size fits all' approach, the ENP supposedly reflects "the existing state of relations with each country, its needs and capacities, as well as common interests".[30]

However, it remains questionable how successfully the ENP will be able to apply this principle to its relationships with the three South Caucasian states. The EU is interested in the South Caucasus as a *region* rather than as three individual states with different expectations and ambitions for co-operation. Thus, even the ENP Strategy Paper points at the importance of the region for both the production and the transportation of energy.[31]

One of the main reasons for the importance of the region as a whole is undoubtedly that of material interest. It goes without saying that Caspian Sea petroleum exports are for the EU a very attractive alternative that would allow for reducing dependence on current sources.[32] For the new EU members whose dependence on Russian sources is even more striking, this interest seems to be all the stronger.[33] Similar to the growing attention that is dedicated to Ukraine and Moldova, the new Member States bring new urgent questions that have until now only been superficially addressed by the EU.[34] In other words, the decision to include the South Caucasian states under the umbrella of this new framework and to put them on an equal level with Ukraine can be primarily seen as a result of a growing awareness on the part of the EU, rather than a result of their repeated quest for closer co-operation, as in the case of Georgia. It has to be pointed out, again, that none of the three South

---

[28] Communication from the Commission, "European Neighbourhood Strategy Policy Paper", COM (2004) 373 final, 7, at <http://ec.europa.eu/world/enp/pdf/strategy/strategy_paper_en.pdf>.

[29] *Popescu*, The EU and South Caucasus: Learning Lessons from Moldova and Ukraine (Paper published for the Central and Eastern European Online Library, 2006), at <http://www.ceeol.com/aspx/getdocument.aspx?logid=5&id=B7746911-5E34-40B0-88B6-81D290AF8BFE>.

[30] COM(2004) 373 final, op. cit. note 28, 3.

[31] Ibid. 11.

[32] Energy security is becoming more and more the driving force in ENP regime building in the South Caucasus. See <http://www.consilium.europa.eu/uedocs/cmsupload/st09971.en06.pdf>.

[33] *MacFarlane*, op. cit. no 12, 63.

[34] *Lynch,* op. cit. no 21, 173.

Caucasian states are actively demanding an increased EU role for purely altruistic and selfless reasons. These states are active only in cases in which it serves their own individual interests and not necessarily if it serves automatically or as by-product the other neighbours in the region at the same time. From this perspective, their wish for a reinforced EU role is not on the same level as that of the states of the Western Balkans. The intensity of their demand for EU membership opportunities is not even comparable to that vocalized by Moldova and Ukraine. The South Caucasian states have beyond a doubt an interest in an EU presence in general, but the attraction expressed is largely utilitarian. The EU is perceived as one more forum (besides the United States, and eventually NATO), in which these states may promote their own interests. Tbilisi in particular sees the EU as another heartily welcomed actor that might counterbalance Russian influence in the region.[35]

Although the ENP initiative in the South Caucasus can be seen as a new development, the engagement of corporate actors of several Member States (notably the United Kingdom, France and Italy)[36] that are involved in exploiting the Caspian resources is by no means new. But the presence of these companies leads to a dangerous situation as well, underlining the fact that energy resources represent a blessing and a curse at the same time: "One of the characteristics of transition created by the resource development before strong democratic institutions are built is that it structurally deprives any leadership of incentive to reform".[37] Hence, policy frameworks aimed at bringing progress to energy-rich countries, as in the case of the ENP in the South Caucasus, have only a small chance of success if they fail to take into account this specific feature of transition countries. To understand this "Caucasian peculiarity," it is worthwhile to look back in time.

The first European strategy to deal with its periphery after the twilight of communism was the implementation of PCAs with the successor states of the Soviet Union.[38] They were concluded for a period of 10 years and defined the scope of co-operation in several pillars: political dialogue, economic trade relations and cultural exchange. In the South Caucasus, with regard to the three countries of Armenia, Georgia and Azerbaijan, the first instrument of co-operation with the EU were PCAs that were signed in 1996, entered into force in 1999 and provided the legal framework for the mutual relations.[39] But apart from a decelerated implementation of this framework, the PCAs, which were due to terminate in 2008, with very limited parameters, lack the much clearer *quid pro quo* philosophy of the ENP. Moreover, they represented the only EU framework with neighbours that did not establish an association between the partners.[40] Yet, while articles in the PCAs dealing with

---

[35] *Lynch*, op. cit. no 21, 177.
[36] Oil companies such as Total, Elf, BP, British Gas, Shell and AGIP.
[37] *Alieva*, op. cit. no 14, 9.
[38] Except the Baltic states.
[39] Find the respective PCAs online at <http://ec.europa.eu/external_relations/ceeca/pca/pca_georgia.pdf> (PCA Georgia), <http://ec.europa.eu/external_relations/ceeca/pca/pca_armenia.pdf> (PCA Armenia), and <http://ec.europa.eu/external_relations/ceeca/pca/pca_azerbaijan.pdf> (PCA Azerbaijan).
[40] *Lipper*, Beefing up the ENP: Toward a Modernisation and Stability Partnership, in *Varwick / Lany* (eds), European Neighbourhood Policy—Challenges for the EU-Policy Towards the New Neighbours 2007, 181 (183).

political dialogue call for governance reforms and attempts to resolve regional conflicts and tensions, these agreements remain only economic and technical.[41] This, of course, augurs poorly in an energy-rich and strategic region with regard to democratization and respect for human rights.

Nevertheless, the Member States of the EU kept declaring for a long time that the PCAs offered the best framework and that there would be no other strategy, no other political role, no other provisions than that offered in the PCAs. Again, the lack of differentiation necessary to understand the Caucasian peculiarities became one of Brussel's major Achilles' heels. Under the sole framework of the PCAs, the mildly phrased value-based stipulations remained an illusionary aspiration blocked by the reality that regional cooperation between the respective states was not achieved. Tbilisi, Yerevan and Baku remained at loggerheads.[42]

Another point of reference to determine whether political frameworks fail or succeed is the available financial resources. The PCAs, based on the declaration of common values and the commitment to market-economy structures, refer to the Technical Aid to the Commonwealth of Independent States (TACIS). TACIS was supposed to provide grant-financed technical assistance to the PCA states. However, the amount of the funding was fairly modest and contributed to the lack of visibility and success of the EU in the region.[43]

To sum up, the PCA/TACIS instrument was increasingly perceived as a failure, both on the part of the EU and by the partner countries.[44] It became apparent that a blanket PCA/TACIS approach applied in particular to the South Caucasus would not be enough to assist the transition of these states and to promote European interests. It placed the burden of transition efforts on the neighbours, which had to adjust to the political, economic and legal rules of the EU without being offered major advantages in terms of cooperation with the EU. Above all, one of the major failings of the PCA/TACIS method that led many in Brussels to reconsider the European strategy was the inability of the EU to differentiate its policies and to adapt to the specific situation of each country. The EU has to recognize the imperative of developing differentiated approaches to states, and in particular, to the fragile region of the South Caucasus and its highly explosive situation. The old concepts of cooperation have not generated substantial progress in terms of stability. Evidently, with Central and Eastern European enlargement completed in 2007 and the Balkan states at its doorstep, the EU finds itself confronted with similar challenges as those faced 16 years ago after the collapse of the Soviet Union.[45]

---

41 *Lynch*, op. cit. note 21, 181.
42 *Lynch*, op. cit. note 21, 183.
43 TACIS, whose budget amounted to nearly 212.1 million euro for the three South Caucasian states between 1991 and 1999, was only slightly increased between 2000 and 2003. See <http://ec.europa.eu/external_relations/ceeca/tacis/figures.pdf>.
44 *Fischer*, op. cit. note 20, 9.
45 *Rhein*, The European Neighbourhood Policy: A Critical Assessment, in *Varwick / Lang* (eds), European Neighbourhood Policy—Challenges for the EU - Policy Towards the New Neighbours 2007, 39 (41).

4. ENP OR "CREATING A RING OF FRIENDS"

We will now turn our attention to a more detailed description of the ENP. This policy, which was discussed and launched between 2002 and 2005, one of the major steps in the long series of EU-driven foreign policy experiments. Yet it is still in its formative stage, on uncharted ground, being shaped first and foremost by the European Commission and the governments of the 17 neighbouring[46] countries.[47] At present, it is still too early to judge the success of the ENP in its entirety, and it will still take much time before the actors involved in the ENP process find and agree on the basic description, what might then be called the "ENP doctrine". Today scholars are already arguing over characteristic traits of this policy. For example, there are some who think that the ENP should be viewed as a foreign policy instrument or, moreover, as the first project of the Common Foreign and Security Policy (CFSP), which represents together with the Common Security and Defence Policy (CSDP) the principal item of European diplomacy.[48] Yet others strongly disagree with this characterization and argue that the ENP is neither foreign policy nor an enlargement policy. They call attention to the fact that it is a mix of domestic policy instruments, foreign policy and enlargement practices.[49] Another theoretical battlefield seems to be the heavily disputed question of the ENP as a policy of "half-open doors". But somehow it seems to remain beyond question that the ENP can be seen as the "EU's new *mission civilisatrice* to externalize its success and export its model to the rest of the world".[50]

The result of the reflection period between 2002 and 2005 is what the European Commission first termed a policy of "Wider Europe",[51] including the former Soviet republics (except for Russia, which expressed the intention not to be part of this policy and to have a special partnership, based on the four common spaces with the EU),[52] as well as the Mediterranean countries and—since 2004—the South Caucasus states. Yet, the fact that the South Caucasus states, having at least somewhat European identities and perceiving themselves to a certain degree as part of Europe,

---

[46] However, the three republics of the South Caucasus do not fall in the scope of the term "neighbour". They are located some 1000 km apart from the nearest EU member country, Romania. But as already mentioned above, all three republics were included in the European Neighborhood Strategy Policy Paper of 2004.

[47] *Rhein*, op. cit. note 45, 39.

[48] *Helmerich*, Die Europäische Nachbarschaftspolitik (ENP) – eine adäquate Außen- und Sicherheitspolitik für die EU? KFIBS-Analyse – Kölner Forum für Internationale Beziehungen und Sicherheitspolitik (2006), 2.

[49] *Popescu*, op. cit. note 29, 2.

[50] *Fröhlich*, The European Neighbourhood Policy: An Adequate Instrument for Democratisation? in *Varwick / Lang* (eds), European Neighbourhood Policy—Challenges for the EU-Policy Towards the New Neighbours 2007, 75 (75).

[51] COM(2003) 104 final, *op.cit.* note 24.

[52] (1) Common economic space; (2) common space of freedom, justice and security; 3) common space on external security; and 4) common space on research, education and culture. For more profound and detailed information on the relations between the EU and Russia, see Fischer, "Die EU und Russland: Konflikte und Potentiale einer schwierigen Partnerschaft" (SWP-Studie, Berlin, 2006).

were united in one policy document together with the states of Maghreb—located on the African continent—sent them a clear message that they were EU neighbours at the periphery, rather than future members.[53] Yet, the ENP is not in the first place about enlargement. Rather, the policy aims at exporting stability to neighbouring countries so that the EU's own peaceful development is not hampered by the new periphery.[54] Moreover, in its intention to "create this ring of friends", or less lyrically, to "develop stability at the Union's periphery", the EU also addresses the necessity of an effective and target-oriented CSDP.

However, despite this bold and ambitious objective, "the European Union is not seeking to establish new bodies or organizations, but rather to support existing entities and encourage their further development".[55] Furthermore, the neighbourhood strategy paper devotes a whole chapter to the issue of co-operation in Eastern Europe and points at the Council of Europe (CoE), the Central European Initiative (CEI), and the Stability Pact as important already-existing structures and bodies of cooperation.[56] In this sense, the ENP process follows the same spirit, since the ENP builds upon several existing policy instruments, in particular the PCAs concluded between the EU and the former Soviet republics in the course of the 1990s, and the AAs with the Mediterranean states.[57] Hence, as the ENP is built into the already-existing institutional framework of the EU's bilateral relation with states at the Union's periphery, yet is supposed to have a more differentiated focus; in contrast to the PCA/TACIS approach, it should by highly flexible and based on individually tailored bilateralism,[58] while providing a common framework for all target countries at the same time.

Following this approach, the form of co-operation between the EU and the respective ENP state differs from country to country, according to each state's needs, capacities, limits and possibilities, as well as the EUs co-operation goals laid down in (APs). All APs concluded with the ENP states have in common that they provide for a number of core priorities at the beginning before defining an agenda of political reform priorities to be implemented and monitored by the European Commission.[59] Taking into account that the states concerned have very different needs and goals to be accomplished through the ENP, APs are set up by the European Commission on a bilateral level, which makes it possible to draft tailor-made APs for each ENP state under their co-operation.[60]

In this regard, the ENP provides four subsequent phases: (1) establishment of treaty-based relations, (2) draft of country reports, (3) agreement on objectives of

[53] *Alieva*, op. cit. note 14, 7.
[54] *Fröhlich*, op. cit. note 50, 77.
[55] COM(2004) 373 final, op. cit. note 28, 21.
[56] Ibid. 20–21.
[57] The existence of a PCA is a precondition for the elaboration of Action Plans; sometimes provisions in Action Plans refer to an existing PCA. For this reason, Belarus, whose PCA was already negotiated but never put into force, does not fall into the scope of the ENP for the time being. This is also the case of Algeria, Libya and Syria. Neither an association agreement nor a PCA came into force in these states, so ENP negotiations have not yet been started.
[58] *Fröhlich*, op. cit. note 50, at 78.
[59] Ibid. 79.
[60] *Helmerich*, op. cit. note 48, 5.

the AP, and finally (4) implementation and the monitoring of the progress.[61] The legal concept of this policy faces occasionally heavy criticism from members of the European Parliament due to the dominant role of the European Commission in this framework. At present, the EP can only execute its co-decisional authority in allocating the European Neighborhood Partnership Instrument (ENPI) budget, but has no say with regard to the priorities of the ENP as such.[62] It seems that the ENP is somewhat "out of reach" for the EP, which again demonstrates that the policy as such is by no means fine-tuned. Apart from this, the Commission underlined that the "ENP should be introduced progressively, and be *conditional* on meeting agreed targets for reform. New benefits should only be offered to reflect the progress made by the partner country in political and economic reform" (emphasis in the original).[63] On the one hand, the EP has stressed on various occasions that the Commission has not yet defined a measurable aim for the ENP, or at least indicators that would help to assess the success of this policy.[64] On the other hand, the concept of soft EU conditionality is not new, in particular not new for the South Caucasian states. We should again examine past experiences, because since 1999, the co-operation between the EU and the South Caucasus states has been based on PCAs which had—regardless of the softly phrased principle of conditionality—no significant positive impact on the promotion of democracy or human rights. Quite the contrary, according to the Freedom in the World ratings, Armenia and Azerbaijan performed worse on democratic development during 2005 to 2006, when even the ENP APs were adopted, than during the early 1990s period before the signing of the PCA.[65] *Schimmelfenning* et al. argue that "the effectiveness of the EU social influence will mainly depend on the degree to which non-member actors identify themselves with the EU community" and their "commitment to Europe".[66] Hence, political elites in ENP states will only pay lip service to values and incentives if the domestic costs are too high.

Procedurally, the EU negotiates with neighbour governments a package of legislative and administrative acts that the respective country agrees to implement in a period of three to five years. The results of these negotiations between the ENP states and the EU are laid down inAPs, whose implementation is subject to joint monitoring.[67] The APs that were negotiated with the South Caucasian states from 2005 to 2006 and entered into force in 2006 placed the reform of democratic institutions and respect for human rights and fundamental freedoms among the top priori-

---

61 Ibid.

62 *Leinen / Weidemann*, How Does ENP Work? A View from the European Parliament, in *Varwick / Lang* (eds), European Neighbourhood Policy—Challenges for the EU-Policy Towards the New Neighbours 2007, 49 (53).

63 COM(2003) 104 final, op. cit. note 24, 16.

64 *Leinen / Weidemann,* op. cit. note 62, 53.

65 Freedom in the World, historical rankings, at <http://www.freedomhouse.org/uploads/fiw/FIWAllSCORES.xls>.

66 *Schimmelfenning / Engert / Knobel*, The Conditions of Conditionality: The Impact of the EU on Democracy and Human Rights in European Non-Member States (ECPR Joint Session of Workshop Papers, Turin, 2002), 6, at <http://www.essex.ac.uk/ECPR/events/jointsessions/paperarchive/turin/ws4/Schimmelfennig.pdf>.

67 *Rhein*, op. cit. note 45, 44.

ties. They automatically expire after 5 years. The protection of minorities is mentioned in practically all APs; however, the EU has considerably less influence on this topic because of the lack of conditionality-related tools. In theory, ENP APs reach well beyond the scope of the current PCAs and AAs by offering the neighbouring countries "a stake in the EU's internal market". But the interesting question, and the real crux of the matter in this regard, is whether this is the only source of motivation for the ENP states to accept the conditionality imposed on them. Why should sovereign states agree to revolutionary and sweeping programmes suggested by an outside actor—and in the case of the South Caucasus, an outside actor that is very far away? This holds in particular true for the EaP, which even emphasizes the element of "partnership" rather than top-down policy instructions.

It goes without saying that there is no single answer. Many researchers point in this regard to the funds that are provided by the EU. Indeed, the EU has earmarked an amount of 12 billion euro from ENPI funds for all neighbouring countries that participate in the ENP framework.[68] There is no doubt that the funds of what was formerly the TACIS budget have been considerably increased in the framework of the ENPI. But one should not overestimate the financial carrot of the ENP. The mentioned amount, distributed among 12 countries with a population of 200 million, over the span of seven years, is certainly not enough to convince ENP state governments to conduct reform that they dislike.[69] The South Caucasus example shows that sometimes neighbour countries want to maintain good relations with the EU as a powerful international actor in order to counterbalance other dominant powers. This alternative explanation has to be increasingly taken into consideration by the Commission and should be kept in mind during negotiations for the implementation of APs.

However, even those modest amounts of funds matter for governments that are keen to continue with reforms. The already-mentioned ENPI compliments the ENP and includes a special cross-border facility that also entails — in contrast to the former TACIS programme — a radical simplification and debureaucratization of the current state of affairs. Moreover, the Commission has also agreed to improve future cross-border cooperation along the EU's external land and sea border.[70] And in this regard, the EU has to take its commitment *vis-à-vis* the establishment of a comprehensive framework for transfrontier co-operation more seriously. For instance, the Lugansk Oblast located in eastern Ukraine cooperates much more intensely in many fields, such as social cohesion and economic partnership, with the neighbouring Rostov Oblast in the Russian Federation than does L'viov, located in the western part of Ukraine, with the eastern administrational units of Hungary or Poland.[71]

From this enumeration of failed strategies and overestimated effects on the part of the EU, one could reason that the first institutionalised attempt to cope with the enormous challenges in the immediate neighbourhood of the EU fell short at re-

---

68 Ibid. 45.

69 Ibid.

70 *Fröhlich,* op. cit. note 50, 79.

71 *Medvedev,* Raskolotaya Ukraina [Divided Ukraine] (Institut ekonomicheskikh strategyj, Mezhdunarodnaya akademiya budushego, Moscow, 2007), 144.

moving the dividing line between West and East in Europe. However, the following section will show that the ENP also has inherent features that limit a real rapprochement towards the neighbourhood, and in particular, towards the South Caucasian states.

5. ROOM FOR IMPROVEMENT?

At present, the ENP leaves many questions open, especially those concerning the challenges that will have to be met in the future. Most of these still unresolved questions gravitate around the issues of possible EU membership perspectives (that is, the ENP or enlargement *vs.* the ENP plus enlargement), technical issues, and the role of Russia and *de facto* regimes. The ways in which these issues will be dealt with will to a large extent determine whether or not the ENP will meet its self-imposed objectives. Regrettably, the EaP has not solved this riddle either: as a complementary policy launched in 2009, which is providing new forums for the Eastern periphery and distinguishing this region from the Mediterranean, it has done little to sketch out a future scenario for coexistence between these states and the EU.

When it comes to the assessment of the ENP in general, many writers follow a paradigm of modernisation by adapting the practice of conditionality from the enlargement experience. But the refusal to consider membership for the ENP states, even in the long term, has led skeptics to argue that the countries at the Union's periphery will not be motivated enough to undertake domestic reforms, and the ENP will therefore fall short of achieving significant results. The EP, for example, seeks to establish a more equal partnership with the ENP states, works seriously on keeping EU membership open as an option, and supports many initiatives to include the partners in various activities of the EU, offering them a seat at the table of relevant EU agencies.[72] Nevertheless, the ENP, which is formulated accurately as "something of a philosophical quest for the EU in which it seeks to answer of how to support the transformation of its neighbours in line with EU standards while not offering membership",[73] is giving very little of what many neighbours want. The ultimate prize—membership—is available for the time being only to Turkey and the states of the Western Balkans. The intense discussion about membership prospects is a signal that the ENP as such has become a subject of polarization and politicization, with dividing lines drawn within the legal bodies of the EU and to a certain degree between 'new' and 'old' EU members.[74] For instance, the former Commissioner on Enlargement Günter Verheugen said that "Ukraine is as close to

---

72 *Leinen / Weidemann*, op. cit. note 62, 50.

73 *Popescu*, op. cit. note 29, 2.

74 We must not lose sight of the fact that the ENP was originally considered a rather technocratic approach with the aim to consolidate existing tools and new instruments in order to develop a more efficient policy for fostering transformation at the EU's periphery. Today it has a growing strategic character. See *Lang*, European Neighbourhood Policy: Where do we Stand – Where are we Heading? in *Varwick / Lang* (eds), European Neighbourhood Policy—Challenges for the EU-Policy Towards the New Neighbours 2007, 15 (15).

joining the EU as Mexico is to joining the US",[75] whereas some EU states, among them mostly Eastern European states, are in favour of dangling a European future in front of states like Georgia, Ukraine and Moldova. But the ENP states also receive different signals from different EU institutions and governments, and even the Commission sends mixed messages.[76] It seems to be clear that the Commission hopes that this new policy will stop neighbouring countries from demanding unrealistic promises of membership for a while.[77] The former President of the Commission, Romano Prodi, has coined the phrase "everything but institutions".[78] Will the ENP, complemented by EaP, hence achieve only "everything but institutions"?

The practical, technical and political obstacles to incorporating the EU's much poorer neighbours into this kind of economic and political area are still enormous, and what the EU is offering at present is far from 'everything but institutions'. The Commission still has to work within the framework of existing EU policies, so it is unable to grant neighbouring countries the two benefits they really want: visa-free access to the EU and free trade in agricultural products. Still today, these policies are extremely sensitive for Member States and national governments, and decisions on them are in the hands of ministries that do not have foreign policy objectives as their first priority.[79]

The EU should be more realistic and ambitious in its periphery policy. It would be naïve to expect that the EU with its softly phrased value policy of the ENP on strengthening of democracy, civil society and rule of law will transform the whole of 'wider Europe' in the way it did the Central and Eastern European states.[80] Unfortunately the EU still sends contradictory messages to its neighbours via the ENP. On the one hand, the ENP promises easier access to the EU market, but on the other hand, because of imprecise incentives and short-term security considerations, the EU tries to impose on its neighbours a number of far-reaching obligations linked with implicit threats of exclusion,[81] although there is no kind of institutional rapprochement between ENP states and the EU. It is hence crucial to understand that the ENP requires a long-term vision. The EU needs to show more patience and understanding with its neighbors at the periphery and should be more than happy if by 2025 the majority of its neighbours uphold standards of governance, democracy and human rights that are comparable with the new EU Member States, prior to their accession in 2004 and 2007.[82] Some argue that as long as explicit membership incentives are absent and ENP countries are governed by authoritarian regimes, there is only a small hope that the ENP will have a positive impact on democracy

---

75 See <http://news.bbc.co.uk/2/hi/talking_point/4061717.stm>.

76 For instance, the Directorate-General for External Relations tries to encourage the neighbours by proposing trade concessions, but is often blocked by the directorates for agriculture and trade. See *Grabbe*, How the EU Should Help Its Neighbors, Policy Brief (Centre for European Reform, London, 2004), 5.

77 *Grabbe*, op. cit. note 76, 1.

78 *Fröhlich,* op. cit. note 50, 80.

79 *Grabbe,* op. cit. note 76, 2.

80 *Grabbe*, op. cit. note 76, 6.

81 *Kahl*, The European Neighbourhood Policy and the Borders of Europe, in *Varwick / Lang* (eds), European Neighbourhood Policy—Challenges for the EU-Policy Towards the New Neighbours 2007, 61 (67).

82 *Rhein,* op. cit. note 45, 47.

and human rights in the future. But with regard to the South Caucasus, the effectiveness of conditionality and socialization mechanisms on a state's behaviour depends on the potential threat of interference and the influence of other external actors in the domestic scene.[83] Thus, the conditionality mechanism, combined with membership prospects, would certainly dilute the EU's strategy in Tbilisi, Yerevan and Baku. Apart from this, a further enlargement of the EU is not possible for the time being. The EU's absorption capacity has definitely reached a critical point, Europe is suffering from an intensified enlargement fatigue. Yet, in the past, it was exactly the possibility of becoming a member of the EU that set in motion reforms in candidate countries.[84] But if the prospect of membership is insufficient to encourage the level of democratic and administrative reforms required by the EU, as it is evident in a couple of candidate countries, why should the golden carrot of membership be more successful in Kiev, Kishinev or Baku?[85] This of course means that the ENP should be strictly separated from membership; instead, it should *really* offer the concerned states visa liberalization and a stake in the EU's internal market by demanding a transformative agenda on the part of the ENP states. Although membership should not be generally ruled out, it should be kept in mind that the EU has designed the ENP as a *permanent alternative* to future enlargements. The EU is afraid to overextend itself,[86] but at the same time it does not want to nourish unrealistic hopes. Silently but steadily, the Union's capability to act became an integral additional part of the Copenhagen criteria (democracy, rule of law, human and minority rights).[87] Accordingly, Brussels must find a way to balance its efforts to increase security and prosperity by inclusion. The only way to accomplish this political high-wire act is to clearly articulate how far the EU is willing to go.[88]

Another important element that is insufficiently considered is the Russian factor. The EU's relationship to Moscow casts to a certain degree dark shadows on its ENP. While Russia tries to reinforce its influence over its "near abroad", Brussels is also trying to widen and deepen its ties with many of the same countries. Potential tensions are already emerging: Russia wants its citizens be able to travel freely in the whole former Soviet Union, but the EU urges its Eastern neighbours via the ENP to reinforce their border controls with other non-EU countries like Russia.[89] At the same time, both have common interests in the region of the South Caucasus. Russia and the EU are first and foremost concerned about stability in the region.

---

83 *Nodar / Kobaladze*, EU-Georgia Neighborhood Relations (Center of EU Enlargement Studies, Central European University, Budapest, 2006), 13.

84 *Leinen / Weidemann*, op. cit. note 62, 55.

85 *Bendiek*, The ENP in a Regime-analytical Perspective: Propositions for a Research Desgin, in *Varwick / Lang* (eds), European Neighbourhood Policy—Challenges for the EU-Policy Towards the New Neighbours 2007, 25 (25).

86 Due to an amendment to the French Constitution, future enlargements will have to be put to a referendum. Similarly, Austrian has pledged to hold a referendum on Turkey's accession. See Lang, op. cit. note 74, at 17.

87 Communication from the European Parliament to the Council (COM 2006) 649, Enlargement Strategy and Main Challenges 2006–2007, at <http://ec.europa.eu/enlargement/pdf/key_documents/2006/nov/com_649_strategy_paper_en.pdf>.

88 *Marchetti*, Widening without Enlarging: The European Neighbourhood Policy and the South Caucasus, Turkish Policy Quarterly 2006, 65 (77).

89 *Grabbe*, op. cit. note 76, 3.

However, stability and the spill-over argument works differently for both sides:[90] Whereas Russia has been directly and manifestly affected by recent ethnopolitical conflicts, terrorist attacks, refugee streams and wars in or from the Caucasus, no similar effect can be proven for the EU. Additionally, the argument about the EU's interest in diversifying its energy imports sounds different from the viewpoint of Moscow, which clearly sees itself as the only alternative for Europe's relative dependence on the Middle East for its gas and petroleum supply. In this sense, the Caucasian transit corridor is—from a purely Russian perspective—even more vital to Moscow than to Brussels. Both actors have to reflect on whether to choose cooperation over conflict: any new ideas in EU initiatives in the Caucasus should be carefully considered against the basic background of EU–Russian relations.[91] But this does not mean that Brussels should grant Russia a veto for its ENP policy: it is the EU that decides how to develop fruitful relations with its periphery. Yet, an EU dialogue on the ENP is absolutely essential. This is not only to convince Moscow that EU–Georgia, EU–Armenia and EU–Azerbaijan relations provide a chance for Russia, but also to find out and discuss areas of EU–Russia and ENP cooperation in which coordination and communication might be useful.[92] The positive side effects of such an approach are obvious: Russia could be convinced by the transformative agenda of the ENP and, on the other hand, this could be helpful in assuring Russia that the ENP is not directed against Moscow.

A remaining typical perception of the Caucasus ruling elites should not remain unmentioned as concerns the Russian aspect: the attempt to reconcile two objectives—to increase the efficiency of the ENP as an incentive for sweeping reforms, without nourishing unrealistic accession hopes, and to promote trilateral cooperation with Russia—creates some confusions on the ground. This is perceived in the Caucasus as the intention of Brussels to keep them in the regional "club".[93]

With regard to the South Caucasus, one of the main shortcomings of the ENP is the fact that not the entire region is included in the ENP. Therefore, the question arises whether ENP objectives can be achieved without involving the breakaway regions of Abkhazia, South Ossetia and Nagorno-Karabakh. These *de facto* subjects of international law, which are not *de jure* states but are nevertheless really existing statelets and therefore enjoy from a legal perspective the provisions of Art 2, clause 4, of the UN charter, remain untouched by the provisions of what Brussels calls "a wider Europe". Hence, it is time for the EU—regardless of technical and political constraints—to think about how these entities can be connected to the ENP. In this regard, the conflict resolution capacity of the ENP in the South Caucasus will be addressed later on.

In the following section we will turn our attention to the issue of which policy the EU pursues in Azerbaijan with briefly selected ENP-related case studies. One of the basic elements of these considerations will be the APs.

---

90 *De Spiegeleire*, Russian Responses to Possible EU Policy Initiatives in the Caucasus, in *Rummel / Zullo* (eds), Rethinking European Union Relations with the Caucasus 1999, 91 (95).

91 Ibid. 111.

92 *Lang*, op. cit. note 74, 22.

93 *Alieva*, op. cit. note 14, 8.

6. ENP IN AZERBAIJAN

In March 2005, the European Commission recommended intensifying relations with Azerbaijan through the conclusion of an AP under the framework of the ENP.[94] However, the first problems and disagreements began to appear: in the drafting period of the AP, the Azerbaijani government and EU officials could not agree on a strongly emphasised wording for democracy, rule of law and human rights, so the Azerbaijani AP remains in this regard rather neutral and weak. However, one of the key issues of the Azerbaijan AP is mentioned as Priority Area 1: "Contribution to the peaceful settlement of the Nagorno-Karabakh conflict". In this respect the Azerbaijan AP contains a strongly worded paragraph on respect and support for sovereignty, territorial integrity and the inviolability of international borders of each other's state and "compliance to international and European norms and principles" in reference to this frozen conflict. This is also underlined by a clause, stating that "any breach of these norms and principles by either party to the Action Plan will result in the immediate suspension of its implementation."[95] There is no doubt that the basic incentive for Azerbaijan to conclude the AP was the concession of the EU to pursue a stronger policy, which aims at resolving the Nagorno-Karabakh conflict under the principle of territorial integrity.[96] From the outset of EU engagement in Azerbaijan, Brussels used the three principal instruments of TACIS, the Food Security Programme and humanitarian aid to assist refugees, along with the rehabilitation of territories damaged during the war over Nagorno-Karabakh. In this respect, Nagorno-Karabakh was the top priority for the EU and the total assistance provided by Brussels has amounted to some € 400 million.[97] Yet, because any directive with regard to a resolution of the Nagorno-Karabakh conflict without the inclusion of the Armenian authorities is very unlikely to succeed, the EU showed once more that its foreign policy capacity and knowledge about the region is very limited: the parallel negotiation process with Baku and Yerevan was not sufficiently used as soft leverage to bring both states, which are at the same time conflict parties, into a convincing dialogue and to pressure them to reach at least a preliminary agreement. In attempting to balance the EU interests, the AP with Armenia and Azerbaijan regarding Nagorno-Karabakh contain fundamentally different language. Whereas the Azerbaijan AP is full of strong wordings and stipulations of state sovereignty, territorial integrity and inviolability of internationally recognised borders and refers to the Karabakh conflict resolution as first priority, the Armenian AP does not contain any par-

---

[94] As a matter of fact, the Commission's suggestion was based on its own country report on Azerbaijan, which provided a detailed overview of the Azerbaijani–European relationship. See Commission Staff Working Paper, SEC(2005) 286/3, Brussels 2 March 2005, at <http://ec.europa.eu/world/enp/pdf/country/azerbaijan_country_report_2005_en.pdf>.

[95] See Azerbaijan AP, 1.

[96] *Bababyev*, Strategie und Demokratie: Azerbajdžan und die EU-Nachbarschaftspolitik, Osteuropa 2007, 201 (204).

[97] *Nuriyev*, EU Policy in the South Caucasus—A View from Azerbaijan, Centre for European Policy Studies, CDEPS Working Document No 272 (July 2007).

ticular reference to territorial integrity, and moreover, the issue of Nagorno-Karabakh comes very late in the Action Plan, only as Priority Area 7. Conversely, the principle of self-determination that was added to the Armenian AP is not included in the parallel Azerbaijan AP.[98]

Most likely, the Commission wanted to get Baku and Yerevan to agree on the very same text with regard to the conflict-ridden region of Stepanakert, but the ineffective result of this obvious inconsistency is a reliance on the lowest common denominator. Only some specific actions are the same in both APs: continued support for a peaceful solution, increased diplomatic efforts, and people-to-people contacts.[99] From another perspective one might say that this inconsistent language is the only feasible way to find an arrangement acceptable to both parties as well as an attempt not to interfere with previously agreed upon principles from negotiations brokered by the OSCE.[100] One can consequently argue that the EU clearly does not see itself as having, or wishing to have, a wider, stronger and more robust role in the Nagorno-Karabakh conflict.

In addition, the Azerbaijan AP mentions the necessity of political dialogue "on security issues that affect the interests of both sides", which certainly refers to European necessities in energy policy as mentioned above.[101] The European interests in energy are crowned by the reference to a possible free trade agreement once Azerbaijan has joined the World Trade Organisation (WTO).[102] Overall, the actions under the respective sections are very general and weak and make a reading like a non-binding shopping list. In the sections regarding strengthening democracy and ensuring respect for human rights and fundamental freedoms, the language of the AP remains again very empty and leaves the interpretational authority to Baku. To sum up, the potential of APs to promote conflict resolution and to push for democracy and the rule of law has not been fully exploited. Measured by the original strategy, the ENP was to "reinforce stability and security and contribute to efforts at conflict resolution" and to strengthen "the EU's contribution to promoting the settlement of regional conflicts."[103] Because the European focus is more on trade relations and economic change, one should not be too surprised that Baku pays only lip service to the soft and vague stipulations of the AP. Accordingly, the EU is regrettably closing its eyes much too often onto undemocratic standards and grave human rights violations and, as a consequence, contributes to the accusation of maintaining double standards. Azerbaijan remains a good example of a post-Soviet autocracy in which a democratic façade only partially masks the full control of a narrow ruling clique.[104]

To sum up, Azerbaijan represents a quite illustrative case study for understanding how the strategic factors of the Caucasus such as the transportation of energy (as

---

98 *Freire / Simao*, The Armenian Road to Democracy – Dimensions of a Tortuous Process, CEPS Working Document No 267 (May 2007), Centre for European Studies, 17.

99 International Crisis Group, Conflict Resolution in the South Caucasus: The EU's Role, Europe Report No. 173 (20 March 2006), 13–14, 14.

100 *Freire / Simao*, op. cit. note 98, 17.

101 Azerbaijan AP, 2.

102 Ibid. 20.

103 ENP Strategy Paper, 4 and 6.

104 *Nation*, op. cit. note 1, 14.

discussed in Section 2. are interrelated with unresolved issues of the nature of the ENP, especially concerning the dilemma of whether to involve *de facto* states (as discussed in Section 4.).

7. CONCLUSION

The August war of 2008 showed the EU two facts quite plainly: the further away conflicts break out, the more likely it becomes that the EU will have to co-ordinate its interests with other key players, be it Russia, Iran or Turkey, and, moreover, without meaningful and comprehensive conflict prevention tools, the concept of state sovereignty will become gradually eroded. One of these tools, the ENP, albeit not conceptually finalized, represents the first serious attempt of the EU to exert positive influence in the volatile region of the South Caucasus. But in view of the unresolved tragedy of Nagorno-Karabakh and other "frozen" conflicts, which showed their potential to unfreeze very quickly as in August 2008, the ENP falls short of effectively contributing to conflict resolution and democracy promotion, because of a number of reasons. First, the ENP was designed as a political framework concentrating on co-operation with governments, enabling the EU to directly negotiate with the states concerned in the region. This forced the Union to co-operate partly with very nationalistic governments, which still have problems recognizing that "breakaway" regions do not simply break away unless there is a reason for it, such as manifestations of nationalism resulting in ethnic cleansing. This is compounded by the dilemma that the various crisis zones of the Caucasus have been out of reach for the respective governments for nearly 20 years and are, therefore, also out of reach for the positive provisions of the ENP. In other words, the concept of the ENP makes it difficult to involve nongovernmental organizations, civil society organizations or even *de facto* governments of the breakaway states. Second, the ENP does not assign Russia a specific role. This does not mean that Russia should be awarded veto rights, but an enhanced and considerably improved relation with Moscow—for instance, by accelerating the process of the formulation of the four common spaces—should be envisaged to make the ENP both more attractive and more efficient. However, technical shortcomings such as relatively vague stipulations of gains for ENP states also dilute the possible success. Finally, the role of other actors, such as the United States, are not sufficiently addressed by the ENP in regions that are "overcrowded" in a sense that the interest of various states and international organizations are aroused with their great cultural influences, contradictory magnitudes and geopolitical potentials.

The way to counteract local disparities in the Caucasus and to prevent these from turning into violence lies beyond a doubt not only in a strategy of pro-active position and intervention. Also, a policy of restraint and non-participation and critical self-reflection is needed.

Vanda Amaro Dias

EU Relations with Eastern Europe and the South Caucasus: Towards the Eastern Partnership Policy

1. Introduction

Since the end of the Cold War, the importance of Eastern Europe and the South Caucasus for the EU security has grown in scope and depth, especially in the political, economic and energetic fields. In fact, relations with the neighbourhood were always of pivotal importance to the EU's foreign and security policies. This follows from the belief that the EU's security starts outside its borders and, thus, it is interested in promoting new frameworks for these countries to come into a gradual integration with the EU. The Union perceives "situations of poverty and under-development as security relevant because they potentially le[a]d to conflict"[1] and create insecurities that can easily affect its internal stability and the main (liberal) principles of the EU's identity. As a consequence, there is a widespread perception that the EU's most visible security challenges – from terrorism to illegal immigration – cannot be properly addressed without external action. Accordingly, the EU has externalised its internal security goals through various forms of external action, namely the various PCAs concluded with the countries of the former Soviet Union, the ENP and its most recent initiatives in Eastern Europe and the South Caucasus: the Black Sea Synergy (BSS) and the EaP. The goal is to bring the countries in these regions into a gradual integration with the EU economy and to foster political reforms to reduce socio-economic imbalances in order to reinforce European security.

However, the EU faces several challenges in its eastern vicinity. Eastern Europe and the South Caucasus are disputed regions where other regional actors – such as Russia, Turkey and Iran – have defined their own neighbouring policies and strategic interests. These often clash with the EU's own approaches towards the region. For these regional powers tend to regard the EU's neighbouring policies with distrust, they try to hamper its ability to transform the political and socio-economic environments in their common neighbourhood.

In order to understand the security dynamics underlying the EU´s relations with Eastern Europe and the South Caucasus, this chapter will provide an overview of EU policies and approaches towards these regions. The goal is to contribute to a

1 *Barnutz*, The EU's Logic of Security: Politics Through Institutionalised Discourses, European Security 2010, 377 (378).

better understanding of these approaches and to identify the main challenges the EU faces when dealing with these countries. For that purpose, the chapter will proceed in the following way. Firstly, it frames EU relations with Eastern Europe and the South Caucasus under the PCAs concluded during the 1990s and technical and assistance programmes (such as TACIS) aiming at encouraging democratisation and the strengthening of the rule of law in the region. Secondly, the chapter analyses the ENP as a new framework for relations with countries in these regions following the EU's last rounds of enlargement. The third part sheds light on regional initiatives under the framework of the ENP, such as the EaP and the BSS, as new attempts to reinforce the EU's footprint in the Eastern neighbourhood. The fourth part briefly assesses the evolution of EU relations with Moldova, Georgia, Armenia and Azerbaijan as an illustration of the EU's approaches towards Eastern Europe and the South Caucasus. The chapter ends with final considerations regarding the EU's overall approach towards the identified regions.

2. LAYING DOWN THE FOUNDATIONS OF EU RELATIONS WITH EASTERN EUROPE AND THE SOUTH CAUCASUS

After the end of the Cold War the EU put in place a system of PCAs with the countries of the former Soviet Union without membership prospects. Their aim was to develop a framework for political dialogue and economic co-operation between these countries and the EU. However, a close examination of the PCAs reveals that they are largely identical, with little differences between them. They failed to acknowledge specific needs of and demands by partner countries and lacked clear incentives to promote change and transformation at a time when these countries were struggling with several difficulties and very much focusing on their internal transitions.[2] Accordingly, the PCAs established during the 1990s were seldom enforced leading to an overall failure to achieve their goals.[3] As a result, this remained a low-profile and generally unsatisfactory framework for relations with the EU's Eastern neighbourhood.

To complement the political framework of the PCAs, in the early 1990s, the Commission launched the TACIS programme aiming at assisting these countries to implement reforms in the administrative, institutional and legal fields, and develop cooperation at the regional level.[4] Technical assistance under the TACIS programme consists mainly of financial contributions that should be allocated to develop new legal frameworks and institutional structures.[5] Under this programme the

---

2 *Joenniemi*, Carving out a "Ring of Friends". The Impact of the ENP on the Shape of Europe, in *Armstrong / Anderson* (eds), Geopolitics of European Union Enlargement 2007, 142 (147).

3 *Ghazaryan*, The ENP and the Southern Caucasus: Meeting the Expectations? in *Whitman / Wolff* (eds) The European Neighbourhood Policy in Perspective: Context, Implementation and Impact, 2010, 223 (226).

4 *Lussac*, Ensuring European Energy Security in Russian "Near Abroad": The Case of the South Caucasus, European Security 2010, 607 (610).

5 *Sodupe / Benito*, The Evolution of the European Union's Tacis Programme, 1991-1996, Journal of Communist Studies and Transition Politics 1998, 51 (55).

EU developed initiatives and approaches towards countries in the region in a number of sectors, including development of human resources, entrepreneurial development and restructuring, transport and communications, energy and nuclear safety, food production and distribution, and environment.[6] Among them TRACECA (Transportation Corridor Europe-Caucasus-Asia) and INOGATE (Interstate Oil and Gas Transport to Europe) are considered to be the most relevant and successful.[7] These programmes allowed the EU to take part in the implementation of hydrocarbons routes in the South Caucasus, thus attracting the countries in the region towards greater integration with the EU.

Despite the development of these initiatives, the EU remained a low-profile player in the region until the development of the ENP. In part, this was due to the fact that the Eastern enlargement was the main focus of the EU's foreign and security policy. However, the fact that Russia and other regional powers preserved an important leverage in the former Soviet space, thus constraining the evolution of EU relations with these countries, should not be disregarded as an explanation for the EU's lack of engagement in the region during the 1990s.

3. The ENP: A new approach towards the EU's Eastern vicinity

Although the EU has always recognised – at least rhetorically – the importance of Eastern Europe and the South Caucasus to its foreign and security policies, it was not until the creation of the ENP in 2004, that the EU started to pay greater attention to countries in these regions. The biggest concern underlying the ENP was that negative security aspects of the new neighbourhood could spill-over into the Union and destabilize its internal order.[8] This policy was thus designed to deal with the security implications of the EU's last rounds of enlargement. Inspired by the enlargement process,[9] the ENP aims at creating a "ring of friends" around the EU, "to avoid new dividing lines in Europe", and to "promote stability and prosperity" across the continent.[10] However, the ENP Strategy Paper strictly recognized that this policy "offers a means to reinforce relations between the EU and partner countries, which is distinct from the possibilities available to European countries under Art 49 of the TEU",[11] i.e. the membership process.

---

6 *Sodupe / Benito*, op. cit. note 5, 59.

7 *Andreev*, The Future of the European Neighbourhood Policy and the Role of Regional Cooperation in the Black Sea Area, Southeast European and Black Sea Studies 2008, 93 (100).

8 *Joenniemi* op. cit. note 2, 143.

9 *Gebhard*, The ENP's Strategic Conception and Design Overstretching the Enlargement Template, in *Whitman / Wolff* (eds), The European Neighbourhood Policy in Perspective: Context, Implementation and Impact 2010, 89 (92).

10 Communication from the Commission to the Council and the European Parliament, Wider Europe — Neighbourhood: A New Framework for Relations with our Eastern and Southern Neighbours, COM (2003) 104 final.

11 Communication from the Commission, European Neighbourhood Policy Strategy Paper, COM (2004) 373 final, 3.

The ENP's roots lie in the European Security Strategy (ESS), developed in 2003 and further reinforced in 2008,[12] recognising that the enlargement brought "the EU closer to troubled areas"[13] and the need to promote stability and good governance in the immediate EU neighbourhood.[14] The document also clearly acknowledges that "the internal and external aspects of security are indissolubly linked"[15] and therefore EU security interests cannot be untied from its overall approach to the neighbourhood.[16] In this regard, both the ESS and the ENP represent a shift from passive to active engagement in the EU's neighbourhood[17] with clear security purposes. Furthermore, the appointment of the EUSR to the South Caucasus, in 2003, and Moldova, 2005, represented an undeniable sign that the EU was ready to undertake a stronger and more active approach towards the region. To accomplish its socioeconomic and political objectives the ENP has also created new policy mechanisms such as the ENPI and the Governance Facility Neighbourhood Investment Fund.[18]

While the PCAs remain, legally and structurally, the basis of the EU's cooperation with the Eastern neighbourhood, the ENP created APs, a new political instrument based on (positive) conditionality and intended to frame the EU's relations with each one of its partners.[19] In fact, conditionality is the ENP's main instrument, whereby the EU offers a share in its internal market and financial support to stimulate economic, political and social reforms, as well as security cooperation in the neighbourhood.[20] The ENP thus establishes a series of bilateral channels between the EU and each neighbour, where the latter is expected to accept European political and economic values in order to be acknowledged as part of the EU's "ring of friends", though this does not guarantee accession to the Union.[21] The overall goal is to address the root causes of instability, crisis and conflict at the EU's borders. In addition, the ENP has a socialization axis relying on social learning processes resulting from institutional and people-to-people contacts and aiming at creating a collectively shared understanding of proper behaviour. This results in a structural foreign policy seeking to influence and transform the political, economic and social systems of the EU's neighbours,[22] as a *sine qua non* condition to preserve EU internal security. However, in practice, socialization has not been extensively applied or has been restricted by domestic constraints,[23] lessening the EU's

---

12 European Council Report on the Implementation of the European Security Strategy – Providing Security in a Changing World, Brussels, 11 December 2008, S407/08.

13 European Council, European Security Strategy: A Secure Europe in a Better World, Brussels, 12 December 2003.

14 *Joenniemi* op. cit. note 2, 143.

15 European Council, 2003, 2.

16 *Browning / Joenniemi*, Geostrategies of the European Neighbourhood Policy, European Journal of International Relations, 2008, 519 (520).

17 *Joenniemi* op. cit. note 2, 145.

18 *Andreev*, op. cit. note 7, 93.

19 COM(2003) 104 final, 16.

20 COM(2003) 104 final, 10-15.

21 *Joffé*, Europe and Islam. Partnership or Peripheral Dependence? in *Armstrong / Anderson* (eds), Geopolitics of European Union Enlargement 2007, 90 (98).

22 *Emerson*, Just Good Friends? The European Union's Multiple Neighbourhood Policies, The International Spectator 2011, 45 (57).

23 *Boonstra / Shapovalova*, The EU's Eastern Partnership: One Year Backwards, FRIDE Working Paper No 99 2010, at 2.

capacity to promote the transformation of the security environment at its borders. Furthermore, the political and financial offers on the table are much less appealing when compared to the enlargement process and the costs of reforms promoted by the EU are too high, which together with the lack of a membership perspective diminishes the EU's transformative potential and decreases the likelihood of a successful strategy based on socialization and conditionality.[24] This propelled the EU to develop regional initiatives aimed at reinforcing its approach towards the Eastern neighbourhood, such as the BSS and the EaP, which are analyzed in closer detail in the next section.

4. Black Sea Synergy and Eastern Partnership: Reinforcing the EU's footprint in Eastern Europe and the South Caucasus

A series of events such as the regression of the democratic progresses in Eastern Europe and the South Caucasus, the lack of democracy improvements in the region, the Russian-Georgian war in 2008, the severe economic crisis experienced by the Eastern neighbourhood in 2009, and the vulnerability of energy supplies from the region, among others, reminded the EU that security, stability and economic development remain key challenges in its Eastern neighbourhood.[25]

After the last rounds of enlargement, the EU became a Black Sea power with undisputed security interests in the region. To fully assume this role, Brussels has been trying to develop a clear and comprehensive strategy towards the region. As a result, in 2007 the EU launched the BSS. This initiative is a facilitation mechanism aiming at promoting the EU's interests in the neighbourhood on a set of policies of regional interest, such as migration, law enforcement, good governance, the protracted conflicts, energy security and the fight against organised crime.[26] One of its main goals is to circumvent the flaws and shortcomings of the EU's bilateral policies towards the region by promoting a regional multilateral framework for co-operation.[27] In addition, it acknowledges that a dynamic regional initiative can further help to address problems in the Black Sea area, "benefit the citizens of the countries concerned as well as to contribute to the overall prosperity, stability and security in Europe".[28]

The initiative promotes variable degrees of co-operation depending on the sector at stake and demands by each country in the region. It identifies thirteen top priority areas for co-operation in the Black Sea region, including: democracy, respect for

---

24 *Ágh*, Regionalisation as a Driving Force of EU Widening: Recovering from the EU "Carrot Crisis"
in the "East", Europe-Asia Studies 2010, 1239 (1241).

25 *Boonstra / Shapovalova*, op. cit. note 23.

26 *Andreev*, op. cit. note 7, 101-102.

27 *Tassinari*, Region-building as Trust-building: The EU's Faltering Involvement in the Black Sea Region, Southeast European and Black Sea Studies 2012, 227 (232).

28 Communication from the Commission, Black Sea Synergy – A New Regional Cooperation Initiative, COM (2007) 160 final, 2.

human rights and good governance; border management and security; the protracted conflicts; energy security; transport; environment; maritime policy; fisheries; trade; research and education networks; science and technology; employment and social affairs; and regional development.[29] Progress in these sectors is understood as an essential contribution to stimulate reforms in the policy and economic realms, support stability and sustainable growth, and promote the resolution of conflicts in the region.[30]

In order to further enhance the EU's relationship with the countries of Eastern Europe and the South Caucasus and address the rampant security challenges in the region, the EaP initiative was endorsed in Prague in 2009, based on a Polish-Swedish proposal.[31] It aims to promote further integration between these countries and the EU, in order to assure European security and stability. For that purpose, the EaP promotes new frameworks for these countries to come into gradual integration with the EU economy and fosters political reforms to reduce socio-economic imbalances. Overall, the goal is to reinforce the framework previously provided under the ENP and complement the BSS initiative[32] giving coherence to the EU's approach towards its Eastern vicinity.

The need to offer further differentiation, ownership and a more ambitious partnership between the EU and its Eastern neighbours, suggesting a greater role for the EU in the region, is at the core of this initiative.[33] For that purpose, it provides a dual-track approach combining the traditional bilateral relations between the EU and its neighbouring countries – that foresees their political association with and economic integration into EU – with a multilateral track that supports regional co-operation and the development of closer ties among the EaP partners.[34]

At the bilateral level the EaP's main goals – "to create a closer relationship between the EU and each of the partner countries to foster their stability and prosperity in our mutual interests" – are to be implemented through AAs, which will supersede the PCAs as the legal basis for EU relations with its Eastern neighbours, deep and comprehensive free trade areas, visa liberalisation, enhanced co-operation in the field of energy security and support to reforms in the EU's partner countries.[35] Conditionality remains the main instrument to promote transformation in the region. However, the EaP's incentives are seen as too vague, distant and costly[36] and therefore hamper the initiative's transformative potential.

The multilateral track, run by the EEAS, is the main novelty of the EaP. Based upon the principle of differentiation, the multilateral dimension is regarded as one of the main strengths of the EaP providing for high-level political support and a number of experts meetings, which may have the potential to ensure its practical

---

29 COM (2007) 160 final.

30 *Tsantoulis*, Geopolitics, (Sub)regionalism, Discourse and a Troubles "Power Triangle" in the Black Sea, Southeast European and Black Sea Studies 2009, 243 (253).

31 Council of the European Union, Joint Declaration of the Prague Eastern Partnership Summit. Prague, 7 May 2009, 8435/09 (Presse 78).

32 *Ágh*, op. cit. note 24, 1255.

33 Communication from the Commission, Eastern Partnership, COM (2008) 823 final.

34 Council of the European Union, 2009, 8435/09 (Presse 78), 6.

35 COM (2008) 823 final, 3.

36 *Boonstra / Shapovalova*,op. cit. note 23, 3.

impact. Furthermore, it opens a number of channels for socialisation and social learning that can impact positively on the EU's approach towards the Eastern neighbourhood and represent an improvement over the original ENP framework.[37] According to the Joint Declaration of the Prague EaP Summit held in 2009 "it will provide a forum to share information and experience on the partner countries' steps towards transition, reform and modernisation and give the EU an additional instrument to accompany these processes. It will facilitate the development of common positions and joint activities".[38]

There are four thematic platforms: 1. democracy, good governance and stability 2. economic integration and convergence with EU policies 3. energy security 4. and contacts between people) and five flagship initiatives outlined within this track but funded by the private sector.[39] Another innovation of the EaP is the Comprehensive Institution-Building Programme "for improving administrative capacity in all relevant sectors of cooperation",[40] "including training, technical assistance and any appropriate innovative measures".[41] The EaP also attempts to create a joint Neighbourhood Economic Community and involve non-state actors into this framework through the creation of EURONEST – the EU-Eastern partners Parliamentary Assembly – and the EaP Civil Society Forum, though their influence in the overall process is not clear.[42] So far, the multilateral track has been successfully implemented and the four multilateral thematic platforms have met regularly since 2009, suggesting that the EaP has the potential to amplify the ENP´s effectiveness in the region.[43]

Along with the BSS, the EaP provides a response to some of the EU's Eastern neighbours complaints regarding the fact that the ENP groups them with countries without membership aspirations and with very different relations with Brussels, i.e. the Mediterranean countries.[44] Simultaneously, it focuses on the areas the EU perceives as vital to preserve its security, namely political capacity-building, socio-economic development, immigration and energy security.[45]

However, the EU's approach eastwards is by no means consensual among EU Member States. Given the historical past and memory of many of the EU's new members, these countries tend to favour a stronger rapprochement towards the East and the inclusion of membership in the frameworks for relations with the Eastern neighbourhood. That position is not shared by France and Germany, which fear that any rapprochement to the East might jeopardise their relations with Russia and thus

---

37 Ibid. 6.

38 Council of the European Union, 2009, 8435/09 (Presse 78), 8.

39 COM (2008) 823 final, 9-12.

40 COM (2008) 823 final, 4.

41 Council of the European Union, 2009, 8435/09 (Presse 78), 7.

42 *Korosteleva*, The Eastern Partnership Initiative: A New Opportunity for Neighbours? Journal of Communist Studies and Transition Politics 2011, 1 (2).

43 Report to the Meeting of Foreign Affairs Ministers, Implementation of the Eastern Partnership, 2010, December, 13. Meeting doc. 336/10 REV 2.

44 *Whitman / Wolff*, Much Ado about Nothing? The European Neighbourhood Policy in Context, in *Whitman / Wolff* (eds), The European Neighbourhood Policy in Perspective: Context, Implementation and Impact (2010), 3 (14).

45 Report to the Meeting of Foreign Affairs Ministers, Implementation of the Eastern Partnership, 2009, December 8. Meeting doc. 319/09.

are reluctant to strengthen the Eastern dimension of the ENP or include a membership perspective within the EaP.[46]

These diverging approaches within the EU have hampered the effective promotion of its norms and values in the Eastern neighbourhood, affecting perceptions *vis-à-vis* the coherence and effectiveness of the EU's foreign and neighbouring policies. The almost simultaneous launching of the BSS and the EaP has further complicated the EU's approach towards the region and indicates a degree of overlapping agendas and policy priorities. Moreover, despite the fact that the EaP is still at a very early-stage and is often praised for providing increased differentiation between the Southern and Eastern neighbourhood,[47] the EU's partners in the region have criticised the initiative for its lack of real added-value compared to the existing frameworks for relations with the EU. They argue that the BSS has the advantage to involve Russia and Turkey, and therefore can play a bigger role in addressing common security issues in the region, something that the EaP lacks.[48] Therefore, a number of questions remain regarding the actual scope and purpose of the EU's multiple frameworks for relations with countries in Eastern Europe and the South Caucasus.[49]

Notwithstanding these critiques, the EU's own evaluation of its neighbouring policies has been rather positive. As stated in the EaP Warsaw Summit: "…much has been achieved already. Political and economic reforms have been implemented in partner countries and relations between the EU and its Eastern European partners have deepened significantly. There is more trade and economic interaction between the EU and the Eastern European partners than ever before".[50] According to the EU significant bilateral and multilateral progresses were made in implementing the EaP. Civil Society Forum platforms have been established in all EaP countries and there has been substantial progress in negotiations on AAs, including DCFTAs. Financial assistance to the EaP partners has also increased considerably in order to support reforms in these countries.[51] The next section sheds light on the evolution of EU relations with Moldova, Georgia, Armenia and Azerbaijan as an illustration of the EU's above-analyzed policies and approaches towards Eastern Europe and the South Caucasus.

---

46 *Nitoiu*, Reconceptualizing "Cooperation" in EU-Russia Relations, Perspectives on European Politics and Security, 2011, 462 (465).

47 *Boonstra / Shapovalova*, op. cit. note 23, 1.

48 *Ágh*, op. cit. note 24, 1255.

49 *Tsantoulis*,op. cit. note 30, 254.

50 Council of the European Union, Joint Declaration of the Eastern Partnership Summit. 2011, Warsaw, 29-30 September. 14983/11 PRESSE 341.

51 European Commission / High Representative of the European Union for Foreign Affairs and Security Policy Joint Communication, European Neighbourhood Policy: Working Towards a Stronger Partnership, JOIN (2013) 4 final, 15.

5. Assessing EU relations with Moldova, Georgia, Armenia and Azerbaijan

As previously mentioned, since the 1990s the EU has developed several frameworks for relations with the countries in Eastern Europe and the South Caucasus. After the dissolution of the Soviet Union, these countries found themselves in complete disarray. Political instability, economic unsustainability and conflicts in the region further contributed to the perception of those countries as a security threat and prompted the EU to engage with them by establishing a number of channels for bilateral and multilateral relations. However, the EU still faces several challenges in the region, such as political instability, socio-economic imbalances and the protracted conflicts – namely the Transnistrian conflict in Moldova, the conflicts in South Ossetia and Abkhazia in Georgia, and the Nagorno-Karabakh conflict between Armenia and Azerbaijan. The EU regards the protracted conflicts in Eastern Europe and the South Caucasus as a threat to regional stability and its own security. For they are often associated with terrorism, organized crime and illegal trafficking, they also undermine efforts to promote regional co-operation and economic development, thus further destabilizing the region.[52]

Under the framework of the CSDP and the ENP, the EU managed to become more active on security issues in the region. It inaugurated the EU Rule of Law Mission to Georgia in 2003 (EUJUST THEMIS), the EU Border Assistance Mission (EUBAM) in co - operation with Moldova and Ukraine in 2005, and the EU Monitoring Mission (EUMM) in Georgia in 2008 following the Russian-Georgian war. Alongside, the EU sees relationships with countries in the region as a means to access the energy deposits of the Caspian Sea and counterweigh its dependence on Russian energy assets. In order to guarantee security of energy transit and supplies the EU has also been involved in mediating gas disputes between Russia and countries in the region.[53]

Another important factor to bear in mind is that the countries in the EU's Eastern vicinity are also part of the sphere of influence of significant regional powers, such as Russia, Turkey and Iran. Among the main challenges these regional actors pose to the EU's security and neighbouring policies in Eastern Europe and the South Caucasus are: Russian active and non-impartial role in the protracted conflicts in the region, its desire to monopolize the energy transportation from the South Caucasus and its foreign policiy interests *vis-à-vis* the countries in the region;[54] Turkish regional pragmatism, its policy of "zero problems with neighbours"[55] and its *status*

---

[52] *German*, Visibly Invisible: EU Engagement in Conflict Resolution in the South Caucasus, European Security 2007, 357 (358).

[53] *Tsantoulis*, op. cit. note 30, 253.

[54] *Abushov*, Policing the Near Abroad: Russian Foreign Policy in the South Caucasus, Australian Journal of International Affairs 2009, 187 (187-188).

[55] *Kahraman*, Turkey and the European Union in the Middle East: Reconciling or Competing with Each Other? Turkish Studies 2011, 699 (700).

quo approach towards the Black Sea region; and the Moscow-backed involvement of Iran in the South Caucasus.[56]

Even though the Union regards Iran as a pariah state, it is very much aware of the need to maintain friendly relationships with Moscow and Ankara and therefore has preferred to follow a pragmatic approach towards Moldova, Georgia, Armenia and Azerbaijan. In this regard, Brussels has adopted a cautious approach towards its Eastern vicinity, mostly because it fears that any successful policy towards the region – and thus any attempt to secure its borders – might conflict with the interests and *modi operandi* of these players, therefore jeopardizing EU relations with these regional powers. The region is, thus, a unique laboratory of overlapping and conflicting power dynamics, which are a root cause of tension in the region and prevent the EU from deepening its relations with the Eastern neighbours. As a result the EU has, so far, opted for a relatively soft and low-profile approach towards the region promoting capacity-building and socio-economic development measures[57] in order to guarantee European security.

EU relations with Moldova, Georgia, Azerbaijan and Armenia are based on the PCAs signed during the 1990s and intended to promote transition to a free democracy and market economy. To do so they provide a framework for co-operation in several areas including political dialogue, trade and investment, economic co-operation, legislative approximation, administration reforms, culture and science.[58] Based on common values and a commitment to promote international peace and security, the PCAs have also institutionalised relations between Brussels and these countries by creating Co-operation Councils, Co-operation Committees and Parliamentary Committees for Cooperation.[59] These institutions focused on reforming specific sectors in order to harmonise these countries legislation with the *acquis communautaire*, and thus change their political and socio-economic environments. To support this process the PCAs set up the basis for the implementation of TACIS, through which the EU's partners received significant financial and technical support for legal and administrative reforms, as well as cross-border cooperation, justice and home affairs. However – and due to distinct political, economic and security realities in the countries in the region[60] and their different strategic interests –, the EU's relations with these countries evolved in different ways and at diverse speeds.

---

[56] *Simão / Freire*, The EU's Neighbourhood Policy and the South Caucasus: Unfolding New Patterns of Cooperation, Caucasian Review of International Affairs 2008, 225 (232).

[57] *Biscop*, The ENP Security and Democracy in Context, in *Whitman / Wolff* (eds), The European Neighbourhood Policy in Perspective: Context, Implementation and Impact (2010), 73 (83).

[58] Commission Staff Working Paper, European Neighbourhood Policy Country Report – Moldova, SEC (2004) 567, 3.

[59] *Bosse*, The EU's Relations with Moldova: Governance, Partnership or Ignorance? Europe-Asia Studies 2010, 1291 (1296).

[60] *Simão / Freire*, op. cit. note 56, 225.

6. MOLDOVA

Overall, Moldova is regarded as one of the EU's best "pupils". Moldova is keen to act on most of the key recommendations addressed by the EU and to implement legal and socio-economic reforms, engage in dialogue with Tiraspol, and reinforce co - operation with the EU on several sectors.[61] Moldova recognizes European integration as its fundamental national objective. Nevertheless, and despite a general positive progression of Moldova, during the 1990s EU-Moldova relations were often characterised by missed opportunities rather than by strategic engagement.[62]

Since 2004, the ENP and the EU-Moldova AP (endorsed in 2005) are the main frameworks for relations between the EU and Moldova. The EU-Moldova co-operation's main goal is to develop close relations in the area of "foreign and security policy and in the resolution of the conflict in Transnistria, and to promote economic growth and poverty reduction",[63] as well as people-to-people contacts. The Transnistria issue and the dialogue on visa-free travel for Moldovan citizens are perhaps the most important topics of the EU-Moldova agenda.[64] Moldova has been actively co-operating with the EU on regional and international issues, including the Transnistrian issue. Chisinau is fully committed to the work of EUBAM[65] and strongly supports the settlement of the conflict.[66] As a sign of its support, the EU opened a European Commission diplomatic mission in Chisinau in 2005 and appointed the first EUSR for Moldova in March 2005. Not only did he work intensively in Brussels and Chisinau to promote the resolution of the conflict, but he also paid several visits to the Transnistrian region in order to establish contacts with local officials and organizations, and increase awareness about what was happening on the ground.[67] Furthermore, the EU has generously sponsored border management and border control projects in the country – that has become the top aid recipient per capita in the region[68] – as a way to contribute to the settlement of the Transnistria conflict.

Despite Chisinau's positive performance and the EU-Moldova political dialogue intensification, there is still significant progresses needed in a number of sensitive areas, namely: "ensuring the fundamental freedoms of citizens, addressing some market and regulatory issues, and enforcing effectively national strategies in areas

---

61 JOIN (2013) 4 final, 4.

62 *Danii / Mascauteanu*, Moldova Under the European Neighbourhood Policy: "Falling Between Stools", Journal of Communist Studies and Transition Politics 2011, 99 (100-101).

63 European Commission, European Neighbourhood and Partnership Instrument – Republic of Moldova: Country Strategy Paper 2007-2013, 2007.Available at: <http://ec.europa.eu/world/enp/pdf/country/enpi_csp_moldova_en.pdf>.

64 Meeting doc. 319/09.

65 *Bosse*, op. cit. note 59,1299.

66 Commission Staff Working Document, Implementation of the European Neighbourhood Policy in 2008: Progress Report Republic of Moldova. 2009, SEC (2009) 514/2, 2.

67 *Bosse*, op. cit. note 59, 1302.

68 *Korosteleva*, Moldova's European Choice: "Between Two Stools"? Europe-Asia Studies 2010, 1267 (1276-1277).

such as the fight against corruption, drugs and trafficking in human beings, or in sectors such as transport and energy".[69]

Although Moldova did not welcome the EaP at first because it perceived the initiative as derogatory and unclear, and condemned the lack of inclusion of a membership prospect,[70] the country is regarded as the EaP's success story and the only country whose relations with the EU have developed dynamically since the launch of the EaP. The EU-Moldova Mobility Partnership is currently in force and progresses have been noted in the fight against illegal migration and the trafficking of human beings.[71] In 2010, Moldova became a full member of the Energy Community Treaty contributing to the EU's aim to promote a secure energy supply system in the neighbourhood.[72] The bilateral co-operation under the framework of the EaP provides the foundations for the AA that will deepen EU-Moldova political association and economic integration by promoting further convergence to EU legislation and standards.[73] The EU and Moldova recently signed the AA that will enhance their relations across all areas of co-operation and provide for establishing a DCFTA with the EU.[74] Furthermore, in 2011 Chisinau confirmed its interest in the Comprehensive Institution Building Programme and the new flagship initiatives envisaged by the EaP. This programme, developed jointly by the Commission and Moldova, intends to assist Moldova with institution-building initiatives needed to prepare the implementation of the AA and DCFTA. In this field, the EU's reports emphasise the good evolution of relations with Chisinau and the positive steps to prepare Moldova for the implementation of a DCFTA.

Perceptions about the EU and European integration remain widely positive stressing the EU's support to political and economic reforms in the country.[75] Therefore, the EU leverage on the country remains high but Moldova's political instability makes it hard to predict for how long the EU will be an attractive partner to Chisinau.[76] This results largely from the fact that Moldova is still overwhelmingly dependent on Russia in the political, economic and energetic fields, not to mention that Moscow remains an active player in the Transnistrian conflict supporting Tiraspol to preserve the *status quo* and keep Chisinau in its sphere of influence.

---

69 SEC (2009) 514/2, 2-3.

70 *Korosteleva*, Change or Continuity: Is the Eastern Partnership an Adequate Tool for the European Neighbourhood? International Relations 2011, 243 (252).

71 Meeting doc. 336/10 REV 2, 2.

72 Meeting doc. 336/10 REV 2, 6.

73 European Commission, European and Partnership Instrument – Republic of Moldova: National Indicative Programme 2011-2013, 2011. Available at: <http://ec.europa.eu/world/enp/pdf/country/2011_enp_nip_moldova_en.pdf>.

74 European Commission, 2011, 8.

75 *Radchuk*, Contested Neighbourhood, or How to Reconcile the Differences, Journal of Communist Studies and Transition Politics 2011, 22 (29).

76 *Boonstra / Shapovalova*, op. cit. note 23, 10.

7. Georgia

Along with Moldova, Georgia is perceived to be one of the EU's closer partners in the region. After the Rose Revolution in 2003, which was strongly welcomed by Brussels, EU-Georgia relations acquired a considerable momentum. Since then, Georgia rapprochement to Western institutions such as the EU, but also NATO, became a clear part of Tbilisi's strategy to balance Russian influence in the South Caucasus.[77] Accordingly, levels of contacts between the EU and Georgia were intensified and the EU provided further assistance to the implementation of reforms in the country.[78] In 2003, the EU appointed an EUSR for the South Caucasus to promote the co-ordinated implementation of EU policies in the region.[79] Moreover, in 2004, the EU launched EUJUST Themis in Georgia using the civilian crisis management arrangements within the CFDP. This rule of law mission was intended to help Georgia to define a long-term strategy to reform the criminal justice sector and successfully accomplished its mission in 2005.[80] That same year, Georgia adopted a National Security Concept that revealed European integration as one of the main axis of its foreign policies. In fact, Georgia is the most pro-Western of the three South Caucasus states and it is actively promoting the implementation of several projects that intend to increase its integration in Western institutions and away from the Russian sphere of influence.[81] Among those are TRACECA, INOGATE, the Baku-Tbilisi-Ceyhan pipeline and other projects aiming to create an EU-Asia corridor via the South Caucasus. These projects also reveal the country's strategic position as a transit route between Europe and Asia, and its important contribution to counter-terrorism in the region further confirmed Georgia's singular relevance to the overall European security.

The secessionist conflicts in South Ossetia and Abkhazia – both of which have existed as *de facto* independent stated since the early 1990s – represent the most serious threats to security and stability in Georgia. The Russian-Georgian war in August 2008 only made this situation clearer, thus providing the momentum for the EU to play a more active role in the region. The EU assumed a mediating position between the parties and created a six-point ceasefire agreement on 12 August. Although the EP acknowledged Georgia's responsibility for starting the war, it was clear that its condemnation rested with Russia alone. In particular, the EU was very critical of Moscow's policy of distributing Russian passports to South Ossetian and Abkhaz citizens and considered it a provocative stance towards Georgia.[82] Even though this was interpreted as a clear sign of the EU's willingness and capability to play a significant role in regional security, the limitations of the ceasefire agreement

---

77 *Abushov*, op. cit. note 54, 197.

78 Commission Staff Working Paper, European Neighbourhood Policy Country Report – Georgia, SEC (2005) 288/3, 3.

79 *Simão / Freire*, op. cit. note 56, 232.

80 SEC (2005) 288/3, 4.

81 *German*, Good Neighbours or Distant Relatives? Regional Identity and Cooperation in the South Caucasus, Central Asia Survey 2012, 137 (143).

82 *Bowker*, The War in Georgia and the Western Response, Central Asia Survey 2011, 197 (201).

were made clear in the discussion about possible sanctions against Russia.[83] Moreover, the fact that the EUMM is not permitted access to the "occupied territories" in Georgia[84] severely restrains its ability to change the grass root causes of the conflict and promote its sustainable resolution. Despite appeals from the Georgian government, the EU's involvement in Abkhazia is far less significant.[85] In general, its main contribution to conflict resolution in the region is still financial as the EU has been providing assistance for the rehabilitation of the conflict zones since 1997 and has become the largest donour to the South Caucasus. Nonetheless, the EUSR is co-chairing the Geneva International Discussions in Georgia, which remains the only forum for dialogue between Tbilisi and the breakaway regions of South Ossetia and Abkhazia.[86]

Under the EaP framework the EU launched regular Human Rights meetings with Georgia[87] and provided technical and financial assistance to mitigate socio-economic imbalances in the country. In 2009, the EU-Georgia Mobility Partnership was launched after the conclusion of negotiations on visa facilitation and readmission agreements.[88] Finally, the EU-Georgia AA [89] opened up a new stage in EU-Georgia relations.

8. ARMENIA AND AZERBAIJAN

The Nagorno-Karabakh conflict dominates the foreign policies of Armenia and Azerbaijan which are still officially at war over the mountainous region. The EU regards the lack of progresses in finding a sustainable solution to the conflict as a destabilizing factor that impacts negatively on European security.[90] However, the EU's involvement in the resolution of this conflict is currently very limited, as the EU is only supporting the ongoing political dialogue under the OSCE Minsk group and providing financial assistance to address the consequences of this dispute.[91] This is despite EUSR Peter Semneby emphasis on the need to expand the EU's mandate in the region and play a more active role in the resolution of the conflict.[92]

Armenia is a landlocked country that has regarded European integration with pragmatism, as the regime in Yerevan believes that European institutions must be balanced against its strategic partnership with Russia[93] and its relations with Iran.

---

83 *Ghazaryan* in *Whitman / Wolff* (eds), The European Neighbourhood Policy, 234-235.
84 *German*, Securing the South Caucasus: Military Aspects of Russian Policy towards the Region since 2008, Europe-Asia Studies 2012, 1650 (1659).
85 *German*, op. cit. note 52, 365.
86 JOIN (2013) 4 final, 17.
87 Meeting doc. 319/09, 3.
88 Meeting doc. 319/09, 4.
89 Meeting doc. 336/10 REV 2, 2.
90 *Nriyev*, Azerbaijan and the European Union: New Landmarks of Strategic Partnership in the South Caucasus, Southeast European and Black Sea Studies 2008, 155 (160).
91 *German*, op. cit. note 52, 366.
92 *Nriyev*, op. cit. note 89, 162.
93 *German*, op. cit. note 81, 144.

As a result, EU-Armenia relations have not been developing as positively as relations with Moldova or Georgia. After a very low-profile engagement in the country during the 1990s and 2000s, in 2009 the European Commission provided a list of key recommendations to be implemented by Armenia before negotiations on a DCFTA could start.[94] That same year an EU Advisory Group started to work with the Armenian administration in order to prepare negotiations on the future EU-Armenia AA, which were launched in July 2010. Preparations for developing a EU-Armenia Mobility Partnership are also currently taking place.[95] Progress on energy co-operation has been noteworthy and Armenia now has an observer status in the European Energy Community.[96] However, Armenia is still regarded as having an ambiguous approach towards European integration. The EU stresses the fact that Yerevan has acted only on some of the key recommendations under the ENP and EaP frameworks, even though it praises the country for the adoption of a roadmap to improve the electoral processes and a set of other measures aiming at improving the human rights situation in the country and to fight corruption and organized crime.[97] Despite these mild improvements, Armenian President Serzh Sargsyan announced in September 2013 that his country would be seeking to join the Russia-led Customs Union, rather than signing the AA under negotiation, thus weakening relations with Brussels.[98]

Azerbaijan is the country with most natural resources and the largest population in the South Caucasus. In order to develop its resources and strengthen its economy, the country has privileged relations with the West. However, due to the Nagorno-Karabakh issue it remains vulnerable to influences from Russia, Turkey and Iran.[99] Aware of this reality Azerbaijan has sought to maintain a multi-level foreign policy in which it is careful to balance these regional powers against deepening co-operation with the West.[100] Moreover, relations with Armenia remain difficult if seldom existent. Accordingly, for Baku the insistence of the EU in having them co-operate with Yerevan has been seen as an interference in domestic politics.[101] Nonetheless, European integration is promoted in Azerbaijan as a key strategic goal of its foreign policies and the country welcomes the increasing role of Western institutions in the region.

Azerbaijan's strategic importance in terms of energy and geographical location reduces the EU's leverage in the country. Furthermore, the fact that the EU is willing to turn a blind eye to the country's authoritarianism reduces its ability to influence and transform Azerbaijan's behaviour. This is a very important element of differentiation regarding EU relations with other countries in the region, which are willing to develop their relations with the EU and benefit from European integra-

---

94 Meeting doc. 319/09, 3.
95 Meeting doc. 336/10 REV 2, 2.
96 Meeting doc. 336/10 REV 2, 3.
97 JOIN (2013) 4 final, 4.
98 *Topouria*, Armenia Chooses Euroasian Union Over the EU: What Now? 2013. Available at: <http://beyondthe.eu/armenia-chooses-euroasian-union-over-the-eu-what-now/>.
99 *Gachechiladze*, Geopolitics in the South Caucasus: Local and External Players, Geopolitics 2002, 113 (120).
100 *German*, op. cit. 81, 144.
101 *Simão / Freire*, op. cit. note 56, 234.

tion, but have very limited bargaining-chips to negotiate the terms of such integration. As a result, the EU has significant potential for leverage to transform their political and socio-economic systems within the ENP framework.

Energy security is an important field in EU-Azerbaijan relations and it is likely to guide their agenda for the coming years. The two sides made significant progresses in energy co-operation that includes the signature of a Memorandum of Understanding in 2006 on the strategic energy partnership between the EU and Azerbaijan.[102] Azerbaijan is actively involved in the implementation of the TRACECA and the "Great Silk Road" project, which aim to link Europe with Asia via the South Caucasus therefore avoiding Russian territory.[103] Under the EaP framework the EU and Azerbaijan signed agreements on energy related projects that will allow the flow of substantial gas supplies from Azerbaijan and the Caspian Sea region to the EU.[104] Negotiations on the EU-Azerbaijan AA were launched in July 2010[105] and negotiations on a possible EU-Azerbaijan Mobility Partnership started to take place between the two parts. However, and even though the country has a singular strategic importance for the EU's security, progress in EU-Azerbaijan relations has been limited[106] revealing the EU's narrow ability to promote changes in the country.

9. CONCLUSION

Although the EU has always recognised the strategic importance of its Eastern vicinity, it was only in the mid-2000s that the Union started to pay greater attention to the countries in Eastern Europe and the South Caucasus. Through the ENP and its related regional initiatives – especially the BSS and the EaP – the EU has been trying to promote stability and prosperity in its Eastern neighbourhood in order to tackle security challenges in the region.

Despite progresses made under these frameworks, Eastern Europe and the South Caucasus have not yet approached the desired levels of security and stability from the EU's perspective. Overall, the impact of the ENP and its related initiatives in promoting reforms in these regions has been limited. Furthermore, the countries have experienced different evolutionary paths and have diverse strategic foreign policy goals that affect their relations with the EU. While Moldova and Georgia are endeavooring to move closer to the EU, Armenia has an ambiguous approach towards European integration and Azerbaijan, though willing to deepen its relations with the EU, is eager to promote a relationship with Brussels on its own terms. The fact that the EU is not the single actor with defined interests in Eastern Europe and the Southern Caucasus compels Brussels to develop a more explicit and nuanced policy towards Russia, Turkey and Iran if it wants to engage itself more actively in

---

[102] *Nriyev*, op. cit. note 90, 162.
[103] *Gachechiladze*, op. cit. note 98, 124.
[104] Meeting doc. 319/09, 4.
[105] Meeting doc. 336/10 REV 2, 2.
[106] JOIN (2013) 4 final, 4.

the region, without antagonising its regional partners.[107] In this regard, the unfolding of relations among the key regional players in Eastern Europe and the South Caucasus is quintessential for the future and success of the EU's policies and initiatives in the neighbourhood. The EU itself acknowledges that shifts in foreign policy orientations of countries in the region and the growing involvement of other actors in its neighbourhood are diminishing the EU's leverage and attractiveness to countries in the region.[108] This will require the EU to make additional efforts to reinforce its frameworks for relations with Eastern Europe and the South Caucasus and to provide them more coherence and content to address security challenges at its borders.

---

[107] *Joenniemi* op. cit. note 2, 148.
[108] JOIN (2013) 4 final, 22.

Gvantsa Davitashvili

Benefits of the New Treaty Basis for "Neighbourhood Agreements" with Moldova, Ukraine and the Countries of the South Caucasus

"Art 1 AA EU-Georgia: Objectives

1. An Association is hereby established between the Union and its Member States, of the one part and Georgia of the other part.

2. The aims of this Association are:

(a) to promote political association and economic integration between the Parties based on common values and close links, including by increasing Georgia's participation in EU policies, programmes and agencies;

(b) to provide a strengthened framework for enhanced political dialogue on all areas of mutual interest, allowing the development of close political relations between the Parties;

(c) to contribute to the strengthening of democracy and to political, economic and institutional stability in Georgia;

(d) to promote, preserve and strengthen peace and stability in the regional and international dimensions, based on the principles of the UN Charter and the Helsinki Final Act of 1975 of the Conference on Security and Cooperation in Europe, including through joining efforts to eliminate sources of tension, enhance border security, and to promote cross-border cooperation and good neighbourly relations;

(e) to promote cooperation aimed at the peaceful conflict resolution;

(f) to enhance cooperation in the area of freedom, security and justice with the aim of reinforcing the rule of law and the respect for human rights and fundamental freedoms;

(g) to support the efforts of Georgia to develop its economic potential via international cooperation, also through the approximation of its legislation to that of the European Union;

(h) to achieve Georgia's gradual economic integration into the EU Internal Market, as stipulated in this Agreement, notably through establishing a Deep and Comprehensive Free Trade Area which will provide for far-reaching market access on the basis of sustained and comprehensive regulatory approximation in compliance with the rights and obligations arising from the WTO membership;

(i) to establish conditions for an increasingly close cooperation in other areas of mutual interest."

"Art 1 AA EU-Republic of Moldova: Objectives

1. An Association is hereby established between the Union and its Member States, of the one part, and the Republic of Moldova of the other part.

2. The aims of this Association are:

(a) to promote political association and economic integration between the Parties based on common values and close links, including by increasing the Republic of Moldova's participation in EU policies, programmes and agencies;

(b) to strengthen the framework for enhanced political dialogue on all areas of mutual interest, providing for the development of close political relations between the Parties;

(c) to contribute to the strengthening of democracy and to political, economic and institutional stability in the Republic of Moldova;

(d) to promote, preserve and strengthen peace and stability in the regional and international dimensions, including through joining efforts to eliminate sources of tension, enhancing border security, promoting cross-border cooperation and good neighbourly relations;

(e) to support and enhance cooperation in the area of justice, freedom and security with the aim of reinforcing the rule of law and respect for human rights and fundamental freedoms as well as in the area of mobility and people-to-people contacts;

(f) to support the efforts of the Republic of Moldova to develop its economic potential via international cooperation, also through the approximation of its legislation to that of the European Union;

(g) to establish conditions for enhanced economic and trade relations leading towards the Republic of Moldova's gradual integration in the EU Internal Market as stipulated in this Agreement, including by setting up a Deep and Comprehensive Free Trade Area, which will provide for far-reaching regulatory approximation and market access liberalisation, in compliance with the rights and obligations arising out of the WTO membership; and to the transparent application of those rights and obligations; and

(h) to establish conditions for increasingly close cooperation in other areas of mutual interest."

1. Introduction

"The EU should be seen not as a static model, but as a dynamic experiment, a process or a laboratory in which new methods of integration, multi-level and multi-centred governance and a new constitutionalism are being worked on and bargained, and are evolving".[1]

There are many legal and political questions around innovations introduced by the Treaty of Lisbon.[2] More effectiveness, efficiency and coherence of external action of the EU is expected after the adoption of the new Treaty. The Lisbon Treaty created additional bases for the progressive development of external action, several changes were made for strengthening the institutional structure of

---

1 *Cremona*, The Union as a Global Actor: Rules, Models and Identity, Common Market Law Review, 2004, 533 (554)

2 Consolidated Version of the Treaty on European Union, C 115/13 09 May 2008 (TEU); and Consolidated Version of the Treaty on the Functioning of the European Union, C 115/47, 09 May 2008 (TFEU).

the EU, for flexibility of the decision making process, for political visibility and effectiveness, and for the general coherence of the EU's external action.[3]

Among other innovative provisions of the TEU, the subject of our research constitutes Art 8 TEU. The increasing importance of that provision derives from its unclear political and legal value. Thus, the contribution focuses on the role of Art 8 TEU for the European integration of Moldova, Ukraine and the countries of the South Caucasus, as a prospective new legal basis for the "new wave" of AAs. More precisely, it tries to find an answer to the question whether the new Art 8 TEU is capable of having an impact on the process of European integration of the neighbouring countries.

2. CO - OPERATION VS. INTEGRATION

2.1. Introduction

Over the last decade, a new dynamism was brought to the external relations of the EU *vis-à-vis* the countries of the South Caucasus, and *vice versa*. This development commenced with the conclusion of PCAs, followed by the development of an external action approach to the South Caucasus region which places "integration" at the center of the debate. However, the understanding what integration means differs widely and varies from deep co - operation to the prospect of membership.

2.2. Co-operation of the EU with transitional states - The PCAs

When the EU established its first contractual relations with Moldova, Ukraine and the countries of the South Caucasus the aims of the PCAs were quite similar to each other and concerned the sharing of European values with the newly independent states.[4] Additionally, the agreement addressed the issues of support of political, economical and democratic processes in third countries.

What constitutes the legal basis of the PCAs, pursuant to EU law? Determination of the legal basis for conclusion of international agreement is an important matter and in that respect the content and objective of the agreement is crucial, as it was defined by the ECJ in *Portugal v Council*.[5] The Court applied the "absorption doctrine" and held that it is important to determine the "essential object" and "ancillary

---

[3] *Sieberson*, Dividing Lines Between the Union and its Member States: The Impact of the Treaty of Lisbon (2008) at 45 - 47.

[4] The Preamble of the PCA with Georgia provides: *"CONSIDERING the links between the Community, its Member States and Georgia and the common values that they share". The same indication is made in the PCA Moldova. Additionally, Art 1 of PCA Georgia and PCA Moldova formulates the necessity of creation of appropriate framework for the political dialogue, economical development, and legislative, economic, social, financial, and cultural cooperation. Koutrakos*, International Agreements, in *Koutrakos* (ed), EU International Relations Law (2006) at 363 – 365.

[5] ECJ case C-268/94 *Portugal/Council*, report 1996, ECR I-6177.

aspects" of the agreement. For determination of the legal basis of the PCA, the objective of the entire agreement prevails over the content of each provision of the PCA. Notwithstanding the fact that a considerable number of EC Treaty provisions are addressed by the PCAs, it becomes obvious that the objective of the entire agreement is important for choosing the proper legal basis of the PCA. Thus, it is commonly agreed that Art 212 TFEU (ex Art 181a EC Treaty), constitutes the legal basis for the PCAs. Since "integration" is clearly not among the objectives of PCA's[6] III of the TFEU – "Cooperation with third countries and humanitarian aid".[7] However, this cannot be said about the ENP and the prospective AAs.

2.3. The impact of the ENP on the European integration of Moldova, Ukraine and the countries of the South Caucasus

A unique policy of the EU towards its neighbouring countries was introduced by the Commission in 2003.[8] Much has been said about the significance, challenges and the methodology of the ENP.[9] The concept of the ENP has established a "privileged relationship" between the EU and its neighbouring states (Newly Independent States and Southern Mediterranean),[10] based on common values which remains distinct from the process of enlargement and offers politi-

---

6 *Maresceau,* A Typology of Mixed Bilateral Agreements, in *Hillion / Koutrakos* (eds), Mixed Agreements Revised: The EU and its Member States (2010); *Hillion*, The EU's Neighbourhood Policy towards Eastern Europe, in *Dashwood / Maresceau* (eds), Law and Practice of EU External Relations – Salient Features of a Changing Landscape (2008) 309-333; *Georgian-European Policy and Legal Advice Center*, Guide to the implementation of the Partnership and Cooperation Agreement between Georgia and the European Communities and their Member States, Tacis DG ER, 2000, 3-7; *Berdiyev*, The EU and Former Soviet Central Asia: An Analysis of the Partnership and Cooperation Agreements, Yearbook of European Law 2003, 463.

7 *Craig / de Búrca*, EU Law: Text, Cases, and Materials[4] (2008) at 187; *Lenaerts / Nuffel*, Constitutional Law of the European Union, in *Bray* (ed), Procedural Law of the European Union[2] (2005) 855.

8 Commission Communication on the Wider European-Neighbourhood: A New Framework for Relations with our Eastern and Southern Neighbours, COM (2003) 104 final, 11 March 2003, 4.

9 *Cremona*, A Constitutional Basis for Effective External Action? An Assessment of the Provisions on EU External Action in the Constitutional Treaty, European University Institute Working Papers, LAW No. 2006/30; *Lynch*, The New Eastern Dimension of the Enlarged EU, Chaillot Paper No.64 (2003), available at <http://www.iss-eu.org/>; *Aliboni*, The Geopolitical Implications of the European Neighbourhood Policy, European Foreign Affairs Review 2005, 1; *Sarto / Schumacher*, From EMP to ENP: What's at Stake with the European Neighbourhood Policy towards the Southern Mediterranean? European Foreign Affairs Review 2005, 17; *Kelley*, New Wine In Old Wineskins: Policy Adaptation In The European Neighbourhood Policy, Journal of Common Market Studies 2006, 29.

10 It was a real shortcoming of the ENP that states of the South Caucasus were not included in the ENP. Armenia, Azerbaijan and Georgia were added to the list of ENP target countries only for political reasons and after the pressure on the part of the CFSP High Representative, the EU Special Representative for the South Caucasus and the European Parliament. See *van Elsuwege / Petrov*, Art 8 TEU: Towards a New Generation of Agreements with the Neighbouring Countries of the European Union, European Law Review 2011, 688; *Labedzka*, The Southern Caucasus (Armenia, Azerbaijan and Georgia), in *Blockmans / Lazowski* (eds), The European Union and its Neighbours: A Legal Appraisal of the EU's Policies of Stabilisation, Partnership and Integration, (2006) at 608.

cal and economic integration to those countries.[11] Thus, the ENP should be considered as a policy somewhere in between co-operation and integration, in other words, the ENP constitutes the policy which remains "more than partnership and less than the membership".[12]

From a legal point of view, the cross-pillar mixture of the relatively innovative and integrated "umbrella" policy – the ENP, raised many questions in terms of its legal certainty, transparency, coherency and accountability.[13] It is arguable whether the Union has the competence to introduce such a policy at all and if yes, what its legal basis was? Abolishment of the pillar structure by the Lisbon Treaty could not be considered as a solution. In practice, the uncertainty of the answer to the question – what is the competence of the EU to act in its neighbourhood? - has never been an impediment for the Union's external action in its neighbourhood.

Pursuant to the case law of the ECJ, the Community has a competence to act on the principle of conferred powers, provided that the Union may also act based on the implied competence. The Court ruled that the Community's legal power "arises not only from an express conferment by the Treaty, but may equally flow implicitly from other provisions of the Treaty, from the act of accession and from measures adopted within the framework of those provisions, by the Community institutions."[14] The case created the "principle of complementary".[15] The mentioned ruling is among other cases through which the Court created the practice of the Unions' implied power to act on the international scene.[16]

Interestingly, the ENP was not enacted by concluding agreements with Moldova, Ukraine and the countries of the South Caucasus, rather it was implemented by adopting Action Plans (APs). The APs have no legally binding force, however they incorporate priorities covering a number of key areas.[17]

Consequently, it should be noticed that mentioning of the term "integration" in the EU instruments within the framework of the ENP has created the ground for assumption of the prospect of membership by third states, among them Georgia, Ukraine and Moldova. The aspiration of the neighbouring countries has particularly

---

11 COM (2004) 373 final, 3.

12 *Prodi*, A Wider Europe. A Proximity Policy as the Key to Stability, Speech 02/619, Brussels, December 2002.

13 *Hillion*, op. cit. note 6, *Christensen*, The Making of the European Neighbourhood Policy (2011) 67; *Labedzka*, op. cit. note 10, 608; *Wichmann*, Rule of Law Promotion in the European Neighbourhood Policy: Normative or Strategic Power Europe? in *Wessels* (ed), The Studies on the European Union, (2010) at 59-60.

14 ECJ, Joined Cases 3, 4, and 6/76, *Cornelis Kramer and others*, report 1976, ECR 1279, margin notes 19-20.

15 *Dashwood*, The Classic Authorities Revised, in *Dashwood / Hillion* (eds), The General Law of EC External Relations (2000).

16 ECJ, case 22/70 *Commission/Council* (AERT/ERTA) report 1971, ECR 263; Opinion 1/76, *European Laying-up Fund for Inland Waterway Vessels*, report 1977, ECR 741.

17 Priority areas according to the ENP AP Georgia constitute: strengthening rule of law; improvement of business and investment climate; encouragement of economic development and enhance poverty reduction efforts and social cohesion, promotion of sustainable development; enhancing co-operation in the field of justice, freedom and security, including in the field of border management; strengthening regional co-operation; promotion of peaceful resolution of internal conflicts; co-operation on foreign and security policy; transport and energy.

been strengthened after opening negotiations on the AAs with Moldova and all states of the South Caucasus (Azerbaijan, Armenia, Georgia). [18]

2.4. Ongoing negotiations on the AAs

When the EaP was announced on 7 May 2009 as a "specific Eastern dimension of the European Neighbourhood Policy", it aimed at "political association and further economic integration between the EU and interested partner countries".[19] This new dimension of the ENP includes also negotiations on a new "wave" of agreements – AAs with Moldova, Ukraine and the countries of the South Caucasus.[20] If the PCAs, the APs and the entire process of neighbouring relations were not promising for Eastern countries, after the negotiations on AAs third countries contemplate their possibilities of the fully beneficial integration process - the prospect of membership. The issue of the legal basis for the new agreements constitutes an essential component of the process of European integration of third countries. "Deepening and widening" of the EU is considered an irreversible development in the never-ending process of European integration. Thus, there is a question: will Art 8 TEU have any impact on the forthcoming bilateral relations between the EU and EaP countries, in other words, will there be a linkage between the process of deepening and widening of the EU on the one hand, and EaP on the other.

3. Art 8 TEU – An innovative legal basis for international agreements of the EU?

3.1. Introduction

The Treaty of Lisbon with its many innovations constitutes the result of a long-lasting process of constitutional reforms.[21] The issue whether or not the European institutions would be adequate to meet the challenges of further integration has arisen from time to time.[22] On the one hand, deepening and widening has always been a challenge for the EU, and on the other hand, it has also always been a response to challenges. What is the EU, what should it be, how far should it expand and what should it do? Those are questions European elites

---

[18] Press Releases 15 July 2010, available at <http://europa.eu/rapid/press-release_IP-10-955_en.htm>.

[19] Available at <http://ec.europa.eu/news/external_relations/090508_en.htm>.

[20] Press Releases 15 July 2010, available at <http://europa.eu/rapid/press-release_IP-10-955_en.htm>.

[21] *Dougan*, The Treaty of Lisbon: Winning Minds, Not Hearts, Common Market Law Review 2008, 617.

[22] *Series*, Flexible Integration: Towards a More Effective and Democratic Europe, Center for Economic Policy Research, 1995 No 6, 1.

were and are still asking themselves.[23] The fact that the EU is a soft power[24] should not be seen as an obstacle for the European integration process of Eastern countries. The EU as an international actor,[25] based on its values and objectives,[26] has been persistently acting at the international scene and especially in its neighbourhood. One of the significant "legal actions" of the Union for fostering the process of European integration is Art 8 TEU.

Before the Treaty of Lisbon, the fundamental treaties of the Union did not contain a clause which refers to the Union's relationship with its neighbours. However, Art 8 TEU should be considered as a reflection of the long lasting practice of external relations of the EU with its neighbours.[27] It should be mentioned that the idea of introducing a very specific provision concerning external relations of the EU to its neighbours was launched within the European Convention, during the preparation of the Draft Treaty establishing a Constitution for Europe. It was presented with the separate title and article on "the Union and its immediate environment" which was stressing the importance of the Union's privileged relations with its neighbours.[28] The new Art 8 TEU obtained its privileged position under the Treaty of Lisbon and is presented in Title I, which provides for "Common Provisions". There is no doubt that systematically Art 8 TEU should not be part of Title I, however that position highlights the significant importance of the provision,[29] which is the most efficient justification. "The position of Art 8 TEU demonstrates the Union's ambivalence. It is not part of the External Action Title in Part III, it is not in Part III at all; it is rather anomalously in Part I, next door to the provisions on the membership of the EU. This implies a separate kind of status for neighbours, rather than merely a field of an action."[30]

3.2. Content of Art 8 TEU

Obviously, Art 8 TEU leaves huge room for interpretation and raises many legal questions. Art 8.(1) TEU provides:

> "*The Union shall develop a special relationship with neighbouring countries, aiming to establish an area of prosperity and good neighbourliness, founded on the values of the Union and characterized by close and peaceful relations based on cooperation.*"

The provision provides, that "*The Union*" is authorised to develop special relations with neighbouring countries. After changes provided by the Treaty of Lisbon,

---

23 *Schmidt*, European Elites on the European Union: What Vision for the Future? in *Gamble / Lane* (eds), The European Union and World Politics: Consensus and Division (2009) at 257.
24 *Telo*, The European Union: Divisions and Unity in the European External Politics, in *Gamble / Lane* (eds), The European Union and World Politics: Consensus and Division (2009) 42.
25 *McGoldrick*, International Relations Law of the European Union (1997) 181.
26 *Sieberson*, Dividing Lines Between the Union and its Member States: The Impact of the Treaty of Lisbon, (2008) at 73- 87.
27 *Ruffert / Schmalenbach*, in *Callies / Ruffert* (eds), AUV/AEUV. Das Verfassungsrecht der Europäischen Union mit Europäischer Grundrechtecharta (2011) Art 8 (Nachbarschaftspolitik)
28 *Van Elsuwege / Petrov*, op. cit. note 10, 688-704.
29 *Ruffert / Schmalenbach*, op. cit. note 27, 162-167.
30 *Cremona*, A Constitutional Basis for Effective External Action? An Assessment of the Provisions on EU External Action in the Constitutional Treaty, 2006 European University Institute Working Paper No 30.

the Union has gained legal personality by Art 47 TEU. Thus, there is no more room for controversy on the capacity of the EU to engage international relations or to conclude international agreements.

It should also be noticed that the Union *"shall"* develop neighbouring relations. Interpretation of this term gives ground for the assumption that the provision obliges the Union to conduct neighbouring relations with proper tools. As that expression has an imperative formulation,[31] it should be considered as an extra added value to the external relations of the EU with its neighbouring countries. The logical consequence of this innovation is increased qualitative criteria of the EUs' neighbouring relations.

Development of a "*special relationship*" with neighbouring countries could be considered as a very general and undeterminable provisional regulation of the EU's external relations with its neighbours. No precise determination exists even in German ("besondere Beziehungen") or in French ("des relations privilégiées") translation. *Special relations* could refer to any instrument of bilateral relations, addressing any issue of common interest, which might positively affect the relations of the EU with its neighbouring countries, having any intensity of closeness. The subject matter of special relations might include very broad range of fields of co-operation.

What does "*neighbouring countries*" mean? It is under the discretion of the EU to determine which countries, group of countries or regions are in its neighbourhood.[32] It is the subject of the discussion, whether a country may have direct land or maritime borders with the EU, or being a neighbour of an EU's direct neighbour could also be considered as being member of the "neighbourhood".[33] That question is definitely the subject of the EU's discretion. Based on the past experience, we assume that the neighbourhood does not only cover the direct neighbours of the EU. Extension of the ENP towards countries which could not be considered as "immediate" neighbourhood of the Union (Azerbaijan, Armenia), but where the Union has "strong interest in the stability and development", makes obvious that the geographical criteria of the neighbouring relations is flexible and may be interpreted in a broad way, according to the policy of the EU.[34] Thus, the "political neighbourhood" is significant and remains as a basis of external relations.

The objective of the Union in relations with its neighbouring countries constitutes establishment of the *"area of prosperity and good neighbourliness"*. That "modest" approach of the EU is not innovative. There is no doubt that the qualitative criteria and potential content of the prospective AAs are not predictable.[35] In this context, classification of the agreements concluded by the Union with third countries has hitherto remained to a large extent a matter of policies, not law.[36] It is interesting whether or not the aim of the "new agreements" will be a "constitutionalising" of the concept of the "integration without membership".[37]

---

31 *Ruffert / Schmalenbach*, op. cit. note 27, 162-167.
32 Ibid.
33 Ibid; *Hanf*, The ENP in the Light of the New 'Neighbourhood Clause' (Art 8 TEU), 2011 European Legal Studies Research Paper in Law, 3.
34 *Van Elsuwege / Petrov*, op. cit. note 10, 688-704.
35 *Hanf*, op. cit. note 33, 5.
36 Ibid. 5; van Elsuwege / Petrov, op. cit. note 10, 688-704.
37 *Hanf*, ibid. 5.

Neighbouring relations should be based on "*the values of the Union*". The EU establishes its neighbouring relations on the "shared" values which is basically the values of the EU. The values of the EU were reflected in the Laeken Declaration, specifically in the context of the Union's external policy:

> *"What is Europe's role in this changed world? Does Europe not, now that it is finally unified, have a leading role to play in a new world order, that of a power able both to play a stabilizing role worldwide and to point the way ahead for many countries and peoples? Europe as the continent of humane values, the Magna Carta, the Bill of Rights, the French Revolution and the fall of the Berlin Wall; the continent of liberty, solidarity and above all diversity, meaning respect for others' languages, cultures and traditions".*[38]

Thus, the values of the EU are part of the Union's own identity, which also characterises the Union's external policy, and Art 8 TEU "constitutionalises" the respect of European values in neighbouring relations.

It has been arguable whether or not the sharing of European values is a precondition for conclusion of international agreements. Pursuant to scholarly opinions, Art 8 TEU does not establish any requirement for the neighbouring countries as a prerequisite or condition, whether political, democratical, or economical for establishing the co - operation and good neighbouring relations.[39] According to others, "respecting the European values" is a conditional statement and the EU addresses contracting parties with this conditional approach.[40] We share the position that the EU aspires to establish peaceful relations with its neighbours based on co-operation, without any conditions but reciprocal consent on sharing *"values of the Union*".[41]

The European integration process - "*characterised by close and peaceful relations based on co-operation*". We consider, that the term "*close"* covers the possibility of any type of co - operation (intensity of co - operation), among them integration without membership or even the membership perspective. The legal or political interpretation of Art 8 TEU should not draw a line between the integration process (enlargement) and co-operation.[42] Rather, is should be used as a framework for the closest co-operation, where the aim of enlargement of the EU in the long run might also be covered. However, that provision is not in itself the basis for the enlargement process (compare to Art 49 TEU). Interpretations of the term "close" can be various. Exclusion of the integration process in the long run for the relations based on Art 8 TEU would undermine the importance of that innovative provision. Moreover, it would decree the motivation of the Eastern states towards the European integration. Therefore, it is under the political discretion of the EU to apply this new article in the most flexible way. Accordingly, a broad interpretation of the provision could be the good "basis" for more enhanced neighbouring relation, which might even lead to a full integration process (based on Art 49 TEU).

---

[38] European Commission, Second Annual Report on the Stabilization and Association Process for South East Europe - 2003, OJ 2003 C 139, 3.
[39] *Ruffert / Schmalenbach*, op. cit. note 27, 162-167.
[40] *Van Elsuwege / Petrov*, op.cit. note 10, 688-704.
[41] *Ruffert / Schmalenbach*, op. cit. note 27, 162-167.
[42] Ibid.

The Conclusion of international agreements, as a means of undertaking international obligations, should have its legal basis in the laws of the contracting parties. Pursuant to the EU law - the legal base for the PCAs (ex Art 181a TEC and new Art 212 TFEU) and AAs (ex Art 310 TEC and new Art 217 TFEU) are provided. After the changes introduced by the Lisbon Treaty, Art. 8 (2) TEU provoked discussions concerning the legal basis of forthcoming new agreements – AAs with Moldova, Ukraine and the countries of the South Caucasus.

Article 8 (2) TEU provides that:

> "*For the purposes of paragraph 1, the Union may conclude specific agreements with the countries concerned. These agreements may contain reciprocal rights and obligations as well as the possibility of undertaking activities jointly. Their implementation shall be subject of periodic consultation.*"

The provision suggests that it may constitute the new legal basis for the "*specific agreements*" concluded with neighbouring countries ("*countries concerned*").[43] "Special privileged links", as a characteristic of the AAs,[44] seems quite similar to the new type of "specific agreements" - provided pursuant to Art 8 (2) TEU. Special relationships in the form of AAs - "can be anything between full membership minus 1% and a trade and co-operation agreement plus 1 %".[45] That 'formula' is still relevant for the prospective AAs with Moldova and countries of the SC region.

Agreements concluded between the EU and the neighbouring country "*may contain reciprocal rights and obligations*" and also "*the possibility of undertaking activities jointly*". "In reality the existing ties with the many different neighbouring countries as well as their interests and expectations with regard to the Union (and also *vice-versa*) differs greatly".[46] Thus, the reciprocal rights and obligations are not (could not) be equal. In fact, the Union is quite dominant in influencing the process of European integration of the Eastern countries.

For the monitoring of the implementation of concluded agreement, "*monitoring*" will be the "*subject of periodic consultations*". Art 8 (2) TEU does not explicitly provide what might be understood as an instrument or institute for consultation. Authorisations of monitoring of implementation of the PCAs were dealt with by Partnership and Cooperation Councils, and their effectiveness has been discussed from the time of its establishment. With regard to AAs, the Association Councils could be authorised as the monitoring institution for the AAs' implementation. After conclusion of the AAs, more effectiveness of Association Councils is expected as a monitoring body.

Consequently, does Art 8 (2) TEU constitute the new legal basis for conclusion of the agreements with the neighbouring countries? According to the opinions of some scholars – Art 8 (2) TEU could be considered as a *lex specialis* to Art 217 TFEU which is the legal basis for the AAs; and that constitutes the substantive side

---

43 After the failed ratification of the Constitutional Treaty, the Commission no longer uses the term "Neighbourhood Agreements", it rather uses DCFTA, "Enhanced Agreements" and speaks of a new generation of AAs; van Elsuwege / Petrov, op. cit. note 10, 688-704.

44 ECJ case 12/86, *Meryem* Demirel *v Stadt Schwäbisch Gmünd*, Report 1987, E.C.R. 3719, 9.

45 *Phinnemore*, Association: Stepping – Stone or Alternative to EU Membership? (1999) at 23.

46 *Hanf*, op. cit. note 33, 10.

of the new Art 8 TEU. [47] According to other scholars – the choice of legal basis (between Art 217 TFEU and Art 8 TEU) should not be left to the discretion of the political institutions, but needs to be established based on objective criteria, ruled by the ECJ. According to this opinion, Art 8 TEU has no intrinsic legal value, but is one among several alternative legal bases.[48]

We share the position that "nothing in the Treaties seems to prevent that Art 8.2 TEU in itself is used to conclude a specific agreement with neighbouring country, after all Art 216.1 TFEU makes clear that legal basis for concluding international agreements can also be found in the TEU".[49] That argument is strengthened by the instruments of the EU, for example the Joint Staff Working Paper of 2011 of the Commission, stating that: "*Along the lines of article 8 of the Lisbon Treaty, of a space involving the EU and its neighbours where political co-operation is as close as possible and economic integration is as deep as possible, supported by high-level political dialogue, legislative approximation and regulatory convergence*".[50] With a high degree of probability, we may assume that the forthcoming AAs aim at intensive relations with neighbouring countries and will be aligned with Art 8 TEU. It is also the expectation of Georgian diplomats that "the legal basis for the prospective AA with Georgia could be Art 8 TEU."[51]

4. THE POLITICAL ASSESSMENT OF ART 8 TEU

Interrelated political positions of the EU institutions, the governments of the Member States and the third countries are determining factors in the European integration process. An assessment of Art 8 TEU would be incomplete without evaluation of its political value. Challenges in the neighbourhood of the EU should be adequately dealt with, - that is the legitimate demand inside and outside of the EU. As we have discussed above, the EU has the treaty obligation to "export" its values outside the Unions' borders. The member states are under the obligation to support the Union's external policy in the spirit of loyalty and mutual solidarity.[52] As a consequence, "*the positions of member states are decisive when the issues of membership rise*",[53] so "*the accession of third states to the EU will not only be decided in Brussels*".[54]

---

47 *Hanf*, ibid. 4.

48 *Thym*, Art 8 EUV, in *Grabitz / Hilf* (eds), Das Recht der Europäischen Union: Kommentar 2010, footnote 1; *Hummer,* in *Vedder / Wolff Heintschel von Heinegg* (eds), Europäischer Verfassungsvertrag (2007) Artikel I-57 EVV footnote 10.

49 *Van Elsuwege / Petrov*, op. cit. note 10, 688-704.

50 Commission Joint Staff Working Paper on a Medium Term Programme for a Renewed European Neighbourhood Policy (2011-2014), COM (2011) 3030, 15.05. 2011, SEC 650, Annex 1.

51 *Tamar Beruchashvili,* Chief Adviser to the State Minister of Georgia on European and Euro-Atlantic Integration, Ambassador, interview by the author of the contribution, 02 November 2011,Tbilisi Georgia.

52 *Craig / de Búrca*, op. cit note 7, 191.

53 *Elmar Brok*, MEP, 21 September 2011 REEES study trip to Brussels.

54 *Monica Macovei*, MEP, 21 September 2011 REEES study trip to Brussels.

The aspiration of the neighbouring countries towards European integration and the process of accession is becoming convincing. In this regard, a Georgian diplomat posits that "*Georgia has a clear aspiration towards membership*", since "*Georgia is not a neighbour of Europe, it is part of Europe*".[55] The EU sets a variety of conditions even before the clear prospect of membership, and the political elites of Eastern countries are asking themselves: *"Whether it is worthy to implement so many acquis without the membership perspective?"*[56] It is clear that the political interest from the Western countries towards the Eastern countries and *vice versa* is increasing, but they are not always equal.

For the process of European Integration, the political interpretations of the new Art 8 TEU has paramount importance. In her assessment of the "neighbouring clause" of the Treaty of Lisbon, a Georgian diplomat mentions: "*Changes and innovations introduced by the Treaty of Lisbon have increasing importance for the EU's external relations with neighbouring countries. The new treaty brought a new dynamism in political relations and fostered the process of European integration of Eastern countries.*"[57] Expectations of the dynamic development of the European integration process of Eastern countries are based on a broad interpretation of Art 8 TEU, which means that it may also cover the perspective of accession even in the long run. This approach concerns the convincing positions of Eastern countries towards the intensive integration to the EU: *"The position of the government of Georgia is to accept the requirements set by the EU, regarding reforms in any field with its widest possible extent."*[58] Obviously, "*Together with political integration, functional and sectoral integration of Georgia to the EU is crucially important. Moreover getting closer to the European values through the transposition of the EU law into Georgian legislation, raises the protection of human rights standards in our country, what is itself in our interests*".[59] Also the government of Georgia posits that "*The process of development of democracy and the intensive reforms are in the interests of Georgia. Once we reach the results necessary for our country, the membership would be a logical consequence of that process in which we are involved now.*"[60]

If we compare the European integration processes of Eastern countries to each other, *"Moldova and Georgia have some common character, however they are very individualistic and unique"*.[61] Moldova is considered to be a "front runner" in the

---

[55] *David Solomonia*, 22 September 2011 REEES study trip to Brussels.

[56] *H.E. Ambassador Selim Küneralp*, Permanent Delegate of Turkey to the European Union, 21 September 2011 REEES study trip to Brussels.

[57] *Tamar Beruchashvili,* Chief Adviser to the State Minister of Georgia on European and Euro-Atlantic Integration, Ambassador, interview by the author, 02 November 2011, Tbilisi Georgia.

[58] *Davit Darchiashvili*, Head of the Committee on European Integration of the Parliament of Georgia, Interview by the author, April 2012, Tbilisi, Georgia.

[59] *Tamar Beruchashvili,* Chief Adviser to the State Minister of Georgia on European and Euro-Atlantic Integration, Ambassador, interview by the author of the contribution, 2November 2011,Tbilisi Georgia.

[60] Ibid.

[61] *Davit Darchiashvili*, Head of the Committee on European Integration of the Parliament of Georgia, Interview by the author, April 2012, Tbilisi, Georgia.

process of integration to the EU.[62] Differently from the South East European countries, "*Multilateral approach has not been helpful in the South Caucasus. Bilateral relations seem to be more effective in this region.*"[63] The Brussels position is also shared by the Georgian policy makers, stating that "*geographically, Georgia is part of the South Caucasus region, however that position should not be exercised against the integration of the individual state to the EU.*"[64] On the one hand, it seems that the political ambitions of Georgia towards the European integration go beyond the borders of the region, and on the other hand, it coincides with the position of the EU, stating a "gradual approach based on a clearer and more rigorous differentiation".[65]

By introducing Art 8 TEU, the EU has recognized the Eastern countries' aspirations towards intensive neighbouring relations and more coherence of the instruments of the Union. However, the discretion of interpretation of Art 8 TEU should be left to the EU. Obviously, Art 8 TEU constitutes the logical response of the EU to the modern challenges of its neighbouring relations. The benefits and positive impact of Art 8 TEU on the European integration of neighbouring countries to the EU will be individualistic. Thus, the principle of 'differentiation' of the ENP will still be actively be concerned.

Consequently, the effectiveness of Art 8 TEU derives from its political flexibility. It should be mentioned that the EU's international agreements (mixed agreements) concluded with third countries are mainly the subject of policies not law.[66] Thus, the political and legal value of Art 8 TEU will firstly be assessed on the basis of the AAs with Moldova, Ukraine and the countries of the South Caucasus.

5. CONCLUSION

The aspiration of the EU toward more legitimacy in its external policy constitutes the basis for the development of EU law. From time to time, the EU improves the content and the context of the legal basis of its external policies. The process has been prolonged with the Treaty of Lisbon and new Art 8 TEU. The benefits of Art 8 TEU in the process of European integration of Moldova and the countries of the South Caucasus should be the following:

1. The new provision establishes the constitutional basis for the EU's external relations with its neighbouring countries.
2. Art 8 TEU is a reflection of existing and long lasting external relations of the EU with its neighbouring countries. It thus confers a constitutional status to the relations of the EU with its neighbouring countries.

---

62 Monica Macovei, MEP, 21 September 2011, REEES study trip to Brussels.
63 Knut Fleckenstein, MEP, 21 September 2011, REEES study trip to Brussels.
64 *Davit Darchiashvili*, Head of the Committee on European Integration of the Parliament of Georgia, Interview by the author of the contribution, April 2012, Tbilisi, Georgia.
65 COM (2011) 3030 Annex 1.
66 *Peers*, EC Frameworks of International Relations: Co-operation, Partnership and Association, in *Dashwood / Hillion* (eds), The General Law of EC External Relations (2000) at 175.

3. The innovative provision highlights the privileged relations of the EU with its neighbouring countries.
4. The broad room for political interpretation of Art 8 TEU leaves discretion for the Union to act in accordance with its political interests near its borders. Also, it increases the motivation of the Eastern countries towards European integration.
5. Art 8 TEU is a political message of the Union, underlining the increasing importance of the relations with neighbours which might acquire any dynamic, among them the prospect of membership. Thus, Art 8 TEU does not aim to draw the lines between co-operation and the integration (enlargement) process, rather it gets closer to those processes.
6. Art 8 TEU might be considered as the new legal basis for the forthcoming AAs with Moldova, Ukraine and the countries of the South Caucasus region.

Part 3:

Regional Powers and Their Interplay with the EU's Strategy in the Black Sea and the South Caucasus Regions

Elizaveta Samoilova

Poking the Bear? - Russia and the EU in the Black Sea Region

"Art 9 (1) AA EU-Georgia

The Parties reiterate their commitment to peaceful conflict resolution in full respect of the sovereignty and territorial integrity of Georgia within its internationally recognized borders as well as to facilitating jointly post-conflict rehabilitation and reconciliation efforts. Pending sustainable solution to conflict and without prejudice to the existing formats for addressing the conflict-related issues, peaceful conflict resolution will constitute one of the central subjects on the agenda of political dialogue between the Parties, as well as in the dialogue with other relevant international actors."

"Art 8 2) AA EU-Republic of Moldova

The Parties reiterate their commitment to a sustainable solution to the Transnistrian issue, in full respect of the sovereignty and territorial integrity of the Republic of Moldova as well as to facilitating jointly post-conflict rehabilitation. Pending its resolution and without prejudice to the established negotiating format, the Transnistrian issue will constitute one of the central subjects on the agenda of political dialogue and cooperation between the Parties, as well as in the dialogue and cooperation with other interested international actors."

1. Introduction

Its new enlarged borders brought the EU closer to some interesting and important regions. The Black Sea region[1] is a distinct geographical area rich in natural resources and strategically located at the junction of Europe, Central Asia and the Middle East. Countries like Moldova, Azerbaijan, Armenia and Georgia are of an increasing importance for the EU since they represent an expanding market with great potential and an important hub for energy and transport flows, but are also faced with challenges like unresolved frozen conflicts, environmental problems as well as illegal migration and organised crime.

---

[1] The Black Sea region, as defined by the European Commission in its documents, includes Greece, Bulgaria, Romania and Moldova in the west, Ukraine and Russia in the north, Georgia, Armenia and Azerbaijan in the East and Turkey in the South. Armenia, Azerbaijan, Moldova and Greece who are not littoral states *per se*, are also included for historical, geographical and political reasons. This article will focus particularly on Armenia, Azerbaijan, Moldova and Georgia.

It is for this reason that the EU has a vital interest in ensuring prosperity, stability and security in its neighbourhood around the Black Sea, thereby also contributing to the overall prosperity, stability and security in Europe.[2]

The EU integration process of South Eastern Europe is a history of success. With its regional approach, which served as basis for the Stability and Association Process, the EU greatly supported necessary reforms in the countries and led them to the status of potential or full candidates for EU membership. In the post-Soviet South Caucasus scenario of the Black Sea region, however, the EU is facing a unique situation which is different from the one in South Eastern Europe and is characterised by a rather complex structure of international actors. Apart from the states involved and the new, partly recognised states like Abkhazia and Nagorno-Karabakh, the key players are international organisations such as the OSCE, NATO and the UN, transnational enterprises and of course states - one of whom is Russia, Europe's by far largest neighbour.

This contribution focuses on Russia's role for the EU and how its influence in the Black Sea region is reflecting in the relations between the EU, Moldova and the countries of the Southern Caucasus by analysing the policy interests of the actors involved and the existing legal and political instruments – or the lack thereof. More precisely, it tries to find an answer to the question: Is the Union's signature approach to the Black Sea area by means of regional co-operation, as pursued in the South Eastern Europe, capable of delivering viable results?

2. RUSSIA'S ROLE IN THE REGION

The Russian Federation is without doubt a very important player for the Black Sea region, as it enjoys an elevated standing resulting not only from its geographical location but also from the fact of being the successor state to the former Soviet Union. Therefore, Russia's policy towards the region – often criticised by South Caucasus scholars as hegemonic[3] – is still to some extent driven by the wish to uphold its weakened influence since the collapse of the Soviet Union.[4] Recent intentions to reintegrate the post-Soviet region resulted in *Putin's* proposal for a new supra-national "Eurasian Union", which would focus primarily on economic issues based on the Customs Union between Russia, Belarus and Kazakhstan and would be open to all former Soviet countries. In the context of Russian policy towards the region over the past ten years, this integration project can be interpreted as a new attempt at installing lost influence and power.[5]

---

2 Communication from the Commission to the Council and the European Parliament, Black Sea Synergy - A New Regional Cooperation Initiative, COM(2007) 160 final, 1.

3 See *Stewart*, Russische Außenpolitik im postsowjetischen Raum. Das Baltikum, die westlichen GUS und der Südkaukasus im Vergleich, SWP Studie S 5 (März 2010) 9.

4 *Delcour / Tulmets*, Pioneer Europe? The ENP as a Test Case for EU's Foreign Policy, European Foreign Affairs Review 2009, 501 (515).

5 See further *Halbach*, Vladimir Putin's Eurasian Union. A New Integration Project for the CIS Region? SWP Comments 1 (January 2012).

Modern Russia's interests in the region can be summarised as follows. Foremost, Russia seems to seek to retain control over the energy sector. The South Caucasus as an important part of the EU energy supply scheme is without doubt still of highest Russian interest. Secondly, Russia concentrates on the management of territorial conflicts,[6] of which there are many in the region, notably in Transnistria, Abkhasia, South Ossetia and Nagorno-Karabakh.

As opposed to these rather unified fields of interest, Russia's relations with the countries concerned are not homogenous and differ widely:

On Moldova, which historically and culturally is more connected to Romania, Russia is exercising its influence in terms of energy supply and the Transnistrian issue. Transnistria, a part of the Moldovan state territory in the east of the Dnjestr river, separated in 1990 and is highly dependent on Russian military support ever since.[7] Based on recent developments, one can say that Russia is acting as a mediator but also tries to preserve the *status quo* for its own benefits.[8]

Russia's relations with Georgia, which has been gravitating towards the West for many years, deteriorated increasingly since the Rose revolution in 2003. The Abkhazian war in the early 1990ies, the ban on Georgian wine and mineral water in 2006 and the military dispute over the separatist region of South Ossetia in 2008 caused the political dialogue to cease completely and showed that Russia is not afraid to use harsh means in order to defend its interests.[9]

In contrast to this, Armenia is considered the only pro-Russian country in the South Caucasus, but not without reason. Armenia is tied to Russia by a political and military alliance. Plus, its economy is controlled by Russian entities which makes it very dependent on its big neighbour.[10]

The relations with Azerbaijan, a country that is close culturally as well as politically to Turkey, another big player in the region, can be characterised as ambivalent: Azerbaijan is the only South Caucasus country that is independent from Russian energy supplies which forces Russia to treat the country as an equal partner. Russia is also engaged as a mediator in the Nagorno-Karabakh conflict.[11]

In terms of legal instruments of co-operation, Russia's policy towards Moldova and the South Caucasus is twofold: On the one hand, Russia greatly emphasises bilateral relations with every country involved. On the other hand, it is also trying to maintain its influence through regional organisations or forms of co-operation like the Commonwealth of Independent States (CIS), the Eurasian Economic Community, the Organisation for Black Sea Economic Cooperation or the Collective Security Treaty Organisation (CSTO). While the CIS has lost its former power quite long ago,[12] all other organisations also show rather little success,[13] especially in the

---

6 See *Stewart,* op. cit. note 3, 24.

7 See *Stewart,* op. cit. note 3, 17.

8 Idid. 23.

9 Ibid. 25 f.

10 *Labedzka*, The Southern Caucasus (Armenia, Azerbaijan and Georgia), in *Blockmans / Lazowski* (eds), The European Union and its Neighbours (2006) 575 (580); *Wojna / Gniazdowski*, Eastern Partnership: The Opening Report (April 2009) 59.

11 See *Stewart,* op. cit. note 3, 29.

12 *Halbach,* op. cit. note 5, 3.

13 *Stewart,*op. cit. note 3, 32.

Caucasus region, simply because most of the South Caucasus countries decline to subscribe to membership in those organisations. Moreover, Russia is trying to marginalise or dissolve other regional organisations in which it does not participate or which call its dominance into question, like the Central Asian Economic Union or the GUAM Organisation for Democracy and Economic Development (short for Georgia, Ukraine, Azerbaijan and Moldova).[14]

Its significant position as a regional power explains the elevated interest the EU expresses towards Russia. Not only is Russia interesting for the Union in terms of trade and energy supply, but especially the EU's ambitions in the field of peacekeeping and conflict resolution require close co-operation. As Russia is a strategic partner, the EU does not want to - as former External Relations Commissioner *Ferrero-Waldner* once put it – "neglect (the EU's) relations with Russia",[15] but rather to strengthen the strategic partnership by stepping up co-operation. Consequently, this would mean that any EU measures taken with respect to the Black Sea region would seem to require consideration of Russia's possible reaction.[16]

However, a common and strategic EU policy towards Russia is not easy to achieve since internally, the EU Member States disagree in this matter. Mostly for historical reasons, the new EU Member States have a different approach *vis-à-vis* Russia than the old ones. Also, the dependence on Russian energy supplies creates a divide between the EU Member States. While e.g. France, Italy and Germany have a quite positive attitude towards Moscow and are eager to advance EU-Russian relations, Member States like Poland and the Baltic states take a significantly more critical position and tend to obstruct negotiations making it a challenge for the Union to develop a more coherent policy towards Russia.[17]

In addition, Russia's own view of the EU and other actors in the region is a very critical one. Russia seems to want to preserve its influence in the region and is declining initiatives of other existing actors,[18] the fear being that fostering links with the West and approaching the Black Sea countries to the European model could push them further away from Russia in the long term.[19] Indeed, it seems that Russia perceives EU initiatives in the region as a potential hindrance to its own closer cooperation with those countries, notably concerning economic integration.[20] In this light, the proposal of a "Eurasian Union" led by Russia can be seen as a countermodel that Russia uses to compete with the EU over integration in the shared neighbourhood region.[21] This so-called *Integrationskonkurrenz* is officially not

---

14 See *Halbach,*op. cit. note 5, 3.

15 See the statement made in the course of the 2755th Council Meeting on General Affairs and External Relations General Affairs, Luxembourg, 17 October 2006.

16 *Labedzka,* op. cit. note 10, 588.

17 *Leal-Arcas*, The EU and Russia as Energy Trading Partners: Friends or Foes? European Foreign Affairs Review 2009, 337 (351); *Timmermann*, EU-Russland: Hintergründe und Perspektiven einer schwierigen Partnerschaft, integration 2008, 159.

18 *Stewart,* op. cit. note 3, 24.

19 *Delcour / Tulmets,* op. cit. note 4, 513.

20 See *Zagorski*, Eastern Partnership from the Russian Perspective, Internationale Politik und Gesellschaft 2011, 41.

21 *Halbach,* op. cit. note 5, 4.

acknowledged by the Kremlin,[22] but reality shows Russia's rather aggressive approach to the region.[23] Then again, Moscow is not convinced by the efficacy or impact of EU multilateral co-operation mechanisms and is apparently not taking them serious.[24] Nevertheless, Russia's government recently expressed the wish to co-operate with the EU and the countries of the Black Sea region as equal partners.[25]

3. OVERVIEW OF THE EU-RUSSIA AND EU-SOUTH CAUCASUS RELATIONS

In order to assess Russia's influence on the EU's policies in the South Caucasus region, it is first necessary to take a closer look at the existing EU-Russia relations.

3.1. Russia

Being the EU's largest neighbour and major trading partner in fossil fuels and metals, Russia has always claimed for itself a special relationship with the EU. After the breakdown of the Soviet Union, the very first PCA[26] was signed with Russia in 1994 and entered into force tree years later after ratification by all EU Member States. This agreement was based on former Art 113 and 235 TEC (now Art 207 and 352 TFEU) and includes the respect of common general principles such as democracy and human rights, but also political dialogue, trade in goods, employment, cross-border supply of services, current payments and capital, protection of intellectual property and economic as well as legislative co-operation. It also provides for institutions where the implementation of the agreement is being supervised and the political dialogue is held. The most important institution is the Co-operation Council on the ministerial level, which was remodelled into the Permanent Partnership Council in 2008. Other institutions are e.g. the Co-operation Committee and the Parliamentary Co-operation Committee. It is also supplemented by a range of sectoral agreements concerning trade in steel,[27] nuclear safety,[28] textile,[29] visa[30] and readmission[31] as well

---

22 See *Tolksdorf*, Russia's Response to the Eastern Partnership in the First Eighteen Months: From Opposition to Gardual Participation? Available at <http://www.easternpartnership.org/community/debate/russia-s-response-eastern-partnership-first-eighteen-months-opposition-gradual-part>.

23 See *Delcour / Tulmets*, op. cit. note 4, 515.

24 *Zagorski*, op. cit. note 20, 46.

25 Ibid. 54.

26 Agreement on partnership and cooperation establishing a partnership between the European Communities and their Member States, of one part, and the Russian Federation, of the other part, OJ 1997 L 327, 3.

27 Agreement between the European Community and the Russian Federation on trade in certain steel products, OJ 2007 L 300, 52.

28 Agreement for cooperation between the European Atomic Energy Community and the Government of the Russian Federation in the field of nuclear safety, OJ 2001 L 287, 24.

as science[32]. Up until today, the PCA, which was initially concluded for a ten year period, is still the basis of all EU-Russia relations, since plans to replace it have not yet succeeded.

In addition, in order to underline Russia's importance and value for the EU, both sides agreed upon a so-called "Strategic Partnership" to develop enhanced bilateral relations outside the main EU approach to its neighbours *via* the ENP. Therefore, in 1999, the EU adopted its first unilateral Common Strategy towards Russia, addressing the consolidation of democracy and the rule of law in Russia, the integration of Russia into a common European economic and social space as well as co-operation to strengthen stability and security in Europe and beyond.[33] Russia responded with a complementary "Strategy for Developing Relations with the EU in the medium-term Perspective (2000 – 2010)", where it also expressed its interest in developing a close partnership with the European Union in order to reinforce their respective positions within the international community and to promote a social market economy.

At the 2003 EU-Russia Summit in St. Petersburg, the parties decided to create the four Common Spaces[34] in order to replace the expiring Strategy and to add new impetus to the stagnating partnership after the Chechen war. The benefit of the spaces – which consist of the Common Economic Space, the Common Space on Freedom, Security and Justice, the Common Space on External Security (CSES), Common Space on Research and Education, including Cultural Aspects – is their reciprocal approach: in their framework, the EU-Russia relations are now being developed on the basis of a mutually agreed agenda, which was set out by a single package of road maps adopted in 2005.[35]

Another proof of Russia's special standing with the EU is the fact that, even though not a member of the ENP, Russia receives technical assistance from EU funds. Most EU financing has been provided by the ENPI,[36] but Russia has also received money from Nuclear Safety Co-operation Instrument,[37] the European In-

---

29 Agreement between the European Community and the Russian Federation on trade in textile products, OJ 1998 L 169, 2.

30 Agreement between the European Community and the Russian Federation on the facilitation of the issuance of visas to the citizens of the European Union and the Russian Federation, OJ 2007 L 129, 27.

31 Agreement between the European Community and the Russian Federation on readmission, OJ 2007 L 129, 40.

32 Agreement renewing the Agreement on cooperation in science and technology between the European Community and the Government of the Russian Federation, OJ 2003 L 299, 21.

33 Common Strategy of the European Union of 4 June 1999 on Russia (1999/414/CFSP), OJ 2000 L 283, 18.

34 Joint Statement of the 11th EU-Russia Summit, St.-Petersburg, 31 May 2003, available at <http://www.consilium.europa.eu/uedocs/cms_data/docs/pressdata/en/er/75969.pdf>.

35 The road maps are available under <http://eeas.europa.eu/delegations/russia/documents/eu_russia/road_maps_en.pdf>. See *van Elsuwege*, The Four Common Spaces: New Impetus to the EU-Russia Strategic Partnership? in *Dashwood / Maresceau* (eds), Law and Practice of EU External Relations (2008) 326 (334).

36 Regulation (EC) No 1638/2006 of the European Parliament and of the Council of 24 October 2006 laying down general provisions establishing a European Neighbourhood and Partnership Instrument, OJ 2006 L 310, 1.

37 Council Regulation (EURATOM) No 300/2007 of 19 February 2007 establishing an Instrument for Nuclear Safety Co-operation, OJ 2007, L 81,1.

strument for Democracy and Human Rights,[38] the EU's Instrument for humanitarian aid[39] and other thematic programmes.

After the Russian-Georgian War in 2008, which brought the EU-Russia relations again to an almost freeze and forced the EU to re-examine its approach towards Moscow, the EU and Russia have been negotiating a new agreement to replace the old PCA and to provide for the contractual framework for EU-Russia relations in the future.[40] The possible options range from a complete abandonment of any treaty basis to a new comprehensive framework agreement.[41] Russia's accession to the WTO in August 2012 opened new perspectives for the negotiations of the new agreement, as it can now build upon the common WTO rules. But the negotiations have been stopped in 2010 because no progress could be made in the Trade and Investment part.[42] In the meantime, at the EU Russia Summit in Rostov-on-Don in May 2010, a Partnership for Modernisation was created to advance both the European and the Russian economies and to contribute to the global recovery and stronger international economic governance.[43]

In the last years, Russia has declined participation in most of the existing EU multilateral initiatives, e.g. the EaP, by stating that it cannot accept neither any norms or standards nor conditionality imposed by a foreign organisation.[44] Nevertheless, Russia takes part in the Northern Dimension policy, established in 1999 by the EU, Norway, Iceland and the Russian Federation in order to provide a common framework for the promotion of dialogue and concrete co-operation, to strengthen stability, intensify economic co-operation, and promote economic integration, competitiveness and sustainable development in Northern Europe, covering the geographic area from the European Arctic and Sub-Arctic to the Southern shores of the Baltic Sea and beyond.[45] In the South, Russia is a member of the BSS, a regional co-operation forum between the countries surrounding the Black Sea which will also be described in the following.

All in all, the EU-Russia relations are based on a variety of policy instruments which are rather complex and overlapping as well as intransparent. However, in view of the strategic partnership envisaged by both parties such multi-layered and close interlacing has to be evaluated generally as positive, its effectiveness being doubtful, of course.

---

38 Regulation (EC) No 1889/2006 of the European Parliament and of the Council of 20 December 2006 on establishing a financing instrument for the promotion of democracy and human rights worldwide, OJ 2006 L 386, 1.

39 Council Regulation (EC) No 1257/96 of 20 June 1996 concerning humanitarian aid, OJ 1996 L 163, 1.

40 Joint Statement on the Launch of Negotiations for a new EU-Russia Agreement, Khanty-Mansiysk, 27 June 2008, available at <www.consilium.europa.eu/ueDocs/cms_Data/docs/pressData/en/er/101524.pdf>.

41 See *van Elsuwege,* op. cit. note 35, 348.

42 See <http://ec.europa.eu/trade/policy/countries-and-regions/countries/russia/>.

43 "EU and Russia launch new partnership for modernization", IP/10/649, Brussels, 1 June 2010.

44 *Delcour / Tulmets,* op. cit. note 4, 516.

45 See the Northern Dimension Policy Framework Document, available at <http://eeas.europa.eu/north_dim/docs/frame_pol_1106_en.pdf>.

3.2. Moldova and the countries of the South Caucasus

With regard to its Eastern neighbours, the EU is using similar instruments as with Russia, although they differ slightly due to particularities of every country/situation. With Moldova and the countries of the South Caucasus, the EU is exercising its bilateral relations also through PCAs which came into force in 1998/1999.[46] Until then, co-operation was limited to technical and humanitarian assistance.[47] Issues covered by the PCAs (again, similar to the PCA with Russia) *inter alia* include trade in goods and services, employment, economic co-operation as well as political dialogue and the respect of general principles. Between the EU and the South Caucasus countries, no bilateral summits are held like with Russia,[48] but regular meetings take place in the institutional framework provided by the PCAs. Also, the Union has already concluded visa facilitation and readmission agreements with Ukraine,[49] Moldova[50] and Georgia.[51]

In addition, within the framework of its Common Foreign and Security Policy, the EU adopted quite a few measures which all underline the region's importance for Brussels:

First, the EU adopted Joint Actions concerning the Georgian border with Chechnya,[52] Ingushetia[53] and South Ossetia[54] in order to provide Georgian authorities with means to support the on-site OSCE Observer Missions.

---

46 Partnership and Cooperation Agreement between the European Communities and their Member States and the Republic of Moldova, OJ 1998 L 181, 3; Partnership and Cooperation Agreement between the European Communities and their Member States, of the one part, and Georgia, of the other part, OJ 1999 L 205, 3; Partnership and Cooperation Agreement between the European Communities and their Member States, of the one part, and the Republic of Armenia, of the other part, OJ 1999 L 239, 3; Partnership and Cooperation Agreement between the European Communities and their Member States, of the one part, and the Republic of Azerbaijan, of the other part, OJ 1999 L 246, 3.

47 This was provided notably through ECHO, Council Regulation 1257/96 concerning humanitarian aid, OJ 1996 L 163, 1, and TACIS, Council Regulation 99/2000, OJ 2000 L 12, 1; see *Labedzka,* op. cit. note 10, 588.

48 Ibid. 599.

49 Agreement between the European Community and Ukraine on the facilitation of the issuance of visas, OJ 2007 L 332, 68; Agreement between the European Community and Ukraine on the readmission of persons, OJ 2007 L 332, 48.

50 Agreement between the European Community and the Republic of Moldova on the facilitation of the issuance of visas, OJ 2007 L 334, 169; Agreement between the European Community and the Republic of Moldova on the readmission of persons residing without authorisation, OJ 2007 L 334, 149.

51 Agreement between the European Union and Georgia on the facilitation of the issuance of visas, OJ 2011 L 52, 34; Agreement between the European Union and Georgia on the readmission of persons residing without authorization, OJ 2011 L 52, 47.

52 Council Joint Action of 20 July 2000 regarding a contribution of the European Union towards reinforcing the capacity of the Georgian authorities to support and protect the OSCE Observer Mission on the border of the Republic of Georgia with the Chechen Republic of the Russian Federation (2000/456/CFSP), OJ 2000 L 183, 3.

53 Council Joint Action of 21 May 2002 regarding a contribution of the European Union towards reinforcing the capacity of the Georgian authorities to support and protect the OSCE observer mission on the border of Georgia with the Ingush and Chechen Republics of the Russian Federation (2002/373/CFSP), OJ 2002 L 134, 1.

54 Council Joint Action of 29 October 2001 regarding a contribution from the European Union to the conflict settlement process in South Ossetia (2001/759/CFSP), OJ 2003 L 157, 72.

Second, two (of currently eight) EU Special Representatives were appointed by the Council in order to increase the Union's presence in the region and to promote the EU's policies and interests in these areas as well as actively contribute to the promotion of peace, stability and the rule of law: One Special Representative deals with issues related to the Southern Caucasus and the crisis in Georgia and another's mandate covers Moldova.[55]

With regard to Moldova, EUBAM was launched in 2005 in order to enhance co-operation between the EU and the Moldovan and Ukrainian authorities in the fight against weapons trafficking, smuggling, organised crime and corruption, thus helping to improve security and stability in the region.[56]

Furthermore, the Union - upon Georgia's invitation - conducted its first Rule of Law Mission in the context of the European Security and Defence Policy towards Georgia (EUJUST THEMIS) in order to support the Georgian authorities in addressing urgent challenges in the criminal justice system.[57]

In addition to that, the EU established a civilian EU Monitoring Mission in Georgia (EUMM), the mandate of which is to monitor compliance in close co-ordination with partners, particularly the UN and the OSCE, with the EU brokered Six-Point Agreement of 12 August 2008, signed by both Georgia and Russia, and the Agreement on Implementing Measures of 8 September 2008 on the territory of Georgia in order to contribute to stabilisation, normalisation and confidence building in the region.[58]

In a multilateral approach towards its Southern as well as its Eastern neighbours and in compliance with the European Security Strategy[59], in 2003 the EU launched the ENP which *inter alia* addresses Moldova and the countries of the South Caucasus.[60] In order to add more depth to this existing policy and to answer the call of the Eastern neighbouring countries for a closer co-operation, in late 2008 it was decided to create the EaP towards the countries of Armenia, Azerbaijan, Belarus, Georgia, Moldova and Ukraine.[61] Furthermore, the EU encourages regional co-operation between Azerbaijan, Armenia, Georgia, Moldova, Russia, Turkey and Ukraine through the Black Sea Synergy[62] that was launched in 2007 in order to

---

[55] EUSR for Georgia Heikki Talvitie (2003 – 2006), then Peter Semneby (2006 – 2011), EUSR for the crisis in Georgia Pierre Morel (2008 – 2011), then Phillippe Lefort (2011 – 2012). EUSR for Moldova Adrijaan Jacobovits de Szeged (2003 – 2006) and Kálmán Mizsei (2007 – 2011). Today, both positions are vacant. See *Labedzka,* op. cit. note 10, 606.

[56] European Union's Border Mission to Moldova and Ukraine. Declaration by the Presidency of the European Union. Odessa, Ukraine, 30 November 2005, 15178/05 (Presse 334).

[57] Council Joint Action of 28 June 2004 on the European Union Rule of Law Mission in Georgia, EUJUST THEMIS (2004/523/CFSP), OJ 2004 L 228, 21; *Labedzka,* op. cit. note 10, 607.

[58] Council Joint Action of 15 September 2008 on the European Union Monitoring Mission in Georgia, EUMM Georgia (2008/736/CFSP), OJ 2008 L 248, 26.

[59] "A Secure Europe in a better World. European Security Strategy", Brussels, 12 December 2003, not published, available at <www.consilium.europa.eu/uedocs/cmsUpload/78367.pdf>.

[60] See 2590th Council Meeting Luxembourg 14 June 2004, 10189/04 (Presse 195), 13.

[61] Communication from the Commission to the Council and the European Parliament, Eastern Partnership, COM(2008) 823 final.

[62] Communication of the Commission to the Council and the European Parliament, Black Sea Synergy – A New Regional Co-operation Initiative, COM(2007) 160 final.

encourage regional co-operation between the countries surrounding the Black Sea.[63]

4. RUSSIA'S INVOLVEMENT IN EU POLICIES AND VICE VERSA

So how does the EU involve Russia, its positions and interests in its policies towards Moldova and the South Caucasus? To answer that, one has to take into account three possibilities: The first one is to examine whether issues concerning the Black Sea countries come up in the bilateral relations between the EU and Russia, whereas the second possibility is to ask: Does Russian influence reflect in the bilateral talks between the EU and the respective countries? A third way to assess Russia's influence in the region is to take a closer look at its engagement via multilateral co-operation forums established by the EU itself or where the Union is a member.

4.1. Issues of South Caucasus and Moldova in the relations between EU and Russia

On a bilateral level, first and foremost the political dialogue - as foreseen in Art 6 of the EU-Russia PCA and the Common Spaces road maps - has a prominent place in involving matters concerning Moldova and the countries of the South Caucasus. This instrument adds flexibility and dynamism to the partnership relations.[64] There are about 40 different dialogues which are either envisaged or have already been initiated.

Topics discussed include *inter alia* energy. The EU-Russia energy dialogue within the Common Economic Space is the most prominent one. This is a truly important issue for the EaP countries, since their geographic location puts them in the position of transit states for Russian oil and gas exports into the EU. Furthermore, Russia is heavily involved in most of their energy sectors[65] in terms of energy supply, economic ties as well as in terms of price policy.

In addition and more importantly for the Black Sea countries, talks about conflict management and conflict resolution between Brussels and Moscow are being held. In this respect it should be noted that the core issues of Moldova and the South Caucasus are the frozen conflicts in Transnistria, Abkhasia, South Ossetia and Nagorno-Karabakh which constitute an important part of this dialogue.[66] However, the

---

[63] For more detailed information see the contributions of *Benedikt Harzl* and *Vanda Amaro Dias* in this issue.

[64] See *Hillion*, Russian Federation, in *Blockmans / Lazowski* (eds), The European Union and its Neighbours (2006) 463 (481).

[65] *Tolksdorf*, op. cit. note 22.

[66] See, e.g., Joint Statement of the 15th EU-Russia Summit (Moscow), 10 May 2005, 8799/05 (Presse 110), available at <http://www.consilium.europa.eu/ueDocs/cms_Data/docs/pressData/en/er/84811.pdf>.

biggest disadvantage of this practice is that the countries concerned are neither heard nor involved.

Furthermore, a Russia-EU visa dialogue has been started in 2007 in order to explore the possibilities of visa-free travel between Russia and the Schengen area as a long-term perspective.[67] These talks raised concerns among the EaP countries that a visa-free regime for Russian citizens without granting the same rights to citizens of EaP countries would effectively create a major imbalance in Russia's favour. So far, little progress has been made in this regard. Apart from this, other forms of involvement of regional issues in the bilateral EU-Russia relations are scarce.

4.2. Russia's influence on the EU-Moldova / South Caucasus relations

In the framework of the bilateral ENP relations with each South Caucasus country Russia is mentioned in every Country Strategy Paper. For instance, the Strategy papers towards Armenia and Azerbaijan contain a brief analysis of the relations of the respective country with Russia underlining its influence in the region in economic and political matters.[68] On the subsequent level of National Indicative Programmes and annual AP, however, there is no more mentioning of aims, instruments, measures etc. involving Russia.

In spite of this, several issues concerning Russia are part of the EU's relations with Georgia and Moldova. The EU is one of the official facilitators of the negotiations on conflict resolution in Transnistria,[69] and it is also involved in the South Ossetian conflict resolution.

On the Transnistria issue, the ENP Action Plan for Moldova contains a briefly stated commitment of the EU "to continue its efforts to ensure the fulfillment by Russia of the Istanbul commitments[70] with regard to Moldova".[71] The EU is trying to contribute to resolving this conflict between Moldova and the Transnistrian Moldavian Republic, which is being supported by Russia in military terms, by participating in the so-called "5+2"-talks under the auspices of the OSCE, which have recently been resumed.[72]

---

67 The first meeting of the EU-Russia visa dialogue was held on 27 September 2007 in Moscow, compare the EU-Russia Common Spaces Progress Report 2007, available at <http://eeas.europa.eu/russia/docs/commonspaces_prog_report2007.pdf>. In 2011, a set of common steps towards visa free short-term travel of Russian and EU citizens was agreed upon, available at <http://ec.europa.eu/dgs/home-affairs/what-we-do/policies/international-affairs/russia/docs/common_steps_towards_visa_free_short_term_travel_en.pdf>.

68 See ENPI, Azerbaijan. Country strategy paper 2007 – 2013, 7, available at <http://ec.europa.eu/world/enp/pdf/country/enpi_csp_azerbaijan_en.pdf>; ENPI, Armenia. Country Strategy Paper 2007 - 2012, 10, available at <http://ec.europa.eu/world/enp/pdf/country/enpi_csp_armenia_en.pdf>.

69 See *Zagorski,* op. cit. note 20, 55.

70 At the 1999 OSCE Summit in Istanbul, Russia committed itself to withdraw its forces from Georgia and Moldova.

71 EU-Moldova Action Plan, 12, available at <http://ec.europa.eu/world/enp/pdf/action_plans/moldova_enp_ap_final_en.pdf>.

72 See the Remarks of Herman Van Rompuy, President of the European Council, following the 28th EU-Russia Summit, Brussels, 15 December 2011, EUCO 162/11, PRESSE 500, PR PCE 121.

Concerning South Ossetia, in the 2006 EU-Georgia AP[73], the EU committed itself to including the issues of settlement of the South Ossetian and Abkhasian conflicts in the EU-Russia political dialogue meetings. After the escalation of the South Ossetia conflict in August 2008, the EU played the role of a mediator and assisted in concluding a ceasefire agreement and the extraordinary Council of 1 September 2008 decided to provide political, financial and practical support to Georgia.[74]

Russia itself is, of course, not directly involved in the political dialogues between the EU and the South Caucasus countries, but issues linked to Russia like visa liberalisation come up at the negotiation table. Brussels has already established visa-free travel with Moldova.[75] The visa liberalisation dialogue with Georgia has started in 2012,[76] but the negotiations are experiencing some difficulties with regard to the EU-Russia visa dialogue. Since most Abkhaz and South Ossetians have Russian citizenship, granting them visa-free entry to the Schengen area would not only "create a clear discrimination within Georgia", as former Georgian Vice-Prime Minister Georgi Baramidze[77] put it, but could also be interpreted as an encouragement of separatism or as approval of the "Russian occupation"[78] of these territories by the EU.[79]

Visa liberalisation and readmission are indeed good examples of the EU practice on an institutional level within the EU. The Union's institutions, especially the EEAS, are forced to pay attention to Russia's policy and need to co-ordinate their own approach towards these countries in accordance with the development of the EU-Russia relations at large.

From all this it becomes obvious that the EU is very hesitant to involve Russian influence into its bilateral relations to the countries concerned. But it also cannot ignore its presence and that is why it is indirectly reflecting on the EU relations to these countries.

4.3. Russia's influence on a multilateral regional level

On a multilateral regional level, the EU's instruments for involving Russia are also limited:

---

73 EU/Georgia AP, available at <http://ec.europa.eu/environment/enlarg/pdf/enp_action_plan_georgia.pdf>.

74 See the Press release on the Extraordinary meeting of the General Affairs and External Relations Council, Brussels, 13 August 2008, 12453/08 (Presse 236).

75 See the press release on Visa liberalisation for Moldova, Brussels, 14 March 2014, 7645/14 (Presse 146).

76 See „The EU starts a visa liberalisation dialogue with Georgia", IP/12/561, Brussels, 4 June 2012.

77 See the statement made by Georgian deputy prime minister Georgi Baramidze in an interview with the EUobserver, available at <http://euobserver.com/24/30131>.

78 The Georgian Government perceives the breakaway regions of Abkhasia and South-Ossetia as occupied by the Russians. This opinion has been approved by the EP. See EP resolution of 17 November 2011 containing the EP's recommendations to the Council, the Commission and the EEAS on the negotiations of the EU-Georgia AA, 2011/2133(INI).

79 *Golunov*, EU-Russia Visa Talks. Open and Hidden Agendas, PONARS Eurasia Policy Memo No 144 (May 2011), 3.

As indicated above, even though Russia was meant to be included in the ENP and is mentioned in the ENP Regional Strategy of 2004[80] where it is described as a key partner of the EU, it is by its own wish not a member of the ENP.

Since regional co-operation in the framework of the EaP is limited to ENP members,[81] Russia is not included in the EaP multilateral platforms' meetings as well. This is especially pitiful because in this framework actors involved also discuss questions of energy security which is, as mentions before, one of Russia's key priorities in the region. Interesting enough, at the Civil Society Forum 2010 in Berlin, there were also participants from Russia (notably the Moscow Helsinki Group, the International Youth Human Rights Movement and the Center for the Development of Democracy and Human Rights), but of course they do not represent the official position of the Russian Federation.

The only regional co-operation forum initiated by the EU where Russia is a member state is the above-mentioned BSS, whose framework also includes non-ENP countries. This initiative, however, has shown very modest impact so far. Whereas the issues discussed in this framework are very broad, the outcome is yet too little (which can be seen from the only progress report of 2008).[82] As a step forward in this initiative, the Black Sea Environmental Partnership was launched in March 2010, but again with low impact so far.

Russia is an observer in the EU "Baku Initiative"[83] that was launched in 2004 in order to facilitate the integration of energy markets of the Black Sea and Caspian Sea regions into the EU market as well as the transportation of the Caucasian/Caspian fossil resources to Europe.[84] Unfortunately, Russia is not taking part in the TRACEA and INOGATE programmes within this framework, even though they involve almost all of Russia's neighbouring countries, but informal consultations with Russian officials apparently do take place.

To sum up, there are virtually no effective or attractive co-operation mechanisms by the EU to involve Russia as well as Moldova and the countries of the South Caucasus.

---

80 Communication of the Commission. European Neighbourhood Policy. Strategy Paper, COM(2004) 373 final.

81 European Commission, Communication to the European Parliament and the Council, Eastern Partnership, COM(2008) 823 final.

82 Communication from the Commission to the Council and the European Parliament, Report on the first year of implementation of the Black Sea Synergy, COM(2008) 391 final.

83 See Ministerial Declaration on Enhanced Energy Co-operation between the EU, the Caspian Littoral States and their neighbouring countries, the so-called "Astana Conclusions" (available at <http://ec.europa.eu/dgs/energy_transport/international/regional/caspian/doc/2006_11_30_astana_conclusions.pdf)>.

84 Ministerial Declaration on Enhanced energy co-operation between the EU, the Littoral States of the Black and Caspian Seas and their neighbouring countries, 30 November 2006, Astana, available at <http://ec.europa.eu/energy/international/international_cooperation/doc/2006_11_30_astana_conclusions.pdf>.

5. POSSIBLE SOLUTIONS AND PROSPECTS

Even though it is obvious from the above that Russia has a big influence on Moldova and the South Caucasus countries, its involvement in the EU integration process of these counties is problematic.

At present, the EU is, on the one hand, compelled to respect Russia as a strategic partner and is influenced by the Kremlin's interests and position in the South Caucasus in the way the EU conducts its own policy in the region. On the other hand, there are almost no EU – induced instruments – not to mention co-ordinated political will – involving Russia in these matters, and certainly no attractive or even satisfactory ones.

This obvious mismatch shows that there is a need for a more effective co-operation mechanism on a solid basis within the EU in order to ensure prosperity, security and stability in the region while at the same time accomodating Russia's economic and political influence in the post-Soviet area.[85] Accordingly, Moscow urges the Union to develop co-operative projects which include the EU itself, Russia and the EaP countries. Therefore, the big challenge for the EU is to find a mechanism that suits its own policy needs and also allows Russia to play a constructive role[86] in the region. This could be achieved through various means:

The first - and easiest - possibility would be the re-ignition of the BSS. This would mean using existing mechanisms and infrastructure and help save resources. In this regard, the EU could, for example, ensure the efficiency of technical assistance and foster concrete projects so that co-ooperation in this framework can improve. Some of the EaP countries are in favour of this possibility considering the advantages at hand. But unfortunately, due to the current overall political situation, this improvement is not likely to happen.

The second solution is the idea of including Russia (together with other key players in the region) in the EaP as a full member. According to the Joint Declaration of the Prague Eastern Partnership Summit, as a third state, Russia "will be eligible for the participation on a case-by-case basis in concrete projects, activities and meetings of thematic platforms, where it contributes to the objectives of particular activities and the general objectives of the Eastern Partnership."[87] Despite Moscow's massive concerns raised at the very launch of the EaP,[88] recent statements by high Russian government officials signalise that Russia does not rule out the possibility of joining the EaP. Considering this, an inclusion of Russia into this initiative

---

85 See *Kremer*, European Partnership and the South Caucasus: Framework Condition for a Grand Bargain in 2025? Caucasus Analytical Digest 19/2010, 15 (16).

86 Ibid.

87 See the Joint Declaration of the Prague Eastern Partnership Summit, Prague, 7 May 2009, 8435/09 (Presse 78).

88 The EaP was then characterised as an EU initiative to establish a sphere of influence in its Eastern neighbourhood forcing the countries concerned to choose between Russia and the EU, see *Stewart*, op. cit. note 3, 2.

could be not as improbable as it seemed a few years ago,[89] but still remains a quite unrealistic scenario.[90]

A third possibility, initially proposed by Poland at an informal foreign ministerial meeting on the EaP in Sopot in May 2010 , is including Russia into the EaP apart from a full membership by organising of a so-called "Group of Friends of Eastern Partnership" (officially named Information and Co-ordination Group), an informal group of states and international financial institutions which officially do not participate in the EaP itself, but are willing to support this initiative on an *ad hoc* basis, e.g. by contributing to concrete projects within its framework. The idea behind the Group was the creation of a forum where EaP members as well as non-members would be able to inform each other about their plans and co-ordinate their respective actions. The official inauguration of the Group took place in Brussels on 29 September 2010 with participation of United States, Russia, Turkey, Norway, Switzerland, Canada, Japan, the EBRD, the EBI and the World Bank.[91] Thus, once the operational framework for the Group is established, Russia will be able to participate in the meetings in the EaP framework while still obtaining its special status for the EU. This could positively contribute to the development of mutual trust.[92]

However, certain EaP countries (first and foremost Georgia) almost instantly expressed their doubts about the idea of Russia participating in any EaP projects as they simply do not consider Moscow as a "friend".[93] Thus it remains to be seen whether the Group of Friends is a viable solution, provided all participants are indeed willing to co-operate.

The fourth possibility is the creation of a totally new multilateral co-operation mechanism involving the EU and Russia as well as the Black Sea countries, which could be carried out on different levels, much as the existing means of co-operation foreseen in the PCAs. This idea is not new, a similar initiative as a sort of Public-Private-Partnership was proposed by *Fischer* and *Zagorski* in 2010.[94]

One could, of course, argue that institutions are not the answer to all tensions on an international political level. The EU has often been criticised about its obsession with institution-building and the experience of nearly 10 years of ENP shows its lack of effectiveness in crucial areas like conflict management. In addition, the latest developments within other co-operation forums initiated by the EU, made it obvious that even if there are multilateral co-operation mechanisms, this does not necessarily mean that they produce viable results. On the contrary, Member States having issues with each other tend to paralyse these forums instead of finding solutions to their mutual problems by way of a constructive dialogue.

---

89 See the statement made by Russian Foreign Minister *Sergei Lavrov* at a news conference on 25 November 2009, available at <www.hurriyetdailynews.com/default.aspx?pageid=438&n=lavrov-russia-could-join-eu-eastern-partnership-2009-11-25>.

90 The same opinion is raised by *Tolksdorf*, op. cit. note 22.

91 See also <www.easternpartnership.org/eap-institutions/group-friends-eastern-partnership>.

92 *Stewart,* op. cit. note 3, 4.

93 See the statement made by Georgian vice prime minister Georgi Baramidze op. cit. note 77.

94 See *Fischer / Zagorski*, Russia, the EU and their Neighbours: Partners in Modernization, in Partnership with Russia in Europe: New Challenges for the EU-Russia-Partnership, Friedrich Ebert Stiftung April 2010, 18.

So the question remains: Is a regional Black Sea co-operation forum at all a realistic possibility? One could critically submit that the actors involved are too heterogeneous and the problems at stake are too complex and not likely to be solved easily. This assessment is not improved by the fact that some countries concerned are simply not willing to co-operate with each other. At the same time, other countries are more than ready to negotiate. Therefore, if there is still a chance, however small, the international community - and first and foremost the EU as the leading example for multilateral co-operation - should not give up on it easily, but rather proactively work towards the establishment of such a mechanism.

In all constellations mentioned above, this would of course also mean for Russia that it would have to give up its hegemonic approach as well as its scepticism against multilateral co-operation and start co-operating with the EU and the South Caucasus countries on an equal footing. Unfortunately, in view of the recent events in the Ukraine and the Crimea this possibility appears less likely. Nevertheless, considering Russia's wish to be treated as equal partner in the framework of the EU-Russia Strategic Partnership, this would be at least worth trying, if not too much to ask.

6. Conclusion

To conclude, it can be said that Russia is an important player for the Black Sea region which makes it also important for the EU. However, the scenario is completely different from the the one the EU has been facing in Southeastern Europe. Being an exceptional neighbour, a regional power and a strategic partner, the EU has to pay attention to Russia's interests as well as actions while developing and implementing its policy towards Moldova and the South Caucasus countries.

The Union disposes of a wide range of instruments for interacting with Russia and the countries of the Black Sea basin, but none is sufficient to balance Russia's influence and to provide for a solid basis for a true regional co-operation between all actors.

There are several possibilities to include Russia into the EU's multilateral co-operation with the countries concerned, which all have their negative and positive aspects. Still the EU has the potential to serve as a mediator for Russia and the Black Sea region and should more actively seek to establish an attractive and effective basis for regional co-operation.

Yet, this strongly depends on the existence of a unified political will of all countries concerned, but first and foremost the EU and its Member States themselves. This implies that the Union, on the one hand, needs to speak with one voice towards Russia and, on the other hand, manage to develop a coherent policy strategy for the Black Sea region that also involves Russia in order to create a genuinely fruitful co-operation and achieve its goal of ensuring prosperity, stability and security for the region in the future.

Sezen Ergen-Breitegger / Ani Harutyunyan

TURKEY, BLACK SEA AND THE EU: WHERE TITANS CLASH

"Art 8 AA EU-Georgia: Regional stability

1. The Parties shall intensify their joint efforts to promote stability, security and democratic development in the region, as well as to work to further promote regional cooperation in various formats and in particular shall work towards peaceful settlement of the unresolved conflicts in the region.

2. These efforts shall follow commonly shared principles of maintaining international peace and security as established by the UN Charter, the Helsinki Final Act of 1975 of the Conference on Security and Cooperation in Europe and other relevant multilateral documents. The Parties shall also make full use of the multilateral framework of the Eastern Partnership that provides for cooperation activities and open and free dialogue, fostering links among partners countries themselves."

"Art 8 AA EU-Republic of Moldova: Regional stability

1. The Parties shall intensify their joint efforts to promote stability, security and democratic development in the region, and in particular shall work together for the peaceful settlement of regional conflicts.

(...)[1]

3. These efforts shall follow commonly shared principles of maintaining international peace and security as established by the UN Charter, the Helsinki Final Act of 1975 of the Conference on Security and Cooperation in Europe and other relevant multilateral documents. "

1. INTRODUCTION

The Black Sea, due to its geographical location, is a strategic region for a number of countries, including not only regional but also global powers. After accession of Bulgaria and Romania to the EU, the region became of crucial importance also to the EU itself. In this paper, we will try to analyse the complex geopolitical features of the Black Sea region, the EU's interests and policies, Turkey's role as a connecting spot for different regions, its foreign policy, as well as the implications of Turkey-EU relations in the region and also the indi-

[1] Para 2 refers to the situation to Transnistria and is quoted at the beginning of the paper of *Samoilova*.

vidual interests of both players. Special attention will be paid to the security and energy issues in the context of EU-Turkey relations, taking into consideration Russian and U.S. interests in the region.

2. GEOPOLITICS OF THE BLACK SEA REGION – DEFINING THE BLACK SEA REGION

Throughout history the Black Sea, by virtue of its geography and natural resources, has been an arena for collision of interests of global powers. Recently, the Black Sea has been attracting more and more attention from international key players and a diverse set of stakeholders, thus, making the role of the coastal states, in particular Turkey, even more important.

There have been many questions on how to define the region. Discussions are typically based on the premise that it is problems that define regions and consequently regionalism.[2] A narrow definition of the Black Sea region is constituted by the six littoral states, namely Bulgaria, Romania, Ukraine, Russia, Georgia, and Turkey.[3] A wider definition includes also non-littoral states such as Armenia, Azerbaijan, Greece and Moldova. The notions of "*Wider* Black Sea area" (a term used by the BSEC) or "Black Sea *region*"[4] (a term used by the EU[5]) first appeared in the programme of the Hellenic Chairmanship of the BSEC in 2004[6] in an effort to accommodate the heterogeneous membership of the BSEC and to indicate the comprehensive and inclusive (in terms of membership) nature of Black Sea subregionalism. The term 'wider' thus reflects the common, collective position that the Black Sea group should not be perceived as an exclusive club and that the Black Sea region extends beyond the strictly defined littoral territories to adjacent areas that are culturally, politically or economically linked to it. Additionally, by stressing the notion of a 'wider' Black Sea region, the BSEC tried to blur geopolitical divisions between a Western European and an Eastern, 'other' Black Sea shore.

No matter which definition is accepted or whether or not a distinct Black Sea region exists, the complexity of the area is revealed when taking into consideration the energy, security, economic and trade interests of global powers like USA, Russia and EU as well as of rising regional powers like Turkey. Moreover, the very composition of the Black Sea states makes the region full of gunpowder that may

---

2 *Manoli*, Where is Black Sea Regionalism Heading? Southeast European and Black Sea Studies 2010,323-339.

3 *Bocutoğlu / Koçer*, Politico-Economic Conflicts in the Black Sea Region in the Post-Cold War Era at 111, available at <http://ifsh.de/file-CORE/documents/yearbook/english/06/BocutogluKocer-en.pdf>.

4 As it is explained in the EU Black Sea Synergy document, The Black Sea region includes Greece, Bulgaria and Moldova in the west, Ukraine and Russia in the north, Georgia, Armenia and Azerbaijan in the east and Turkey in the south. Though Armenia, Azerbaijan, Moldova and Greece are not littoral states, proximity and close ties make them natural regional actors.

5 Communication from the Commission to the Council and the European Parliament, Black Sea Synergy – A new regional co-operation initiative, Brussels, 11 April 2007, COM(2007) 160 final, p. 2.

6 *Manoli,* op. cit. note 2, 325.

explode at any time by just a single spark, changing the balance of power not only on the regional, but also on a global level. The reason for this explosiveness is that almost all of these countries have disputes or conflicts with one another, and those conflicts reverberate into other regions adjacent to the Black Sea, where interests of global and regional powers collide. Thus, the Mediterranean, South Caucasus, Middle Eastern, Black Sea regions coalesce due to Turkey's geopolitical position, economic strength and its active role in the Black Sea area. In this sense the Black Sea region and especially Turkey become both a bridge and sometimes a dividing line between those regions.

The Black Sea basin has been considered a gift and a curse and the ''backyard of one power or the other''[7] throughout history. In the more recent past and in geopolitical terms, the Black Sea region took shape after the dissolution of the Soviet Union. First of all, there was the security and power vacuum that appeared after the dissolution of the Soviet Union. Secondly, the interest of the region's countries to be more closely involved with the Western world has drawn the EU's attention more towards the area. EU and NATO enlargement processes have made bilateral and regional relations more complex. Third, the proximity to the Middle East, especially after 9/11, underlined the importance of the security of the area and the democratisation of its nations as a key element to a peaceful future. Fourth, energy sources of the Caspian Sea and the ability to compete with Middle Eastern energy sources have become much more important. Finally, we might address the resurrection of dormant conflicts in the area.[8] All these problems shape the Black Sea and Turkey's role in the region.

3. TURKEY'S NEW FOREIGN POLICY AND ITS ROLE IN THE REGION

3.1. Neo-Ottomanism

Turkey's domestic situation has always been reflected in its foreign policy. In this sense, when analysing Turkish foreign policy, it is of utmost importance to take into account the fact which groups representing which ideologies are in power in the country.

The new era of Turkey's foreign policy began with its domestic transformation since 2002 when representatives of the Justice and Development Party (APK) came to power. *Davutoğlu*, the Chief Advisor to the Prime Minister since 2002 and Minister of Foreign Affairs of Turkey since 2009, developed a new foreign policy vision that was supposed to deepen Turkey's involvement in regional politics, international organisations, and world politics. Turkey's new foreign policy has been driven by three key factors: re-conceptualising Turkey's identity and international role, de-securitising its foreign relations ('zero problems with neighbours'), and

---

7 *Aydın*, Europe's Next Shore: The Black Sea Region After EU Enlargement, Occasional Paper, 2004 at 6, available at <www.peacepalacelibrary.nl/ebooks/files/ISS_EU_occ53.pdf>.

8 *Yılmaz*, Karadeniz'de Değişen Dengeler ve Türkiye, Karadeniz Araştırmaları, Sayı:15, Güz 2007, at 47.

increasing its strength as a trading state.[9] Since the AKP came to power in late 2002, its foreign policy has been based on what *Davutoğlu* calls 'strategic depth'. His main argument is that Turkey is a great power that has neglected its historic ties and diplomatic, economic and political relationships with its neighbouring regions (Middle East, North Africa, the Balkans, and Eurasia), dating back to the Ottoman era.[10]

This Neo-Ottoman approach reminds Turks that they once had a great multinational empire that ruled the Middle East, North Africa, the Balkans and parts of Central Europe. Such emphasis on the Ottoman legacy is not part of a plan to islamise Turkey and its foreign policy. Rather it is an attempt to balance and broaden the geo - strategic horizons of a country which in the past has been obsessed by following an exclusively Western trajectory[11]

The second characteristic of neo-Ottomanism is a sense of grandeur and self-confidence in foreign policy. Neo-Ottomanism sees Turkey as a regional superpower. Its strategic vision and culture reflects the geographic reach of the Ottoman and Byzantine Empires. According to this neo-Ottoman vision, Turkey is a pivotal state which should play a very active diplomatic, political, and economic role in a wide region of which it is the "centre." Moreover, Turkey's role is not only in the centre of regional, but also of global politics. *Davutoğlu* points out that Turkey promises to contribute to security, stability and prosperity in a wide range of territories that go beyond Turkey's immediate neighbourhood.[12] Such grand ambitions, in turn, require a nation-state at peace with its multiple identities, including its Muslim and multinational past.

The third aspect of neo- Ottomanism is its goal of embracing the West as much as the Islamic world. Like the imperial city of Istanbul, which straddles Europe and Asia, neo-Ottomanism is Janus-faced. In that sense, the fact that the Ottoman Empire was part of Europe matters a great deal to AKP's neo-Ottoman vision.13 It should also be noted that this 'neo-Ottoman' vision does not have an imperialist agenda. AKP leaders want to reach out to non-Western regions to complement their ties to the West - not to replace them.[14] In the context of de-securitisation of its foreign relations, Turkey's new neighbourhood policy appropriated a vision of minimising the problems in its neighbourhood which has been called 'zero problems policy' by *Davutoğlu* himself.[15]

In the context of the active involvement of international politics and the policy of 'zero problems' with neighbours, Turkey tries to be pro-active during times of crisis. For instance, during the Russia-Georgia crisis in 2008 Prime Minister *Erdoğan*

---

9 *Ulgen*, A Place in the Sun or Fifteen Minutes of Fame? Understanding Turkey's New Foreign Policy, Carnegie Papers, No 1, December 2010, at 4.

10 *Taşpinar,* The Three Strategic Visions of Turkey, US – Europe Analysis Series No 50, March 8, 2011, at 1.

11 Ibid. at 2.

12 Aras, Davutoğlu Era in Turkish Foreign Policy, SETA, Foundation for Political, Economic and Social Research, Policy Brief No 32, May 2009, at 6; see also Davutoğlu, Turkey's New Foreign Policy Vision, Insight Turkey (2008) at 78.

13 *Taşpinar,* op. cit. note 10, at 2.

14 *Taşpinar,* op. cit. note 10, at 1.

15 *Aras*, op. cit. note 12, at 6; see also Davutoğlu, op. cit. note 12, at 78.

visited Georgia, Azerbaijan and Russia before any other leader in the region and in Europe. Turkey offered a stability platform and carefully managed a potential NATO-Russia crisis in the Black Sea. Second, *Erdoğan* visited four influential Arab countries in the immediate aftermath of Israel's Gaza offensive, and a Turkish team led by *Davutoğlu* himself pursued a shuttle diplomacy between Damascus and Cairo during the crisis.[16] However, it should also be admitted that in spite of Turkey's economic growth and desire to become a regional and global power, its foreign policy of active involvement in crisis mediations and conducting good neighbourly relations were not always successful (e.g. the "Football diplomacy" with Armenia did not succeed in the end because of Turkey's close relations with Azerbaijan and the latter's demands to solve the Nagorno-Karabakh issue as a precondition to the opening of the Armenian-Turkish border). This policy approach is currently facing challenges and obstacles. The crisis around Ukraine, which will be discussed below, was just recent evidence of this.

Although Turkey's "new" foreign policy is not really new because previous Turkish leaders, including former presidents *Ozal* and *Demirel*, charted similar courses for Turkish foreign policy, it is worth mentioning that *Ozal* wanted Turkey to acquire a more influential role in the Middle East, while *Demirel* wanted to develop a larger role for Turkey in the Black Sea, the Caucasus, and Central Asia. The differences are *Davutoglu's* much broader take on the idea, coupled with Turkey's newly de-securitised international context and its economic growth.[17]

3.2. Turkey's role in the Black Sea region

3.2.1. Economic co-operation: the BSEC

During the Cold War era, Turkey was the only NATO member in the area to secure the Black Sea region against the Eastern Bloc.[18] After the collapse of the Soviet Union, the region became even more important for Turkey. To act more pro-actively after the demise of communism, Turkey took initiatives already in the early 1990's.

Turkey started multiple institutions for regional co-operation in the area. One of those initiatives was the BSEC. It was established in 1992 by Albania, Armenia, Azerbaijan, Bulgaria, Georgia, Greece, Moldova, Romania, the Russian Federation, Turkey and Ukraine,[19] covering a vast economic area from the Adriatic to the Pacific with a total population of 325 million.[20] In the early 1990's, most of the founding members were trying to adapt their centrally planned economies to world markets. However, political and economic obstacles did not hinder the founding mem-

---

16 Aras, op. cit. note 12, at 9.

17 Ibid. 15.

18 *Kasımr*, Türkiye'nin Karadeniz Politikası: Temel Parametreler ve Stratejiler, at 172, available at <www.usak.org.tr/dosyalar/dergi/eVRqmB4CKUXHvPJTAUQF9U6skITPdp.pdf>.

19 The Republic of Serbia joined BSEC in 2004 which led total members to 12 countries.

20 *Özer*, Black Sea Economic Co-operation and the EU, at 1, available at <http://www.sam.gov.tr/wp-content/uploads/2012/01/11.-THE-BLACK-SEA-ECONOMIC-COOPERATION-ANDTHE-EU.pdf>.

bers to have future reflections on the area.[21] The "Summit Declaration on Black Sea Economic Cooperation"[22] and the "Bosphorus Statement"[23] established the BSEC, starting as an economic regional co-operation organisation. The political framework was set by the Summit Declaration whereas the Bosphorus Statement underlined the scope of co-operation.[24]

In 1998, with the adoption of its Charter,[25] the BSEC acquired international legal identity and became an international organisation.[26] This can be considered a huge achievement for a regional initiative.[27] The BSEC Charter established bodies to rule in three main areas: governmental, parliamentary and economic relations. On the Parliamentary level, Art 20 of the Charter established the Parliamentary Assembly of the BSEC, an international non-governmental level has been established by BSEC itself, and the economic perspective is completed by the Black Sea Trade and Development Bank, founded on the basis of Art 22 BSEC Charter.[28]

Initially inspired by the EEC, the BSEC is different from other free trade areas. Its aim is not just to establish free trade,[29] it shall provide a secure, peaceful and prosperous region for its members.[30] It engages in many co-operation areas such as agriculture, banking and finance, combating crime, education and energy.[31] In each of these areas a working group is created and they are all gathered under a Committee of Senior Officials. This Committee of Senior Officials represents the Ministers of Foreign Affairs of the Member States and acts on their behalf. Turkey is hosting the BSEC Permanent International Secretariat (PERMISI) in Istanbul. Ultimately, it is difficult to estimate the effectiveness of the BSEC. One commentator holds that the BSEC has not fully answered the expectations that existed, but it nevertheless forms an important instrument for co-operation in the region.[32]

---

21 *Apakan*, Turkey´s Approach to the Black Sea Region and to the Organization of the Black Sea Economic Cooperation (BSEC), see <www.mfa.gov.tr/turkey_s-approach-to-the-black-sea-region-and-to-the-organization-of-the-black-sea-economic-cooperation-bsec-.tr.mfa>.

22 Full text available at <www.bsec-organization.org/documents/declaration/summit/Reports/Istanbul1992.pdf>.

23 Full text available at <www.bsecorganization.org/documents/declaration/summit/Reports/Bosphorus%201992.pdf>

24 *Hartwig*, The Black Sea Economic Cooperation Process, at 3, available at <http://aei.pitt.edu/812/1/scop97_1_2.pdf>.

25 Full text available at <www.bsecorganization.org/documents/LegalDocuments/statutory/charter/Download/CHARTER%20web%20080630.pdf>.

26 *Aral*, The Black Sea Economic Co-operation after Ten Years: What Went Wrong, Alternatives Turkish Journal of International Relations, 2002 at 74.

27 See <http://politikaakademisi.org/turkey-black-sea-economic-cooperation-bsec-relations/>.

28 *Hartwig*, op. cit. note 24, 3.

29 Ibid. 1.

30 For futher information check <http://www.mfa.gov.tr/karadeniz-ekonomik-isbirligi-orgutu-_kei_.tr.mfa>.

31 For a full list of co-operation areas, check BSEC's webpage at <www.bsec-organization.org>.

32 *Zeyno*, Turkey and the Wider Black Sea Region, The Wider Black Sea Region in the 21st Century: Strategic, Economic and Energy Perspectives 2008 at 87.

3.2.2. Security

The region also represents a key security matter for Turkey. Turkey's role and policy in the Black Sea region should be analysed taking into consideration the strategic interests of the USA (NATO), Russia and their competing relationships on the one hand and ambiguous relations between Russia and Turkey on the other. The regime of the Turkish Straits (Bosporus and Dardanelles) is governed by the Montreux Convention of 1936. This treaty recognises the sovereignty of Turkey over the two straits, allows for free passage of commercial ships and limits the stay of military ships from non-littoral states to 21 days[33] in the Black Sea. Turkey's main interest is to avoid any foreign intervention (including that of the USA) to the Straits regime which grants Turkey the right to ban any foreign battleship to get into the Black Sea basin.

The U.S. strategic interests in the region have grown recently. Observing the delicate balances of the Cold War, the USA and NATO did not play any active role in the Black Sea region. In fact, even in the first decade of the post-Cold War era, the USA maintained a rather low profile when Black Sea issues were considered. However, with the events of 9/11 as well as with Bulgaria and Romania becoming NATO members, the transatlantic security focus shifted from Central and Eastern Europe to what is now called 'greater Middle East' or 'wider Black Sea'.[34]

One of the reasons that the USA have shifted their attention to the region is energy security. For the USA, minimising the western markets' energy dependency on Russia is of great importance. Therefore, the USA aims to diminish the Russian role as a major energy supplier to the markets. Thus, the Black Sea becomes vital as the key transit region for natural gas and, to some extent, oil.[35]

The USA also recognises the region as a strategic asset for the control of the so-called 'greater Middle East'. To increase its influence over the region and to facilitate the war on terrorism, the new U.S. security perceptions require control over the wider Black Sea with its strategic position between Europe and the Middle East. These aims can only be achieved via an increased political and military presence in the region. In this regard, the USA attempted to extend *Operation Active Endeavour*[36] from the Mediterranean to the Black Sea. However, in 2004 Turkey proposed *Black Sea Harmony*[37] operated by the Turkish Navy. Lately, in 2006 Russia and in 2007 Ukraine joined the operation. This initiative allows Turkey to retain control over the Turkish straits. Russia supports this operation as well, as it keeps the major NATO actors out of the Black Sea.

---

33 Art 18 (2) Montreux Convention regarding the regime of the straits, 20 July 1936, available at <http://sam.baskent.edu.tr/belge/Montreux_ENG.pdf>.

34 *Özdamar*, Security and Military Balance in the Black Sea Region, Southeast European and Black Sea Studies 2010, 341 (344).

35 Ibid.

36 Under this operation, NATO ships deployed in the Mediterranian were to control the sea and to prevent terrorist activities in the region.

37 This is a naval operation initiated by Turkey in March 2004 in accordance with the UN SC resolutions 1373, 1540 and 1566 and aims at deterring terrorism and asymmetric threats worldwide and ensuring the security of the Turkish Straits.

As another alternative to *Active Endeavour*, Turkey initiated BLACKSEAFOR. In April 2001, a Black Sea Naval Co-Operation Task Group was established by the 6 littoral states in Istanbul. For the first time in history, those six states came together in order to enhance the realisation of some common tasks.[38] BLACKSEAFOR is bringing together the naval forces of the Member States. The principles of BLACKSEAFOR have been established in Art 2 of the Founding Agreement.[39] Member States undertake to act in line with the purposes and principles of the UN Charter. It has been clearly stated that BLACKSEAFOR's activities are neither directed against any state nor intended to form a military alliance against any state or a group of states. Moreover, Member States agreed that BLACKSEAFOR should contribute to strengthening co-operation and good-neighbourly relations among nations. BLACKSEAFOR shall be a transparent, regional and stand-alone force. According to these principles, all decisions regarding BLACKSEAFOR shall be taken by consensus of the Parties, and the provisions of the Agreement shall not affect in any way the rights and obligations of the Parties deriving from other international agreements. Beyond the co-ordination of naval forces, over time and especially after 9/11 BLACKSEAFOR became an important force in combating crime and terrorism. Currently, however, conditions do not allow the operation to become a fully functional mechanism. Under Ukraine's term presidency the programmes of BLACKSEAFOR were recently cancelled due to the tensions between Russia and Ukraine.

Turkey also uses the Montreux regime as a balancing tool between NATO (USA) and Russia. This policy of power balance was reflected in the aftermath of the 2008 Russian-Georgian War when Turkey constrained NATO naval ships deployment in the Black Sea straits. Moreover, Turkey didn't allow the transit of a U.S. 69.552-ton hospital ship that was to be sent to Georgia, as according to the Montreux Convention "In the event that one or more countries without a shore on the Black Sea desire to send naval forces into the Black Sea, for a humanitarian purpose, the said forces cannot exceed 8.000 tons."[40] In spite of the fact that Turkey is a NATO Member State with a sizable presence of U.S. military installations on its territory, the reason for its support to Russia was the economic and energy interdependence between Turkey and Russia as well as Turkey's realisation that the regional security of the Black Sea region cannot be guaranteed via exclusion of another global power's, namely Russia's interests.

As part of this regional policy, Turkey after the Georgian-Russian war of 2008 initiated the Caucasian Stability and Co-operation Platform. However, this platform never really materialised due to the problems between the countries involved. Turkey's main aim in establishing this initiative was to create a secure Black Sea region and to enhance further co-operation in the area.[41] But at the same time, this initia-

[38] *Ulusoy*, A New Formation in the Black Sea: BLACKSEAFOR, Perceptions Journal of International Affairs, 2001 – 2002, 1, available at <http://sam.gov.tr/wp-content/uploads/2012/01/Hasan-Ulusoy1.pdf>.

[39] Full text available at <www.dzkk.tsk.tr/denizweb/blackseafor/english/agreement/agreement.php>.

[40] Art 18 (1) (d) Montreux Convention.

[41] A 2020 Vision for the Black Sea Region: A Report by the Commission on the Black Sea, at 29, available at

tive was an attempt to strengthen Turkey's reputation and position as an independent (from the USA mainly) regional power in the Black Sea. The platform should have been in the format of 3+2 (Armenia, Azerbaijan, Georgia, plus Russia and Turkey as regional stakeholders), taking into account that Russia perceives NATO expansion to the East and deployments of military installations in its immediate neighbourhood as a security threat. Thus, as Turkey emphasised, Russia must be incorporated into security arrangements in order to protect the fragile balance and prevent more assertive Russian foreign policies.[42] However, sharing the Black Sea region with Turkey was not in Russia's plans. The Caucasian Stability and Cooperation Platform failed also because the interests of not all the stakeholders in the region were taken into consideration: neither the EU, the USA, nor Iran (another regional power) were included in the initiative.

With regard to the recent Ukraine crisis it should be noted that the events put Turkey in a challenging situation: at stake for officials in Ankara are Turkey's commitments to its Western allies and its cultural kin, Crimean Tatars, pitted against its economic and political relationship with Moscow. As recently as 2010, Russia and Ukraine signed a treaty leasing the Crimean port of Sevastopol to Moscow for use by the Russian navy until 2042.[43] Now that Crimea is under Russia's control there is no longer a need to pay for its presence in the field. From a military perspective, the peninsula can serve as an outpost for extending power projection towards southern Ukraine, the Balkans and Turkey. Now that Moscow's military presence is no longer constrained by legal agreements with the Ukrainian side, it can fully utilise the geostrategic potential of Crimea by implementing a broad spectrum of mutually reinforcing instruments.[44]

Russian control over Crimea has significantly changed the balance of power in the region. From the Turkish point-of-view, the immediate impact of the crisis is rather negative since the country now has to face a more powerful and assertive Russian presence in the Black Sea region resulting in the deterioration of Ankara's relative position versus Moscow. In recent years, Ankara has often voiced concerns about Russian actions in the region, but avoided challenging Moscow directly. Such an approach was driven by Turkey's 'zero problems with neighbours' foreign policy, growing economic exchange between the two countries and significant dependence on energy supplies from Russia. Both countries also recognise each other's strength and position in the region and understand that a direct confrontation would have far reaching consequences, potentially destabilising vast areas across the Black Sea, Middle East, Caucasus and Central Asia.[45] Turkey's ambitions for an active foreign policy collide with the challenges brought by the security and en-

---

<www.blackseacom.eu/fileadmin/user_upload/Paper/A%202020%20Vision%20for%20the%20Black%20Sea.pdf>.

42 *Özdamar*, op. cit. note 34, 345.

43 *Cagaptay / Jeffrey*, Turkey's Muted Reaction to the Crimean Crisis, 4 March 2014, The Washington Institute Policy Watch 2219, available at <www.washingtoninstitute.org/policy-analysis/view/turkeys-muted-reaction-to-the-crimean-crisis>.

44 *Klus*, The New Strategic Realities in the Black Sea, New Eastern Europe Article, 22 April 2014, available at <www.neweasterneurope.eu/articles-and-commentary/1197-the-new-strategic-reality-in-the-black-sea>.

45 Ibid.

ergy, economic interests of global powers, thus, constraining Turkey's geopolitical position. The crisis in Ukraine may even become the last trigger for Turkey to move away from its policy of 'strategic depth'.

Another concern for the Turkish side relates to energy matters. Turkey's and Russia's trade in energy has massively developed over the years. Turkey imports more than 98 % of its gas needs. In 2009, 52 % of gas imports came from Russia.[46] Turkey also imports 92 % of its domestic oil demand, where Russia had the share of 32 % of the total imports[47]. Turkey's and Russia's interests, despite the important size of energy commerce in the Black Sea Basin, are not always in line.[48] Especially when Turkey and Russia' interests regarding Central Asia, Caucasus and the Straits are considered, it is safe to say that there is a conflict of interest between these two countries. Being active in the Black Sea area is crucial for Turkey since Russia is sometimes trying to bypass Turkey in defining the routes for energy transfer. The energy issues will be more elaborated below.

4. THE EU'S INTERESTS AND POLICIES IN THE REGION

4.1. Overview

The Black Sea region was of secondary importance to the EU during most of the 1990's,[49] taking a back seat against the Yugoslav conflicts. However, the EU had to change this approach and paid greater attention to the area starting by the early 2000s. Already in 2002, then Head of the EU Commission *Prodi* underlined the importance of the Black Sea for the EU.[50] Unresolved conflicts in the wider Black Sea region, including the South Caucasus, frequent Russian-Ukrainian crises, EU-Russia economic interdependence, in particular EU dependence on Russian energy supplies, the EU's search for new energy sources, including diversification of energy suppliers - all these factors contributed to the wider Black Sea region being seen as an important component of European policies and strategies. This was even more true after the sixth expansion round of the EU which granted accession to the Black Sea littoral countries Romania and

---

46 International Energy Agency, Energy Policies of IEA Countries, Turkey Review 2009, 67, available at <www.iea.org/publications/freepublications/publication/turkey2009.pdf>.

47 Ibid.

48 *Yılmaz*, op. cit. note 8, 58.

49 *Emerson*, The EU's New Black Sea Policy: What Kind of Regionalism is this? CEPS Working Document, No. 297, July 2008, at 1, available at <http://www.harvard-bssp.org/static/files/381/Michael%20Emerson%20EU%20New%20Black%20Sea%20policy.pdf>;
Çelikpala, Security in the Black Sea, Policy Report II, at 7, available at <www.bertelsmann-stiftung.de/bst/en/media/xcms_bst_dms_30921_30922_2.pdf>.

50 *Prodi*, A Wider Europe - A Proximity Policy as the Key to Stability, "Peace, Security And Stability – International Dialogue and the Role of the EU, Sixth ECSA-World Conference, Jean Monnet Project, Brussels, 5-6 December 2002, at 4, available at <http://europa.eu/rapid/press-release_SPEECH-02-619_en.htm>.

Bulgaria in 2007. As a result, the EU was transformed from an external to a local-regional stakeholder. Taking into account the 2004 NATO enlargement where Romania and Bulgaria were among the states which joined the Alliance, the role of the Black Sea region became even more vital in the security sense.

Unlike other players, the EU has no 'national' ambition in the Black Sea basin. Therefore the EU's policy towards the area is informed by its general principles such as promoting stability, economic prosperity, security, democracy and peace.[51] The EU has two major interests along with many other minor ones in the region. First, the EU aims to secure energy supplies from the region to its markets. European dependency on Russian energy creates a vital need for transiting gas and oil to the EU markets through the Black Sea and Turkey. Second, the stabilisation and democratisation of the ex-Soviet republics in the region will strengthen the security of Europe. The fragile republics in the region are seen as sources of instability, conflict and terrorism that have the potential to affect the EU's security.[52] The European Security Strategy lists five key threats that the EU is confronted with in the twenty-first century and all are applicable to the Black Sea region: the proliferation of weapons of mass destruction, terrorism, regional conflicts, state failure and organised crime.[53] Despite having political and security interests in the Black sea area, the EU has also become a centre of gravity for the region's economic activities. Since 2004, the EU has become the main trade partner of each country in the Black Sea region. Trade with the EU amounted to 29.7 % of overall trade for Armenia[54], 42.4 % for Azerbaijan[55] and 29 % for Georgia.[56] The EU is also by far Russia's main trading partner, accounting for 50 % of its overall trade turnover.[57] Moreover, the EU is the most important investor in Russia. It is estimated that up to 75 % of foreign direct investment stocks in Russia come from EU Member States (including Cyprus).[58]

---

51 *Mkrtchyan / Huseynow / Gogolashvili*, The European Union and the South Caucasus. Three Perspectives on the Future of the European Project from the Caucasus, Europe in Dialogue 2009/1, at 94, available at <www.bertelsmann-stiftung.de/bst/de/media/xcms_bst_dms_28297_28302_2.pdf>; *Aydin*, op. cit. note 7, 12.

52 Özdamar, op cit. note 42, 344.

53 European Security Strategy, Brussels, 12 December 2003, 3-5, available at <https://www.consilium.europa.eu/uedocs/cmsUpload/78367.pdf>.

54 European Commission, Trade Picture Armenia, available at <http://ec.europa.eu/trade/policy/countries-and-regions/countries/armenia/>.

55 European Commission, Trade picture Azerbaijan, available at <http://ec.europa.eu/trade/policy/countries-and-regions/countries/azerbaijan/>.

56 The EU's Black Sea Synergy: Results and possible Ways forward, Standard briefing, EP Directorate general for external policies, Policy Departmeny, 2010, at 12, available at <http://www.iris-france.org/docs/kfm_docs/docs/observatoire-voisinage-europeen/bl-sea-1010-way-forward-final-published.pdf>.

57 Source: Permament Mission of the Russian Federation to the EU website, available at <www.russianmission.eu/en/trade>.

58 European Commission, Trade Picture Russia, available at <http://ec.europa.eu/trade/policy/countries-and-regions/countries/russia/>.

4.2. EU Black Sea Synergy

On 11 April 2007 the European Commission launched the BSS as a new regional co-operation initiative.[59] As explained under "The Need for a Regional Policy" title of the Communication of the Commission, right after two Black Sea regional and also littoral states joined the EU on 1 January 2007 (i.e. Bulgaria and Romania), the EU´s interest regarding the region increased: "More than ever before, the prosperity, stability and security of our neighbours around the Black Sea are of immediate concern to the EU."[60]

In this Communication, the Commission underlined the need for regional co-operation rather than an individualistic approach. Main co-operation areas, namely 'Democracy, respect for human rights and good governance', 'Managing movement and improving security', 'the Frozen Conflicts', 'Energy', 'Transport', 'Environment', 'Maritime Policy', 'Fisheries', 'Trade' 'Research and Education Networks', 'Science and Technology', 'Employment and Social Affairs' and 'Regional Development' were highlighted in the Conclusions of the Commission. These areas have been chosen according to the EU's priorities and to the level where the EU was already actively involved in the area. In this sense, the BSS is a flexible framework complementary to the strategic partnership with Russia, the pre-accession policy with Turkey and EaP.

The novelty of the BSS framework was its consideration of the Black Sea as a distinct region (geographical area) in a wider sense, rich in natural resources and strategically located at the junction of Europe, Central Asia and the Middle East.[61] According to the BSS Communication, in order to address the challenges of this region (unresolved conflicts, environmental problems, insufficient border controls encouraging illegal migration and organized crimes) and to utilize its development potential, a dynamic regional response was necessary.[62] As a result, this co-operation both inside the Black Sea region and between the region and the EU might contribute to the overall prosperity, stability and security in Europe.

However, the BSS was not successful either: its limits and the lack of strategic vision as well its fragmented approach for implementation were highlighted by the EP in 2011.[63] Since the launch of the BSS only one progress report had been issued (in 2008), which had not been followed up with any regular reporting mechanism,[64] as well as no ministerial conference had been held since 2008.[65] In January 2011 the EP adopted a resolution calling on the European Commission and the then-soon-to-be-launched EEAS to prepare an EU Strategy for the Black Sea region. The EP even called for the creation of a specific budget line for the Black Sea Strate-

---

59 Communication from the Commission to the Council and the European Parliament, Black Sea Synergy – A new regional co-operation initiative, Brussels, 11 April 2007, COM(2007) 160 final, 2.

60 Ibid.

61 Ibid. 1.

62 Ibid. 2.

63 An EU Strategy for the Black Sea, EP resolution of 20 January 2011 on an EU Strategy for the Black Sea (2010/2087(INI)), P7_TA(2011)0025, para. D.

64 Ibid. para. F.

65 Ibid. para. G.

gy.[66] However, the EU Black Sea Strategy has still not been drafted. There are a number of obstacles for the implementation of the BSS in particular and the EU Black Sea Strategy in general: along with a lot of institutional, financial and policy challenges inside the EU that constrain the implementation of the BSS, one of the challenges for its implementation is Russia's and Turkey's attitude towards the EU as a "large newcomer"[67] and potential competitor in the Black Sea region. Turkey's reinvigourated foreign policy priorities include becoming a clear regional power, drawing on its strategic location between two continents and on the Black Sea in particular. In this regard, the EP in its Black Sea Strategy called on the EU to properly include Russia and Turkey in the Black Sea regional co-operation framework.[68]

Besides, the economic and trade blockades between several pairs of Black Sea states (Russia-Georgia, Turkey-Armenia and Armenia-Azerbaijan) as well as protracted conflicts in the region (Transnistria / Moldova, South Ossetia / Georgia, Abkhazia / Georgia and Armenia / Nagorno-Karabakh / Azerbaijan, Turkey's problems with the Kurdish minority) and the 2008 Russo-Georgian war have fragmented the regional economy and generated distortions. The energy disputes of 2006 and 2009, as well as the recent crisis between Russia and Ukraine have raised concerns about Europe's energy security. In addition the EU's ability to engage further in the Black Sea region has been conditioned by the deterioration of Russian-transatlantic relations over the NATO expansion and the issue of deployment of ballistic anti-missiles systems in Central Europe. Russia perceives the Black Sea region as strategically important for its security interests. Therefore, it resists an increased EU influence around the Black Sea. All these challenges and recent developments have been reflected in the EU's lowering the level of its ambition in the Black Sea region.

4.3. EU-BSEC

As discussed before, it took time for the BSEC to catch the EU's attention. Since taking an observer status in 2007 the EU has been in contact with BSEC whenever it thought that it would be useful. However, it is safe to say that the BSEC was considered as an ''inefficient talking shop'' by the EU.[69] In particular, it was criticised for not reaching its initial goals, for being disturbed by internal disagreements and such.

Nevertheless, the EU had to take an interest in the organisation when BSEC members joined the EU. In 2008, the EU and BSEC adopted a Declaration on en-

---

66 Ibid. para. 9.

67 Policy Briefing, The EU Black Sea Policy: Where do we stand? September 2013, DG EXPO/B/PolDep/Note/2013_221, EP 491.519, available at <www.europarl.europa.eu/RegData/etudes/briefing_note/join/2013/491519/EXPO-AFET_SP(2013)491519_EN.pdf> at 12.

68 An EU Strategy for the Black Sea, op. cit. note 69, para. 12

69 *Mecar / Kordos / Stefkova* : EU and Black Sea Regional Cooperation: Current Prospects of BSEC, available at <www.mfa.gov.tr/eu-and-black-sea-regional-cooperation-cureent-prospects-of-bsec-.tr.mfa>.

hanced co-operation[70] in a special meeting of the Council of the Ministers of the BSEC and the EU Presidency and the European Commission. The aim of this declaration was for BSEC members to manage to bring the EU into a more institutionalised co-operation, especially in its priority areas. However, joining the EU did not hinder Member States' ambitions to play an important role in the Black Sea basin. For example, Romania is one of the three BSEC countries to support PERMISI[71] by providing diplomatic staff.[72]

Turkey acted as a link between BSEC and the EU especially during its presidency of the BSEC during 2012. The BSEC Troika which consists of former, present and future presidencies, held a second informal meeting with the Working Party on Eastern Europe and Central Asia under the EU Council of Ministers.[73] According to the BSEC Permanent International Secretariat Secretary General Victor Tvircun, the relation between the EU and BSEC could not reach the level that has been aimed at due to the individualistic approach of the EU towards BSEC Member States.[74] On the 20th anniversary of the establishment of BSEC, Commissioner *Damanaki* in her speech in Istanbul underlined once more that the EU's ambitions are not dormant, on the contrary that there will be more involvement by the EU in the Black Sea basin.[75]

5. EU-TURKEY RELATIONS AND THEIR IMPLICATIONS IN THE REGION

The character of EU-Turkey relations should be understood in the context of the role of other global powers and the collision of their interests (like USA, Russia) in the Black Sea region, in the context of Russian influence, as well as Russian-Turkish both competitive and co-operative relations. As two major players in the area, the relationship between Turkey and the EU has a long history, and a detailed analysis of this process would be beyond the scope of this paper. We will therefore shortly summarize the past events and the implication of the accession negotiations for the Black Sea area.

Turkey's attempts to co-operate with the EU date back to 1959, when Turkey made its first application to join the EEC. This led to the signature of the Ankara

---

70 Full text available at <www.bsec-organization.org/aoc/Energy/Pages/ANNEX%20III%20FINALDECL%209APRIL%20ADOPTEDBYMINISTERS.pdf>.

71 The BSEC Headquarters were established in March 1994 in Istanbul.

72 *Aurescu*, The Role of The European Union in the Wider Black Sea Region, Turkish Policy Quarterly, 2011, 39.

73 Press Release on BSEC-EU Interaction, available at <www.bsec-organization.org/bsecnews/PressReleases/PressReleases/20121213%20BSEC-EU%20Interaction.pdf>.

74 Ibid.

75 Speech of European Commissioner for Maritime Affairs and Fisheries *Damanaki* at the Black Sea Economic Cooperation: The Goals for the Future. Black Sea Economic Cooperation, 2012, Istanbul, availble at <http://europa.eu/rapid/press-release_SPEECH-12-497_en.htm?locale=en>.

Agreement on Creating an Association between the Republic of Turkey and the EEC in 1963 which constitutes the legal basis for the relations between the EU and Turkey. Turkey applied in 1987 for full membership which revived the relations with the EU. One major step was without doubt the entry of Turkey into its Customs Union with the EC in 1995 which abolished all kind of duties on imports of European goods.[76] Between 1987 and 1999 Turkey prepared for membership, in 1999 it announced that it was "ready" to be a candidate for full membership. However candidacy is not enough to start negotiations between the candidate country and the EU. Turkey only could start negotiations 5 years after announcing its candidacy, in 2004 it has been decided that negotiations would start.[77]

Since then and especially during the last years, Turkey-EU relations have entered into a difficult phase. The reluctance of the EU to grant full membership to Turkey started to cause negative impacts. The EU's progress report on Turkey of 2012 has been harshly criticized as 'biased', 'one sided' and 'baseless' by the Turkish EU Minister *Bağış*.[78] The Turkish Minister of Foreign Affairs *Davutoglu* claimed that Turkey's accession to the EU is a strategic goal, however in case of Europe's rejection, Turkey will choose its own path.[79] On 22 October 2013 EU-Turkey decided to resume the accession negotiations.[80]

In the light of these developments, the Black Sea region acquires crucial importance for both parties. Any move forward from the EU in the Black Sea basin would also have consequences for Turkey. It has been debated that Turkish membership in the EU would play a very important role for the energy supplies to Europe by creating an alternative to Europe's dependency on Russia.[81] However, it must be borne in mind that Turkey without EU perspective will tend to enter into different alliances with different countries. In this sense a fundamental consequence of Turkey's policy of 'strategic depth' is that Turkey "is no longer perceived as a state at the periphery of the European system or as a front state firmly rooted in the West." As Turkey's Western orientation loses primacy in its web of relationships, the necessity that its policy choices line up with Western priorities diminishes. Turkey thus increasingly defines co-operation with the United States and the EU through the prism of its regional priorities.[82] This idea has been underlined by Turkish Prime Minister *Erdoğan*'s attempt to join the Shanghai Five instead of the EU.[83] Further Turkish-Russian co-operation is also on the Turkish agenda in case of a rejection by the EU.[84] But Turkey's active policy in the East does not mean its alienation from the EU. Just the opposite, EU needs Turkey in the Middle East. Turk-

---

76 For further information, check <www.abgs.gov.tr/index.php?p=111&l=2>.

77 For a background see <http://ec.europa.eu/enlargement/pdf/turkey/st20002_05_tr_framedoc_en.pdf>.

78 See <www.bbc.co.uk/news/world-europe-20882239>.

79 See <www.haberturk.com/gundem/haber/832196-turkiye-abye-rest-cekti>.

80 *Dombey / Spiegel*, EU to resume membership talks with Turkey, 22 October 2013, Financial Times, available at <www.ft.com/cms/s/0/4de2c362-3b20-11e3-87fa-00144feab7de.html#axzz36QAukxvD>.

81 See <www.turkishpolicy.com/images/stories/2008-02-policy/james.pdf>.

82 *Ulgen*, op. cit. note 9, at 5.

83 See <www.haberturk.com/dunya/haber/814564-bizi-sangay-beslisine-alin-abyi-unutalim>.

84 *Celikpala*, Security in the Black Sea, Policy Report II, at 13, available at <www.bertelsmann-stiftung.de/bst/en/media/xcms_bst_dms_30921_30922_2.pdf>.

ish influence in the Middle East may contribute to the strengthening of EU influence there.

It is worth emphasising that the relations between the EU and Turkey and the international political situation in the Black Sea region cannot be analysed without taking into consideration energy issues, especially that of concerning the production, consumption and transfer of natural gas. In 2006 the EU Green Paper proposed an energy security policy[85] which was finalised in the Lisbon Treaty. This policy envisions the future of energy for the Union to be based on three principles: sustainability, competitiveness and security of supply in energy provision.[86]

Along with the contribution to the environmental sustainability, in order to safeguard the security of energy supply and ensure competitiveness in the EU markets the European Commission developed the Southern Gas Corridor (SGC) initiative.[87] In this context, the SGC is aimed at enhancing the diversification of the routes and sources of gas imported into Europe. The SGC is envisaged as supplying a significant amount of gas from the Caspian Basin and the Middle East to meet the Union's future energy needs.

On 13 November 2008 the EU Commission published its EU Security and Solidarity Action Plan outlining its initiative for the SGC.[88] It signaled that Brussels would support more independence from Russia as was made clear by former EU Commission President *Barroso's* statement that the EU needs "a collective approach to key infrastructure to diversify our energy supply – pipelines in particular. Today eight Member States are reliant on just one supplier for 100% of their gas needs – this is a problem we must address. We must shield European citizens from the risk that external supplies cannot honour their commitments."[89]

Due to its geographical location Turkey occupies a vital position in the EU SGC. There were many projects included in the SGC, such as NABUCCO, Turkmenistan-Caspian Sea-Turkey-Europe gas pipelines that were expected to be realised. By its initiatives, Turkey is aiming to secure its influence over the energy corridor in this area,[90] thus becoming a centre of the diversification plans of EU.

One of the options to diversify natural gas routes and sources, excluding Russia and including Turkey, was the NABUCCO project. NABUCCO was supposed to transfer Caspian natural gas (from Turkmenistan) to Europe through Turkey. But it failed because of a number of factors. Turkey initially supported NABUCCO as it

---

85 European Commission, An Energy Policy for Europe (COM(2007) 1 final), 10 January 2007, available at <http://ec.europa.eu/energy/energy_policy/doc/01_energy_policy_for_europe_en.pdf>.

86 *Erdogdu*, Turkey's Energy Strategy and its Role in the EU's Southern Gas Corridor, Instituto Affari Internazionali, IAI working papers 14/01, February 2014, p. 2.

87 An EU Energy Security and Solidarity Action Plan, Communication from the Commission to the European Parliament, the Council, the European Economic and Social Committee and the Committee of the regions, Second Strategic Energy Review, Brussels, 13.11.2008, COM(2008) 781 final, available at <http://eur-lex.europa.eu/LexUriServ/LexUriServ.do?uri=COM:2008:0781:FIN:EN:PDF>.

88 Ibid. 4.

89 BBC News, EU seeks to expand energy grids, 13 November 2008, available at <http://news.bbc.co.uk/2/hi/europe/7727028.stm>.

90 *Kamalov* , Some Current Issues in the Blacksea Region (translated from Turkish, Karadeniz Bölgesindeki Bazı Güncel Sorunlar, Karadeniz Araştırmaları), at 6.

would not only strengthen its geo - political importance and provide huge transit revenues, but also improve its position as a bridge between the Caspian and Middle East regions and Europe. In the course of time, however, Turkey became an obstacle because it insisted on the right to consume 15 percent of the gas from any pipeline built on its territory, to be purchased at a "reasonable price",[91] and wanted to tax gas in transit and play the role of middleman in the Caspian-EU gas trade, rather than being merely a transit state. Turkey's becoming a major energy hub, rather than energy transit could not be approved by the EU, especially taking into consideration the fact that during the NABUCCO negotiations Turkey sought to link approval of NABUCCO to the opening of the energy chapter in its EU accession talks (which was blocked by Cyprus).[92] Another obstacle for the success of NABUCCO was the disputes over the legal status of the Caspian Sea and consequently the exploitation of its natural resources (including energy).

In addition to the NABUCCO case, Turkey's attempts to be at the centre of energy supplies and to bypass Russia were also reflected in other projects in the context of SGC, such as the Trans-Adriatic Pipeline (TAP) and Trans-Anatolian Pipeline (TANAP)[93]. With the discovery of the Shah Deniz Field,[94] the core "driver" behind the SGC concept shifted from Turkmenistan to Azerbaijan. The EU's failure to secure additional gas supplies for the SGC (from Iraq and Turkmenistan) left Azerbaijan as the only secure supplier for the whole project which increased Azerbaijan's bargaining power enormously. The close co-operation between Azerbaijan (the most important gas supplier to the SGC initiative) and Turkey (the most important transit country in the SGC project) gave them considerable influence over the EU. Since then, these two countries have effectively begun to define the shape of the SGC. This became particularly clear when the TANAP Agreement was signed on June 26, 2012.[95] In order to understand the features, the reasons behind, opportunities and challenges of the idea of SGC, the role of the Russian natural gas and Russia's gas pipelines policy towards Europe in the context of Black Sea region should be discussed.

Russia holds about 1/3 of the world's proven gas reserves (62 % of which is held by the Kremlin controlled Gazprom: the latter also holds the export and gas network monopoly). Europe is very much dependent on the Russia's natural gas supplies. In 2013, 30 % of EU's gas consumption was supplied by Gazprom.[96] Around the half of the Russian gas imported in 2013 crossed Ukraine which amounts to approximately 15 % of European consumption,[97] thus, making Russia a lot dependent on the Ukraine. Although currently, Ukraine is a major transit country for Rus-

---

[91] *Erdogdu*, op. cit. note 86, 8.

[92] Ibid. 9.

[93] More on TANAP at <www.tanap.com/en/what-is-tanap>.

[94] British Petroleum, Shah Deniz Stage 2, available at <www.bp.com/en_az/caspian/operationsprojects/Shahdeniz/SDstage2.html>.

[95] *Erdogdu*, op. cit. note 86, 11.

[96] Gazprom Export, Delivery Statistics, Gas supplies to Europe, 2013, available at <www.gazpromexport.ru/en/statistics/>.

[97] Russian Gas Imports to Europe and Security of Supply – Factsheet, CIEP, Clingendael International Energy Programme, at 1, available at <www.clingendaelenergy.com/files.cfm?event=files.download&ui=9C1DEEC1-5254-00CF-FD0318660498970>.

sian gas and cannot be replaced even by maximum loading of alternative routes,[98] after the 2006 and 2009 as well as the recent Ukraine crisis, Russia is advancing rapidly in implementing its gas route diversification policy. Gazprom already has a strategy to diversify supply routes and to bypass transit countries (including those both to the West and to the East). Discussing all potential routes of exporting Russian gas is out of the scope of the current paper, but some of the gas projects will be elaborated further in the context of the Black Sea region and Turkey's role in Russia's and EU's energy routes and sources diversification plans.

As Russia's economy is quite complicated and not diverse, it relies mostly on its energy, primarily gas exports. Thus, the geo - politics of natural gas (natural gas pipelines) is of utmost importance to Russia's foreign policy. 50 % of Russia's gas export to EU goes through Ukraine. Therefore, Russia will do everything possible to avoid too much escalation with Ukraine. But as the conflict has escalated already, Russia may also look for other routes for gas export to Europe, for example the so-called *Blue Stream* (one of the several options). Russia claims to have lost about 2 billion dollars during the two weeks of gas flow interruption in January 2009. So, for Russia, even though building South Stream is very expensive, it is like 'buying an insurance against potential future gas flow interruptions'.[99] With this option there will be little dependence on the Ukrainian political situation, the transit risk will be eliminated, Russia will not pay transit fees, sell gas at low prices and from a Russian point of view, it will increase its influence in Central and Eastern Europe and the Balkans.[100]

Russia introduced *South Stream* as a direct reaction to the January 2006 gas crisis with Ukraine and also to Europe's NABUCCO visions, which Russia believed to be a serious threat to their monopoly to supply Europe with pipeline gas from Eurasia.

These gas pipelines are very important because they also reveal both the co-operative and the competitive character of Russian-Turkish relations. Although *Erdogan* pointed out that NABUCCO and *South Stream* were not rivals and in combination would offer diversity, and *Putin* reaffirmed that the *South Stream* project would not shut out NABUCCO,[101] the initiation of TANAP and *South Stream* almost simultaneously proves the competitive relations between Russia and Turkey in the energy sphere. But it should also be noted that to avoid Ukraine's position of exclusivity, the *South Stream* pipeline was re-routed through Turkish waters.[102] On the one hand, Turkey is an energy bridge between the Middle East, the Caspian and to Europe: a wide range of gas and oil pipelines pass through Turkey and Black Sea. On the other hand as a result of rapid population growth and economic development (Turkey is the 17th largest economy in the world), Turkey's energy de-

---

98 *Hafner*, FEEM, Russian Strategy on Infrastructure and Gas Flows to Europe, POLINARES Working Paper No 73, at 8, available at <www.polinares.eu/docs/d5-1/polinares_wp5_chapter5_2.pdf>.

99 Ibid. at 21.

100 Ibid.

101 *Pronina /Berat Meric*, Turkey Offers Route for Gazprom's South Stream Gas Pipeline, 6 August 2009, available at <www.bloomberg.com/apps/news?pid=newsarchive&sid=a.TM4QijmIMk>.

102 South Stream Route: Business Hand in Hand with Politics, The Voice of Russia, 24 June 2014, available at <http://voiceofrussia.com/radio_broadcast/no_program/273881750/>.

mands increased in recent years. Turkey is heavily dependent on fossil fuels (especially natural gas, with 32 %) to meet its energy requirements. However, its domestic energy resources are very limited, making the country even too dependent on energy imports. For instance, in 2011 Turkey imported 98.2 % of its primary gas needs.[103]

Turkey is Russia's third-largest gas customer after Germany and Italy, buying from 24.5 billion cubic meters to 9.6 billion cubic meters, according to Gazprom data.[104] Turkey tried to diversify its energy dependence on Russia also by buying liquefied natural gas LNGs from Algeria and Nigeria. In addition, especially after the 2008 Russian-Georgian war, Turkey moved to intensify its gas imports from Azerbaijan.[105] For Turkey, there are two significant obstacles in the way of realising its pipeline ambitions – high costs and Russian interests. Moscow clearly would prefer to maintain its strong energy position both in Turkey and in the EU. In April, for example, the deputy head of Russia's state-run energy giant Gazprom, *Medvedev*, met with Turkish Energy Minister *Yıldız* to explore the possibility of expanding the company's exports to Turkey, which, at 26.61 billion cubic meters, currently ranks second only to Germany (40.18 bcm) as a Gazprom market.[106]

Not only Turkey, but also the EU faces obstacles in the diversification of energy (in particular, natural gas) routes or sources because of a high dependence on Russia. Russia's recent move to cut natural gas supplies to Ukraine[107] was a terse reminder to Europe that, if it continues to put pressure on Russia regarding to what it considers its backyard, then the disruption of Europe's vulnerable gas supplies might be next, especially if we take into account the fact that the 2009 gas crisis between Ukraine and Russia resulted in supply disruptions in 18 European countries, reporting major drops in or complete cut-offs of their gas supplies transported through Ukraine from Russia.[108] It even caused a humanitarian crisis in several Central and Eastern European countries.[109] This dramatic move, coupled with Russia's recent $ 400 bn natural gas deal with China, is meant to deliver a blunt message to Europe, as the United States pressures it to impose more sanctions on Russia. Simply put, *Putin*'s response to toothless US and EU sanctions is that Russia has other options.[110]

It should be noted that Russia, too, depends on the EU and its capital investments in Russia. Russia is also dependent on the EU in sense of its gas export because it depends on revenues it gets from its gas and oil supplies to Europe. Both partners (EU and Russia) do not have any serious alternatives. In this sense, Turkey may be

---

[103] *Erdogdu*, op. cit. note 86, 4.
[104] *Pronina / Berat Meric*, op cit. note 101.
[105] *International Energy Agency*, Energy Policies of IEA Countries, Turkey Review 2009, at 67-84, available at <www.iea.org/publications/freepublications/publication/turkey2009.pdf>.
[106] *Jones*, Ukraine Crisis Puts Strain on Turkey-Russia Ties, 7 May 2014, available at <www.eurasianet.org/node/68351>.
[107] *Handjani*, Breaking Europe's Putin Addiction, Aljazeera Opinion, 20 June 2014, available at <www.aljazeera.com/indepth/opinion/2014/06/europe-russia-gas-dependency-201461710261232130З.html>.
[108] *Hafner*, op. cit. note 98, 9.
[109] Ibid. 4.
[110] *Handjani*, op. cit. note 107.

a good partner for Russia in diversifying its gas transfers to Europe, avoiding Ukraine. But on the other hand, Turkey's ambitions to act as a regional power make Russia nervous.

6. Conclusion

In conclusion, we might say that the Black Sea region will be of pioneering importance in the near future. Surrounded by powerful littoral states such as Russia and Turkey and also with the influence of the EU, the region remains to be a centre for clashes of different interests. Turkey plays a very important role, based on its geographical position and initiatives it has taken after the power vacuum that occurred with the collapse of the Soviet Union. Those initiatives put the country in a leading position in the region, although the BSEC could not function as expected and the efforts were insufficient to enhance a very active regional co-operation. In spite of its growing economic and political power, Turkey's policy initiatives in its neighbourhood and on the global level were not always successful due to the competitions among other regional powers.

The relations between the EU and Turkey are reflected not only in the accession negotiations, but first and foremost in the field of security issues (also related to the U.S. presence in the region) and in energy challenges (in the context of Russia's natural gas pipelines policy in the region). The recent crisis in Ukraine and the intensification of the *South Stream* gas pipeline are reminders of the fact that although Turkey is a promising alternative to diversify the European energy sources, both the EU and Turkey very much depend on the Russian energy resources. Thus, any Black Sea regional initiative (security, energy, or otherwise) should not exclude regional states, namely Russia and Turkey.

Part 4:

Signature Issues in the EU Integration of South Eastern Europe and Their Relevance for the Black Sea and South Caucasus Regions

Lorin – Johannes Wagner

AWARDING UNION CITIZENSHIP: NATIONAL CITIZENSHIP IN THE CONTEXT OF A "COMMON" EU IMMIGRATION POLICY

1. INTRODUCTION

> *"Union citizenship is destined to be the fundamental status of nationals of the Member States"*[1]

The wording of this recital, which is taken from the ECJ's judgement in *Grzelczyk*, encapsulates a promise: a promise that the Union citizenship is destined to be more than national citizenship, warranting a status of freedom in the EU at large. And though Union citizenship is by the very wording of Art 20 (1) TFEU "additional to and not [to] replace national citizenship", the value of Union citizenship as such has become a most sensitive issue of late. When Malta announced that it would sell its citizenship and thereby also grant Union citizenship to third-country nationals, an outcry followed.[2] Only after the Commission threatened to instigate proceedings to bring Malta before the ECJ[3] was it that Malta altered it citizenship selling scheme.[4] This scheme which aims to help to consolidate Malta's budget outrightly draws on the advantages and hence the value of the "destined" status of Union citizenship. And albeit Malta has been the first Member State to openly monetize Union citizenship, Malta is not the first Member State where the awarding of national citizenship and hence

---

1 See ECJ, C-184/99, *Grzelczyk,* report 2001, I-06193, margin note 31.

2 For an overview see e.g. *Hilpold,* Die Verkaufte Unionsbürgerschaft, Neue Juristische Wochenschrift 2014, 1071; and especially *Sachar / Bauböck* (eds), EUI-Working Papers – Should Citizenship be for Sale? available at <http://eudo-citizenship.eu/images/docs/Citizenship-for-Sale-RSCAS_2014_01.pdf>. See, however, also the EP's Resolution P7_TA-PROV(2014)0038 of 16 January 2014, available at <http://eudo-citizenship.eu/images/docs/EP-Malta-news%2016%20January%202014.pdf>.

3 See the joint press release of the European Commission and the Maltese Authorities of 29 January 2014, available at <http://europa.eu/rapid/press-release_MEMO-14-70_en.htm> as well as *euobserver.com,* EU commission prepares legal challenge on Malta passport sales, 23 January 2014, available at <http://euobserver.com/justice/122843> and <http://euobserver.com/justice/122925>; and *euobserver.com,* Malta bows to EU 'pressure' on passport sales, available at <http://euobserver.com/justice/122925>.

4 Additional to an investment of – in total – one Million Euro, "new citizens" are now required to reside in Malta for at least one year.

Union citizenship has led to a critical view of the inherent linkage between national and Union citizenship.

Before the Maltese "citizenship for sale" outcry, it was the practice of Romania to grant its citizenship to Moldovans which spurred critique. The intriguing assumption was that Moldovans were entering the EU "through the back door", side-lining visa requirements and other more burdensome obstacles in order to reside and work in the Union.[5] This in general prompts the question if awarding national citizenship faces any constraints under EU Law. It is in this light that the following analysis aims to provide a legal assessment of the Member States' regulative discretion when awarding their national citizenship from the point of EU Law, placing a special emphasis on restrictions which might derive from the aim to establish a common immigration policy.

To this end, the first part of this article briefly covers the EU's Area of Freedom, Security and Justice in general to subsequently address the development of a common immigration policy in particular. The second part is devoted to the fundamental status of Union citizenship and the legal status of third-country nationals under EU Law. The third part covers the issue of national citizenship in the context of EU Law, focusing firstly on the question whether national citizenship is *per se* beyond the realms of EU Law or is just to be considered an element of national identity, warranting special respect under EU Law. In another subsection of this third part, possible limitations of awarding national citizenship to third-country nationals are discussed from an individualistic point of view, questioning the Member States' discretion in light of the ECJ's case law in the field of Union citizenship. The same question is further on also dealt with in a more general context, asking whether Member States face certain limitations with respect to general principles of EU Law and the right of the Member States "to determine volumes of admission of third-country nationals coming from third countries in order to seek work, whether employed or self-employed".[6] The subsequent subsection addresses the issue of proportionality and how a test of proportionality must be construed in order to balance competing principles of EU Law in the context of awarding national citizenship. Finally, the conclusion provides a short assessment of the findings.

2. THE AREA OF FREEDOM, SECURITY AND JUSTICE AND A COMMON MIGRATION POLICY

2.1. EU migration policy in general

With the entry into force of the Treaty of Lisbon the EU lost its architecturally cherished pillar-structure becoming a monolithic sculpture with a little appendix in the front and a somewhat inconclusive bulge in the middle. The skilled art

---

[5] *SpiegelOnline*, Romanian Passports for Moldovans – Entering the EU Through the Back Door, 7 March 2010, available at <http://www.spiegel.de/international/europe/0,1518,706338,00.html>.

[6] Art 79 (5) TFEU.

connoisseur will be able to picture this absurdly modern deconstruction of a once ancient Greek temple as a profound architectonical description of the Union's legal *status quo*. For the passionate ignorant of modern art, however, a more legal description may be better served to depict that the Union's policy in the field of the CSFP still adheres to the intergovernmental *modus vivendi* and that the policy in the Area of Freedom, Security and Justice has not yet cut all ties with intergovernmentalism. Though the Union's aim to "offer its citizens an area of freedom and justice without internal frontiers, in which the free movement of persons is ensured in conjunction with appropriate measures with respect to external border controls, asylum, immigration and the prevention and combating of crime"[7] now effectively covers all the aspects that were split between the third pillar and Title IV TEC, the Member States' stronghold can still be detected in various forms.[8] The changes brought by the Treaty of Lisbon are, however, more than a unification under the umbrella of the TFEU but also comprise an extension of Union competences.[9] For the purpose of the present analysis not all the changes but merely the gradual development of a common immigration policy is of special interest.

2.2. Art 79 TFEU – Towards a "common" immigration policy

The first aspect to be highlighted in this regard is the very notion of a "common" immigration policy that in the far-fetched meaning of developing an "efficient management of migration flows, fair treatment of third-country nationals residing legally in Member States and the prevention of" and enhanced combat of illegal immigration and human trafficking has been set as an aim for the Union only with the coming into force of the Treaty of Lisbon.[10] Immigration policy under the TEC was purpose-limited to measures on immigration policy within certain areas,[11] implying that the competences of the then EC were not intended to be developed into something like a "common" immigration policy. The new elevation in the very aim underlying the Union's competences in the field of immigration policy certainly thus asks for an extension of competences to match.

The difference between Art 79 (2) TFEU and Art 63 (1) no 3 and 4 TEC, the respective core provisions of immigration policy, at first sight suggest however little change to this end. Apart from the competence to adopt measures to combat trafficking in persons in Art 79 (2) lit d TFEU, Art 79 (2) TFEU resembles the already

---

7 Art 3 (2) TEU.

8 Eg Art 76 TFEU derogates the Commission's monopoly on initiative as also a quarter of the Member States can initiate the adoption of measures referred to in the field of judicial co-operation in criminal matters, police co-operation and Art 74 TFEU. Further examples can be found in Arts 69, 72, 73, 81 (3) (3), Art 82 (3), Art 83 (3) and Art 87 (3) TFEU.

9 Besides some minor changes in the field of judicial co-operation in civil matters and police co-operation the changes in the field of judicial co-operation in criminal matters including new competences to harmonise criminal procedural law, criminal law and to establish a European Public Prosecutor's Office have been praised as a substantial widening of Union competences.

10 Art 79 (1) TFEU.

11 Art 63 (1) no 3 TEC.

known.[12] The essential difference then is that the already wide competences of the Union have been set into the context of a holistic approach. Part of this approach is that the Union shall not only develop a common immigration policy in the sense of determining the requirements, conditions, rights as well as the removal and repatriation of (il-)legal third-country nationals pursuing a long-term stay within the Union and the fight against human trafficking, but shall moreover develop a common immigration policy "at all stages"[13] providing for an differentiated and yet integrated approach in relation to short-term measures based on Art 77 TFEU.[14] The common immigration policy thus goes hand in hand with the Union's short-term visa policy, essentially covering all aspects of migration from short-term stay to long-term residence.[15]

2.3. Restrictions of a "common" immigration policy – The issue of labour migration

Considering this primary legal framework, the question arises: What powers are left for the Member States in the field of immigration policy? Any assessment of this question must keep in mind that immigration policy and the Area of Freedom, Security and Justice at large are shared competences[16] of the EU and that moreover Art 79 (4) and (5) TFEU enshrine certain restriction of the Union's common immigration policy. While the former aspect evidently protects the Member States' power only in a relative sense, the latter provisions demand further attention.

Art 79 (4) TFEU allows for the adoption of measures promoting the integration of third-country nationals residing legally in a Member State, giving way for the inclusion of yet another important aspect of immigration policy, but at the same time "excluding any harmonisation of the laws and regulation of the Member States." For this very aspect of immigration policy the Union is thus rendered to merely support the actions of the Member States who remain in charge of their own integration policy.[17]

The meaning and relevance of Art 79 (5) TFEU, stipulating that Member States ultimately retain the power "to determine volumes of admission of third-country nationals coming from third countries to their territory in order to seek work,

---

12 As far as Art 79 (2) lit d TFEU goes it should be noted that this provision essentially stipulates a competence that has already been implicitly assumed by the EC; see *Hoppe* in *Lenz / Borchardt* (eds), EU-Verträge/ Kommentar nach dem Vertrag von Lissabon[6] (2012) Art 79 AEUV margin note 5.

13 Art 79 (1) TFEU.

14 In this sense *Thym* in *Grabitz / Hilf / Nettesheim* (eds), Das Recht der Europäischen Union EL 52 (2014) Art 79 AEUV margin notes 16 and 23.

15 The distinction between short and long term stays is not predetermined by the treaty itself. However, in line with Art 62 (2) no 2 EC and the already adopted secondary law on short term visa intended for stays not exceeding three months (eg Council Regulation (EC) No 539/2001 listing the third countries whose nationals must be in possession of visas when crossing the external borders and those whose nationals are exempt from that requirement, OJ 2001 L 81, 1), it seems wise to assume a continuity along this three months criterion.

16 Art 4 (2) lit j TFEU.

17 For a critical assessment *Thym* op. cit. note 14, Art 79 AEUV margin note 41.

whether employed or self-employed", is harder to assess. In principle, Art 79 (5) TFEU reads like a contradiction of the aim of a holistic common immigration policy, as labour migration undoubtedly constitutes an essential part of any immigration policy. So how can the aspiration of a "common" immigration policy then be upheld against the background of Art 79 (5) TFEU? To give the answer right away: In a true sense it cannot.

However, as with most legal problems, the way leading to the answer is more complex than the answer itself. That is to say that Art 79 (5) TFEU intends to clarify the general scope of the Union's immigration policy, which in the absence of the clause enshrined in para 5 could also be understood to include all aspects of labour migration.[18] But at the same time it is obviously meant to restrict the Union's competences in this very field.

The Member States' power to determine the volumes of third-country nationals seeking work is nevertheless relative, as the Union by virtue of Art 79 (2) lit a TFEU may still regulate the conditions for access to the labour market of third-country nationals who legally immigrated to the Member States of the EU for other reasons than to seek work[19] and, moreover, the Union may also regulate the legal status of those third-country nationals that have legally taken residence in the territory of the Member States based on the prerogatives of Art 79 (5) TFEU.[20] So although the Union's means may fall short in the light of the aim of developing a truly common immigration policy,[21] it is no exaggeration to conclude that there is little in this field that is left beyond a possible Europeaninsation of immigration policy,[22] but the very basis of labour migration. One should nevertheless also note that taking a look at the already existing secondary legislation the emphasis is on "possible", as the Union so far has only partially made use of these competences.[23]

2.4. The legal status of third-country nationals in light of Art 79 (5) TFEU

For the analysis at hand it is important to see that the Member States' prerogative to determine the volume of admission of third-country nationals seeking work on their territory does not automatically correspond with a legal status for these third-country nationals under EU Law. As opposed to citizens of the Member States who by virtue of Art 20 TEU are citizens of the Union and thus *ratione personae* can rely on the right of free movement within the territory of Member States and the fundamental freedoms, third-country nationals are sub-

---

18 See *Thym* op. cit. note 14, Art 79 AEUV margin note 43.
19 Ibid, margin note 44.
20 *Hoppe* op. cit. note 12, Art 79 AEUV margin note 10.
21 See *Rossi* in *Calliess / Ruffert* (eds), EUV/AEUV. Verfassungsrecht der Europäischen Union mit Europäischer Grundrechtecharta[4] (2011) Art 79 AEUV margin note 34; *Hoppe* op. cit. note 12, Art 79 AEUV margin note 10.
22 *Hecker*, Zur Europäisierung des Ausländerrechts, Zeitschrift für Ausländerrecht 2011, 46 (47).
23 For an intuitive overview see Hecker ibid. at 48 who estimates that roughly one third of the regulations governing immigration of third-country nationals, excluding the right of free-movement of Union citizens and their relatives as well as asylum and refugee laws, is in the one or the other way influenced by EU Law.

ject to further conditions and requirements to acquire certain rights under secondary EU legislation.

The difference is most intriguing when trying to assess the requirements and conditions for moving to another Member States in order to pursue employed or self-employed work for a Union citizen on the one hand and a third-country national on the other hand. For Union citizens such a situation is in principle governed by the freedom of movement of workers under Art 45 TFEU or the freedom of establishment under Art 49 TFEU, granting them equal access and rights with nationals. Whereas third-country nationals in line with Council Directive 2003/109/EC concerning the status of third-country nationals who are long-term residents[24] must have been legally and continuously residing in a Member State for five years[25] and furthermore provide evidence "of stable and regular resources to maintain himself / herself and the members of his / her family, without recourse to the social assistance system", must have a health insurance and must comply with integration conditions, if foreseen by national law, to acquire a long-term status in the first place,[26] which under the conditions set out in Art 15 of Directive 2003/109/EC entitles them to take residence in another Member State in order exercise an economic activity in an employed or self-employed capacity.[27] The right to take residence in another Member State is however not absolute, as Member States "may limit the total number of persons entitled to be granted right of residence, provided that such limitations are already set out for the admission of third-country nationals in the existing legislation at the time of the adoption of the directive". [28] Even if allowed to take residence in another Member State, third-country nationals may face certain disadvantages in respect of gaining access to the labour market or self-employment, as for labour policy reasons Member States "may give preference to Union citizens, to third-country nationals, when provided for by Community legislation, as well as to third-country nationals who reside legally and receive unemployment benefits in the Member State concerned".[29] It is thus obvious that the hurdles to overcome are much more manifold and burdensome for third-country nationals than they are for Union citizens.

The competence of Member States to determine the volume of admission of third-country nationals seeking work and everything that follows from it entails some important implications which need to be taken into account in the context of this analysis. The power of the Member State to decide upon who is given admission to its territory in order to reside and work there comprehends the logic that the respective Member State also remains individually responsible for these third-country nationals. Phrased differently, third-country nationals under Art 79 para 5 TFEU in principle remain legal subjects of the respective national legal orders and only gradually develop to become common legal subjects under secondary EU Law

24 OJ 2003 L 16, 44.

25 Art 4 para 1 Directive 2003/109/EC.

26 Ibid. Art 5.

27 Ibid. Art 14 (1).

28 Ibid. Art 14 (4).

29 Ibid. Art 14 (3) (2). Equal treatment of third-country nationals may also be derogated for reasons set out in Art 11 (3) and Art 21 (2) ibid.

and thus gain rights that stretch beyond the respective host Member State. The measures of secondary EU Law are however bound to respect the Member States' prerogative under Art 79 (5) TFEU, meaning that none of the measures adopted by the Union is to eradicate the Member States' competence to decide on the admission of labour migrants. The principle of mutual recognition thus does not apply in the field of labour migration *strictu sensu* but is rather subject to secondary legislation, which is to define the further requirements and conditions opening the ambit of EU Law for third-country nationals *rationae personae*. From a different point of view, this very aspect translates into an obligation of Member States *inter alia* to procure each other from an interference of their respective labour migration policies.

3. THE FUNDAMENTAL STATUS OF NATIONALS OF THE MEMBER STATE UNDER EU LAW

An assessment of Union citizenship in the same light provides not only for some interesting but also for some rather different conclusions. First of all, Union citizenship is granted based on Art 20 (1) TFEU, stipulating that "[e]very person holding the nationality of a Member State shall be a citizen of the Union", which according to the new wording introduced by the Treaty of Lisbon shall be "additional" to national citizenship.[30] The mere fact that Union citizenship as well as the principal rights of Union citizens, listed in Art 21 to Art 24 TFEU, are established on a treaty basis reflects the specific legal quality of Union citizenship.

This is further fortified in the face of the case law of the ECJ. In its famous ruling *van Gend en Loos* the ECJ held that the then EEC "constitutes a new legal order of international law for the benefit of which the States have limited their sovereign rights, albeit within limited fields, and the subject of which comprise not only Member States but also their nationals".[31] Needless to say that this ruling on the direct applicability of EU Law is at the core of the fundamental freedoms and all other individual rights granted by EU Law, but what is especially noteworthy for the present context is that the ECJ used individual rights and rights of nationals, and thus Union citizens, interchangeably.

The special nature of national citizenship and consequently Union citizenship under EU Law has ultimately been distilled in *Grzelczyk*,[32] where the ECJ defined Union citizenship as "the fundamental status of nationals of the Member States, enabling those who find themselves in the same situation to enjoy the same treatment in law irrespective of their nationality". So although Art 20 (2) (2) TFEU stipulates that the rights of Union citizenship enlisted in Art 20 (2) (1) lit a to d TFEU shall be exercised in accordance with the conditions and limits defined by the Trea-

[30] Art 17 (1) TEC provided that Union citizenship was to "complement" national citizenship rather than being "additional".

[31] ECJ, C-26/62, *Van Gend en Loos,* report 1963, 1, 12.

[32] ECJ, C-184/99, *Grzelczyk*, margin note 31.

ties and by the measures adopted thereunder, the fundamental status of Union citizenship is as such not subject to secondary EU Law but forms a core part of the Union's legal order.

Another aspect highlighting the difference between the legal status of national citizens of the Member State and third-country nationals under EU Law is the simple fact that national citizenship of Member States is understood as a formal criterion, meaning that while third-country nationals are bound to fulfil specific (individual) conditions and requirements in order to acquire a legal status under EU Law, nationals of the Member State can simply rely on the triggering momentum of their citizenship to acquire the fundamental status under EU Law, irrespective of the requirements, conditions, rights and obligations that arise from national citizenship.

The individual rights of nationals of the Member State under EU Law differ from the rights of third-country nationals not only by their legal quality, but also rely on the principle of mutual recognition. In *Micheletti* the ECJ affirmed that "it is for each Member State, having due regard to Community law, to lay down the conditions for the acquisition and loss of nationality" and that it is not permissible under EU Law (then Community Law) for another Member State to "make recognition of the status of Community national" that follows from national citizenship of Member States subject to further conditions.[33]

It is nevertheless obvious that an unfettered practice of granting national citizenship by one Member State bears implication for all other Member States. But in contrast to immigration policy, where Member States have retained the power to determine – and hence also to restrict – the volume of admission of third-country nationals entering their territory in order to seek work, Member States have no legal means to deny Union citizens' rights granted by EU Law on a general basis. A practice of a Member States to grant admission to its territory only to certain Union citizens would render the individual rights, such as the right of free movement, the freedom of establishment or the freedom of movement of workers of those excluded nugatory and would therefore constitute a breach of EU Law.

The question thus arises if the practice of a Member State pursuing a *laissez-faire* citizenship policy in the first place is compatible with EU Law. In order to assess the possible limitations on Member States in the field of national citizenship, especially in the context of a common immigration policy, it is necessary to take a closer look at the status of national citizenship and to determine whether this very status warrants special guarantees under EU Law. To this end, the obligation of the Union to respect the national identities of the Member States stipulated in Art 4 (2) TEU will be given scrutiny.

[33] ECJ, C-369/90, *Micheletti*, report 1992, I-4239, margin notes 10 and 11.

4. NATURALISATION OF THIRD-COUNTRY NATIONALS UNDER EU LAW

4.1. National citizenship as part of the national identity of a Member State

The conditions for acquiring citizenship established by a Member State reflect its own historical, cultural, and social background which does not necessarily have to be shared by all Member States. The competence for defining the conditions for acquisition and loss of citizenship remains with the Member State and have not been transferred explicitly, either in whole or in part, to the EU, either within the context of the Area of Freedom, Security and Justice or as part of its competence in another policy field. In line with the case law of the ECJ it is important to note that "the fact that a matter falls within the competence of the Member States does not alter the fact that, in situations covered by EU law, the national rules concerned must have due regard to the latter".[34] The Union for its part shall, however, respect the national identities of Member States, "inherent in their fundamental structures, political and constitutional, inclusive of regional and local self-government".[35] The acquisition of a Member State citizenship, as citizenship policy in general, is obviously linked to national identity, triggering the question what the obligation of the Union to respect national identities amounts to.

If citizenship policy and the respective national regulations represent a part of the national identity of a Member State, are the measures it undertakes to protect its identity *per se* immune from any influence of EU Law? The rather weak term "respect" used to define the obligation of the Union seems to stand in the way of an interpretation granting immunity *per se* thus implying that any measure must be compatible with EU Law and thus stand a test of proportionality.

The difference between these two approaches can also be assessed when trying to define the meaning of national identity. In this sense, the latter approach, immunising all measures relating to the protection of national identity, could be understood as a general exemption clause, thus warranting a delimiting definition of the very notion of national identity. As any other exemption clause enshrined in the Treaties, the definition is subject to an interpretation within the context of the Treaties. The meaning and hence the scope of this clause would thus be uniform for all 28 Member States of the EU. If, however, the clause in Art 4 para 2 TEU is understood as a mere principle that relies on the Member States' endogenous "national identity", a final definition would neither be subject to a restrictive Treaty interpretation nor would it be possible. The principle to respect the national identity would thus resemble a means for the Member States to bring into play their national identities according to their own perceptions. That is to say that the EU as a consequence would be under an obligation to weigh any measure against the underlying interests of a Member State deemed to form a part of the respective national identity.

---

[34] See ECJ, C-135/08, *Rottmann*, report 2010, I-1449, margin note 41 and the herein quoted cases.

[35] Art 4 (2) TEU.

Both approaches are subject to severe limitations, as the notion of national identity is either rendered to be a uniform yardstick, irrespective of the peculiarities of the Member State or diffuses into a heterogeneous cacophony. A solution to this dilemma is hinted by the fact that the very wording of Art 4 (2) TEU refers to a plurality of "national identities" while at the same time linking these identities to the inherent "fundamental structures, political and constitutional, inclusive of regional and local self-government". It seems though that Art 4 (2) TEU provides for an intertwined approach whereby EU Law erects the very skeleton for the concept of "national identities",[36] but leaves it to the Member States to put flesh on these bones. In practical terms, Art 4 (2) TEU thus constitutes an opening clause that reimburses respect for certain fundamental identities and differences of the 28 Member States in the context of an ever-expanding EU Law.

The room for manoeuvre under this norm is nevertheless restricted in a twofold way. Firstly, the concept of national identity only relates to the "fundamental structures, political and constitutional, inclusive of regional and local self-government" and therefore does not correspond to a wider cultural concept of national identity[37] and secondly, any measure concerning the national identity of a Member State is not *per se* exempted from the scope of EU law, but must rather stand a test of proportionality.[38] Respect for national identity in this sense warrants an open-ended act of balancing of the EU's interest in a uniform application of EU Law on the one side and the Member States' interest to preserve the core of their national identities on the other side. Any such act of balancing may however only take place if a measure of a Member State falls within the ambit of EU law and the concept of national identity likewise, as it is only then when the obligation for the Union to respect the national identities of Member States arises.

When assessing the issue of citizenship, we are therefore confronted with two separate questions: (a) Does a Member States' decision to award national citizenship to an individual fall within the scope of EU Law and (b) can any such measure be considered a matter of national identity as protected by Art 4 (2) TEU?

The latter question refers back to the very scope of national identity, respectively the 'framework' of this concept. For the further analysis it is thus not to ask if citizenship constitutes a matter of national identity from the point of view of Member States in the first place, but rather if this issue can be subsumed to be a part of one of the aspects narrowing down the concept of national identity from the Union – Treaty – point of view. Albeit the issue of citizenship is not explicitly mentioned in Art 4 (2) TEU, the context as well as the abstraction of the mentioned aspects allows for an inclusive understanding. When looking at the context, we find that Art 4 (2) TEU does not only stipulate respect for the national identities of Member States but furthermore obliges the Union to "respect their essential State functions, including ensuring the territorial integrity of the State, maintaining law and order and

[36] For an insightful differentiation between the concept of national identity and national sovereignty see *von Bogdandy / Schill,* Overcoming Absolute Primacy: Respect for National Identity under the Lisbon Treaty, Common Market Law Review 2011, 1417 (1425).

[37] Ibid. 1427.

[38] Ibid. 1417. For an absolute supremacy of national identity see *Puttler* in *Calliess/Ruffert*, EUV/AEUV[4] Art 4 EUV (22).

safeguard national security." The final sentence additionally sets out that "in particular, national security remains the sole responsibility of each Member State." From an overall perspective, the core theme and aim of this provision is to procure an erosion of essential "State competences". It seems worth remembering at this point that the overarching ratio of Art 4 (2) and Art 4 TEU is to determine the relation between the Union and the Member States being States in their own right. This necessarily entails the capacity to legally determine the bond between a Nation and its nationals or, in other words, a State and its citizens.

Additionally, one might also be tempted to read Art 4 (2) TEU in the light of international law, linking the concept of national identity and the interrelated question of essential State functions to the classical doctrine of statehood and sovereignty. This line of thought bears some resemblance to the arguments put forward by Advocate General (AG) *Maduro* in the *Rottmann* case, as he recalls the traditional concept of citizenship under international law[39] in order to subsequently conclude that the "question of nationality are in principle within the reserved domain of States"[40] and that the "Union does not deviate from the solution adopted under International Law".[41] *Maduro* is, however, quick to bolster this "outside the EU Law box" argument by inferring that also Declaration No 2 on nationality of a Member State[42] implies the same conclusion.[43] Though, knowing that the concept of *domaine réservé* under international law is relative itself, it is not difficult to see that the concept of *domaine réservé*, used in the context of *Rottmann* to (in principle) deliminate the Member States' competence in the field of citizenship, and the concept of national identity enshrined in Art 4 (2) TEU run in the same veins. In essence, both concepts encapsulate the logic that a sovereign State must preserve at least some (essential) matters within his regulatory competence.[44] The annotations of *Maduro* in *Rottmann,* though given before the entry into force of the Treaty of Lisbon, may therefore be looked upon as to provide a yardstick for assessing the issue of citizenship within the context of Art 4 (2) TEU. The aforegiven answer that the issue of citizenship falls very well within the ambit of Art 4 (2) TEU is thus not only supported by employing a deductive contextual line of thought but can also be fortified by a wider inductive assessment. As a side note it is, however, to be kept in mind that respect for national citizenship under Art 4 (2) TEU does cover the legal bond between an individual and a Member State but does in principle neither attribute specific weight to certain features of this special bond nor in a broader sense define the essential rights and obligations of a Member State's citizenship.

---

39 Opinion AG *Maduro*, C-135/08, Rottmann, report 2010, I-01449, margin notes 16 ff.
40 Ibid. margin note 18.
41 Ibid. margin note 19.
42 As the Opinion was written before the entry into force of the Treaty of Lisbon the Declaration referred to is the Declaration No 2 on nationality of Member States, annexed by the Member States to the Final Act of the Treaty of the European Union, OJ 1992 C 191, at 45.
43 Opinion AG *Maduro,* C-135/08, Rottmann, margin note 19.
44 *Ziegler,* Domaine Réservé, in *Wolfrum* (ed), Max Planck Encyclopedia of Public International Law, margin note 1, available at <www.mpepil.com/subscriber_article?script=yes&id=/epil/entries/law-9780199231690-e1398&recno=1&searchType=Quick&query=Domaine+r%C3%A9serv%C3%A9>.

To this end it is therefore possible to conclude that the special bond of citizenship between an individual and a Member State which specifically materializes in the process of naturalisation warrants special respect under EU Law.

4.2. Naturalisation of third-country nationals and individual rights

As stated above, the obligation of the Union to respect the national identity of a Member State arises only if the process of naturalisation falls within the scope of EU Law. Henceforth, it is to question when – if at all - the awarding of a Member State's citizenship bears momentum under EU Law.

This question is to be distinguished from the mere fact of competences, as it is unequivocal that the competence for awarding citizenship remains solely with the Member State.[45] The question hence essentially boils down to the fact whether there are any obligations under EU Law that interfere with this competence of Member States and hence could trigger the ambit of EU Law.

When looking at the relevant case law, albeit none of which deals with the issue of awarding citizenship, we always find that the actual background entails a possible impediment of individual rights granted under EU Law. In *Micheletti*[46], for example, the right of establishment was called into question and in *Rottmann* not a single right, but almost all rights as a Union citizen were on the spot. Also, in *Kaur*[47] the ECJ was asked if EU Law provided for directly applicable rights that could be invoked before national courts in order set aside restrictive national regulations and therefore questioned the conformity of national law. At first sight, this implies that EU Law only comes into play if issues of national citizenship interfere with directly applicable individual rights under EU Law. It is submitted that this observation, though sketchy, seems to hold quite well with the broader approach of the ECJ. Ever since the ECJ established that EU Law constitutes "a new legal order" that is intended to confer rights upon individuals,[48] has the ECJ emphasized and substantially widened the individual dimension of EU Law against the Member States' regulatory authority.[49] Still, any such protection, as can be seen from *Kaur,* rests upon the fact that the respective individual possesses a legal status under EU Law in the first place.[50] Obviously, in most cases this means being a Union citizen and hence enjoying "the fundamental status of nationals of the Member States, enabling those who find themselves in the same situation to enjoy the same treatment in law irrespective of their nationality".[51]

But what about those individuals who only by their naturalisation acquire this fundamental (legal) status? Well, the answer is as intuitive as forthright: An indi-

---

45 See ECJ, C-135/08, Rottmann, margin notes 39 and 41.

46 See ECJ, C-369/90, *Micheletti,* report 1992, I-4239.

47 See ECJ, C-192/99, *Kaur,* report 2001, I-1237.

48 See ECJ, C-26/62, *Van Gend en Loos*, 12.

49 For an insightful analysis on the expansion of individual rights in light of the latest case law of the ECJ see *Hailbronner / Thym,* Case C-34/09, *Gerardo Ruiz Zambrano v. Office national de l'emploi (ONEm)*, Judgment of the Court of Justice (Grand Chamber) of 8 March 2011, Common Market Law Review 2011, 1253.

50 See ECJ, C-192/99, *Kaur,* margin note 25.

51 See ECJ, C-184/99, *Grzelczyk,* margin note 31.

vidual who has no legal status yet cannot possibly be infringed in his or her yet inexistent rights under EU Law.

The same conclusion, although on a different line of thought, can be drawn for individuals who possess a (certain) legal status within the EU prior to their naturalisation. In line with Council Directive 2003/109/EC concerning the status of third-country nationals who are long-term residents,[52] third-country nationals may under certain conditions, as has been pointed out above, acquire the right to take residence in another Member State and work. These rights are however minor to the rights of Union citizens as they may be restricted by the Member State under certain conditions. Naturalisation by a Member State thus implies more and not less rights for the respective individual, making it very difficult to see where the change of status under EU Law could be used to encroach on those lesser rights. From this point of view, the process of naturalisation is hence not only an element intrinsically linked to the national identity of the Member State but at the same time seems to be beyond the realms of EU Law.

4.3. Naturalisation of third-country nationals in the light of general principles of EU Law

Naturalisation may, however, also be examined from a more general perspective. A conflict with EU Law may not only stem from an impediment of individual rights but may well be the result of the neglect of general principles of EU Law.

What comes to mind in this respect is the principle of loyalty and sincere co-operation stipulated in Art 4 para 3 subpara 1 to 3 TEU warranting Member States to mutually respect and assist each other when "carrying out tasks which flow from the Treaties", "to ensure fulfilment of the obligations arising out of the Treaties or resulting from the acts of the institutions of the Union as well as "to facilitate the achievement of the Union's tasks and to refrain from any measures which could jeopardise the attainment of the Union's objectives".

Assuming that a Member State effectively uses naturalisation to provide a means for third-country nationals to more easily overcome the hurdles that these individuals face when trying to seek work in a Member State of the EU, we are therefore again to ask if such measures are compatible with EU Law. Though difficult it would be to prove any such "circumvential" approach, it is quite intuitive that such measures would obstruct a common immigration policy that still comprehends the basic logic that the individual Member States are free to determine the volumes of admission of third-country nationals coming to their territory in order to seek work. In case of an excessive use of naturalisation by one Member State the different legal status of third-country nationals and EU citizens would effectively topple the freedom of the other Member States enshrined in Art 79 para 5 TFEU.

When looking at the principle of loyalty and sincere co-operation we are nevertheless confronted with the fact that the primary purpose of this principle is to compel Member States to ensure the fulfilment of the obligations arising from the Trea-

[52] OJ 2003 L 16, 44.

ties or resulting from the acts of the EU institutions.[53] However, the Member States' power to determine the volume of admission of third-country nationals seeking work in itself constitutes no obligation under EU Law but is rather meant to limit the competences of the Union. The same conclusion pertains when assessing the problem in light of the principle of loyalty and sincere co-operation between the Member States, as Art 4 (3) (1) TEU warrants mutual respect and assistance amongst Member States where obligations flow from the Treaties. In this context, it is nonetheless submitted that any limited interpretation of the principle of loyalty and sincere co-operation would ignore that the legal order of the EU is not simply construed as a set of obligations and duties of the Member States *vis-à-vis* the Union, but has rather been established as a multidimensional integrated legal order attributing (new) rights and duties on all its entities and subjects. The consequence, namely that the right of the one embodies the duty of someone else, demands mutual respect and assistance in a broader sense. And although the principle of loyalty and sincere co-operation enshrined in Art 4 (3) TEU is limited by its wording we find reassurance throughout the Treaties in various articles calling for solidarity between the Member States.[54] For the example at hand Art 80 TFEU states that "[t]he policies of the Union set out in this Chapter […] shall be governed by the principle of solidarity and fair sharing of responsibilities […] between the Member States". The rather obvious background of this provision is that a common border, asylum and immigration policy also requires a fair burden-sharing between those Member States with extended external borders and those without.[55] In a broader sense the principle of solidarity must be understood as a means to enhance and complement the principle of loyalty and sincere co-operation between Member States.[56] Solidarity by the very wording of Art 80 TFEU stretches beyond the obligations enshrined in the Treaties, including explicitly a fair sharing of responsibilities and burdens of the financial implications of a common border, asylum and immigration policy.[57] It is thus only forthright to conclude that Member States must also adhere to the principle of solidarity in other areas that are left in their responsi-

---

[53] In this context *Streinz* argues that the principle of sincere co-operation is essentially "vertragsakzessorisch" (obligations ancillary to a treaty); *Streinz* in *Streinz* (ed), EUV/AEUV. Vertrag über die Europäische Union und Vertrag über die Arbeitsweise der Europäischen Union[2] (2012) Art 4 EUV margin note 25.

[54] See especially Art 222 TFEU, but also Art 24 (2) and (3), Art 31 (1) (2) and Art 32 TEU as well as Art 122 (1) and Art 194 TFEU. *Calliess* also points out that solidarity is a "Leitwert" of the Union that shines through in variety of rules and mechanisms that do not explicitly refer to the solidarity, see *Calliess* in *Calliess/Ruffert*, EUV/AEUV[4] Art 222 AEUV margin no 5.

[55] See amongst others *Rosenau / Petrus* in *Vedder / Heintschel von Heinegg* (eds), Europäisches Unionsrecht. EUV/AEUV/Grundrechte-Charta (2012) Art 80 AEUV (1); and *Rossi* op. cit. note 21, Art 80 AEUV margin note 3.

[56] *Vedder* in *Vedder / Heintschel von Heinegg*, Europäisches Unionsrecht Art 4 EUV margin note 22, argues that solidarity between the Member States constitutes a concretisation of the principle of sincere co-operation whereas *Rossi* perceives solidarity as a complementation of the principle of solidarity, that in this is context is however only political appellative rather than legally binding; *Rossi* op. cit. note 21, Art 80 EUV margin notes 1 and 2.

[57] A practical example of solidarity on the Union level is the so-called European Refugee Fund for the period 2008-2013, aimed at supporting Member States in the field of asylum; Decision No 573/2007/EC of the EP and the Council establishing the European Refugee Fund for the period 2008 to 2013 as part of the General program 'Solidarity and Management of Migration Flows' and repealing Council Decision 2004/904/EC, OJ 2007 L 144, 1.

bility but bear severe implications for a common border, asylum and immigration policy. Clearly, Art 79 (5) TFEU and the herein enshrined freedom of Member States to determine the volumes of admission of third-country nationals coming to their territory in order to seek work qualifies under the given pretext, warranting Member States *inter alia* to respect their remaining competences. Any *laissez-faire* naturalisation policy that is intended to by-pass or which effectively by-passes the (limits of a) common immigration policy would thus encroach on the principle of solidarity under EU Law. This line of thought bears some resemblance to the argument AG *Maduro* raised in *Rottmann* where he indicated that "an unjustified mass naturalisation of nationals of non-member States", could affect the principle of sincere co-operation (Art 4 (3) TFEU), and that the legislative power of a Member State in the sphere of nationality was thus subject to restrictions under "primary Community legislation and the general principles of Community law".[58]

However, the mere fact that a Member State pursues a *laissez-faire* naturalisation policy seemingly contradicting Art 79 (5) TFEU is in itself not conclusive to finally answer the question whether such a measure is compatible with EU Law. In light of the aforesaid such an assessment can however clarify two things: firstly, by relying on the principle of solidarity in connection with Art 79 (5) TFEU it becomes clear that a Member States' citizenship policy is not *per se* beyond the realms of EU Law; and secondly, by the same token possible limitations to this policy field of the Member State rooted in EU Law appear on the horizon. Although the argument that an encroachment of the principle of solidarity in connection with Art 79 (5) TFEU might still be compatible with EU Law may seem illogical at first sight, one must not forget that also the Member States' citizenship policy as an aspect of national identity warrants respect under Art 4 (2) TEU. The question of EU Law compatibility of a Member States' naturalisation policy seen from this angle can hence neither be answered by relying just on one of these competing principles nor can it be answered in the abstract. Compatibility can only be assessed in the light of the facts at hand and by employing a test of proportionality. Practically, this means assessing whether the measures taken are capable of achieving a valid aim, are necessary to this end and are proportional in light of the principle of solidarity and the freedom of the other Member States to determine the volume of admission of third-country nationals coming to their territory to seek work.

4.4. The question of proportionality

Certainly, the application of a test of proportionality is no easy task. Theoretically, however, the question about the proportionality of a measure boils down to whether the following scheme can be applied to the measures of a Member State:

1. Identification of the objective that is pursued by the Member State on the basis of the national legal framework;

[58] See Opinion AG *Maduro*, C-135/08, *Rottmann*, margin note 30.

2. assessment of the measures in respect of capability and necessity, asking whether the national measures represent a part of a coherent set of measures aimed at the achievement of the same objective and whether there are other less intrusive measures through which it could be achieved;
3. weighing the measures and their impact against other competing objectives.

In general, one might assume that the focus of any test of proportionality rests upon the last point as it at is this level where the conflicting principles go head to head. For the specific context, however, also the second and the first point in this scheme entail crucial elements, as the application of a proportionality test relies on the fact that the measures of a Member States are intended, capable and necessary to establish a special bond of citizenship between an individual and a Member State that is protected by Art 4 (2) TEU. This is to say, that any assessment of a Member States' citizenship policy in the very context of a test of proportionality has to take into account the legal measures and its underlying motives. So albeit EU Law is not to define or determine the elements of national citizenship, respect under Art 4 (2) TEU is subject to the fact that the respective Member State pursues a coherent and objective-related policy.

To this end, international law may provide some useful hints: In the famous *Nottebohm* case the ICJ ruled that naturalisation was an act under national law but that the right of a State to exercise diplomatic protection for an individual under international law rests upon the fact that "nationality must correspond to the factual situation" and that according to international practice, nationality was "a legal bond having as its basis a social fact of attachment, a genuine connection of existence, interests and sentiments, together with the existence of reciprocal rights and duties".[59] In a case where such a "genuine connection" could not be established a State was not entitled under International Law to exercise diplomatic protection.

In line with the ratio of this ruling one can draw the conclusion that also under EU Law respect for a Member States' citizenship policy under Art 4 (2) TEU relies on the fact that the respective national legal framework of a Member State as well as the facts on the ground provide for the establishment of a genuine bond between the Member State and its citizens defining the primary individual subjects of that very State. It should be remembered that this conclusion does in no way interfere with the Member States' competence in the field of citizenship policy, but merely limits the possibility of a Member State to invoke respect for its national identity. A *laissez-faire* citizenship policy of a Member State undermining the competence of the other Member State to determine the very parameters of their labour migration policies that bears no validity in this sense can thus not be deemed compatible with the principle of solidarity and EU Law at large.

Things are however different, if the objectives and means are to meet the criteria outlined before, as the clash of interests then becomes an outright clash of principles

[59] ICJ, *Liechtenstein v Guatemala (Nottebohm),* Judgment, second phase, [1955] ICJ Rep 4 margin notes 22 and 23.

under EU Law: on the one side the principle of solidarity and on the other side the principle of respect for the national identities of the Member States. Which of these principles is eventually to prevail in the process of weighing and balancing is ultimately subject to the facts of the very case at hand.

And though any abstract assessment cannot predetermine a convincing conclusion for this problem, it should be born in mind that the principle of solidarity, as described above, is in its essence a peripheral means of the EU's legal order to shield and maximise the effects of EU Law, meaning that solidarity as a prohibitive principle only prevails where the Treaties fall short in formulating concrete legal obligations for the Member States *inter alia*, but where an unfettered use of a Member States' regulative powers might still bear severe implications for other Member States. The principle of respect for the national identities of the Member States, which is moreover also linked to the concept of Union citizenship as a common status of citizens of the Member States on the other hand is a principle at the core of the Union's legal order, essentially defining the relationship between the Union and the Member State (*inter alia*) as sovereign States.[60] As a consequence, the intrinsic value of these conflicting principles must be taken into account, thus making it rather difficult to imagine a situation whereby a Member State's citizenship policy aimed at establishing a special bond of citizenship could be deemed incompatible with EU Law.

5. CONCLUSION

Union citizenship is a concept which despite being additional to national citizenship is still built upon the formal criterion of being a citizen of a Member State. National citizenship and its comprising elements in turn are solely defined by the respective Member State. Furthermore, the presumption that citizenship of a State establishes a special bond defining the individual subjects of a State prompts the argument that citizenship is not only a requirement for Union citizenship but constitutes an inherent part of national identity and therefore warrants protection under Art 4 (2) TEU.

Union citizenship and thus citizenship of a Member State as such has been described by the ECJ as the fundamental status of individuals under EU Law, attributing rights and duties on the respective individuals. At the core of the privileges that come with Union citizenship is the right to rely on the fundamental freedoms and the right to move and reside freely within the territory of the Member States, granting citizens of a Member State an equal legal status in all the Member States of the Union.

Third-country nationals coming to a Member State seeking work enjoy no such favourable status, as under Art 79 (5) TFEU Member States remain free to decide upon the volume of admission of third-country nationals coming to their territory seeking employed or self-employed work. Moreover, under secondary EU Law

---

[60] *Puttler* op. cit. note 38, Art 4 EUV margin note 8.

respective third-country nationals are given only a less favourable status in other Member States of the Union than Union citizens.

The differences between these two concepts and the underlying ratio are at the heart of the question whether Member States face certain limits under EU Law when awarding their citizenship to third-country nationals. In the assessment at hand it has been argued that, albeit citizenship policy remains an exclusive competence of the Member States, EU Law is triggered if a Member State pursues a naturalisation policy which undermines Art 79 (5) TFEU, as Member States under the principle of solidarity are bound to use their regulative powers without repercussions on other Member States. Such an encroachment of the principle of solidarity is however not *per se* incompatible with EU Law, as the field of citizenship policy and hence naturalisation of third-country nationals must be respected as part of the national identities of the Member States. A solution for this clash of principles can only be derived through the application of a proportionality test which eventually and in light of the specific circumstances of the case must weigh the specific interests and the effects of the measures adopted against each other.

Eugenia Mocanu

EU VISA LIBERALIATION VS. NATIONAL CITIZENSHIP LAWS AND POLICIES

"Preamble AA EU-Georgia

- COMMITTED to deepening their dialogue and cooperation on mobility, migration, asylum and border management taking also into account the EU-Georgia Mobility Partnership, with a comprehensive approach paying attention to legal migration, including circular migration, and to cooperation aimed at tackling illegal migration, trafficking in human beings and efficient implementation of the readmission agreement; (...)

Art 16 (2) AA EU-Georgia: Movement of persons and readmission

2. The Parties shall continue to endeavour to enhance mobility of citizens and shall take gradual steps towards the shared objective of visa-free regime in due course, provided that the conditions for well-managed and secure mobility set out in the two-phase Action Plan on Visa Liberalization are in place."

"Preamble AA EU-Republic of Moldova

- RECOGNISING the gradual steps being taken towards a visa-free regime for the citizens of the Republic of Moldova in due course, provided that the conditions for well-managed and secure mobility are in place;

Art 15 (2) AA EU-Republic of Moldova: Movement of persons

2. The Parties shall also endeavour to enhance mobility of citizens and shall take gradual steps towards the shared objective of a visa-free regime in due course, provided that the conditions for well-managed and secure mobility, set out in the Action Plan on Visa Liberalisation, are in place."

1. INTRODUCTION

The Republic of Moldova[1] is widely considered a success story in terms of its participation in the EaP, particularly with respect to migration - related issues. Indeed, in July 2010 the EU and Moldova started negotiations on visa-free trav-

1 For the purpose of this work, the author will use the term Moldova and Moldovan, referring to the Republic of Moldova and its citizens. It is not to be confused with the part of Romania, bearing the same name and bordering with the Republic of Moldova (which is an independent state).

el for Moldovan citizens to the EU which resulted in the adoption of a Visa Liberalisation Action Plan (VLAP) of January 2011. According to the reports presented by the European Commission, Moldova has made significant progress in strengthening its migration services' capacities when compared to its fellow countries from the EaP region. As a result, the European Commission proposed a visa-free regime for Moldovan citizens, traveling to the Schengen area and holding a biometric passport.[2] On 27 February 2014, the EP voted for the abolishment of visas for Moldovan citizens. Moldova is thus the first EaP country to meet all the requirements for visa-free travel as provided in the Visa Liberalisation Plan.[3] As of 28 April 2014, the visa requirements have been abolished for Moldovan citizens who want to travel to the Schengen zone for a short stay and hold biometric passports.[4]

Despite the fears of some EU Member States that a visa-free regime will cause an increase of immigration flows (illegal migration) and of cross-border crime, granting a visa-free regime to Moldova will have a significant impact, as the country will not only come closer to the EU, but will also become more attractive to the EU Member States. At the same time, visa liberalisation is important due to the historically close relations with Romania, the sister-country that fully supports and promotes Moldova on its way to EU integration. Romania has a preferential policy of granting citizenship to its former nationals who lost it against their own will. This policy is primarily aimed at Moldovans living on the other side of the Prut River (dividing the two states); it shows an increasing number of citizenships granted annually by the Romanian authorities to Moldovan citizens. It is important to note that Moldovans may acquire a second citizenship, as both countries allow multiple citizenships and, thus, the statehood of Moldova is not endangered. However, this process is not viewed in a positive light by some EU Member States. There are many who believe that the visa liberalisation dialogue between Moldova and the EU has started through the back door by turning Moldovans into "new" Romanian citizens.

So what are the citizenship laws and policies in the EU? What are the rules for third country nationals to exercise their "freedom of movement" in the EU? Which way should Moldova choose to go? And, what are the relations between the EU, Moldova and Romania?

---

2 European Commission Press Release IP/13/1170, "Commission proposes visa-free regime to Moldova", 27 November 2013.

3 European Parliament Press Release, REF. 20140221IPR36646, "Parliament gives green light to visa-free travel for Moldovan citizens", 27 February 2014.

4 European Commission Statement 14/101, "Commissioner Malmström on visa-free travel for Moldova", 3 April 2014.

2. EU CITIZENSHIP

2.1. General notions

The EU is a partnership of 28 Member States. It works 24/7, 365 days a year. Its aim is the benefit of its people, its citizens. Without them, the Union would not make any sense, it would not serve any purpose. The Treaties instituted the citizenship of the Union, stating that it is additional to the national citizenships. Thus, the first is linked to the second and ceases to exist without it.

The concept of a European citizenship was considered from a very early stage in the development of the Communities and may be said to begin with the birth of the "market citizen", a "reduced functionalist concept of an individual"[5] which conferred certain individual rights under the Treaty Establishing the European Economic Community (TEC). It is a concept that is essentially based upon the economic objectives set forth in the Treaty. Among the reasons for introducing Community citizenship, three are of particular importance: (1) encouraging free movement, (2) reducing the EU's democratic deficit, and (3) forming a base for the construction of a European identity.[6] Community citizenship gave economic actors under Art 18 TEC the right of free movement and residence within the territory of the Member States. In particular, the right of residence throughout the Community was given to employees, self-employed workers and to their family members by secondary legislation, in conjunction with the right to work.[7] Nevertheless, these rights did not in any way provide a condition of citizenship.

EU citizenship is evolutionary and can expand to include new rights together with the expansion of the scope of the Treaties. Thus, the benefits of Union citizenship are not limited to the rights conferred by Art 21-24 TFEU. In fact, Art 25 TFEU makes it plain that the concept of citizenship was explicitly designed to be developed further. The main features of the Union citizenship, according to the Treaty of Lisbon, are as follows: firstly, since it is expressly stated that the Union citizenship is *additional* to the national citizenship, it is therefore necessary in the first instance to be a a citizen of a Member State; secondly, Union citizenship *does not replace* national citizenship – it is *prima facie* Member States who determine the conditions under which citizenship is conferred,[8] and the other Member States

---

5 *O'Keeffe,* Union Citizenship, in *O'Keeffe / Twomey* (eds), Legal Issues of the Maastricht Treaty 87; *Kadelbach*, Union Citizenship, in *Bogdandy / Bast* (eds), Principles of European Constitutional Law, (2010), at 455; *Kadelbach*, European Citizenship Rights, in *Ehlers* (ed), European Fundamental Rights and Freedoms,(2007) at 542.

6 *Rostek / Davies*, The Impact of Union Citizenship on National Citizenship Policies" European Integration online Papers 2006 at 6, available at <http://eiop.or.at/eiop/index.php/eiop/article/view/2006_005a>.

7 European Union, Summaries of EU Legislation, "Citizenship of the European Union", at <http://europa.eu/legislation_summaries/institutional_affairs/treaties/amsterdam_treaty/a12000_en.htm>.

8 European Council (1992), Denmark and the Treaty on European Union, OJ 1992 C 348; Case C-192/99 *The Queen v. Secretary of State for the Home Department, ex parte: Manjit Kaur*

are required to recognise the citizenship duly granted by another Member State;[9] thirdly, Union citizenship comprises a number of rights and duties in addition to those stemming from citizenship of a Member State; however, there are no obvious duties or obligations imposed by the Treaty on individuals.[10]

Moreover, as stated in Declaration no 2 on Nationality of a Member State,[11] "the question whether an individual possesses the citizenship of a Member State shall be settled solely by reference to the national law of the Member State concerned". However, one cannot state that there is no connection between the national citizenship of Member States and the Union citizenship. Indeed, the Union citizenship confers rights (Arts 20-25 TFEU); at same time, it does not replace the national citizenship, but adds to it (Art 20 TFEU). They go hand in hand: one cannot be a Union citizen without holding the citizenship of a Member State. Member States, by virtue of their monopoly in determining who qualifies as their citizens, enjoy freedom in deciding who should be granted the status of EU citizenship. In this respect, Member States are sovereign actors: even if national legislation distinguishes several categories of citizenship, the right to decide who is ultimately entitled to Union citizenship lies with the Member States themselves.[12]

Granting citizenship is a constant process that directly affects people and states through immigration / emigration and goes beyond the limits of only one state: (1) it affects the neighbouring countries, on the regional level and (2) it influences the migration policies and sets up certain standards on the Union level. Indeed, every Member State has the sovereignty to decide on its internal citizenship policies. However, the Union also has a say in this process, being directly affected through waves of new citizens. Thus, the national citizenship laws are not independent of EU Law and must respect its rules and principles. Member States have the primary competence to determine their own laws concerning access to and deprivation of national citizenship, nevertheless subject to the principle that where this competence impacts on EU Law rights – which it usually does, since every national citizen is a Union citizen – they must respect EU Law and its rules and principles.[13] Thus, EU membership has an influence on the national sovereignty of Member States in the field of citizenship. Firstly, pursuant to Art 4 (3) TEU based on the principle of

---

[2001] ECR I-01237; Case C-369/90 *Micheletti and others v. Delegacion del Gobierno en Cantabria* [1992] ECR I-4239, para 10.

9 *Craig / de Burca*, EU Law. Text, Cases, and Materials (4th ed 2008) at 848; *Lenaerts / Nuffel / Bray* (eds), Constitutional Law of European Union (2nd ed 2005) at 544; Case C-369/90 *Micheletti and Others* [1992].

10 Ibid. 849; *Besson / Utzinger*, Toward European Citizenship, Journal of Social Philosophy 2008, 191; *Shaw*, Citizenship Within and Across the Boundaries of the European Union" Transitions, 2011, 45; European Union, Summaries of EU legislation "Citizenship of the European Union" at <http://europa.eu/legislation_summaries/institutional_affairs/treaties/amsterdam_treaty/a12000_en.htm>.

11 Declaration no. 2 on Nationality of a Member State annexed to the Treaty on European Union OJ 1992 C 191.

12 Case 192/99 *Kaur* 2001; *Rostek / Davies*, op. cit. note 6, 11.

13 *Davies*, The Entirely Conventional Supremacy of Union Citizenship and Rights, in *Shaw* (ed) Has the European Court of Justice Challenged Member State Sovereignty in National Law European University Institute Working Paper RSCAS 2011 no. 62, 6; Case no 135/08, *Rottmann v. Freistaat Bayern* 2010 ECR I-1449, Opinion of AG Maduro, paras 23, 26.

sincere co - operation, the Member States and the Union shall assist each other in carrying out the tasks which flow from the Treaties. Consequently, citizenship regimes within the Union are interconnected: nationals of Member States are also citizens of the Union and thus can claim extensive social, economic and even political rights associated with their EU citizenship in other Member States.[14] Secondly, certain EU- related laws and policies[15] have an inevitable impact on the formation of the citizenship regimes of EU Member States, even without any specific legal obligations or external political pressure.[16] Thirdly, as indicated by ECJ case law, there is a need for Member States to respect certain EU standards when adopting decisions in the field of citizenship.[17]

2.2. Dual citizenship in the EU

In recent years, dual citizenship has become a more and more common phenomenon: though it had been highly disfavoured in the past, today it plays a more positive role. Traditionally, the main reason for the existence of dual citizenship was the concurrent application of the two ways of acquiring citizenship at birth: *jus soli* and *jus sanguinis*. Another reason for accepting dual citizenship is the equality of sexes in citizenship laws. As *Joppke* asserts, the reason for states to allow multiple citizenship is "de-ethnicisation" and "re-ethnicisation" of citizenship laws.[18] The de-ethnicisation process, characteristic of receiving states, entails facilitation of the access to citizenship, either through opening it at the margins, in terms of liberalised naturalisation procedures or through adding a *jus soli* element to the main road of birth-attributed citizenship.[19] Meanwhile, sending states take the position of re-ethnicisation, i.e. that of dual citizenship,[20] perceiving multiple citizenship as an important instrument in maintaining links with their emigrant population.[21]

The right of Member States to confer certain people a special treatment due to historical reasons is accepted at the European level, as the provisions on conferring citizenship are not uniform in the EU and are not part of supranational legal norms.[22] However, principle 11 of Bolzano/Bozen Recommendations [23] reads as follows:

---

[14] *Swider*, Pre-Accession Changes to Residence Based Naturalisation Requirements in ten new EU Member States", European University Institute Working Papers RSCAS 2011 no. 18, 3.

[15] Namely EU laws on immigration, asylum, long-term resident and EU documents on third-country nationals.

[16] *Swider*, op. cit. note 14, 3.

[17] *Rottmann* op. cit. note 13.

[18] *Joppke*, Citizenship Between De- and Re-Ethnicization, Sage Foundation Working Paper 2003 no. 204.

[19] Ibid., 7.

[20] Ibid. 11; *Joppke*, Citizenship and Immigration, Polity 2010, 63-66.

[21] *Margiotta / Vonk*, Nationality Law and European Citizenship: The Role of Dual Nationality, European University Institute Working Papers RSCAS 2010 no 66, 3.

[22] *Dimulescu / Avram*, Banali in EU: Politica romaneasca de redobindire a cetateniei in comparative cu alte state din UE Policy Memo 2011, no. 22, 4.

> *"[...]States should, however, ensure that such a conferral of citizenship respects the principles of friendly, including good neighbourly, relations and territorial sovereignty, and should refrain from conferring citizenship en masse, even if dual citizenship is allowed by the State of residence. If a State does accept dual citizenship as part of its legal system, it should not discriminate against dual nationals."*

The *Micheletti* case has established the principle of non-discrimination based on multiple citizenships on the Union level. The Court held that when the host Member State is faced with a person who has double citizenship of a Member State and also the citizenship of a third state, it is obliged to recognise that part of a person's dual (or multiple) citizenship and cannot restrict the effects of the citizenship of another Member State by imposing an additional condition for recognition of that citizenship with a view to the exercise of the fundamental freedoms provided for in the Treaties. Consequently, Member States must recognise the Union citizenship of citizens of other Member States also holding the citizenship of a third state: the Member State citizenship of a dual citizenship holder who also possesses a non-Member State citizenship will always prevail.[24]

Some countries may seem more restrictive when granting citizenship, whilst others are more liberal. Nonetheless, all countries tend to keep links with their communities abroad and maintain this relationship by offering the possibility of reintegrating them into the country which at a certain point in time was their homeland. Moreover, some countries extend this opportunity to their offsprings, whilst other countries, by their facilitated naturalisation policies, "pay" their former citizens for the political mistakes of the past. This is the case of Bulgaria, France, Germany, Italy, Spain, United Kingdom. Also, countries with a ban on dual citizenship, such as Germany and Austria, offer a possibility to derogate from this rule.

2.2 EU Citizens vs. Third-Country Citizens

European citizenship is marked by a tension: between a citizenship that is a derivative of the nation-state and a citizenship that is defined by free movement.[25] On the one hand, citizenship rights are primarily granted to citizens of Member States and are only partially or differentially extended to third-country citizens. On the other hand, citizenship rights in the Union are primarily activated through practices of free movement, rendering the mobility of citizens central to the effective institution of European citizenship.[26] As it is well established, a Member State cannot, in the case of a dual citizen with the citizenship of anoth-

---

[23] The Bolzano/Bozen Recommendations on National Minorities in Inter-state Relations 2008 OSCE High Commissioner on National Minorities, principle 11.

[24] *Shaw*, Citizenship: Contrasting Dynamics at the Interface of Integration and Constitutionalism, European University Institute Working Paper RSCAS 2010 No 60, 16; *Margiotta / Vonk* op. cit. note 21, at 12.

[25] *Aradau / Huysmans / Squire*, Acts of European Citizenship: A Political Sociology of Mobility, Journal of Common Market Studies 2010, 945.

[26] Ibid 946. *Maas*, Migrants, States and EU Citizenships Unfulfilled Promise", Citizenship Studies 2008, 6.

er Member State and that of a third state, refuse to recognize such a person as an EU citizen. To do so, it would deny such a person the benefit of the free movement rights under the Treaty.[27] One of the major achievements of European integration has been the expansion of citizenship of the Union and the freedom of movement, as *Carrera and Wiesbrock*, note. When the European citizenship was officially instituted in 1993, the EU has arguably played a decisive role in transforming foreigners into citizens and dismantling internal border controls among its Member States.[28] It has also been suggested that the Union has promoted a "rather revolutionary understanding of citizenship," whose freedoms and benefits are no longer exclusively attached to a citizenship status, but closely intertwined with the mobility of individuals beyond their state's territory. One distinctive feature of European citizenship lies in the encouragement that it gives individuals to move and benefit from some of its most symbolic features and components. In most cases, it is at the moment of moving, crossing an EU internal border, when the individual becomes a beneficiary of a full set of EU (citizenship-related) rights and freedoms.[29]

The connectivity between citizenship of the Union and that of an EU Member State constituted a condition for national governments to agree on its very establishment by the TEU. It is therefore surprising that this connecting factor has not prevented the expansion of citizenship rights and freedoms to third-country citizens. That said, the EU Member States largely retain a monopoly over determining "who qualifies" as a European citizen and the question of whether an individual possesses the citizenship of a Member State is still to be settled "solely by reference to the national law of the Member State concerned".[30] Recently, however, the degree of national discretion has transformed the status of those who can benefit from the set of supranational civil, social, political and economic freedoms and benefits. In fact, it seems that third-country citizens have acquired certain EU freedoms that, while perhaps not formally falling within the legal landscape of European citizenship, are of a similar nature.[31]

Initially, the Treaty of Amsterdam recognised the principle of free movement of third-country citizens, which was included in Title IV of TEC, dealing with "Visas, asylum, immigration and other policies related to free movement of persons". Despite the recognition given to the rights of third-country citizens, such references in the TFEU were not maintained. However, Art 26 TFEU still defines an internal market as "an area without frontiers"[32] in which free movement of persons is en-

---

[27] *Shaw*, Setting the Scene: The Rottmann Case Introduced" in *Shaw* (ed), Has the European Court of Justice Challenged Member State Sovereignty in National Law? European University Institute Working Paper RSCAS 2011 No 62, at 2.

[28] *Carrera / Wiesbrock*, Whose Citizenship to Empower in the Area of Freedom, Security and Justice? The Act of Mobility and Litigation in the Enactment of European Citizenship (Justice and Home Affairs, CEPS Liberty and Security in Europe 2010 No 12, at 3.

[29] Ibid.

[30] Op. cit. note 11.

[31] Op. cit. note 28.

[32] In practice, this are only exists on the continental part of the EU. Ireland and United Kingdom have consistently abstained from taking part in abolishing internal border controls.

sured in accordance with the provisions of the Treaties, without specifying whether or not these persons should be EU citizens.[33] The provisions of Art 26 TFEU as applied to the internal market may be addressed with specific reference to two areas which both have direct implications on the rights of third-country citizens residing inside and outside the EU: first, the absence of internal frontiers – denoting the absence of all border controls on all persons, whether as citizens of the Union or of third countries, and, second, the realisation of free movement of persons. In contrast to the abolition of border controls, which does not distinguish citizens of the EU from third-country citizens, the EU law on free movement clearly sets these two categories apart and, third-country citizens might be regarded as only benefitting from freedom of movement in a way that could be described as indirect and partial.[34]

3. VISA FACILITATION AGREEMENTS AND VISA LIBERALISATION

Many countries that are subject to visa requirements by the EU are pressing for relaxation or abolition of these requirements.[35] Relaxation of visa requirements is also called visa liberalisation, i.e. facilitation of visa procedures, whilst the abolition of visa requirements means that a visa-free regime is established. In order to achieve any of these two regimes, the EU negotiates with each country individually, because a country is only eligible for relaxation or abolition of the visa requirement if it meets certain conditions. The purpose of visa facilitation agreements is to promote interaction between the citizens of the EU and the contracting States.[36] Visa abolition entails a lifting of the visa requirements, thus the third-country citizen can enter and leave the EU without any visa. The decision on granting visa-free travel is not based on a treaty, but is subject to the European legislative procedure. Such decisions are adopted by a special qualified majority.[37] However, both visa facilitation and visa liberalisation relate to short term-visas, i.e. those with a maximum duration of three months.

Visa facilitation agreements have been signed with nine non-EU countries: Albania, Bosnia and Herzegovina, Georgia, Macedonia, Moldova, Montenegro, Rus-

---

[33] *Boeles / Heijer / Lodder*, *European Migration Law* (2009) at 115.

[34] *Cornelisse*, European Integration and Immigration by Third-country Nationals: The Obduracy of the National Border, 12, at <http://www.libertysecurity.org/IMG/pdf_CORNELISSE_obduracy_of_the_national_border.pdf>.

[35] For the purpose of this work, the term "visa facilitation agreement" will be used which is the Agreement between European Community and [respective country] on the facilitation of issuance of visas. Belgian Presidency of the Council of the EU, "EU External Visa Policy", at <http://www.eutrio.be/files/bveu/media/documents/EU_external_visa_policy.pdf>.

[36] Ibid.

[37] European Stability Initiative, "The EU Decision Making Process", at <http://www.esiweb.org/index.php?lang=en&id=354>.

sia, Serbia, Ukraine.[38] Visa facilitation agreements bind all EU Member States except Denmark, the United Kingdom and Ireland. The Schengen associated states are not covered by visa facilitation agreements.[39] One common point in all visa facilitation agreements is the prospect of a visa-free travel regime, as it is recognised as a long-term objective. The visa facilitation agreement with Moldova is the only one that declares the intention to improve the EU presence in the country and to set up a Common Application Centre in Chisinau.[40]

In some agreements, a special reference is made to Regulation no 1931/2006 concerning the establishment of a system of local border traffic.[41] Hungary, Poland, Slovakia and Romania declared their willingness to negotiate a local border traffic regime with Ukraine. In the Western Balkans, Macedonia was to negotiate one with Bulgaria, Serbia another with Bulgaria, Hungary and Romania. Moldova and Romania also declared their willingness to establish a local border traffic regime which was completed by signing the agreement on local border traffic on 13 November 2009 in Bucharest.[42] Only the Romania-Moldova agreement fully complies with Regulation 1931/2006. The other agreements either have a border area that goes beyond what is allowed by the Regulation (Hungary-Ukraine; Slovakia-Ukraine, albeit in a limited area), or require travel medical insurance contrary to the Regulation (Poland-Ukraine).[43]

Acquiring a visa is a cumbersome process and very often the residents of border regions try to find easier ways of moving freely into the EU. Good examples in this respect are offered by Moldova and Macedonia. Both countries try to benefit from their neighbouring countries' status as EU Member States. Many Macedonians have applied for a Bulgarian passport, many Moldovans for a Romanian or Bulgarian one. *Angel Marin*, Bulgaria's former Vice President, announced in January 2008 that "between 2002 and 2007, some 39,000 Macedonians and as many Moldovans applied for Bulgarian passports. [...] Of those, some 13,925 Macedonians and 10,613 Moldovans were granted passports". In Moldova, there is a Bulgarian

---

38 Macedonia, Montenegro and Serbia have been granted visa-free regime in December 2009, Albania and Bosnia and Herzegovina – one year later, Albania, in 2010. European Stability Initiative, The Visa Facilitation and Readmission Agreements, at <http://www.esiweb.org/index.php?lang=en&id=351>.

39 European Commission (2011), Consolidated Version of the Handbook for Processing of Visa Applications and the Modifications of Issued Visas Based on Commission Decision C (2010) 1620 final, Commission Implementing Decision C (2011) 5501 final of 4 August 2011 amending Commissions Decision no C (2010) 1620 final of 19 March 2010 establishing the Handbook for the Processing of Visa Applications and the Modifications of Issued Visas, 63.

40 European Commission Declaration on Representation and the Common Application Centre in Chisinau, annexed to Visa Facilitation Agreement with Moldova.

41 Regulation (EC) no 1931/2006 of the European Parliament and of the Council of 20 December 2006 laying down the rules on local border traffic at the external land borders of the Member States and amending the provisions of the Schengen Convention OJ 2006 L 405, 1.

42 Agreement between the Government of Romania and the Government of the Republic of Moldova on local border traffic, Official Gazette of Romania 52/2010, 22 January 2010.

43 European Commission (2011), Second report on the implementation of the and functioning of the local border traffic regime set up by Regulation no 1931/2006, (Communication) COM (2011) 47 final.

minority of 60,000 to 80,000 (1.9 %)[44]; and in Macedonia, Bulgaria considers the Slavic population as being of Bulgarian origin and therefore easily grants passports. EU officials are aware of the seriousness of this problem.[45] In an interview, a high diplomat of an EU Member State voiced concerns that:

> *"the Bulgarians will come sooner or later to claim territory from the Macedonian state when one day the majority [in some border regions to Bulgaria] will possess a Bulgarian citizenship. Once, they will even somehow understandably pose the question: What is the foundation of statehood in these areas?"*[46]

Nevertheless, the local border traffic is an asset of many residents living at the EU's external border.

Because visa liberalisation is more far-reaching than visa facilitation, the EU expects third countries to make extra efforts to meet specific conditions because, once the visa obligation has been abolished, it is impossible to prevent (illegal) immigration by passport holders from those countries. The EU therefore "requests" the concerned countries to develop and implement the conditions presented by the EU, relating to the effective administrative and policing system. Moreover, this relation is based on mutual respect between the EU and the third country. The conditions that a country has to put into effect are key to the visa liberalisation and are of a dual character: on the one hand, the EU is trying to achieve its strategic objective of supporting and stabilising the countries that surround it, in accordance with the ENP; on the other hand, it wants to avoid the situation where abolition of the visa obligation leads to a surge in unfounded applications for asylum, illegal (transit) migration from countries which still have a visa obligation, and an increase in international crime.[47]

4. EU – MOLDOVA

One of the countries that struggles with the nature of citizenship, on the one hand, and visa liberalisation, on the other hand, is the Republic of Moldova: Ever since its independence from the Soviet Union, Moldova has been on a dif-

44 Biroul National de Statistica al Republicii Moldova (National Bureau of Statistics of the Republic of Moldova), Anuarul Statistic al Moldovei 2012 (Statistical Yearbook of Moldova), Statistica, 2012, p. 40. The data refers to the population census in 2004.

45 *Trauner / Kruse*, EC Visa Facilitation and Readmission Agreements: Implementing a new EU Security Approach in the Neighbourhood" (2008), CEPS Working Document 2008 no 290, 22-23, at <http://aei.pitt.edu/9374/>.

46 Ibid. 23.

47 Belgian Presidency of the Council of the EU, "EU External Visa Policy".

ficult and bumpy transformation process. It is a partner country in the ENP and since the accession of Romania in 2007, it has direct border with the EU.[48]

Moldova has strong ties with the EU: its legal relationship is based on a PCA,[49] establishing the legal and institutional framework for bilateral relations setting up the principal common objectives and encouraging and supporting Moldova's objective of further integration into European economic and social structures.[50] The implementation of the PCA is done through the EU-Moldova ENP AP,[51] a political document laying out the strategic objectives of co-operation between Moldova and the EU while recognising the aspiration of Moldova to further integration. At the same time, it states that the relations between the two parties will depend on the readiness of Moldova to commit to common values and its capacity to implement all established priorities.[52] *Inter alia*, the AP contains perspectives on establishing a constructive dialogue on visa co-operation between the EU and Moldova, including an exchange of views on possibilities of visa facilitation in compliance with the *acquis*.[53]

In 2007, Moldova unilaterally abolished the visa regime for EU Member States citizens.[54] In the same year, Brussels and Chisinau concluded the Visa Facilitation[55] and Readmission Agreements[56] that made it easier to obtain visa for 15 categories of professionals and disadvantaged people.[57] At the same time, Moldova and the EU took the responsibility of bringing back people who illegally reside on the territories covered by the agreement.[58]

---

48 *Niemann / Wekker*, Normative Power in Europe? EU Relations with Moldova, European Integration online Papers 2010, available at <http://eiop.or.at/eiop/index.php/eiop/article/view/2010_014a>.

49 Partnership and Cooperation Agreement between European Communities and their Member States and the Republic of Moldova OJ 1994 L 181, 1.

50 EEAS, "EU-Moldova Relations" <http://eeas.europa.eu/moldova/index_en.htm>.

51 Proposal for a Council Decision on the position to be adopted by the European Communities and their Member States within the Cooperation Council established by the Partnership and Cooperation Agreement establishing a partnership between the European Communities and their Member States, of one part, and the Republic of Moldova, of the other part, with regard to the adoption of a Recommendation on the implementation of the EU-Moldova Action Plan, COM(2004) 787 final.

52 Euractiv, Dosar: Relatiile UE-Moldova Orientarea Declarativ Europeana, in contrast cu apropierea de Moscova (Dossier: EU-Moldova Relations the European orientation, in contrast to proximity with Moscow) (23 November 2007), at <http://www.euractiv.ro/uniunea-europeana/articles%7CdisplayArticle/articleID_11945/Dosar-Relatiile-UE-Moldova-Orientarea-declarativ-europeana-in-contrast-cu-apropierea-de-Moscova.html>.

53 EU / MD ENP AP, New Partnership Perspectives.

54 *Litra*, Moldova on the EU Visa Liberalisation Path: Tacking Stock Achievements and Failures. In-depth Study, Institutul pentru Dezvoltare si Initiative Sociale IDIS Viitorul, 2012, 7.

55 Agreement between the European Community and the Republic of Moldova on the Facilitation of the Issuance of Visas OJ 2007 L 334, 169.

56 Council Decision 2007/826/EC of 22 November 2007 on the Conclusion of the Agreement between the European Community and the Republic of Moldova on the Readmission of Persons Residing without Authorisation OJ 2007 L 334, 148.

57 Art 6, Visa Facilitation Agreement with Moldova.

58 European Council, European Union Joint Press Release, EU-Moldova Agreements on the Facilitation of the Issuance of Visa and Readmission, 10 October 2007.

In January 2010, the EU and Moldova started negotiations on an AA.[59] The AA, as a successor to the PCA, is a concrete way of exploiting the very positive dynamics in EU-Moldova relations, focusing on support to core reforms, on economic recovery, governance and sector co-operation.[60] It can also be seen as a reform agenda for Moldova, based on a comprehensive programme of regulatory approximation, around which Moldova's assistance partners can align themselves and focus their assistance.[61] When in force, the AA will replace the EU-Moldova PCA. On 27 June 2014, the EU and Moldova signed the text of the AA, which includes provisions on the establishment of a DCFTA as an integral part. Both sides expressed their common commitment to undertake further technical steps, required to prepare the AA, including the DCFTA for signature.[62]

Moldova is a priority partner within the EaP. The EaP was officially launched in May 2009 and it is part of the ENP. It responds to the desire of the EU's Eastern neighbours to move closer to the Union and should bring about a significant strengthening of EU policies towards the Eastern Partners (Armenia, Azerbaijan, Georgia, Moldova, Ukraine and Belarus).[63] During the Vilnius Summit, the participants welcomed the achievements by Moldova in fulfilling the benchmarks set out in its VLAP and the presentation of the European Commission's latest progress report in this regard.[64] As a result, the European Commission proposed a visa-free regime for Moldovan citizens, travelling to the Schengen area and holding a biometric passport.[65] On 27 February 2014, the European Parliament voted for the abolishment of visas for the Moldovan citizens. Moldova is the first EaP country to meet all the requirements for visa-free travel as provided in the VLAP.[66]

---

[59] EP (2011), Negotiations of the EU-Moldova Association Agreement. Recommendations to the Council, the Commission and the EEAS, 2011/2079(INI); Council of the European Union, Press Release, "EU-Moldova Cooperation Council" (Brussels 21 December 2009) 17732/09 (Presse 388).

[60] EP Resolution of 15 September 2011 containing the EP's recommendations to the Council, the Commission and the EEAS on the negotiations between the EU and the Republic of Moldova on the Association Agreement (A7-0289/2011).

[61] *EEAS*, EU-Moldova Association Agreement, at <http://eeas.europa.eu/moldova/assoagreement/index_en.htm>.

[62] *EEAS*, EU-Moldova Association Agreement: What does the Association Agreement Offer? at <http://eeas.europa.eu/moldova/pdf/quick_guide_eu_md_aa_en.pdf>.

[63] EU Neighbourhood Info Centre, Eastern Partnership, at <http://www.enpi-info.eu/eastportal/content//506/Eastern%20Partnership>.

[64] Council of the European Union, Joint Declaration of the Eastern Partnership Summit, Vilnius, 28 - 29 November 2013, "Eastern Partnership: The Way Ahead", Vilnius, 29 November 2013, 17130/13, Presse 516.

[65] European Commission Press Release IP/13/1170, Commission Proposes Visa-free Regime to Moldova, 27 November 2013.

[66] EP Press Release, REF. 20140221IPR36646, Parliament Gives Green Light to Visa-free Travel for Moldovan Citizens, 27 February 2014.

5. NATIONAL CITIZENSHIP PROVISIONS: MOLDOVA AND ROMANIA

5.1. Introduction

Moldova and Romania have a long history together, as being one country once. However, due to historical reasons, the two states were set apart and developed in different directions. Since 2007 Romania is a member of the EU, whilst Moldova is a neighbour of it. Nonetheless, Romania is fully supporting Moldova on its way to EU integration. Moreover, through its policy on re-acquisition of Romanian citizenship, mainly aimed at Moldovans who meet the requirements set out by Romanian legislation, it tries to bring people closer to the Union and benefit from EU citizenship and rights conferred by it. Thus, it can be seen as a two-fold process: firstly, the integration of Moldova into the EU through EU-Moldova joint activities, and, secondly, integration of Moldovan people, even before the integration of the country itself.

5.2. Citizenship provisions in Moldovan legislation

The terms "citizenship" and "nationality" have a different usage in the Romanian language. "Citizenship" (*cetăţenie* in Romanian) is used to describe the legal status of nationals, their legal link with the state, their rights, freedoms and duties. Whilst "nationality" in Romanian language (*naţionalitate*) has a strong ethnic underpinning and its use remains a highly sensitive issue in Moldova. This is because the term "nationality" was used legally and politically in the Soviet Union to distinguish the fifteen ethnicities of the Union Republics.[67]

Moldova became a sovereign and independent state on 27 August 1991 with the adoption by Parliament of the Declaration of Independence.[68] However, the institution of citizenship was established even earlier, through the Declaration of Sovereignty of the Republic of Moldova on 23 June 1990 which provided for the establishment of the republic citizenship.[69] Also, it guaranteed rights and freedoms to the republic citizens, foreign citizens and stateless people who live on the territory of the Soviet Socialist Republic of Moldova. Inclusion of these provisions in the Declaration had its legal basis in the Law of 5 May 1990 of the USSR that guaranteed the Union Republics the right to adopt their own laws on citizenship.[70]

---

67 *EUDO Citizenship Observatory*, Citizenship or Nationality? Moldova, at <http://eudo-citizenship.eu/databases/citizenship-glossary/terminology#Moldova>.

68 Law on Declaration of Independence of the Republic of Moldova nr 691-XII from 27 August 1991, Official Gazette no 11-12/103, 118 from 1991.

69 Art 8 Declaration of Sovereignty of the Republic of Moldova, 23 June 1990, no 148-XII, Supreme Soviet of the Soviet Socialist Republic of Moldova.

70 *Arseni*, Drept constituţional şi instituţii politice. Volumul I. Tratat elementar (CEP USM, 2005), 353; *Arseni / Suholitco*, Cetăţenia – o nouă viziune şi reglementare europeană (Chişinău: Litera, 2002), 20.

Nowadays, the citizenship has its fundament in the Constitution of the Republic of Moldova[71] (Art 17):

> (1) The citizenship of the Republic of Moldova shall be acquired, maintained or withdrawn under the conditions provided for by the organic law.[72]
>
> (2) No one may be arbitrarily deprived of his/her citizenship or of the right to change the citizenship.

Moldova ratified the European Convention on Nationality of the Council of Europe in 1999, which brought a new provision in the matter of citizenship – multiple citizenship.[73] As a consequence, Moldova was confronted with a twofold dilemma: a *de jure* prohibition of dual citizenship and a *de facto* increase in the number of Moldovan citizens applying for the restitution (re-acquisition) of Romanian citizenship.[74] Thus, the Moldovan Parliament adopted a new Law on Citizenship in June 2000,[75] providing for cases of multiple citizenships, including in some cases of naturalisation (Art 24 - 26 Law no 1024). However, the Parliament has amended the Law on Citizenship in 2003[76] and repealed the provisions prohibiting Moldovan citizens from possessing the citizenship of other states.

One of the innovations brought by the amendments in 2003 provides explicitly that the acquisition of another citizenship by a Moldovan citizen does not lead to the loss of Moldovan citizenship (Art 24 (3) of the Law on Citizenship). At the same time, the acquisition of the Moldovan citizenship by a foreigner through naturalisation is subject to the renunciation or loss of any previous citizenship, except where such renunciation or loss is not possible or cannot reasonably be required (Art 17 (1) (g) of the Law on Citizenship).[77]

5.3. Citizenship provisions in Romanian legislation

Romania acceded to the EU in January 2007 and brought a rich historical experience into the Union that goes all the way back to long-lasting Byzantine and Ottoman imperial legacies and to the more recent successive waves of Western and Soviet-style modernisation. Thus, the history of Romanian citizenship chal-

---

71 Constitution of the Republic of Moldova of 29 July 1994, Official Gazette no 1.

72 Law no 1024-XIV of 2 June 2000 on the Citizenship of the Republic of Moldova, Official Gazette no 98 from 10 August 2000.

73 Chapter V of the European Convention on Nationality. The Convention uses the term "nationality" instead of "citizenship" which are to be regarded as the same notions. See Explanatory Report to the European Convention on Nationality.

74 Following the Romanian adoption of a law on citizenship in 1991 which made special provisions for the re-acquisition of Romanian citizenship, an increasing number of Moldovan citizens started applying for Romanian citizenship. See *EUDO Citizenship Observatory*, Country Report Moldova, RSCAS/EUDO-CIT-CR 2010/18.

75 Law no 1024-XIV of 2 June 2000 on the Citizenship of the Republic of Moldova, Official Gazette no 98 from 10 August 2000.

76 Law no 232-XV from 5 June 2003 on the Amendment of the Law on Citizenship no 1024-XIV from 2 June 2000, Official Gazette no 149-152.

77 *EUDO Citizenship Observatory*, Country Report Moldova, RSCAS/EUDO-CIT-CR 2010/18, p. 13; *Arseni / Suholitco*, op. cit. note 70, 73-75; *Arseni*, op. cit. note 70, 393-395.

lenges the clear-cut and neatly defined analytical dichotomies, such as "old" versus "new" states and "civic" versus "ethnic" or "inclusive" versus "exclusive" citizenship doctrines, which are erroneously regarded as corresponding to "Western" versus "Eastern" historical experiences.[78] In the context of Moldovan-Romanian relations, the Romanian policy on citizenship did not only intersect with that of state border, but reflected very well the modality in which the Romanian state knew how to balance the main strategic objective of its foreign affairs – Euro-Atlantic integration – and relations with Moldova, always seen by Bucharest as a priority and a special one.[79] Romania was the first state to recognise the independence of Moldova, only few hours after Moldova declared its independence on 27 August 1991. Diplomatic relations were established on 29 August 1991.[80]

One important element is that the Romanian legislation on acquiring citizenship is based on the principle of *jus sanguinis*, thus, someone becomes a Romanian citizen if at least one of the parents is Romanian citizen. The principle of *jus sanguinis* is applicable also in the case of re-acquisition of Romanian citizenship of those who lost it for "reasons non-imputable to them" or those to whom "this citizenship has been taken against their own will", provided by Art 37 Law on Citizenship adopted in 1991, with an implied reference (only) to inhabitants of the former Moldovan Soviet Socialist Republic, as well as to Northern Bucovina or Southern Dobruja, because their successors also benefit from the right of re-acquisition of Romanian citizenship.[81]

Adopted in March 1991, the new Law on Romanian Citizenship no 21/1991[82] was built on the 1939 Law, which was abrogated by the communist regime in 1952.[83] The law prohibited dual citizenship with one important exception (see below), at the same time providing for three methods of re-acquisition of Romanian citizenship:

1. by repatriation (Art 8);
2. by request without repatriation (Art 11); and
3. by "restoration" of citizenship to former Romanian citizens (Art 35) living in the lost territories of interwar Greater Romania.

The 1991 Law brought some innovations in this respect. Firstly, the law guaranteed former citizens the right to re-naturalisation through repatriation: "*the person who has lost Romanian citizenship can reacquire it through repatriation, if he or she expresses a manifest desire to do so*" (Art 8). Secondly, in line with the 1990

78 *Iordachi*, Politics of Citizenship in Post-Communist Romania: Legal Traditions, Restitution of Nationality and Multiple Memberships, in *Baubock / Perchinig / Sievers* (eds), Citizenship Policies in the New Europe (2nd ed 2009) at 175.

79 *Dimulescu / Avram*, op. cit. note 22, 5.

80 Romanian Embassy in Chisinau, Bilateral Relations, at <http://chisinau.mae.ro/node/221>.

81 *Dimulescu / Avram*, op. cit. note 22, 5.

82 Law 21/1991 on Romanian Citizenship, Romanian Official Gazette part I no 576.

83 *Iordachi*, op. cit. note 78, 6.

Decree,[84] the 1991 Law allowed reacquisition of citizenship by former Romanian citizens even without repatriation: "*former Romanian citizens who, before 22 December 1989, have lost their Romanian citizenship for different reasons*" can reacquire Romanian citizenship by request even if they retain their foreign citizenship and their domicile abroad (Art 37).[85] Thirdly, and most importantly, the 1991 Law introduced a new form of access to Romanian citizenship that can be generically called "restoration" or "restitution". An additional para to Art 37 stipulated that the right to reacquisition of citizenship is also granted to all those who "*were stripped of Romanian citizenship against their will or for reasons beyond their control, and their descendants*".

However, two of the provisions in the law create confusion, as the difference between them is not evident. One of them relates to those who had lost Romanian citizenship "for various reasons", while the other one refers to those who had lost citizenship "against their will for reasons beyond their control". Only the official interpretation of the Law explains the difference. The first provision refers to those who lost citizenship as a result of individual actions that unilaterally breached their citizenship contract with the Romanian state, while the second provision relates to those citizens denaturalised *en masse* as a result of territorial changes.[86] Thus, due to historical developments, the introduction of these provisions into Romanian legislation on citizenship brought several major innovations. Consequently, the right to re-acquisition of citizenship was not restricted to those who had emigrated due to political persecution or were stripped of citizenship by the communist regime; it was also granted to "all former citizens and their descendants" regardless of when or under what conditions they had lost Romanian citizenship. Although the Law does not provide expressly, the main beneficiaries of the policy of restoration and re-acquisition of citizenship have been the inhabitants of the former Soviet Socialist Republic of Moldova, and those of the provinces of Northern Bucovina and Southern Bessarabia in the Ukraine. Due to Soviet occupation, the inhabitants of these regions were forcefully stripped of their Romanian citizenship and the 1991 Law allowed to restore their legal status.[87]

It is important to note that, as initially mentioned, dual citizenship was not allowed under the 1991 Law on Citizenship. However, there was an exception – renaturalisation of former Romanian citizens holding the citizenship of another country and keeping their domicile abroad. Thus, a new category of non-resident dual citizens living in neighbouring countries was created. Moreover, the re-acquisition of the Romanian citizenship by former citizens was achieved by a simpler procedure of application in comparison with the regular naturalisation.[88]

[84] Decree Law 137 from 11 May 1990, Official Gazette of Romania 75 from 21 May 1990.
[85] *Iordachi*, op. cit. note 78, 10.
[86] *Iordachi*, EUDO Citizenship Observatory, Country Report Romania, RSCAS/EUDO-CIT-CR 2010/20, 10.
[87] *Iordachi*, op. cit. note 78, 10-11.
[88] Ibid., 11.

Similar to the Moldovan legislation, but adopted much earlier, the 1991 Constitution of Romania[89] included a provision in Art 16 (3) according to which "public functions or dignitary positions, civil or military, may be held by persons who have only Romanian citizenship and who have their domicile in Romania". But the provision did not survive over time and the amendments to the Constitution in 2003 lifted this restriction. Currently, in order to hold a public function, the requirements relate to holding Romanian citizenship and residing on the territory of Romania.[90]

5.4. Re-acquisition of Romanian citizenship by Moldovans

The Romanian Government recognised the right of re-acquisition of Romanian citizenship by those who have been deprived of this status, and adopted different forms of its transposition. Currently, the biggest number of applicants is coming from Moldova. In 2009, Moldovans constituted 67. 2% of the total amount of applications for citizenship.[91]

Moldovan citizens may re-acquire Romanian citizenship in accordance with Art 11 (1) Law on Citizenship which provides as follows:

> *(1) Persons who have acquired Romanian citizenship by birth or adoption and have lost it for reasons that are not imputable to them or whose Romanian citizenship has been withdrawn against their will, as well as their descendants to the third degree, may apply for reacquisition of Romanian citizenship or it may be granted to them, and they may keep their foreign citizenship also, and either establish their domicile in Romania or keep their domicile abroad, provided that they meet the conditions in Art 8 para (1) b),[92] c)[93] and e).[94]*

Until 2001, there was not a big number of applications for re-acquisition of Romanian citizenship compared to the total population of the Republic of Moldova: about 95.000 of Moldovans made use of this right.[95] However, the situation changed once Romania was granted a visa-free regime for the Schengen zone. Thus, the status of a Romanian citizen became very attractive to Moldovans, who continued to undergo the procedures of visa application in order to travel to the

---

89 Romanian Official Gazette, part I, No 233.

90 Art 16 (3) of the Romanian Constitution, as amended in 2003, reads as follows: "*access to public, civil, or military positions or dignities may be granted, according to the law, to persons whose citizenship is Romanian and whose domicile is in Romania.*"

91 *Eurostat News Release*, Acquisition of Citizenship in the EU: EU27 Member States Granted Citizenship to 776.000 persons in 2009, 83/2011 – 10 June 2011, at <http://epp.eurostat.ec.europa.eu/cache/ITY_PUBLIC/3-10062011-AP/EN/3-10062011-AP-EN.PDF>.

92 Art 8 b) requires that their conduct shows loyalty to the Romanian State, they do not engage in or support actions against the rule of law or national security and they declare that they have not done so in the past.

93 Art 8 c) requires that they have reached the age of 18.

94 Art 8 e) requires that they are known to have good conduct and they have not been sentenced, in Romania or abroad, for any criminal offence that would make them unworthy to be Romanian citizens.

95 *Dimulescu / Avram*, op. cit. note 22, 5.

Schengen zone. As a consequence, the Commission on Citizenship started to receive about 300 requests per day, bringing its activity to a standstill.[96] Subsequently, the Romanian Government adopted two ordinances,[97] by which the process of re-acquisition of Romanian citizenship was suspended. In particular, the application of the following articles was suspended:

1. Art 35 Law on Citizenship: "Persons who have been granted Romanian citizenship under the law shall have all the rights and freedoms, as well as the obligations provided in the Constitution and in the laws of Romania for Romanian citizens".
2. Art 10 (2) Law on Citizenship: "Para (1) shall apply also to stateless persons who are former Romanian citizens and to their descendants to the second degree inclusively."[98]
3. Art 36 (2) Law on Citizenship: "Persons who have acquired honourable citizenship shall enjoy all the civil and political rights that are acknowledged to Romanian citizens, except for the right to elect and be elected and to hold a public office."

Moreover, in 2003 the Romanian Government adopted the Emergency Ordinance no 43,[99] thus hardening the requirements on re-acquisition of citizenship, by introducing Art 10^1 into the Law on Citizenship. *Inter alia*, it stipulated that the applicant should prove knowledge of the Romanian language and its traditions in order to be integrated into the social life of Romania. Thus, the applicants had to meet all requirements imposed to aliens for naturalisation. Until 2003, these conditions were not imposed on former citizens and their descendants who lost their Romanian citizenship against their will. Moreover, all the applications had to be lodged in person, except in thoroughly justified cases, either to the Ministry of Justice, or Romanian diplomatic missions abroad; thus, lodging the request through third-party intermediaries was not possible. In addition, the introduction of Art 37 led to a sort of discrimination, by stipulating that the citizens who re-acquired Romanian citizenship and live in Romania cannot exercise their right to free movement with a Romanian passport during the first four years after their naturalisation, except in cases of studies abroad, family reunification, medical treatment or travels related to activities in Romania. Moreover, as stated in the Reasoning for the adop-

---

96 Expunere de motive pentru aprobarea Ordonantei de Urgenta a Guvernului no 160/2002 (Reasoning for the adoption of Government Emergency Ordinance no 160/2002).

97 Government Emergency Ordinance no 167/2001 on Suspension of Application of Art 35 Law on Citizenship no 21/1991, republished Official Gazette no 802 from 14 December 2001 and Government Emergency Ordinance no 160/2002 on Suspension of Application of some Provisions from Law on Citizenship no 21/1991, Official Gazette no 850 from 25 November 2002.

98 Art 10 (1) Law on Citizenship provides as follows: "Romanian citizenship may be granted also to persons who have lost such citizenship, as well as to their descendants to the second degree inclusively who apply to acquire it again, and they may keep their foreign citizenship and establish their domicile in Romania or keep their domicile abroad, provided that they meet the conditions in Art 8 (1) b) - e) accordingly.

99 Government Emergency Ordinance no 43/2003 on Amendments to Law on Citizenship 21/1991, Official Gazette Part I, no 399 from 9 June 2003.

tion of Law no. 165/2003,[100] these amendments were imposed due to the fact that most of the re-naturalisation demands were opportunistic, especially in the context of visa-free regime for Romanian citizens who wished to travel in the Schengen zone.[101]

The amendments to the Romanian legislation on citizenship were interpreted as a way of interrupting *de facto* the process of re-acquisition of Romanian citizenship. Although the European Commission repeatedly stated that the policy of re-acquisition is an internal matter of Romania, several EU agencies voiced their concerns that upon Romania's accession in January 2007, the country's policy on re-acquisition of citizenship could become an uncontrollable gate of access to the Schengen space for non-EU citizens, bypassing restrictive immigration policies.[102]

Thus, for the first time, a link was created between Romanian citizenship policy and the problem of immigration of Moldovans into the EU by means of Romanian passport. However, being caught between the upcoming EU integration and its special relationship with the Republic of Moldova, Romania chose the EU in this pre-accession period.[103] Between 2004 and 2007, only 3019 persons re-acquired Romanian citizenship, based on Art 11 of the Law on Citizenship, and 90% of them were originally from Moldova.[104]

In 2007, when Romania entered the EU, a visa regime for Moldovan citizens was introduced by Romania. This created even more controversy. Many Moldovans who were travelling to Romania either for studies, work or family issues were faced with the difficult process of acquiring Romanian visa. As a consequence, the number of applicants wishing to re-acquire the Romanian citizenship increased. However, applicants faced difficulties due to the imposed restrictions by the Romanian Government. Some citizens even tried to re-acquire the status of Romanian citizens by legal action.

As a result of domestic public and political pressure, the Law on Citizenship was modified accordingly, starting with 2007. The latest amendments to the Law, introduced in 2009,[105] relate to the degree of eligible candidates (from second-degree to third-degree of descendants of former citizens); a period of five months for examination of applications; the requests for re-acquisition of citizenship could be lodged without a residence requirement of four years (as introduced in 2002). In 2010, the Romanian Government created the National Authority for Citizenship in order to process the large number of applications for Romanian citizenship, in particular those coming from Moldova.[106]

---

[100] Expunere de motive la Legea 165/2003 pentru aprobarea Ordonantei de urgenta a Guvernului no 160/2002 privind suspendarea aplicarii unor dispozitii din Legea cetateniei romana no 21/1991 (Reasoning to the Law no 165/2003 on the adoption of the Government Emergency Ordinance no 160/2002 on the suspension of application of certain provisions from the Law no 21/1991).

[101] *Dimulescu / Avram*, op. cit. note 22, 5.

[102] *Iordachi*, op. cit. note 86, 6; *Dimulescu / Avram* ibid. 6; *Iordachi*, op. cit. note 78, 14.

[103] *Dimulescu / Avram*, op. cit. note 22, 7.

[104] Ibid. 7.

[105] Government Emergency Ordinance no 36/2009 on Amending the Law on Citizenship no 21/1991, Official Gazette no 781 from 16 November 2009.

[106] Romanian National Authority for Citizenship.

Thus, Romania was making steps ahead in its relations with Moldova. Some even considered that the policy on re-acquisition of Romanian citizenship was a possible process of political reunification.[107] Officials from Chisinau reiterated that the unification with Romania is not a subject to be discussed, as the two countries will not unite and "the integration into the EU means that the Republic of Moldova stays as Republic of Moldova."[108]

6. MOLDOVA, ROMANIA AND THE EU

Due to the close relations between Romania and Moldova, Romania pursues one priority in the ENP: to bring Moldova on a solid EU accession path. One of the diplomatic successes of Romania was setting up a group of EU Member States that would support Moldova in its attempt to achieve European integration.[109] It was originally called "Group of Friends", and later renamed to "Group for the European Action of the Republic of Moldova". Launched at the beginning of 2010 as an informal ministerial mechanism, it constitutes a platform for dialogue and an exchange of ideas on advancing relations between the EU and Moldova. It is an informal and open initiative and any Member State can participate.[110] Initially, it was co-chaired by France which was an important step in order not to create the impression that only countries from Eastern Europe supported this idea. The group consisted of Romania, France, Austria, Estonia, Lithuania, Latvia, Sweden, Hungary, Poland, Germany, United Kingdom, Czech Republic, Slovakia, Slovenia and Italy. Up to date (April 2014), it had eight meetings. It might be observed that the level of interest differs from state to state. For example, the position of France has changed over time. It gradually turned its back on Moldova in the visa dialogue and opposed the accession of Romania to the Schengen zone, seeing the strong ties between Moldova and Romania and the Romanian citizenship policy as critical issues.[111]

During the eighth meeting, on 10 February 2014, the officials tackled issues of the political situation in Moldova, as well as the positive evolution of the dialogue

---

[107] *Culic*, Dual Citizenship Policies in Central and Eastern Europe, Working Papers in Romanian Minority Studies, Institutul pentru studierea problemelor minoritatilor nationale, 2009, 17; "Russian Press: President of the Parliament, Supporter of Unification with Romania" (29 August 2009), at <http://www.ziare.com/international/al-qaida/presa-rusa-presedintele-parlamentului-moldovean-sustinator-al-unirii-cu-romania-869165>.

[108] "Mihai Ghimpu spune ca nu va promova of politica de unire cu Romania" (6 September 2009) at <http://www.ziare.com/international/stiri-externe/mihai-ghimpu-spune-ca-nu-va-promova-o-politica-de-unire-cu-romania-877258>.

[109] The Mission of the Republic of Moldova to the European Union, Political Dialogue RM – EU.

[110] Ministry of Foreign Affairs of Romania, "Sixth Meeting of the Group for the European Action of the Republic of Moldova" Press Release, 25 May 2012.

[111] *Ghinea / Dinu / Ivan*, Cum am folosit fereastra de oportunitate. Bilantul unui an de relansare a relatiilor Romania – Republica Moldova, CRPE (Centrul Român de Politici Europene) Policy Memo 19, December 2010, 15-16.

with the EU. All sides expressed support for the signing of the EU-Moldova AA, as well as the completion of visa liberalisation in the nearest future. The European officials conveyed consolidated messages on continuous support for Moldova's European integration, as well as for the reform process, and assured of their political and financial support for Moldova to this end.[112]

As previously noted, the relationship between the EU and Moldova has advanced significantly in recent years. However, at present the EU does not appear to attach much priority to granting Moldova a completely visa-free regime, perhaps due to the fear in some quarters about large scale immigration of Moldovan citizens into the EU. However, as has been proven by the Western Balkans' visa-free regime, such a step would not negatively affect the EU. For example, Macedonia did not face an exodus of its population after receiving visa liberalisation. In the case of Moldova, there is a strong case to be made that the situation would be the same, and it may be questioned who would actually leave the country if those members of the labour force that were willing to leave are already living in the EU. According to some estimates, the number of people who can eventually migrate is around 100,000 people, while, interestingly, the Moldovan authorities expect that many Moldovans, especially those who are illegally residing in the EU, will return to Moldova. That said, it may be noted that a considerable number of Moldovans already hold Romanian passports and many have also requested Romanian citizenship.[113]

On 27 March 2011, Romania, together with Bulgaria, were meant to accede to the Schengen zone, based on a report prepared by the Schengen Evaluation Group, thus concluding the phase of implementation of the Schengen *acquis*. The Council, in its conclusions from its meetings from 9-10 June 2011, certified the preparedness of both countries to join the Schengen zone, reiterating that this process should take place no later than September 2011.[114] The integration of the countries into the Schengen zone should be effected by the Council, by unanimous decision of all Governments of the States members of the Schengen Zone.[115] However, during the JHA Council meeting of 22 September 2011, France and Germany opposed Romania's and Bulgaria's accession to the Schengen zone.[116]

One of the reasons of this postponement supported by officials from Paris referred specifically to Moldova: in November 2010, the Secretary of State for European Affairs (at that time), *Pierre Lellouche*, stated that the border between Roma-

---

112 Embassy of the Republic of Moldova to the Republic of Portugal, News from Moldova, "Foreign Minister attends meeting of the European Action Group for Moldova", <http://www.portugalia.mfa.md/news-from-moldova-en/?news=496464>.

113 *Litra*, Visa-Free Perspectives for Moldova: A Never Ending Story or an Accomplishable Task? Moldova's Foreign Policy Statewatch, 2010 no 5, Institutul pentru Dezvoltare si Initiative Sociale IDIS Viitorul, p. 3.

114 Council of the European Union, Justice and Home Affairs, 3096th Meeting, Luxembourg 9 - 10 June 2011, Doc 11008/1, Presse 161, PR CO 7.

115 European Parliament, Parliamentary Question for Oral Answer: Accession of Bulgaria and Romania to Schengen, O-000221/2011.

116 European Parliament, Parliamentary Question for Oral Answer: Accession of Bulgaria and Romania to Schengen, O-000221/2011; Council of the European Union, Justice and Home Affairs, 3096th meeting, Luxembourg 9-10 June 2011, Doc 14464/11, Presse 320, PR CO 53.

nia and Moldova is badly monitored, due to the distribution of thousands of Romanian passports across the border (i.e. in Moldova). *Laurent Wauquiez*, who succeeded *Lellouche*, adopted a similar position.[117] Moreover, during the summer of 2010, several Western newspapers[118] published articles insinuating that Romania has pulled Moldova into the EU through the back door, granting citizenship to a large number of Moldovans.[119] Furthermore, it was argued that Romania has not complied with EU legislation on the granting of citizenship and that Moldovans will "invade" Europe, and, as a result, crime will increase in the Member States.[120] Indeed, in the context of Romania's accession to the EU and considering all benefits, an increasing number of Moldovans are applying for Romanian citizenship.

In December 2010, *Brice Hortefeux*, former French Minister of Interior, and *Thomas de Maiziere*, former German Federal Minister of Interior, asked the European Commission, in a joint letter, to postpone the expansion of the Schengen Area, pointing out that

> *"[...] it would not be realistic nor responsible to neglect the deficiencies identified. [...] The absence of a satisfactory juridical and administrative environment in the fields of security and justice, persisting corruption at different levels and worrying levels of organised crime. We consider that the decision should be taken when the main causes of worries would be removed and when the two countries would begin irreversible progress in their fight against corruption, of organised crime, as well as of reforming their judicial systems".*[121]

Consequently, the two states pleaded, in 2011, for a postponement of Romania and Bulgaria's Schengen accession to a later date (1 January 2014).

Furthermore, when the Romanian Government opposed the simplification of procedure of re-acquisition of Romanian citizenship, the Senate made reference to Romania's obligations under the EU Treaty of Accession[122], arguing that it would lead to potential conflicts with the European Commission.[123] However, the Treaty of Accession is silent on this particular issue, as it is *prima facie* Member States who determine the conditions under which citizenship is conferred. Thus, the Ro-

---

[117] *Dimulescu / Avram*, op. cit. note 22, 4.

[118] Der Spiegel, Le Figaro, Daily Star.

[119] Der Spiegel, "Romanian Passports for Moldovans Entering through the Back Door" (13 July 2010) <http://www.spiegel.de/international/europe/romanian-passports-for-moldovans-entering-the-eu-through-the-back-door-a-706338.html>.

[120] *Litra*, Are the Moldovans Who Hold Romanian Passports a Devastating Threat for EU? Moldova's Foreign Policy Statewatch, Issue 10, Institutul pentru Dezvoltare si Initiative Sociale IDIS Viitorul September 2010

[121] Euractiv, Romania Fumes at Franco-German Schengen Blockade (22 December 2010), <http://www.euractiv.com/enlargement/france-germany-block-romanias-schengen-bid-news-500856>.

[122] Treaty between (Member States of the European Union) and the Republic of Bulgaria and Romania concerning the accession of the Republic of Bulgaria and Romania to the European Union OJ 2005 L157, 11 and the Protocol concerning the conditions and arrangements for admission of the Republic of Bulgaria and Romania to the European Union OJ 2005 L 157, 29.

[123] *Iordachi*, op. cit. note 86, 17.

manian policy of granting citizenship to its former citizens is strictly and exclusively regulated by the Romanian legislation and there is no formal or legal connection between the Schengen acquis and legislation on conferring citizenship.[124] Moreover, in its pre-accession negotiations, the European Commission did not interfere with the citizenship regime of Romania, as it was the case of Latvia, Estonia and, to some extent, the Czech Republic.[125]

As discussed previously, there is no legal instrument at the European level that would regulate the policies of Member States on conferring citizenship, as it is directly connected to the sovereignty of states. At the same time, the other Member States are required to recognise the nationality duly granted by another Member State.

Some Member States[126] argued that the Romanian policy on re-acquisition of citizenship created "new" Romanian nationals and this process may impact both the demographic equilibrium and immigration fluxes in Europe.[127] Moreover, there is a particular concern in Italy that the immigration flow of Romanian nationals increased after its accession to the EU.[128] In the absence of a concrete EU action and the probability that Italy might, at some point, refuse to recognise the "new" Romanian nationals and invoke that Romania infringes provisions of Art 4 (2) TFEU on loyal co-operation, by granting "en masse" naturalisation to Moldovan citizens. Romania, on the other hand, will rebut that its autonomy in the domain of nationality law follows from the principle that the EU respects the national identities of the Member States as laid down in Art 4 (3) TEU. Furthermore, the re-acquisition policy for former nationals and their descendants living outside its territory is an element in the reconstruction of Romanian identity. Nonetheless, Italy uses a similar line of reasoning to justify its own preferential regime for co-ethnics living in Latin America. After all, the state which claims to suffer negative effects to its demographic equilibrium as a result of the nationality policies of other Member States will, by invoking the principle of loyal co - operation, claim that these policies "ought not change its own national identity by devious means".[129]

However, with due regard to all statements, there is no accepted policy on the Union level as regards citizenship laws and policies, due to the lack of experience within the EU and universally accepted standards. Moreover, it should be reiterated that the few existing international standards on nationality laws are by no means followed through by the "old" Member States.[130]

---

[124] *Dimulescu / Avram*, op. cit. note 22.
[125] *Swider*, op. cit. note 14, 4.
[126] France, Italy, Germany.
[127] Department of European Affairs of Italy, Andrea Ronchi, Preoccupazioni su cittadinanza romena e moldavi (29 April 2009) at <http://www.politicheeuropee.it/comunicazione/16576/moldova-ronchi-preoccupazione-su-cittadinanza-romena-a-moldavi>.
[128] *Uccellini*, Outsiders after Accession: The Case of Romanian Migrants in Italy, 1989 – 2009, Political Perspectives 2010, Vol. 4(2), 70-85.
[129] *Margiotta / Vonk*, op. cit. note 21, 18 - 19.
[130] *Swider*, op. cit. note 14, 5.

7. CONCLUSION

As the Moldovan case has shown, a small country can make further progress on migration issues, due to the strong political will of its government, as well as the involvement of Moldovan civil society – its own citizens. While it is indeed a success story that within a relatively short period of time Moldova managed to leave behind its partners from the EaP. Currently, Moldova is the only EaP country to have been granted visa-free travel to the EU, based solely on its merits in meeting the benchmarks of the VLAP.

While some countries were reluctant to move towards a visa-free regime, as it might cause new possible waves of illegal migrants, others have debated the re-acquisition of Romanian citizenship by Moldovan nationals. It may be concluded from this research that Romania and Moldova are not exceptional cases. Indeed, many other EU Member States have similar policies of naturalisation of their former nationals and, if the question is ever raised, it is possible that they would use the same reasoning as Romania to reconstruct their national identity. Therefore, Romanian citizenship policy does not contravene any standards, either at international or at European levels. Moreover, as observed, the EU does not have any powers to interfere with a Member State's policy on granting citizenship. However, it has been noted that national citizenship policy affects the Union and this process is not left unseen: it influences the EU in its policy making, particularly with respect to migration or asylum issues.

Moldova and the EU have developed a very positive relationship in recent years, with the former receiving support of the Union institutions and some Member States to assist with its integration into the EU. Lastly, this leaves the question of whether Moldova should choose visa liberalisation or Romanian citizenship? Although visa liberalisation arguably brings citizens closer to the EU, it does not confer any comprehensive rights as provided for in the Treaties. Meanwhile, Romania is a Member of the EU and its citizens enjoy a full range of rights and freedoms. This in turn raises a further question: should the Romanian policy be seen as a gate to the EU? This question should be answered in the affirmative. It is clear that by applying for Romanian citizenship, Moldovan citizens exercise their rights conferred by Romanian law – and it may be seen as a re-acquisition of citizenship previously lost against their own will. Moldovan citizens have taken significant steps in integrating themselves into the EU. Now it is time for Moldova to integrate itself into the EU.

Aleqsandre Devidze

Judicial Activism of Constitutional Courts as a Means of Promoting EU Integration: The Case of Georgia

"Art 13 AA EU-Georgia: Rule of law and respect for human rights and fundamental freedoms

1. In their cooperation in the area of freedom, security and justice the Parties shall attach particular importance to further promoting the rule of law, including the independence of the judiciary, access to justice, and the right to a fair trial.

2. The Parties will cooperate fully on the effective functioning of institutions in the areas of law enforcement and the administration of justice.

3. The respect for human rights and fundamental freedoms will guide all cooperation on freedom, security and justice."

"Art 12 AA EU-Republic of Moldova: Rule of law

1. In their cooperation in the area of freedom, security and justice the Parties shall attach particular importance to the promotion of the rule of law, including the independence of the judiciary, access to justice, and the right to a fair trial.

2. The Parties will cooperate fully on the effective functioning of institutions in the areas of law enforcement and the administration of justice.

3. The respect for human rights and fundamental freedoms will guide all cooperation on freedom, security and justice."

1. Introduction

The proliferation of constitutional courts in the 20th century throughout Europe and their impact on legal and political processes is highly evident. Constitutional courts in Europe went far beyond the traditional paradigm of judicial bodies and catalysed transition processes from planned to market economy, from communism and authoritarian regimes to democracy and rule of law based governance. The courts in certain cases fostered the process of "returning to Europe" and contributed to the realisation of aspirations of their respective countries towards European integration. Several courts from Central and East European and South East European countries are best examples in this regard, in particular the Constitutional Courts of Hungary, Poland, Slovenia and Croatia.

On the other hand, the first generation constitutional courts[1] of Germany, Italy and Spain are characterised as strong and activist national courts in Europe. At the regional level in Europe, two strong and activist "quasi constitutional courts" – the ECtHR and the ECJ - are operating, and it is obvious that possessing activist and strong constitutional courts is part of European constitutionalism.

From the EU's perspective and according to certain MEPs, "efficient and independent judiciary (*inter alia* with constitutional courts) is significant and has principal meaning in the EU's relation with third countries."[2] However, possessing an activist constitutional court is not and has never been a precondition for countries aspiring towards the EU. Rather, the preconditions in the integration process are a commitment to strengthening the rule of law, consolidating democracy and respecting human rights and fundamental freedoms, which are enshrined and reflected in the relevant external policies of EU towards third states, for instance in the ENP AP for Georgia,[3] in the EaP[4] and in the EU's agreements with third countries (for instance objectives and / or human rights clauses in AAs). It is noteworthy that one of the objectives of the EU - Georgia AA is to "enhance cooperation in the area of freedom, security and justice with the aim of reinforcing the rule of law and the respect for human rights and fundamental freedoms[5] in addition. Art 13 of EU – Georgia AA contains the condition that "In their cooperation in the area of freedom, security and justice the Parties shall attach particular importance to further promoting the rule of law, including the independence of the judiciary, access to justice, and the right to a fair trial"[6] and "The respect for human rights and fundamental freedoms will guide all cooperation on freedom, security and justice."[7] Accordingly, attainment of ENP objectives, observing AA objectives and application of EU *acquis* will be impossible if the constitutional courts disregard their countries' will to align themselves with the EU. "Engines of European integration" of third states are basically the legislative and executive branches, however as the experience of countries from Central, Eastern and South Eastern Europe illustrates, European integration of third countries requires active participation of the constitutional courts in the process as well. Therefore, this paper attempts to explore the significance of

---

1 *Sólyom*, The Role of Constitutional Courts in the Transition to Democracy With Special Reference to Hungary, International Sociology, 2003, 133 (135).

2 *Werner Schulz and Knut Fleckenstein* - personal interview with MEPs during a REEES study trip to Brussels (21 September 2011). See also *Cremona*, The European Neighbourhood Policy: Legal and Institutional Issues, Working Paper of Center on Democracy, Development, and the Rule of Law Stanford Institute for International Studies, 2004, No 25.

3 Commission Communication to the Council on European Neighbourhood Policy Recommendations for Armenia, Azerbaijan, Georgia and for Egypt and Lebanon COM (2005) 72 final of 2.3.2005. Also ENP AP for Georgia (2006), available at <http://ec.europa.eu/world/enp/documents_en.htm#2>.

4 Commission Communication to the European Parliament, the Council, the European Economic and Social Committee and the Committee of the Regions, on Cooperation in the Area of Justice and Home Affairs within the Eastern Partnership, COM (2011) 564 final of 26 September 2011, 15-16.

5 Association Agreement between the EU and the EURATOM and their Member States, of the one part, and Georgia, of the other part, Art 1 (2.F).

6 Ibid. Art 13 para 1.

7 Ibid. Art 13 para 3.

constitutional – judicial review in the European integration process and to find an answer to the normative question whether judicial activism of constitutional courts and, in particular, activism of the Constitutional Court of Georgia, may foster the European integration of the country.

2. THE CONCEPT OF JUDICIAL ACTIVISM

2.1. The specific relevance of judicial activism for EU integration

Judicial activism is closely connected to the dynamic-objective reading of constitutional texts by the relevant courts, or in other words, to constitutional interpretation which requires continual updating of the Constitution in line with the perceived community and social expectations. Judicial activism implies active reception of foreign constitutional standards by the courts as well.[8]

Most of the constitutional courts of the countries of Central and Eastern Europe were judicially activist courts and carried out an essential role in the political, economic and social reforms of their respective countries in the transition phase. Constitutional Courts of Hungary and Croatia, for instance, were actively applying comparative constitutional law, in particular European constitutional law,[9] and, in addition, after the first years of judicial activism which were mainly related to internal reforms and the fashioning of a new democratic system, these courts have shown that they turned into important actors of the European integration process as well, in response to a new social demand – the alignment with and the return to Europe.[10] The Constitutional Court of Hungary relied on and constructed itself even a "national imagery." The idea behind this was that Hungary always belonged to Europe and was currently returning to it and there was a necessity to adapt to European legal norms and values.[11] "According to *Scheppele*, in Hungary Europe was seen as the base of liberal constitutionalism, and having a powerful court was part of being European."[12]

---

[8] *French*, Judicial Activists – Mythical Monsters? Southern Cross University Law Review 2008, 59 (71).

[9] *Sólyom*, op cit. note 1, 136. See also the speech of the President of Constitutional Court of Republic of Croatia at the 20th Anniversary of the Constitutional Court of Republic of Hungary, 24 November, 2009: *Omejec*, Abstract Review of Laws by the Croatian Constitutional Court: Between the Poles of Judicial Activism and Self-Restraint, available at <http://mkab.hu/index.php?id=conference>.

[10] *Piqani*, Constitutional Courts in Central and Eastern Europe and their Attitude towards European Integration, European Journal of Legal Studies 2007, 1 (2).

[11] *Boulanger,* A Government of Judges or Better Democracy? Normative and Empirical Aspects of Post-Communist Judicial Activism: The Hungarian Experience, paper presented at European Consortium for Political Research Conference, Marburg (2003) 19.

[12] *Scheppele*, Imagined Europe, paper presented at plenary address, Law and Society Association Meeting, Glasgow, 1996.

2.2. Legality and legitimacy of judicial activism

Every year a vast number of articles and research papers is dedicated to the issue of judicial activism. This is one of the most contested terms in constitutional law and it is often said to be "a court's decision one does not like."[13] Judicial activism of constitutional courts, which we advocate as one of the significant attributes in Georgia's European integration process, is attacked from two fronts. The first is the counter-majoritarian arguments to constitutional-judicial review which challenges the legitimacy of constitutional justice itself (institutional challenge). The second argument indicates that judicial activism is in contrast to and departs from constitutional intent (substantive challenge). As for the institutional issue, while holding the occupation in the constitutional courts, judges overrule laws and policies of directly elected governments and legislatures, that is to say, "judges who are not politically responsible are telling the people's elected representatives that they cannot govern as they'd like, because constitutional-judicial review gives unelected judges a special position above and inside the political system and accordingly they can declare decisions produced by elected governments and legislatures."[14] Here the question - where is peoples' say? – arises. This is known as the counter-majoritarian objection to judicial review. Therefore, the more a court is activist and a strong institution, the more the questions arise concerning its legitimacy.

In response to the counter-majoritarian objection to judicial review, it is often held that "courts can be more democratic ... than legislatures."[15] The fact that parliament is elected, while on the other hand, judges are not, is not sufficient to assume that the former is more democratic than the latter because "majorities sometimes do not have power to decide... And in addition quite often the realization of political equality through elections, representation, and legislative process is imperfect. Electoral systems are often flawed... All in all, it should be said in all fairness that the election is not the end of democratic society or democracy. One should also bear in mind that democratic legitimacy of the judge may be attained not only through democratic election but if the judge defends democracy itself. "[16] The constitution is the people's instrument on giving their say, therefore the review of legality of an act against compliance with the constitution would in fact be the supervision of the acts' conformity with the people's say.[17] Furthermore, judges are select-

---

[13] *Kline*, Judicial Independence: Rebuffing Congressional Attacks on the Third Branch, Kentucky Law Journal 1998, 679 (688).

[14] *Doli / Korenica,* A Comparison Between Judicial-Constitutional Review Models: Towards a Hypothetical Approach on the Logic of Each Model, Group for Legal and Political Studies Press, available at <http://www.ceeol.com/aspx/issuedetails.aspx?issueid=32445dac-1399-40e3-a244-35f409cea397&articleId=32ded6af-8a91-4e65-8bde-68ced50d99fc>.

[15] *Boulanger*, Europeanisation Through Judicial Activism, Hungarian Constitutional Court's Legitimacy and "Return to Europe," in *Sadurski* (ed), Spreading Democracy and Rule of Law? The Impact of EU Enlargement on the Rule of Law, Democracy and Constitutionalism in Post-communist Legal Orders, 2005, 276.

[16] *Leon / Rivera,* The Counter-Majoritarian Difficulties, Bickel and Mexican Case, Mexican Law Review 2010, 25 (33).

[17] Doli / Korenica, op. cit. note 14, 1 (3).

ed from the "people that are not segregated by lines of race, religion, income and wealth, for instance."[18] In addition, judges do have qualities that other public servants do not possess and they exercise their duties transparently.

Concerning judicial activism of constitutional courts, we think that activism is justified to the extent that the court safeguards and promotes fundamental rights and freedoms. Therefore, the decisions in which the Constitutional Court of Georgia imported (or in the future will import) a high level of human rights protection standards and by means of teleological interpretation will recognise rights that are not indicated in the Constitution, even though they are a product of judicial activism, will still remain legal and legitimate.

As far as Georgia is concerned, the answer on legality and legitimacy has to be found in the Constitution of Georgia itself. Three articles of the Constitution of Georgia give the Court the possibility to be activist. The first is Art 6 according to which: "The legislation of Georgia shall correspond to universally recognized principles and rules of international law. An international treaty or agreement of Georgia unless it contradicts the Constitution of Georgia, the Constitutional Agreement,[19] shall take precedence over domestic normative acts."

Another article which might "legalize" judicial activism is Art 7 of the Constitution of Georgia: "The state shall recognize and protect universally recognized human rights and freedoms as eternal and supreme human values. While exercising authority, the people and the state shall be bound by these rights and freedoms as directly applicable law." Finally, Art 39 of the Constitution will always justify recognition and importing of rights that were not expressly laid down in the Constitution: "The Constitution of Georgia shall not deny other universally recognised rights, freedoms and guarantees of an individual and a citizen, which are not referred to herein but stem inherently from the principles of the Constitution."

These are legal grounds that *might* be referred to as the "legal basis" for judicial activism. Without any doubt what is legal is not legitimate *per se.* Legitimacy in political sociology is described as a capacity of the system to engender and maintain the belief that the existing political institutions are the most appropriate ones for society or, in other words, a value whereby decisions and acts of institutions or public officials are recognised and accepted as right and proper.[20] In reality, there is no textbook answer on the legitimacy of judicial activism, because it greatly depends on various circumstances, *inter alia,* on the society's assessment of the activity of the Court.

In conclusion, it should be noted that activism of the Constitutional Court of Georgia will be justified and legitimate as long as it preserves constitutional rights and freedoms. The analysis of the practice of the Constitutional Court of Georgia below illustrates that it tries to expand and evaluate human rights in the Georgian constitutional legal order and this attitude has to be maintained and developed further, since it supports, on the one hand, enhancing human rights standards in na-

---

[18] *Lever,* Democracy and Judicial Review: Are They Really Incompatible? Perspective on Politics, 2009, 805 (809).

[19] There is only one constitutional agreement in Georgian constitutional legal order – Constitutional Agreement between Georgia and Apostle Autocephalous Orthodox Church of Georgia.

[20] *Lipset*, Political Man: The Social Bases of Politics (1960) at 77.

tional legal order, and on the other hand, contributes to the integration process in a manner described below.

3. GEORGIA'S ASPIRATION TOWARDS EUROPEAN INTEGRATION AND THE ROLE OF THE CONSTITUTIONAL COURT OF GEORGIA IN THE INTEGRATION PROCESS

3.1. Introduction

The concept of European integration is strongly attached to the idea of establishing a "kind of United States of Europe,"[21] to the idea of Unity of European countries, which was articulated long before the arrival of the twentieth century.[22] The CoE and the EU, notwithstanding the fact that they are different institutions and hold two different vocations, both stem from and are results of this idea. The unification of Europe is a continuous process.[23] This process together with its results might be called European integration. Hence, whenever we refer to a certain country's aspiration towards European integration we refer to that country's will and intention to align itself closely to the prime European structures – such as the CoE and in particular the EU.

It should be said in all fairness that Georgia's European vector had already taken shape before the "Rose Revolution" of 2003. Georgia became the first country in the Caucasus region to join the CoE in 1999. But in the EU–Georgia relations the determining factor was the "Rose Revolution", and since then both the legislative and executive branches of the Government of Georgia reflect their European aspirations in their official statements or in their respective legislations.[24] When discussing the issue of certain countries' aspiration towards European integration, it is also important to take into account public opinion. The UNDP public opinion survey on the attitude of Georgians towards the EU shows that 79 % of respondents would vote for EU membership if there was a referendum. On the question "which organisation should Georgia join first – NATO or the EU" the majority of respondents answered in favour of the EU.[25] The former President of Georgia, *Saakashvili*, meeting with the EU High Representative for Foreign Affairs and Security Policy, on the occasion of launching the AAs for the South Caucasus countries, stated:

---

[21] Winston Churchill's speech at the University of Zurich in 1946, cited in *Lenaerts / Van Nuffel*, Constitutional Law of the European Union (2005) 24.

[22] *Graig / De Burca,* EU Law - Text Cases and Materials (2008) 4.

[23] *Huber / Esterbauer,* The European Neutrals, The Council of Europe and the European Communities, Centre International de Formation Européenne - Austria Publications, 1998 Vol 9, 9.

[24] The Parliament of Georgia, Resolution N 828, 1997. See also De Waal, Georgia's Choices - Charting the Future in Uncertain Times, Carnegie Endowment for International Peace (2011) 33, available at <www.carnegieendowment.org/files/georgias_choices.pdf>.

[25] *Eurasian Partnership Foundation*, Public Opinion Survey on Attitudes towards European Integration in Georgia (2010) available at <www.epfound.ge/files/eusurveyappendix_georgia_aug09.pdf>.

"Georgia is not paving the way to Europe, rather Georgia is part of Europe and is returning to the European institutions."[26] This approach is similar to the attitude of countries from Central and Eastern Europe towards the EU and reminds us of the case of Hungary, since in Hungary public officials were also indicating that Hungary was always part of Europe and returning to European constitutionalism. The EU clearly expressed its attitude towards its neighbouring countries by apprising the relations as "more than partnership but less than membership".[27] However, the recent Resolution of the EP adopted on 17 April 2014 "On EaP countries and in particular destabilisation of Eastern Ukraine" indicates that Georgia, like any other European country, has a European perspective. According to the resolution, "AAs with Ukraine and the other EaP countries do not constitute the final goal in their relations with the EU... pursuant to Article 49 of the TEU, Georgia, Moldova and Ukraine – like any other European state – have a European perspective and may apply to become members of the Union provided that they adhere to the principles of democracy, respect fundamental freedoms and human and minority rights and ensure the rule of law."[28] Declaring the recognition of Georgia's European perspective based on Art 49 TEU is *inter alia* an outcome of Georgia's aspirations and great will to deepen and intensify EU integration. Henceforth the core question is how and by which legal means is the Constitutional Court able to realise Georgia's goal and its aspiration towards the EU?

3.2. The role of the Constitutional Court of Georgia in the European integration process

"Scarcely any political question arises ... that is not resolved sooner or later into a judicial question."[29] EU–Georgian relations are based on a contractual relationship, a policy relationship, and each of them sets its obligations and objectives which should be observed in order to deepen relations with the EU.

For instance, the ENP AP for Georgia of 2006 determined "strengthening rule of law and democratic institutions, respect for human rights and fundamental freedoms in compliance with international commitments of Georgia (such as the PCA and membership in the CoE, OSCE and the UN)"[30] as the first priority area. In accordance with the ENP AP, respecting and promoting human rights in accordance with European and international standards still remains the challenge in the 2011 – 2013 ENP National Indicative Programme.[31]

---

26 *Mikheil Saakashvili's* speech on the occasion of launching negotiations on AA with Georgia, Batumi, 15 July 2010, joint press conference of *Katherine Ashton* available at <www.president.gov.ge/ge/PressOffice/News/SpeechesAndStatements?p=5318&i=6>.

27 *Prodi,* Speech on A Wider Europe - A Proximity Policy as the Key to Stability, (2002) available at <http://europa.eu/rapid/pressReleasesAction.do?reference=SPEECH/02/619>.

28 EP, Resolution of 17 April 2014 on Russian Pressure on Eastern Partnership Countries and in particular Destabilisation of Eastern Ukraine, (2014/2699(RSP).

29 *Schwartz*, The Struggle for Constitutional Justice in Post-Communist Europe (2000) 4.

30 ENP AP for Georgia, 2006.

31 ENPI , National Indicative Programme for Georgia, 2011 – 2013, para 2.3.1.1, 11.

In a similar vein, the Commission Communication on Cooperation in the Area of Justice and Home Affairs within the EaP indicates that "the promotion and mainstreaming of gender equality and fight against discrimination, as fundamental principles of EU law, shall also be included in the objectives of the co-operation plan, and the co-operation with EaP countries should focus on strengthening the respect for human rights, including respect for the rights of the child, freedom of expression, freedom of assembly, and the rights of persons belonging to minorities."[32] Hence, EU integration will *inter alia* depend on the implementation of international and regional human rights standards which are highly relevant to the co-operation with EaP partner countries, and with Georgia as well.[33]

Since the early nineties agreements concluded between the EC and third countries systematically contain a clause stating that human rights constitute an essential element of the agreement and disregarding of that essential element might result in the suspension of the agreement. The EC / EU has concluded agreements containing human rights and democracy clauses with approximately 150 countries.[34] Scholars are questioning whether human rights and democracy clauses impose any obligation to comply with human rights and democratic principles.[35] However, *Fierro* argues that human rights clauses envisage that positive measures have to be taken by third countries since European Council and Council of Ministers first mandated human rights clauses in 1991.[36] In a landmark resolution of November 1991 the Council of Ministers stated that "the Community and its Member States will give high priority to a positive approach to the conditionality that stimulates respect for human rights and encourages democracy."[37] *Fierro* further argues that teleological interpretation (which is also supported by the Vienna Convention on the Law Treaties) will lead to the understanding of human rights clauses as a positive conditionality.[38] The resolution of the EP of 2011 on Georgia recommended to the Council, the Commission and the EEAS "incorporation in the Association Agreement of clauses on the protection and promotion of human rights reflecting the highest international and European standards, taking full advantage of the Council of Europe and OSCE framework and insisting particularly on the rights of internally-displaced persons (IDPs) and persons belonging to national and other minorities."[39] Accordingly, the EU–Georgia AA contains human rights and democracy clauses. In the preamble of the AA parties express their commitment to the abundant international standards of human rights protection,[40] and in its objectives the AA sets the goal strengthening democracy and reinforcing the rule of law and the respect for human rights and fundamental freedoms in Georgia.[41] According to

[32] COM(2011) 564 final, para 3.5.2, 15.
[33] COM(2011) 564 final para 3.5.2, 16.
[34] *Bartels,* Human Rights and Democracy Clauses in the EU's International Agreements (2005) 5, available at <www.pedz.uni-mannheim.de/daten/edz-ma/ep/05/pe363.284-en.pdf>.
[35] Ibid. 65.
[36] *Fierro*, The EU's Approach to Human Rights Conditionality in Practice (2003) 386.
[37] Council of Ministers, Resolution of the Council and of the Member States meeting in the Council on Human Rights, Democracy and Development, 28 November 1991, No 10107/91.
[38] *Fierro*, op. cit. note 36, 386.
[39] EP, Resolution of 17 November 2011, (1) (r).
[40] Draft EU – Georgia AA, 2.
[41] Ibid. Art 1 (2) (C, F).

Art 2 AA, "Respect for the democratic principles, human rights and fundamental freedoms is an essential element of the agreement", and therefore it creates the obligation on Georgia to take positive measures in this regard. Positive measures in the human rights field have to be taken by the executive and legislative branches of government. Nevertheless, the issue of protection of fundamental rights and freedoms very often leads to judicial questions and, in particular, to constitutional question. While adjudicating a case, the Constitutional Court of Georgia may adhere strictly to the Constitution, simply because judges have sworn that they would be subject and bound by the Constitution, to nobody and nothing, save the Constitution.[42] Therefore, any constitutional decision which is based strictly on the constitutional text without referring to the abundant international practice will be legal. However, reception of comparative constitutional law (referring to decisions of foreign courts) and interpreting fundamental rights and freedoms in accordance with European and international standards, also treatment of the constitution as a living instrument in order to respond to new social demands, requires activism of the constitutional court. Henceforth, we think that attainment of ENP and EaP objectives and clauses on promoting human rights protection in the AA will be observed if the Constitutional Court of Georgia is a strong and activist court. The Court is best placed to attain ENP and EaP objectives by means of respecting fundamental rights and freedoms in compliance with Georgia's international commitment. But in order to discuss the benefits of activism of a constitutional court for European integration we have to define the term "judicial activism" itself.

4. JUDICIAL ACTIVISM OF THE CONSTITUTIONAL COURT OF GEORGIA AS A CATALYST OF EUROPEAN INTEGRATION

We think that judicial activism of the Constitutional Court of Georgia should be expressed in three principal ways: 1) reception and active application of European human rights protection standards; 2) judicial activism by means of teleological interpretation of the Constitution; and 3) readiness and willingness to apply and explore the EU *acquis*. We will discuss each of them in details below.

4.1. Fostering European integration by applying European standards of human rights protection:

> *"Toute Société dans laquelle la garantie des Droits n'est pas assure... n'a point de Constitution."*[43]

The EU sees countries as reliable partners if they share the EU's goals and values and express their readiness to act in their support.[44] The core values, protection of

[42] Art 9 of the Organic Law on the Constitutional Court of Georgia (1996); Art 8 of the Constitutional Act on the Constitutional Court of the Republic of Croatia (2002); Art 7 of the Law on the Constitutional Court of the Republic of Lithuania (1993).

[43] Déclaration des Droits de l'Homme et du Citoyen de 1789 Art 16.

fundamental rights and freedoms and respect for democracy and rule of law, are essentially interdependent and complement each other.[45] Since Georgia is aspiring to European integration, the Constitutional Court of Georgia while interpreting fundamental rights and freedoms has to be focused and oriented on the EU's human rights protection standards.

Following the Lisbon amendments, Art 6 TEU now views the human rights protection system from three angles: the first is the EU Charter of Fundamental Rights which has the same legal value as treaties; the second is the ECHR to which the EU shall accede; and finally fundamental freedoms as they result from the constitutional traditions common to the Member States, shall constitute general principles of the Union's law. As mentioned above, the EU will accede to the ECHR and, according to the EU Charter of Fundamental Rights, in particular according to Art 52 (3) of the Charter "in so far as the Charter contains rights which correspond to rights guaranteed by the Convention, the meaning and scope of those [Charter] rights shall be the same."[46] Also taking into account the Memorandum of Understanding between the CoE and the EU the latter "regards the Council of Europe as the Europe-wide reference source for human rights[47] and ... recognizes the unique contribution of the ECHR in human rights protection field ...".[48] Hence whenever we refer to the European standard of human rights protection we basically refer to the ECHR and the case law of the ECtHR since the Convention, together with the case law of the ECt HR and the EU Charter of Fundamental Human Rights, constitutes the European human rights protection standard.[49]

The ECHR has to be distinguished from the international treaties, since *a)* it is the human rights treaty which itself deserves a distinctive approach; *b)* it is the European human rights treaty which sets as its objective the unity and integration of European states (to which Georgia is aspiring) through evaluating common human rights protection standards in Europe; *c) pacta sunt servanda* requires that states apply the case law of the ECtHR since achieving the Convention objectives would be jeopardised without taking case law into consideration. Georgia ratified the ECHR in 1999. According to the Law of Georgia on International Treaties, the international agreements of Georgia are an integral part of the legislation of Georgia."[50] Therefore, the ECHR is directly applicable law in Georgia's constitutional legal order and the courts are bound by it. However applying the ECHR without recognising the case law of the ECtHR, which formally has no binding force upon the judiciary, is meaningless. Scholars argue that ECtHR case law has *de facto erga omnes* effect on the Member States, because "the case law - especially that of the Grand Chamber's judgments - creates a body of law which encompasses 'common

---

44 *Solana,* A Secure Europe in a Better World, SO 138/03, Thessaloniki European Council, June (2003) 15.

45 Commission Communication on the External Dimension of the EU's Human Rights Policy: From Rome to Maastricht and Beyond (1995) 567 final, 6.

46 Charter of Fundamental Rights of the European Union, OJ (2010) C 83/02, Art 52.3.

47 Memorandum of Understanding between the CoE and the EU (2007) para 17, available at <www.coe.int/t/der/docs/MoU_EN.pdf>.

48 Ibid. paras 2, 16.

49 Ibid. para 2.

50 Law of Georgia on International Treaties of Georgia (1997) Art 6 (1).

European standards' by which states, and in particular their judicial authorities, are bound."[51] In other words, the ECHR seeks general solutions to general problems with which it is confronted.[52] And last but not least, most European countries treat the Convention at least supplementary as a guiding instrument for interpreting their national constitutional standards and, on the other hand, in certain countries the ECHR is treated as a surrogate or shadow constitution. The Convention perceives itself, as expressed by the ECtHR, as the "constitutional instrument of European public order and nucleus of a common European constitutionalisation process in the area of human rights."[53]

Furthermore, the EU's accession to the ECHR creates a "European triangle" which is one of the best possibilities for Georgia (and for other EU-aspiring countries as well) to approximate its human rights protection standards with EU standards.

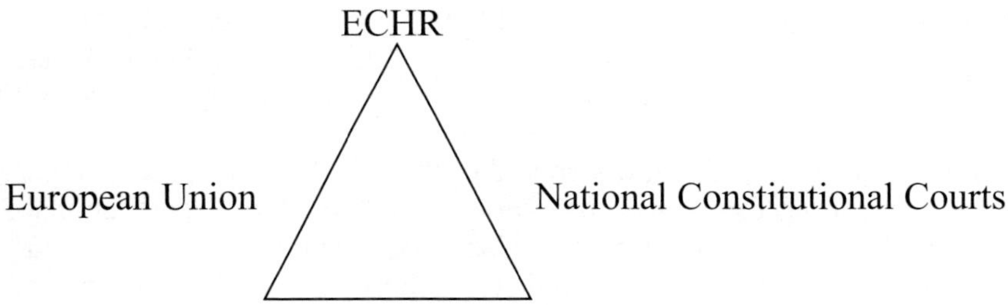

Hence the necessity and importance of application and implementation of the ECHR and the ECtHR's case law in non–Member States aspiring to the EU is obvious: if they apply and implement the ECHR they will apply EU human rights protection standards. The aim is not to catalyze European integration, but the objective is to enhance human rights protection which will itself contribute to the European integration process. The Constitutional Court of Georgia in collaboration with ordinary courts may facilitate Georgia's inclusion in the "European constitutionalisation mainstream" by means of applying European human rights protection standards.

As mentioned above, the Constitutional Court is best placed and has the pertinent competences to attain ENP objectives by means of respecting fundamental rights and freedoms in compliance with Georgia's international commitments. For in-

---

[51] Committee on Legal Affairs and Human Rights' Contribution to the Conference on the Principle of Subsidiarity, Skopje, (2010): "Strengthening Subsidiarity: Integrating the Strasbourg Court's Case Law into National Law and Judicial Practice", at 8.

[52] Judgment on the merits delivered by Chamber *Rantsev v. Cyprus and Russia,* Application No 25965/04, ECHR, (2010) para 197. The ECtHR held that "The Court's judgments in fact serve not only to decide those cases brought before the Court but, more generally, to elucidate, safeguard and develop the rules instituted by the Convention, thereby contributing to the observance by the States of the engagements undertaken by them as Contracting Parties."

[53] Judgment on the Preliminary Objections delivered by Chamber, *Case of Loizidou vs. Turkey* (preliminary objections) Appl. No 15318/89, (1995) para. 75, cited in *Weiß,* Human Rights in the EU: Rethinking the Role of the European Convention on Human Rights After Lisbon, European Constitutional Law Review 2011, 64 (76).

stance, the Joint Communication on "A New Response to a Changing Neighbourhood" indicates that the new approach aims at providing better protection *inter alia* of the freedom of thought, conscience and religion.[54] In order to illustrate the practical importance of the reception of European standards we will refer to a recently adopted decision of the Constitutional Court of Georgia. Constitutional complaint N477 concerned the right to conscientious objection to military service. An applicant argued that the Law on Military Reserve Service contradicted the Constitution of Georgia, in particular Art 19, guaranteeing freedom of speech, thought, conscience, religion and belief, since the Law on Military Reserve Service did not provide for the possibility of applying an alternative service. Art 19 of the Constitution does not explicitly answer the question, whether the right to conscientious objection to military service is constitutionally protected. The Court, by treating the Constitution as a living instrument and by referring to the recent judgment of the ECtHR Grand Chamber's decision in *Bayatyan* v. *Armenia*, came to the conclusion that the right to conscientious objection to military service is protected by the Constitution of Georgia.[55] At the European level, only the EU Charter of Fundamental Rights in Art 10 explicitly recognises the right to conscientious objection to military service.[56]

Implementation of the new standard of the ECHR in this particular case, in fact, has approximated Georgian constitutional standards to the constitutional standards of the CoE and EU Member States. Therefore, in similar cases application of European standards is a "must", and judicial authorities should implement these standards in their national legal orders.

4.2. Practice of activism in application of ECHR and ECtHR case law by constitutional courts of certain countries in South Eastern Europe and in Georgia

4.2.1. Slovenia

As in most European legal orders the ECHR in Slovenia is superior to the legislation and inferior to the Constitution. With regard to the case law of the ECtHR it has to be noted that formally it is not binding upon the Constitutional Court however, there is almost no decision without reference to the ECHR and its respective case law.[57] According to statistical data, the Constitutional Court of

---

[54] Joint Communication by the High Representative of the Union for Foreign Affairs and Security Policy and the European Commission, "A New Response to a Changing Neighbourhood" (2011) final 303, at 2.

[55] Decision of the Constitutional Court of Georgia N 1/1/477, *Public Defender of Georgia vs. Parliament of Georgia*, (2011) para 19.

[56] Charter of Fundamental Rights of the European Union, OJ (2010) C 83/02, Art 10, para 2.

[57] *Ribičić*, Implementing European Standards into the Case Law of the Constitutional Court, Contribution to the International Conference on the Position of Constitutional Courts Following Integration into the European Union, Bled, (2004), available at <http://www.us-rs.si/en/about-the-court/conferences/pcceu-bled-30-september-2-october-2004/presentation-by-dr-ciril-ribicic-judge-of-the-cons/>.

Slovenia has untill now referred to the case law of the ECtHR in its 600 decisions and relied on the ECHR jurisprudence in more than 100 cases.[58]

4.2.2. Croatia

The Constitutional Court of the Republic of Croatia accepts the binding interpretative authority of all the judgments and decisions of the ECtHR.[59] Formally, the ECHR has a sub-constitutional status, it is above law in terms of legal effect, but lower than the Constitution of Croatia. However, the ECHR has a quasi-constitutional status in Croatian legal order according to the case law of the Court.[60] The Constitutional Court of Croatia has so far referred to the ECtHR and its case law in more than 750 decisions and rulings.[61] Furthermore, the Court in decision U-I/988/1998 of 17 March 2010 checked the constitutionality of the Pension Insurance Act and came to the conclusion that the Court's own case law was not relevant anymore and directly referred to the ECHR stating that the ECtHR has a developed case law on this subject.[62] The internal organisation of the Constitutional Court of the Republic of Croatia includes monitoring the judgments of the European Court through a Senior Legal Advisor who observes the case law, selects important judgments that could have implications for Croatia, and makes written reports to the judges and legal advisers.

4.2.3. Georgia

The practice in Georgia is quite different concerning reception and integration of ECtHR case law. As illustrated above, Croatia fully satisfies the demand of the CoE with regard to integrating the Court's case law into its own national case law and seems to be quite effective. We think that this lesson could be learned, and the practice and approach of the Constitutional Court of Croatia have to be taken into account and shared by its counterpart from Georgia.

From 1996 till 2007 the Constitutional Court of Georgia adjudicated 445 cases and applied the ECHR and its case law only in 7 decisions. From 2007 till now the Court adjudicated approximately 130 cases and referred to the European standards in its 16 decisions.[63] The progress is obvious. However, applicants base their argu-

---

58 *Cernec / Avbelj,* Implementation of the European Convention on Human Rights and Fundamental Freedoms in Slovenia, in *Alleweldt / Hammer/ Marcus* (eds), The European Convention on Human Rights and Fundamental Freedoms in Central and Eastern Europe, (2012) 545.

59 *Omejec,* Ways and Means to Recognize the Interpretative Authority of Judgments against other States - The Experience of the Constitutional Court of Croatia, paper presented at the conference "The Principle of Subsidiarity: Strengthening Subsidiarity: Integrating the Court's Case-law into National Law and Judicial Practice" Skopje, October, Venice Commission Report (2010) 019, 3–4.

60 Ibid. 4.

61 Ibid. 5.

62 Decision of the Constitutional Court of Republic of Croatia U-I/988/1998, Decision of Constitutional Court of Republic of Croatia U-III-1897/2008.

63 According to the decisions provided at the official website of the Constitutional Court of Georgia, not all decisions are uploaded onto the official website of the Court , and even though

mentation on the Strasbourg Court more often than the Constitutional Court does in its decisions. There are some cases where the applicant based the argumentation on European standards, but the Court did not draw attention to the applicants arguments and decided the case without applying European standards.[64] This does not mean *a priori* that the Constitutional Court in a certain case refused to enhance a human rights standard. For instance, constitutional claims N 482, 483, 487, 502 (combined cases) were partially upheld and certain unconstitutional provisions in the Law of Georgia on Assemblage and Manifestation were abolished without reference to the European human rights standards.

In the judgment *Public defender vs. Parliament of Georgia* in 2009, the Constitutional Court of Georgia stated that "the Board thinks that deciding the constitutional issue should be done with giving the maximum respect to the requirements of international law, especially international human rights law, considering abundant international experience. However, this does not imply that the Constitutional Court should upgrade any international agreement or covenant to the rank of the Constitution and should replace the constitutional norms with international law norms during its reasoning."[65]

We share this opinion and agree with the statement that an international agreement should not replace constitutional norms, but, on the other hand, when interpreting certain constitutional rights and freedoms and while building the argumentation the Court should not only "respect," rather be willing and ready to actively implement international and European standards where the circumstances of the case give the possibility to do so. In conclusion, it should be noted that reception of European standards by the Constitutional Court of Georgia has to be the rule in its judicial activity, rather than the exception.

4.3. Judicial activism of the Constitutional Court by means of teleological interpretation

4.3.1. Overview

Judicial activism may be expressed not only by active application of European standards of human rights protection but also by means of employing teleological interpretation of constitutional text. Scholars[66] classify three basic types of judicial activism: 1) Judicial activism as conflict with classical policymakers; 2) methodological activism – methods and arguments used in constitutional interpretation; and 3) procedural activism of the courts which in practice means dis-

---

this statistical data reflects the overall situation, it might still not be precise, <www.constcourt.gov.ge>.

64 Decision of Constitutional Court of Georgia 482, 483, 487, 502 (combined cases), *Citizens and Political Parties of Georgia vs. Parliament of Georgia* 2011.

65 Decision of Constitutional Court of Georgia N 2/1/415, Public Defender vs. Parliament of Georgia, (2009) para 5, Section II. available at <http://constcourt.ge/index.php?lang_id=ENG&sec_id=74&id=563&action=show>.

66 For example *Aaviksoo*, Judicial Activism in Constitutional Review Decisions of the Supreme Court of Estonia, Juridica International, (2007), 60 (69).

regarding procedural limits that allow more extensive intervention of the judiciary[67] – for instance, opening the door to more litigants.

4.3.2. Methodological activism

The subject of our interest is methodological activism. Methodological activism is basically related to the issue of constitutional interpretation, and it signifies judicial argumentation that does not entirely rely on the text of the Constitution or which diverges from the intention of the authors of the Constitution. The Australian constitutional law scholar *Craven* equated judicial activism with constitutional interpretation, and he appraised activism as "progressivism"[68] as well. According to *Barak*, the ultimate purpose of interpretation is modernisation, updating the constitution in accordance with new social demands[69] while treating the legal text as a living instrument.[70]

We think that the Constitutional Court of Georgia should apply methodological activism in order to realise Georgia's goal and aspiration towards European integration. But the question is, which interpretation method of the Constitution will better contribute to Georgia's integration within EU.

Since the goal of interpretation is to find the right answer to the hard cases,[71] to achieve and realise social goals, and also to realise the purpose of the text, it is not difficult to conclude that it is the purposive interpretation, or in other words teleological interpretation, which should be employed by constitutional courts. Nevertheless, purposive interpretation does not disregard other methods of interpretation, for instance, historical or systematic interpretation of the constitution, because any theory of interpretation of constitutional law aims at perfecting the constitution. Any approach to the founding document must ultimately be perfectionist in the sense that it attempts to make that document as good as it can possibly be.[72] However, we would like to emphasise the importance and necessity of the purposive interpretation as an emanation of judicial activism, because "primacy must be accorded to the spirit and not the letter of the text."[73] Purposive interpretation is closely connected to the objective-dynamic understanding of legal texts. It tries to read the text in dynamic and to investigate the objective of the constitutional text. Justice *Brennan* expressed this idea in the following remarks: 'We current Justices read the constitution in the only way that we can: as twentieth Century Americans."[74] In 1977 the German Federal Constitutional Court in the life imprisonment case stated: "Neither original history nor ideas and intentions of the framers are of the decisive

67 Ibid. 61.
68 *French*, op. cit. note 9, 70-71.
69 *Barak*, The Judge in a Democracy, Princeton University Press USA, (2006) 132.
70 *Dickson*, A Life in the Law: The Process of Judging, Saskatchewan Law Review 2000, 373 (388).
71 *Dworkin,* A Matter of Principle (1985) at 119.
72 *Sunstein,* A Constitution of Many Minds (2009) at 23.
73 *Fennely*, Legal Interpretation at the European Court of Justice, Fordham International Law Journal, 1996, 656 (670).
74 *J. Brennan*, United States Supreme Court, University of California at Davis Law Review 1985, 7.

importance in interpreting particular provisions of the Basic Law. Since adoption of the Basic Law, our understanding of the content, function and effect of basic rights has deepened. Current attitudes are important in assessing the constitutionality of life imprisonment. New insight can influence and even change the evolution of this punishment in terms of human dignity and principles of constitutional state."[75] Hence, Constitutional Courts of Spain,[76] Italy[77] and Germany[78] interpret constitutional texts in up–to–date manner, responding to the demands of contemporary society.

Continental law has long recognised teleological interpretation.[79] The good illustration is ECJ and ECtHR acting as "constitutional courts." The shifting of these two courts towards teleological interpretation has characterised the last decades in Europe. It won't be excessive if we refer to the teleological interpretation as a European standard of interpretation. The ECtHR treats the Convention as a "living instrument" and establishes different human rights standards periodically. On the other hand, the ECJ, before the development of the teleological method, employed the doctrine of "effectiveness", called by its French name, "effet utile".[80] The *effet utile* doctrine provides that once the purpose of a provision is clearly identified, its detailed terms will be interpreted so "as to ensure that the provision retains its effectiveness."[81] The ECJ in *van Gend en Loos* pronounced the essence of the method of interpretation: it applies to the Treaties, stating that "it is necessary to consider the spirit, the general scheme and the wording"[82] of the provision in question.[83] The "spirit" – purposive interpretation used by the ECJ in its further case law gave critics reason to qualify the Court as an "activist court" or "engine of European Integration". Judge *Constantinos Kakouris* of the ECJ stated "[t]he Court constantly uses teleological interpretation ... [and] seeks to apprehend the meaning of law in the light of its purpose ..." The Court, he said, "must arrive at criteria by reference to the beliefs and common values of the people of Europe."[84]

Purposive interpretation is applicable and advantageous not only for international treaties (such as ECHR, EEC, TEC, and TFEU) but for constitutions as well, since constitutions, roughly speaking, are also "contracts", "agreements" between people and those who are in charge of exercising collective will - the governments. Purposive interpretation has to be preferred because each constitution is a unique legal document. "It reflects events of the past, lays down the foundation for the present and determines how the future ought to look like. It must therefore be capable of growth and development over time to meet new social, political and historical reali-

---

75 45 BVerfGE 187 (1977), available at <http://www.hrcr.org/safrica/dignity/45bverfge187.html>.

76 *Sweet,* Governing With Judges - Constitutional Politics in Europe, (2000) at 99.

77 Ibid. 100–102.

78 *Kommers*, Germany: Balancing Rights and Duties, in *Goldsworth* (ed), Interpreting Constitutions - A Comparative Study, (2006) at 201.

79 *Barak*, Purposive Interpretation in the Law, (2005) at 86.

80 *Fennely*, Legal Interpretation at the European Court of Justice, Fordham International Law Journal, 1996, 656 (674).

81 Ibid. 674.

82 ECJ, Case 26/62, (*Van Gend en Loos vs Netherlands)* 1963.

83 *Fennely*, op. cit. note 73, 660.

84 Ibid. 668.

ties."[85] Using purposive interpretation contributes to the attainment of the objective and fundamental values enshrined in the constitution. The ECtHR and the ECJ are good examples for EU-aspiring countries. These two courts, by means of teleological interpretation of their founding documents, have built the two biggest successful systems on the continent – a human rights protection system on the one hand, and a closer union between the peoples of Europe on the other hand. We think that the advantages and benefits of these two systems, for the peoples of Europe, are beyond doubts. Therefore, it is much more desirable and important that the constitutional courts of EU–aspiring countries are activist in such a manner that they use European standard of interpretation – purposive interpretation of the constitutions since countries of South Caucasus, *inter alia* Georgia, are post–communist countries (even though several decades passed) and dynamic–objective interpretation will assist to leave "post–communist constitutionalism."[86] Accordingly, if constitutional courts employ the European method of legal interpretation this will support the ordinary judiciary to follow the constitutional court's practice and Soviet–born methods of legal interpretation might simply be left behind.

Recently, an article concerning the Europeanisation of third country judiciaries was published which ascertained the role of the Russian and Ukrainian judiciary in the European integration process. This article illustrates *inter alia* the importance of teleological interpretation in the Europeanisation process. However, as in most post–Soviet states "Homogeneity of the legal systems of both Russia and the Ukraine with the EU has not yet been achieved, because the Russian and Ukrainian judiciaries are not yet acquainted with European methods of teleological interpretation."[87]

Therefore, in order to make ties with European legal traditions and to realise Georgia's goal "to return to Europe," the Constitutional Court of Georgia besides active interpretation of the Constitution of Georgia in line with European human rights protection standards, has to employ teleological interpretation in its judicial activities.

4.3.3. Procedural activism

In contrast to methodological activism, procedural activism means expanding the standing requirement and allowing more applicants to lodge complaints with the court. Scholars define it in the following way: "The procedural approaches to judicial activism identify judicial activism according to procedural criteria without considering the substance of the matter. In this approach, judicial activism is defined as disregard for procedural limits or the interpretation of theirs that allows for more extensive intervention of the judiciary. The main procedur-

---

85 Supreme Court of Canada, *Hunter v. Southam* Inc. (1984) 2 145 (156).

86 Omejec, op. cit. note 59.

87 *Petrov / Kalinichenko*, The Europeanization of Third Country Judiciaries through the Application of the EU acquis: The Cases of Russia and Ukraine, International and Comparative Law Quarterly, 2011, 325 (353).

al limits that are tackled within the framework of that dimension are the doctrine of standing..."[88]

The Constitutional Court of Georgia encountered procedural judicial activism only recently. The Court was asked to recognise as unconstitutional a norm of the "Organic law on the Constitutional Court of Georgia" which enumerated who was entitled to apply to the Court. It excluded foreigners and stateless persons from the list of potential petitioners. The case was particularly complicated by the fact that the respondent, the Parliament of Georgia, argued that the norm of the Constitution which sets forth competences of the Constitutional Court did not grant the right to apply to the Constitutional Court to foreigners and stateless persons. The Court declared that everyone disregarding his / her citizenship has the right to apply to the Court, and the Constitution expresses the will of the citizens that individuals shall have the remedy to protect their rights and this aim may not be achieved through the approach differentiating between citizens and foreigners since they are equally entitled to the fundamental human rights recognised by the Constitution.[89] Accordingly, the disputed norm which omitted foreigners and stateless persons from the list of potential petitioners was declared unconstitutional. Consequently, the Court's door is now open to much more litigants than a year before. Several constitutional complaints were submitted to the Court by foreigners after this decision had been rendered by the Court. The decision in question is a manifestation not only of procedural judicial activism, but of substantive judicial activism as well - i.e. interpreting constitutional text in a teleological way. An analysis of the of case law of the Constitutional Court of Georgia shows that there are not many cases where the Court in such a bold manner used teleological interpretation and exposed procedural activism. Although, the Court has to follow this practice, i.e. apply European methods of interpretation in its future decisions.

It is only by actively applying European human rights standards and interpreting the Constitution by means of European methods of interpretation that the Constitutional Court of Georgia may contribute to Georgia's integration process.

4.4. Application of the EU *acquis* by constitutional courts – the case of the AA with Georgia

Negotiations on the AA with Georgia were launched in July 2010, the find text of the EU-Georgia AA was signed in June 2014 and is now undergoing ratification. This new contractual relationship between Georgia and the EU creates a strong political bond and promote further convergence by establishing a closer link to EU legislation and standards.[90] It is obvious that the AA will boost EU-Georgian relations through "creating a higher level of political association"[91] and gradual integration into the EU's economy through establishing access to

---

[88] *Aaviksoo*, op. cit. note 66.

[89] Decision of Constitutional Court of Georgia N 1/466, *Public Defender of Georgia vs. Parliament of Georgia*, 2010, para. II. 16.

[90] Communication from the Commission on Eastern Partnership, COM(2008) 823 final, 3 December 2008, 4.

[91] COM(2008) 823 final, 3.

the common market. Hence, in this section we intend to examine the legal rank of the AA in Georgia's constitutional legal order and how the judiciary and, in particular, the Constitutional Court of Georgia, can apply the EU *acquis* after signing the AA. We will try to find some legal background in this regard in Croatia and Hungary as lessons for Georgia.

Art 6.2 of the Constitution of Georgia (1995) states that: "an international treaty or agreement of Georgia unless it contradicts the Constitution of Georgia, the Constitutional Agreement,[92] shall take precedence over domestic normative acts." Henceforth, the AA will have superior legal force in the domestic legislation of Georgia. Furthermore, the Law of Georgia on International Treaties of Georgia reiterates the provision of the Constitution and declares that: "International agreements of Georgia are an integral part of the legislation of Georgia."[93]

Hence, we have to explore what are the mechanisms for the Constitutional Court of Georgia to apply the AA. In contrast to Croatia and Hungary, the Constitutional Court of Georgia is not authorised to decide on the conformity of laws with international treaties. Therefore, there are basically three possibilities for the Court to look inside and apply the AA. Firstly, the Constitutional Court may generally apply the AA as an integral part of the legislation of Georgia and exploit the AA for its argumentation while deciding cases. Secondly, an international agreement may be challenged in the Constitutional Court if it is alleged to violate constitutional rights and freedoms, therefore by means of the constitutional complaint the ombudsman of Georgia, citizens and other individuals have the right to apply to the Court.[94] The third way for the Constitutional Court to look inside the AA is by checking the constitutionality of international treaties of Georgia. However, there are two mechanisms for this: through *ex ante* and ex *post* review. We think that the Constitutional Court should be given opportunity to check the constitutionality of the AA *ex ante* since prior checking is essential for three basic reasons: 1) it will fortify reliability and security of the constitutional legal order of Georgia (legal certainty); 2) it will instruct ordinary courts and public administration in applying the AA; 3) it will support the European integration process. We will discuss each reason in greater detail below.

4.4.1. Security of the constitutional legal order of Georgia

According to the Constitution of Georgia, "Apart from the international treaties and agreements providing for ratification, it shall also be obligatory to ratify an international treaty and agreement which *inter alia* requires a change of domestic legislation, adoption of necessary laws and acts in order to fulfill international obligations."[95] Since the EU-Georgia AA contains binding hamonisation clauses, it has to be ratified by the Parliament of Georgia. The Parliament may submit constitutional submissions to the Constitutional Court before ratification,

---

[92] Constitutional Agreement Between Georgia and Apostle Autocephalous Orthodox Church of Georgia (2002).

[93] Law of Georgia on International Treaties of Georgia (1997) Art 6 (1).

[94] Organic Law on Constitutional Court of Georgia (1996) Art 19 (E) and Art 39 (1).

[95] Art 65 of Constitution of Georgia (1995).

and the ratification process will be temporarily stopped, henceforth ratification of the respective international treaty or agreement shall be impermissible before adjudication by the Constitutional Court.[96] If the Court concludes that an international agreement or a provision of it is unconstitutional, then according to the Organic Law on the Constitutional Court of Georgia recognition of an international treaty or agreement or certain parts thereof as unconstitutional shall result in the inadmissibility of ratification of that international treaty or the agreement.[97] In this case, the Law on International Treaties of Georgia gives the solution to the legislature by providing that the agreement in question will be binding on Georgia only after appropriate amendments to the Constitution. It is theoretically possible that certain provisions of the AA might appear in contradiction to the Constitution of Georgia. Therefore, it is better that this nonconformity is eradicated at the early stage by means of amending the Constitution or re - negotiating certain provisions[98] rather than by dealing with a Treaty that is signed or entered into force. If the Treaty is signed and then the Constitutional Court through *a posterior* abstract review will establish unconstitutionality of a certain provision of the agreement, this will endanger the legal security principle, because an international agreement (or its provision) will lose binding effect at domestic level, i.e. in the Georgian constitutional legal order, but still it will be binding at international level. Therefore, non - execution of an international treaty at the domestic level will necessarily lead to a violation of international obligations.

A similar situation existed in Hungary regarding the Europe (EA). The Constitutional Court of Hungary through *a posterior* review established that a certain competition provision of the EA was not directly applicable, and implementing rules of the EA were unconstitutional. Art 62 of the EA reiterated Arts 85 and 86 of the EEC treaty concerning competition rules. The Constitutional Court of Hungary recognised that the implementing rules of Art 62 of the EA were unconstitutional,[99] but it did not annul the rules. In contrast, the Court saved Art 62 of the EA. *Volkai* criticised the Court's decision stating that: "Although the Court's decision not to annul Article 62 (2) EA might at first glance show genuine self-restraint, by giving guidelines on how that implicitly unconstitutional article could be applied in a constitutional way, the Court acted in an activist manner. Undoubtedly, the Court lacks any kind of legislative power to do so, since it may only decide on a provision's constitutionality or unconstitutionality. In other words, it may declare Article 62 (2) EA unconstitutional or may save it, but it cannot save it and at the same time limit its applicability."[100]

---

[96] Organic Law on Constitutional Court of Georgia (1996) Art 38 (2) and Art 65 (4).
[97] Organic Law on Constitutional Court of Georgia (1996) Art 23 (5).
[98] Renegotiation of certain provisions is, of course, a not efficient way of solving the problem in question, since it highly depends on the parties' will and takes quite long time.
[99] Decision is available at the official website of the Constitutional Court of the Republic of Hungary <http://www.mkab.hu>.
[100] *Volkai*, The Application of Europe Agreement and European Law in Hungary: The Judgment of Activist Constitutional Court on Activist Notions, Jean Monnet Working Paper 8/99 (2000) at 23.

As mentioned above, checking an international treaty after its ratification and finding it unconstitutional creates quite an inconvenient legal situation which might adversely affect legal security. Therefore, it is better if these issues are resolved before ratification of the treaty. Prior checking will not eradicate but reduce the risk of challenging the treaty in the constitutional court afterwards. Furthermore, it will also serve as guidance for ordinary courts and public administration in applying the agreement.

4.4.2. Instructing ordinary courts and public administration in applying the Association Agreement

Prior checking of the AA will instruct the courts and public administration in applying the treaty in their cases. There are lots of issues which might be difficult for ordinary courts and public administration to deal with, for instance, whether AA provisions may have direct effect or not, issue of direct effect of secondary treaty legislation, Association Council's decisions, application of EU's secondary legislation etc. Application of AAs and secondary association law in associated states generally requires recourse to Community law. For instance, the Constitutional Court of Croatia adopted a teleological interpretation of the country's SAA with the EU by stating: "... SAA and Interim Agreement oblige Croatian bodies in charge of protection of competition, that when resolving cases, not only to apply Croatian competition law, but also take into consideration the rules of competition law of the European Community."[101] *Stanić* appreciates this decision as a long-awaited judgment and attributes to it great importance since it instructs the Croatian judiciary how and when the criteria and standards of the comparative law of the European Community should be applied.[102]

All above mentioned issues (direct effect of treaty provisions, application of secondary treaty law and EU's *acquis* in general) are very essential in constitutional legal orders of associated states and we think that constitutional courts are in the best position as ultimate arbiters to decide these issues.

4.5. Supporting European integration

We have already discussed the reasons why *ex ante* review of the AA with Georgia might support the integration process. Nevertheless, in this part we shall sum up these arguments. First of all, *ex ante* review will reduce the risk of challenging the treaty in the Constitutional Court after it is ratified. Hence, *ex ante* review fortifies reliability that the agreement in question is deemed to be constitutional. On the other hand, since the Constitutional Court is the ultimate arbiter in deciding constitutional issues and its decisions are highly circulated in

---

[101] Decision of Constitutional Court of Republic of Croatia U-III /1410/2007, Official Gazette No 25/08, also cited in *Stanić*, The Interpretative Effect of European Law in the Judgment of the Croatian Constitutional Court U-iii-1410/2007, Croatian Yearbook of European Law and Policy, 2008, 247 (261).

[102] Ibid. (260).

the judiciary, and since decisions of the Court are electronically available for everyone, the decision of the Court will be the guidance for concerned individuals, ordinary courts and other public authorities while applying the AA in their cases.

The active application of the EU *acquis* is currently debated in the Ukrainian judiciary as well. "Some Constitutional Court judges advocate the necessity of applying more elements of the EU *acquis* in their decisions, due to Ukraine's pro-European policies and its aspirations for EU membership."[103] The Constitutional Court of Ukraine has several times referred to EU law in its decisions as a persuasive source of law.[104]

In conclusion, *ex ante* review of the AA with Georgia will inevitably make the Constitutional Court explore the case law of the ECJ, its attitude towards the AA, importance of the AA in the EU's legal order and its interpretative tools while deciding cases, which might lead the Constitutional Court towards Europe-friendly decisions in the future.[105]

5. CONCLUSION

The idea of this research paper was to explore the significance of constitutional-judicial review in European integration processes and to find an answer to the normative question whether judicial activism of constitutional courts and, in particular, of the Constitutional Court of Georgia, may foster the European integration process. We came to the conclusion that judicial activism of the Constitutional Court of Georgia, if expressed in the active reception of European human rights standards, as well as in employing teleological interpretation and application of the EU *acquis*, may in fact catalyse the European integration of Georgia.

The research contains valuable recommendations that might be interesting and useful for constitutional courts and in particular for the Constitutional Court of Georgia since Georgia has clearly made its choice – paving the way towards the EU. On the other hand, our study has shown that the Constitutional Court of Georgia also has competences and legitimacy to realise Georgia's choice – align Georgia with the EU.

[103] *Petrov and Kalinichenko,* op. cit. note 87, 346.
[104] Ibid.
[105] Ibid.

Romina Beqiri and Sloboda Midorović

ENDING IMPUNITY IN THE SOUTH CAUCASUS: THE CHALLENGES AHEAD

"Art 6 AA EU - Georgia: Serious crimes of international concern

1. The Parties reaffirm that the most serious crimes of concern to the international community as a whole must not go unpunished and that impunity for such crimes must be avoided by taking measures at the national and international level including the International Criminal Court.

2. The Parties consider that the establishment and effective functioning of the International Criminal Court constitutes an important development for international peace and justice. The Parties reaffirm their commitment to continue to cooperate with the International Criminal Court by implementing the Rome Statute and its related instruments, giving due regard to preserving its integrity"

"Art 6 AA EU - Republic of Moldova: International Criminal Court

1. The Parties reaffirm that the most serious crimes of concern to the international community as a whole must not go unpunished and that their effective prosecution must be ensured by taking measures at the national and international level, including the International Criminal Court (ICC).

2. The Parties consider that the establishment and effective functioning of the ICC constitutes an important development for international peace and justice. The Parties agree to support the ICC by implementing the Rome Statute of the International Criminal Court and its related instruments, giving due regard to preserving its integrity."

1. INTRODUCTION

"Punishment is now unfashionable, because it creates moral distinctions among men, which, to the democratic mind, are odious. We prefer a meaningless collective guilt to a meaningful individual responsibility", - Thomas Szasz[1]

The South Caucasus' so-called "frozen" conflicts are anything but frozen, and very often the situation is on a knife's edge, threatening not only the military forces on the ceasefire lines, but also the civilian populations in the region. The

---

1 *Thomas Szasz* (15 April 1920 – 8 September 2012) was a psychiatrist and academic.

conflicts are also far more than domestic or territorial controversies[2] because they have both regional and international implications and represent one of the principal obstacles to the development of the region.

This research does not aim at presenting a comprehensive history of the South Caucasus conflicts on the basis of international law or at examining the causes that brought these disputes about. Rather it highlights the consequences that came out of these conflicts and sheds light on the serious crimes and military hostilities committed by the belligerent parties. Ultimately, this paper aims at analysing the question whether the ENP in the South Caucasus demands a more serious commitment to prosecute the perpetrators of the atrocities which occurred during the conflicts in the region. The research focuses on the 2008 war between Russia and Georgia because this situation is currently under preliminary examinations by the ICC, taking into consideration the fact that only Georgia is party to the ICC, among other South Caucasian countries (Armenia, Azerbaijan).

We will examine the ICTY experience in the Western Balkans and compare the co-operation by the Balkan states with the ICTY and the co-operation by the South Caucasus countries with the ICC in the context of EU integration. The lack of progress in talks[3] would make it difficult for the parties involved to reach an effective compromise without the intervention of the international community. Hence, it needs to be discussed whether the South Caucasus countries would agree with SEE solutions for EU integration. Is it possible to draw a parallel between South Caucasus-ICC-EU and the Western Balkans-ICTY-EU strategy?

2. SOUTH CAUCASUS AND WESTERN BALKANS IN A COMPARATIVE EU APPROACH TOWARDS PEACE, SECURITY AND JUSTICE

One of the principal aims of the EU in the 2004 enlargement process was to expand the zone of "prosperity, stability and security" that its citizens enjoy to also include the neighbours of the EU. This approach has developed from an understanding that the EU cannot keep enlarging *ad infinitum* and there is a need to find new ways of spreading security beyond its borders to ensure the long-term stability and security for the EU and its citizens.

The bloody wars in the Balkans during the 1990s prompted the EU as an international actor to realise that peace and stability on the periphery are crucial to the security of the Union. Consequently, the EU has taken steps towards boosting its involvement in conflict resolution efforts not only in the Balkans but also in the South Caucasus. The importance of interacting with the South Caucasus is reflected also in the EU's gradual economic and political engagement with certain countries, notably with regard to conflict resolution. In February 2001 the General Affairs and External Relations Council (GAERC) declared that the EU was willing to play a

---

2 *German,* Visibly Invisible: EU Engagement in Conflict Resolution in the South Caucasus, European Security 2007, 363.

3 Ibid. 4-5.

more active political role in the South Caucasus, stating that it would seek ways of lending its support "to prevent and resolve conflicts" and to assist in post-conflict rehabilitation.[4] In addition, further co-operation with other international organisations such as the OSCE, UN and CoE would reinforce the bilateral and multilateral dialogue within the South Caucasus states. In the European Security Strategy (ESS) of 2003 the region was identified as an area in which the EU would be taking a "stronger and more active interest".[5]

The path of integration into the EU of the Western Balkan countries is individual and depends on the merits of each one of them with regard, in particular, to the determination to satisfy all the requirements, meet all the obligations, carry out the reforms and adopt the necessary measures that EU membership implies. The EU maintains a principled and consistent approach towards Serbia in relation to its co-operation with the ICTY.[6] It is necessary to affirm that for the EU and its institutions, impunity for war crimes and genocide is incompatible with the values of the Union, and that full co-operation with the ICTY was the key for Serbia to have closer ties to the EU.[7]

The SAA negotiations with Serbia and Montenegro were officially opened on 10 October 2005.[8] There have been many tensions, hence in May 2006 the Commission, supported by GAERC, decided to suspend the negotiations of the SAA with Serbia in light of the successive governments' continuous failure to co-operate with the Tribunal, in particular, Serbia's failure to transfer to the custody of the ICTY wartime Bosnian Serb Commander *Ratko Mladić*. The Commission's annual progress report on Serbia in November 2006 emphasised that full co-operation with the ICTY is a precondition for the resumption of SAA talks:

1. The Council regretted that Serbia and Montenegro were still not fully co-operating with the ICTY and it therefore supported the Commission's decision to call off the negotiating round on an SAA scheduled for 11 May, in line with its Conclusions of 3 October 2005 and 27 February 2006.
2. The Council reiterated its firm commitment to the European perspective of Serbia and Montenegro. In this context, the Council indicated its support to resume negotiations as soon as full co-operation with the ICTY is achieved. It once again urged the authorities in Belgrade to ensure that all remaining fugitive ICTY indictees, notably *Ratko Mladić*, are brought to justice without further delay.

---

4 See 2331st Council Meeting, General Affairs, 26 February 2001, Press Release 6506/01 (Presse 61) Brussels, at <www.ue.eu.int>; *German*, op. cit. note 2, 358.

5 European Union, European Security Strategy: A Secure Europe in a Better World, EU, Brussels, 12 December 2003, at 8.; German op. cit. note 2, 358.

6 The ICTY was established pursuant to Security Council Resolution 827 (23 May 1993) S/Res/827 (1993).

7 *Human Rights Watch*, Letter to the EU on Relations with Serbia and ICTY Co-operation, Brussels, 26 March 2007, <http://www.hrw.org/news/2007/03/25/letter-eu-relations-serbia-and-icty-cooperation>.

8 Serbia Progress Report 2006, 5, at <http://ec.europa.eu/enlargement/pdf/key_documents/2006/Nov/sr_sec_1389_en.pdf>.

3. If the necessary conditions are met and negotiations can resume rapidly, the Council underlines that a swift conclusion of the negotiations according to the timetable envisaged by the Commission is still within reach.[9]

On 26 February 2007, the ICJ ruled that Serbia's failure to transfer *Ratko Mladić* to the ICTY amounted to a violation of its obligations under the Convention on Genocide. The Court also ordered Serbia to transfer to the ICTY individuals indicted for genocide and to co-operate fully with the Tribunal for *Ratko Mladić*, and Bosnian Serb wartime President, *Radovan Karadzić.*

In the 2007 report, the Commission indicated that SAA negotiations with Serbia resumed, following a clear commitment by the country to achieve full co-operation with the ICTY, and concrete actions undertaken by the country that have matched this commitment.[10]

To transfer Mladić as a condition for resuming SAA negotiations demanded more from Belgrade than was expected of Croatia, for whom the transfer to the ICTY of Croatian General *Ante Gotovina* was a precondition for EU candidate status rather than SAA talks. What the case of Gotovina actually demonstrates is the value of a clear, firm and consistent position on the part of the EU as regards ICTY co-operation, since there is little doubt that without firm EU pressure *Gotovina* would never have been brought to justice.[11]

In July 2006, the Serbian Government adopted an AP on co-operation with the ICTY. The implementation of the AP suffered from a number of deficiencies, as regards the co-ordination between the civilian and military security services and the role and power of the prosecution. The inclusion of provisions concerning the co-operation of Serbia with the ICTY in the SAA indicates the importance of the effective functioning of the international judicial institution in the context of the Serbia's EU integration. Considering the strong links between the EU and Serbia to establish a relationship based on reciprocity and mutual interest, which should allow Serbia to further strengthen and extend its relations with EU Member States, in March 2012 Serbia was granted EU candidate status and in September 2013, the SAA[12] entered into force. Besides, Serbia continues to have a positive attitude towards the ICC: it did not conclude bilateral agreements granting exemptions from ICC jurisdiction.It is important that Serbia continues to support fully the ICC and the integrity of its Statute in line with relevant EU decisions.[13]

---

9 GAERC, Conclusions on the Western Balkans. Brussels, 15 May 2006, <http://www.consilium.europa.eu/ueDocs/cms_Data/docs/pressData/en/gena/89618.pdf>

10 SEC (2007) 1435, Serbia 2007 Progress Report, 16.

11 Human Rights Watch, Letter to the EU on Relations with Serbia and ICTY Co-operation, 26 March 2007 <http://www.hrw.org/news/2007/03/25/letter-eu-relations-serbia-and-icty-cooperation#_edn2>

12 SAA between the European Communities and their Member States of the one part and the Republic of Serbia, of the other part.

13 Ibid. "The Commission stressed its readiness to resume negotiations as soon as full co-operation with the ICTY is achieved" at 5. Link: <http://ec.europa.eu/enlargement/pdf/key_documents/2006/Nov/sr_sec_1389_en.pdf>

The EU's approach to the South Caucasus shares the same philosophy, as the countries should enhance regional co-operation and good-neighbourly relations as key elements of the PCAs which coherently addresses political, economic and assistance-related issues, as well as promotion of peace, strengthening of democratic processes and protection of human rights, enhancing bilateral and regional co-operation, and so forth.

Both Western Balkans and South Caucasus countries play a decisive role in the process of transformation into an area of longstanding stability and security in the region. The EU itself is based on principles such as reconciliation, compromise and peaceful coexistence; and it condemned all war crimes that took place in the former Yugoslavia and South Caucasus. The EU supports the work of the ICTY and of the local War Crimes Chambers in their effort to ensure justice and accountability, but is also the main promoter of the ICC.

Actually, the similarities and differences between the two regions in relation to the EU are at variance. The EU has not been involved in all the conflicts in the South Caucasus as it was in the Western Balkans, but only in ascertaining a settlement between South Ossetia (Tskhinvali), Abkhazia and Tbilisi. South Ossetia is not seeking to become an independent state, but it is calling for reunification to become a constituent part of the Russian Federation,[14] which is different from the countries of former Yugoslavia which declared independence.

The situation in Abkhazia[15] is somewhat different to South Ossetia and the EU is far less involved in the search for a negotiated solution, lending its support to on-going negotiations and providing financial assistance for rehabilitation.[16] Abkhazia is seeking full independence based on close political and economic integration with the Russian Federation.

The accountability for serious past crimes through fair trials is the foundation for successful post-conflict reconstruction based on the rule of law and respect for human rights.[17] The Western Balkans' full co-operation with the ICTY, as well as a commitment to fair domestic war crimes trials demonstrated the States' maturity and commitment to embrace fully the values of the EU. Given the successful position of the EU towards the Western Balkans for a European, democratic future including a commitment to justice and prosecuting war criminals, the EU cannot ignore the plight of thousands of victims and their families still waiting for justice in the South Caucasus. This position puts in doubt the seriousness of the EU's demands towards Member States, candidate states and those countries which aim at EU integration, regarding the commitment to justice, to rule of law and respect for human rights. That in turn depends on the EU providing principled and consistent leadership on these matters in the South Caucasus other than political and economic.

---

14 Novye Izvestiya, 4 February 2004, 1-4. In February 2004 the South Ossetian leader Eduard Kokoity proclaimed that 95 % of the Republic's population of approximately 100,000 had adopted Russian citizenship.

15 See *German,* op. cit. note 2, 373.

16 Ibid.

17 Human Rights Watch, op. cit. note 11.

Considering Serbia and Georgia, the EU's position is rather different. The EU strongly reaffirmed that it would be ready to consider any concrete measures which would help Serbia to integrate swiftly into the family of European nations[18]through full co-operation with the ICTY. In the EP Resolution 2011[19] full co-operation with the ICTY was a fundamental condition for Serbia to progress on the path to EU membership. This statement underlines the fact that all the states of the Western Balkans could only gain candidate status and/or open accession negotiations with the EU if the ICTY Office of the Prosecutor assesses that these countries had offered full co-operation.[20]

In case of the South Caucasus, the co-operation with the ICC is more complex. The reasons are, firstly, that not all the South Caucasus countries are parties to the Rome statute, thus, have no obligation to co-operate, but may do it voluntarily, secondly, the conflicts in the region and the consequences of those conflicts occurred long before the creation of the ICC in the 1990s, which makes it more difficult and even impossible to impose ICC jurisdiction on the crimes committed.

3. SOUTH CAUCASUS CONFLICTS AND THE ROLE OF THE EU

After the Cold War when the Soviet Union collapsed, a number of violent conflicts occurred in the post-Soviet area. In practice, individuals involved and responsibility for the crimes committed during those armed conflicts remained unpunished. The conflicts escalated and became violent especially in South Ossetia (Georgia), Transnistria (Moldova), Abkhazia (Georgia), Chechnya (Russian Federation) Nagorno-Karabakh (Armenia, Azerbaijanand Nagorno-Karabakh) and the conflict between Georgia, South Ossetia / Abkhazia and Russia in August 2008.

The armed conflict that occurred in Georgia in August 2008 has its roots in the Soviet era, in which Georgia was divided into three political-territorial entities, including the Autonomous Republic of Abkhazia and the Autonomous Oblast' (district) of South Ossetia. The conflicts arose during the period of the country's first President, Zviad Gamsakhurdia, who promoted nationalistic ethno-centrist slogans such as "Georgia for Georgians" towards the two political-territorial entities of Abkhazia and South Ossetia. Tensions arose and the conflict occurred between Georgian forces and separatist forces, first in South Ossetia in 1991 - 1992 and then in Abkhazia 1992 – 1994. The conflict ended with a peace agreement signed on 24 June 1992 in Sochi by Russian and Georgian Presidents, Boris Yeltsin and Eduard Shevardnadze. At the time, South Ossetia became a semi-autonomous area with a separate administration. One of the reasons why Georgia lost control over large

18 GAERC, Conclusions on the Western Balkans, 12 February 2007, 13, at <http://www.consilium.europa.eu/ueDocs/cms_Data/docs/pressData/en/gena/92758.pdf>(accessed on 3 January 2013).

19 EP resolution of 19 January 2011 on the European integration process of Serbia, P7TA (2011)0014.

20 This political imperative has been clearly formulated vis-à-vis in the South Caucasus countries through ENP action plans.

parts of both territories was notably because of the support from Russia to South Ossetia and Abkhazia.

Significant similarities exist between these conflicts.[21] Firstly, in each case, ceasefire agreements have been settled since 1992. They are monitored by a variety of international organisations and enshrine the victory of the separatist forces on the battlefield. Secondly, a fragile stability level emerged in the region, but the governments are still weak and the international community does not recognize the newly emerged states. Thirdly, the EU perspective reflects in the development of institution-building and economic policies. The conflicts present an ethno-political dimension characteristic at the post-Soviet era. The Georgia-Abkhazia conflict has a distinctly ethnic character and the roots of this conflict lie partly in the Soviet period.[22]

The current stage of the conflict between Azerbaijan and the former autonomous region of Nagorno-Karabakh began in the late 1980s and turned into a vicious war where Armenia was also involved later. It started when in response to the self-determination claims of the Nagorno-Karabakh population the Azerbaijani authorities organised massacres and ethnic cleansing of the Armenian population on the entire territory of Azerbaijan. 25.000 people died in the war and over 700.000 people were displaced from the sides.[23] Russia played a critical role in all of the separatist conflicts, as a mediator-cum-supporter-cum-combatant.[24] The *de facto* states of Abkhazia, South Ossetia and Nagorno-Karabakh, on the one hand, and their "home countries", Georgia and Azerbaijan, on the other, can survive without conflict settlement, but none of them will prosper.[25]

As the EU has expanded, the Eastern European and the South Caucasus countries became closer neighbours, and their security, stability and prosperity increasingly affect that of the EU. Thus, closer co-operation between the EU and its Eastern European partners – Armenia, Azerbaijan, Belarus, Georgia, the Republic of Moldova and Ukraine – is vital for the EU's external relations.

After the 2008 Russian-Georgian war, on 2 December 2008, the Council of the EU appointed Ambassador *Heidi Tagliavini* head of the IIFFMCG.The Mission was mandated by the Council to investigate the origins and the course of the conflict in Georgia with regard to international law (including the Helsinki Final Act), humanitarian law and human rights, and the accusations made in that context (including allegations of war crimes).

On 30 September 2009, the Mission formally presented the results of its investigation in the form of a Report to the Council of the EU, the OSCE and the UN, as well as to the parties of the conflict. In the context of the 2008 war the EU Fact-Finding Mission stated that "[for] the first time in its history [that] the European Union has decided to intervene actively in a serious armed conflict".[26]

---

21 *Lynch*, Engaging Eurasia's Separatist States: Unresolved Conflicts and de facto States. United States Institute of Peace (Washington D.C. 2004), at 6.

22 Ibid. 27.

23 Ibid. 35.

24 Ibid. 21.

25 Ibid. 9.

26 The key materials used for constructing the arguments are the "Tagliavini Report" or the IIFFMCG by the EU.

4. ICC AND THE SOUTH CAUCASUS

4.1. The ICC as an instrument to establish justice

In order to end the adverse effect of the prevalence of impunity,[27] the international community established international criminal courts such as the ICTY, ICTR, and ICC. The ICC as a manifestation of the establishment of criminal justice proclaimed as its main objective "to prosecute and investigate committed core international crimes and punish the perpetrators in order to "put an end to impunity and to contribute to the prevention of the [most serious]crimes"[28] of international concern, such as genocide, crimes against humanity and war crimes.

The ICC relies on State parties to the Rome Statute based:

1. on the principle of complementarity (which ensures that states will have both the right and an incentive to prosecute crimes within their jurisdiction); and
2. on the obligation of Member States to co-operate (which presupposes effective implementation of the Rome Statute into national law).

International criminal law does not contain abstract norms about crimes but it provides certain actions that shall be prohibited and punishable directly under international law, if there is a concrete threat to legally protected values and interests of the community of nations.[29]

Only one country of the South Caucasus – Georgia – took the step to ratify the Rome Statute of the ICC which establishes that every signatory vows to respect the non-impunity principles for all the crimes that occurred after the entry into force of the Statute on 1 July 2002.[30] The ICC is considered as a last resort, a complement to national courts, and has jurisdiction over serious crimes: genocide, crimes against humanity, war crimes and aggression, if national courts are unwilling or unable to investigate or persecute.

Co-operation with the ICC is not the same in case of State Parties compared to states which are not parties of the Rome statute. This makes a difference especially for the conflicts in the South Caucasus, as not all the states in the region are parties

---

27 Impunity is defined as "the impossibility, de jure or de facto, of bringing the perpetrators of human rights violations to account – whether in criminal, civil, administrative or disciplinary proceedings – since they are not subject to any inquiry that might lead to their being accused, arrested, tried, and, if found guilty ." in: Updated Set of principles for the protection and promotion of human rights through action to combat impunity, 08 February 2005, UN ECOSOC E/CN.4/2005/102/Add.1, p. 6.

28 Triffterer (ed), Commentary on the Rome Statute of the International Criminal Court: Observer's Note, Article by Article (2008) at 16.

29 Ibid. 31.

30 See the Preamble of the Rome Statute: "[...] that the most serious crimes of concern to the international community as a whole must not go unpunished and that their effective prosecution must be ensured by taking measures at the national level and by enhancing international co-operation."

to the statute. To State Parties, the ICC ''is entitled'' to present ''co-operation requests'' and they are obliged to ''co-operate fully' (art 86)' with it in ICC investigations and prosecutions of crimes. But as for non-party states, the ICC only ''may invite'' (art 87/5) them to ''provide assistance'' on the basis of an *ad hoc* arrangement. The word ''invite'' shows that co-operation by states which are not parties to the ICC is in the legal category of co-operation of a ''voluntary nature''.

4.2 Implementation of the Rome Statute: Georgia

Georgia signed the Rome Statute on 18 July 1998 and ratified it on 5 September 2003. A legislative package of five bills was passed by Georgia's Parliament on August 14, 2003:

1. regarding co-operation with the ICC;
2. amending the Code of Criminal Procedure;
3. amending the Criminal Code;
4. amending the law of Georgia on custody;
5. amending the law on executive actions.

No problems arose regarding the surrender of its own nationals, sentencing or the principle of *ne bis in idem*. No incompatibility was found between the Statute requirement and Georgian law.[31] The Georgian Constitution was not amended as it was compatible with the Rome Statute although the Constitution does provide for immunities (Arts. 63, 75), but from the legal point of view "these [the immunities] are not absolute and if necessary can be lifted by the Parliament."[32]

Parliament amended Art 9 (2) of the Code of Criminal Procedure which provides that prosecution, detention or any other procedural means regarding certain officially accorded immunities or similar protections by Georgian law or its Constitution, as well as persons enjoying diplomatic immunity and representatives of the ICC, are determined by the Constitution, by international agreements to which Georgia is party, as well as the Code of Criminal Procedure and other laws.

In addressing possible inconsistencies between the Georgian Criminal Code and the Code of Criminal Procedural, Georgia chose not to adopt a separate law but rather to proceed with a series of amendments to certain provisions. The crimes within the jurisdiction of the Court are now included in the Georgian Criminal Code as follows: genocide under Art 407, crimes against humanity under Art 408, and war crimes under Arts 411, 412 and 413.[33]

---

31 Art 13 of the Constitution of Georgia provides that Georgian nationals cannot be extradited except when otherwise established by international treaties to which it is a party. The distinction in the Rome Statute (Art 102) between extradition (to another State) and surrender (to the ICC) was recognised. See also: "Workshop on the Ratification and Implementation of the Rome Statute of the International Criminal Court in the Southern Caucasus" 29 February - 1 March 2004, Tbilisi, Georgia.

32 Ibid. Prof. *Kvachadze* and *Turava* of the Supreme Court of Georgia summarised the steps that were taken by Georgia towards ratification and implementation of the Statute.

33 Ibid.

4.3 Steps undertaken towards the implementation of the Rome Statute

4.3.1 Armenia

Armenia signed the Rome Statute on 1 October 1999[34] and took a number of steps towards ratification and implementation. In August 2004, the Armenian Constitutional Court delivered a negative opinion[35] on the compatibility of the Rome Statute with the national legislation. The reasons were: *a)* the ICC is seen as supplementing the national judicial system of Armenia (contradicting Arts 91 and 92 of the Constitution); *b)* national authorities would be deprived of the right to grant amnesty (Arts 40, Art 55 para 17, Art 81 para 1).[36]

In the Constitution, it is stated that once ratified international agreements become part of national law, they prevail over conflicting laws of Armenia. In order to harmonise the Statute with domestic laws, there was a need to amend the Criminal Code and the Code of Criminal Procedure regarding the surrender or extradition of Armenian citizens but whilst the Rome Statute is ratified, it would have primacy over national laws. A new Criminal Code was adopted on 18 April 2003. This provides for some changes in section 13 ("Crimes against peace and human security") which gives the definition of: *a)* serious breaches of international humanitarian law during armed conflicts (Art 391); *b)* crimes against human security (Art 392); *c)* genocide (Art 393).[37]

4.3.2 Azerbaijan

Azerbaijan's position concerning implementation of the Rome Statute has been more influenced by a lack of political interest rather than by serious incompatibilities between the Statute and domestic legislation. A new Criminal Code entered into force on 1 September 2000. However, Azerbaijan did not sign the Rome Statute.[38] On September 2002, a discussion on signing began in the Parliament, but it was impeded by constitutional provisions on extradition, immunity and trial by jury.

Crimes enumerated in the ICC Statute are not fully provided for in the Criminal Code. The latter criminalises genocide[39] and the crime of aggression[40] as defined in

---

34 Country Summary - Georgia: <http://www.iccnow.org/?mod=newsdetail&news=15>.

35 SDO-502, 13 August 2004, Constitutional Court of the Republic of Armenia, Decision in English is available at <http://www.icrc.org/applic/ihl/ihl-nat.nsf/39a82e2ca42b52974125673e00508144/b07416492992a833c12576500051dd64?openDocument>.

36 5 July 1995, Constitution of the Republic of Armenia. The Constitution was amended in 2005.

37 English translation of the Armenian Criminal Code at: <www.legislationline.org/data/Documents/Armenia_Criminal_Code_2003.htm>.

38 Country Summary- Azerbaijan: <http://www.iccnow.org/?mod=country&iduct=11>.

39 Criminal Code of the Republic of Azerbaijan, 1 September 2000, Arts 103, 104 available in English at <www.carimeast.eu/media/legal%20module/natfr/AZ_1.2%20Criminal%20Code%20of%20AR_EN.pdf>.

40 Ibid. Arts 100, 101, 102.

the Rome Statute, and partially war crimes[41] and crimes against humanity.[42] Azerbaijan's hierarchy between national and international law is confusing: state authorities are bound by international law when addressing international issues and by national law when addressing national ones.[43] Hence, it is the Constitutional Court that has the duty to interpret the law and establish the applicable hierarchy.

4.3.3 Russian Federation

As Russia was involved in the 2008 war in Georgia and because the situation is currently under preliminary examination by the ICC, the analysis of Russia's attitude towards the ratification of the Rome Statute is also essential in the context of the South Caucasus conflicts. The Russian Federation signed the Rome Statute on 13 September 2000.[44] In September 2002, there were some attempts to submit the ratification bill to the Duma for approval, but sources reported that ratification was not on the Duma's legislative agenda[45] mostly because of political reasons. State Duma deputy speaker *Vladimir Lukin* stated, "I'm deeply convinced that we should ratify the [Rome] Statute without looking at the US stance. We should carry out not pro-American or anti-American policy, but pro-Russian policy, proceeding from our own views and beliefs."[46]

The national legislation of Russia does not fully comply with the Statute, thus the Criminal Code and Criminal Procedural Code would have to be adapted to include crimes under the jurisdiction of the Rome Statute. Co-operation legislation must also be incorporated into implementing legislation. However, a comparative study[47] of national legislation and provisions of the Rome Statute was conducted to deal with constitutional issues, criminal law and co-operation with the Court. With regard to surrender and extradition, the legal study concluded that no constitutional amendments are required.

5. Case study: The August 2008 armed conflict

5.1 The obligation of States to investigate

According to international humanitarian law, States have an obligation to investigate war crimes allegedly committed by their nationals or armed forces or on

41 Ibid. Chapter 17, Arts 114-119.
42 Ibid. Arts 105-113.
43 The Law on Extradition of Criminals on 15 May 2001 does not enable the surrender to the ICC. In respect to the extradition of nationals, there is a linguistic particularity in the Azerbaijan legislation as it refers to "extradition" and "surrender" with the same meaning differently as the Statute provides. Another difference is related to the maximum term of provisional detention: under Azerbaijan law it is limited to 48 hours and under Rome Statute the limit is 96 hours.
44 Country Summary ICC: <http://www.iccnow.org/?mod=country&iduct=143>.
45 Ibid.
46 Ibid.
47 Ibid., Country Summary ICC: <http://www.iccnow.org/?mod=country&iduct=143>.

their territory, and, if appropriate, prosecute the suspects falling under their jurisdiction.[48] The obligation to investigate and prosecute applies to both international and non-international armed conflict.[49] It is also confirmed by the UN Security Council and General Assembly that States should take measures to ensure the investigation of war crimes and crimes against humanity and the punishment of the perpetrators.[50] In 1946, the UN General Assembly recommended that all States, including those not members of the UN, arrest persons who allegedly committed war crimes in the Second World War and send them back for prosecution to the State where the crimes were committed.[51]

A number of human rights treaties include an obligation on States to prosecute persons suspected of having committed serious violations of human rights such as the ICCPR and the Convention Against Torture and Other Cruel, Inhuman or Degrading Treatment or Punishment which impose a general obligation on all States Parties to provide an effective remedy against violations of the rights and freedoms contained in these two core human rights treaties. This includes not only a duty to investigate but also to punish the individuals held criminally responsible for the crimes committed.

The preamble to the Statute of the ICC recalls "the duty of every State to exercise its criminal jurisdiction over those responsible for international crimes". As the ICC former Prosecutor *Moreno-Ocampo* stated "The Rome Statute ensures the end of impunity and that … States have the primary responsibility to investigate and prosecute; the Court only steps in if there are no genuine national proceedings."

Article 1 of the Rome Statute emphasises that "… the International Criminal Court established under this Statute shall be complementary to national criminal jurisdictions". The ICC principle of complementarity governs the exercise of the Court's jurisdiction. This distinguishes the Court in several significant ways from other known institutions, including the ICTY and the ICTR. The Statute recognises that States have the first responsibility and right to prosecute international crimes. The ICC may only exercise jurisdiction where national legal systems fail to do so, including where they purport to act but in reality are unwilling or unable to genuinely carry out proceedings.

The complementarity regime serves as a mechanism to encourage and facilitate the compliance of States with their primary responsibility to investigate and prosecute core crimes. Where States fail to genuinely carry out proceedings, the Prosecutor must be ready to move decisively with ICC proceedings.

---

48 First Geneva Convention, Art 49; Second Geneva Convention, Art 50; Third Geneva Convention, Art 129; Fourth Geneva Convention, Art 146.

49 Genocide Convention, Art VI; Hague Convention for the Protection of Cultural Property, Art 28; Convention against Torture, Art 7; Chemical Weapons Convention, Art VII (1); Amended Protocol II to the Convention on Certain Conventional Weapons, Art 14 ; Ottawa Convention, Art 9; Second Protocol to the Hague Convention for the Protection of Cultural Property, Arts 15–17.

50 See: UN General Assembly, Res. 2583 (XXIV) and 2712 (XXV), Res. 2840 (XXVI) and Res. 3074 (XXVIII).

51 UN General Assembly, Res. 3 (I) para 570.

5.2 The EU Fact-finding Mission to Georgia

Considering the sensitive situation in Georgia, on 1 September 2008 the EU Council pledged its commitment to support firstly every effort to "secure a peaceful and lasting solution" and secondly "confidence-building measures" to the conflict in Georgia.[52] Therefore on 2 December 2008, the EU Council of Ministers decided to establish the IIFFMCG which would aim, as provided in Art 1 (2) of the Rome Statute, "to investigate the origins and of the course of the conflict in Georgia, including with regard to international law, humanitarian law and human rights, and the accusation made in that context"[53] including allegations of war crimes.

The *Tagliavini* report, concluded by the Fact-Finding Mission, noted that: "[...] guided by the principles of fairness, impartiality, even-handedness and balance for the report, the Mission's purpose was to present the sequence of events to discuss the responsibility and will make a contribution to the stable and peaceful environment the South Caucasus as a prerequisite for the development of all the countries and nations sharing the region."[54]

As for the conflict in South Ossetia and adjacent parts of the territory of Georgia, the Mission established that all sides to the conflict - Georgian forces, Russian forces and South Ossetian forces - committed violations of international humanitarian law and human rights law. Numerous violations were committed by South Ossetian irregular armed groups, by volunteers, mercenaries, and by armed individuals. One of the main problems which was stated in the Report was that "it is difficult to identify the responsibilities for and the perpetrators of these crimes" because both Georgian and Russian forces in many cases used similar armament, further complicating the attribution of certain acts. Therefore, many crimes committed during the conflict have significant elements which might be described as war crimes, if it were not for the difficulties of identification and attribution.[55]

Apart from war crimes, one of the most serious allegations was made by Russia and South Ossetia against Georgia: the charge of genocide.[56] Hence the Mission urgently started to examine this allegation, due to the grave connotations conjured up by the term genocide in public opinion and conscience, and also due to its very specific legal definition and to the ensuing serious consequences under international law.[57] Genocide is described as a specific act (killing, serious bodily or mental harm, etc) "committed with intent to destroy, in whole or in part, a national, ethnical, religious or racial group, as such".[58] Moreover, the Mission reaffirmed the legal

---

52 IIFFMCG, Vol 1, margin 3, at 6.
53 Council Decision 2008/901/CFSP of 2 December 2008 concerning an independent international fact-finding mission on the conflict in Georgia.
54 IIFFMCG, Vol 1, margin 10, at 9.
55 IIFFMCG, Vol 1, margin 26, at 26.
56 IIFFMCG, Vol 1, margin 27, at 27.
57 Ibid.
58 Convention on the Prevention and Punishment of the Crime of Genocide, adopted on 9 December 1948 by the United Nations General Assembly.

argumentation that international law requires proof of specific intent for the crime of genocide to be constituted.[59]

According to international law, all the acts that constitute genocide are grave breaches of the Geneva Conventions and represent war crimes if they are committed in the course of an international armed conflict.[60] Also, any act that constitutes genocide and is committed in the course of a non-international armed conflict is a violation of common Art 3 and of Protocol II. The Mission concluded: "After having carefully reviewed the facts in the light of the relevant law, to the best of its knowledge allegations of genocide committed by the Georgian side in the context of the August 2008 conflict and its aftermath are neither founded in law nor substantiated by factual evidence.[61]

Several testimonies by direct eyewitnesses and indirect sources stated extrajudicial killings[62] of ethnic Georgians by Ossetian forces during the torching of villages in South Ossetia. Amnesty International documented "unlawful killings, beatings, threats, arson and looting perpetrated by armed groups associated with the South Ossetian side.[63] Although several international organisations documented different numbers of people killed in the war,[64] an exact number of summary executions has not been established by the Mission even though it "declared that there is credible evidence of cases of summary executions carried out by South Ossetian forces."[65]

Unfortunately, the August 2008 armed conflict saw many crimes committed in violation of international law, international humanitarian law and human rights law[66] from all the parts involved in the conflict by the Georgian forces, Russian forces and South Ossetian irregular armed groups, by volunteers or mercenaries or by armed individuals. Beyond those acts committed during the five days of hostilities from 7-8 to 12 August, additional acts were perpetrated after the ceasefire came into effect, raising serious concerns about the co-responsibility of those forces in control of the situation, whose duty was to protect the civilian population.

The Report demonstrated that "most of the violations committed during the August 2008 conflict and the ceasefire period were committed in South Ossetia and in the adjacent so-called buffer zone. By contrast, few violations were reported in the upper Kodori Valley and Abkhazia. This exception does not relate, however, to the situation of ethnic Georgians in the Gali district of Abkhazia and the upper Kodori Valley, where their rights as a minority seem to be endangered."[67]

---

59 IIFFMCG Vol 1, margin 27, at 26.

60 Art 50/51/130/147 of the Geneva Conventions; Art 85 of Protocol I.

61 Ibid.

62 IIFFMCG, Vol 2, at 353.

63 See also *Human Rights Watch*, Up In Flames – Humanitarian Law Violations and Civilian Victims in the Conflict over South Ossetia, 2009, at <www.hrw.org/sites/default/files/reports/georgia0109web.pdf>; *Amnesty International*, Civilians in the line of Fire - The Georgia-Russia Conflict, 18 January 2008, at 39.

64 "During and in the immediate aftermath of the war, at least 14 people were deliberately killed by Ossetian militias in territory controlled by Russian forces. Human Rights Watch documented six deliberate killings in Georgian settlements controlled by Russian forces, and received credible allegations of another six cases. Human Rights Watch also heard allegations of two such killings in South Ossetia." Ibid., 154.

65 IIFFMCG Vol 2, at 355.

66 IIFFMCG Vol 1, margin 25, at 26.

67 IIFFMCG, Vol 1, margin 25-26, at 26.

With regard to allegations of ethnic cleansing committed by South Ossetian forces or irregular armed groups, the Mission reported continuing forced displacements of ethnic Georgians who had remained in their homes after the hostilities. It found evidence of systematic looting and destruction of ethnic Georgian villages in South Ossetia. Consequently, the Report concluded that ethnic cleansing of ethnic Georgians in South Ossetia was indeed practised both during and after the August 2008 conflict.[68]

In respect to international humanitarian law on the conduct of hostilities and the protection of non-combatants, the violations during the armed conflict concern the ill-treatment of persons, the destruction of property and forced displacement. More specifically, the violations include indiscriminate attacks in terms of the type of weaponry used and their targeting, the lack of adequate protection by Russia and Georgia, widespread campaigns of looting and destruction of ethnic Georgian settlements by South Ossetians, as well as ill-treatment, gender-related violence including rape, assault, hostage-taking and arbitrary arrests, together with the failure by Russian forces to prevent and stop violations by South Ossetian forces, armed irregular groups and armed individuals before and after the ceasefire in South Ossetia and the adjacent territories.

There was a considerable flow of IDPs and refugees which confirms the severity of the conflict. Reportedly about 135,000 persons fled their homes, most of them from regions in and near South Ossetia.[69] While most persons fled to other parts of Georgia, a significant number also sought refuge in Russia. The majority fled because of the dangers and the insecurity connected to the conflict situation. In addition, numerous cases of forced displacements in violation of international humanitarian and human rights law were noted. The Report highlighted that more than 35,000 IDPs/refugees are not expected to return to their homes in the foreseeable future, owing to the continued insecurity of the situation or to the destruction of their homes and property.

Mullins identified the variation in the type and frequency of the violations of the Geneva Conventions by the parties in the August 2008 conflict (see table below). This conflict produced 199 incidents in which South Ossetians (94 crimes) and Russian forces (82 crimes) were responsible for both the largest number and the most grave crimes recorded.

---

[68] IIFFMCG, Vol 1, margin 27, at 27.
[69] Ibid. margin 28, at 27.

Table: Violations of the Geneva Conventions (Mullins 2011)

Crime	Georgia	Russia	South Ossetia	Abkhazian	To-tals
Failure to maintain order in an occupied territory	0	14	n/a	n/a	14
Rape	1	0	5	0	6
Indiscriminate/disproportionate: artillery/air strikes	7	13	0	0	20
Indiscriminate/disproportionate: vehicle/small arms	4	1	0	0	5
Looting	1	3	30	2	36
Destruction of property	1	5	27	0	33
Inappropriate targets (civilian)	6	17	0	0	23
Murder (civilian)	1	5	17	0	23
Ill-treatment/torture (civilian)	0	3	8	0	11
Detentions	0	1	3	0	4
POW violations	0	3	4	0	7
Destruction of cultural objects	0	17	0	0	17
Total	21	82	94	2	199

Given the evidence, Russian forces were responsible for failure to maintain order in 14 incidents, inappropriate targeting and using indiscriminate and disproportionate artillery and air strikes. Of the four parties involved in the conflict, two (namely Russia and South Ossetia) clearly committed more crimes.[70]

[70] *Mullins,* War Crimes in the 2008 Georgia–Russia Conflict, British Journal of Criminology 2011, 918 (924).

5.3 Office of the Prosecutor: No impunity for crimes committed in Georgia

5.3.1 National investigations into alleged crimes

Georgia is a State Party to the Rome Statute since 2003, thus the ICC has jurisdiction over the crimes committed on the territory of Georgia or by its nationals from 1 December 2003 onwards. This includes forced displacement of civilians, killing of peacekeepers and attacks against civilian targets.

The Office of the Prosecutor (OTP) received 3,830 communications in relation to the Georgian situation and made its preliminary examination public on August 2008. The Office conducted a visit to Georgia in November 2008 and to Russia in March 2010; both Russian and Georgian authorities provided substantial information from their national investigations before. In February 2011, the OTP conducted a second visit to the Russian Federation and received a comprehensive update on the progress of national investigations. In September 2011, both Governments of Russia and Georgia were requested to provide a written update on the progress and failures of their respective investigations.

On 18 October 2011, the Russian Embassy replied to the OTP that "factors create an obstacle to genuine advancements in the national investigation of the criminal case, preventing the possibility to properly bring to justice alleged perpetrators of crimes within the jurisdiction of the Russian Federation".[71] According to Russian authorities, "the Georgian side had refused to provide legal assistance in relation to the criminal case" and "senior officials of foreign states including those of Georgia enjoy immunity from the criminal jurisdiction of the Russian Federation".[72]

On 12 December 2011, the Georgian Government provided the OTP with an updated report concerning the national criminal proceedings related to the August 2008 armed conflict. On 15 May 2013, the Chief Prosecutor of Georgia officially confirmed that the investigation would focus on allegations of war crimes, including "attacks against Russian peacekeepers by the Georgian troops, attacks against civilians both by the Georgian and Russian troops, destruction of civilian properties, forcible displacement of civilian population, torture and other ill-treatment, and pillage of ethnic Georgian villages".[73] Georgia as a State Party to the Rome Statute in fulfilling its obligation to co-operate with the ICC "stressed its willingness to fulfil its obligations to investigate and prosecute those responsible for committing crimes within the jurisdiction of the Court, regardless of nationality or status".[74]

---

71 Report on Preliminary Examination Activities 2012, The Office of Prosecutor ICC, November 2012, §133, 31, <http://www.icc-cpi.int/NR/rdonlyres/C433C462-7C4E-4358-8A72-8D99FD00E8CD/285209/OTP2012ReportonPreliminaryExaminations22Nov2012.pdf>.

72 Ibid.

73 Report on Preliminary Examination Activities 2013, The Office of Prosecutor ICC, November 2013, §168, 40, <http://www.icc-cpi.int/en_menus/icc/press%20and%20media/press%20releases/Documents/OTP%20Preliminary%20Examinations/OTP%20-%20Report%20%20Preliminary%20Examination%20Activities%202013.PDF>.

74 Ibid. para 172, at 41.

Apart from the Russian and Georgian governments' reports, the OTP received reports by different NGOs and participated in meetings with these organisations in which additional facts of the alleged crimes committed during the August 2008 conflict were provided.

5.3.2 OTP Report on Preliminary Examinations

In its latest 2013 Report on the Preliminary Examinations, the OTP identified serious crimes allegedly committed in the August 2008 conflict as following:

1. Forcible displacement of Georgian population: Through systematic and widespread destruction and pillaging of houses and property, South Ossetian forces allegedly forced 30,000 ethnic Georgians to flee from villages within and outside South Ossetia.

2. *Attacks against peacekeepers*: According to available information, Georgian forces allegedly attacked Russian peacekeepers' positions in Tskhinvali.

3. *Unlawful attacks:* There are allegations that both Georgian and Russian forces might have used indiscriminate or disproportionate force and/or failed to take the required precautions to spare civilian losses.

4. *Pillaging and destruction of property*: Allegedly, South Ossetian forces, not prevented by Russian forces, looted, burned and systematically destroyed ethnic Georgian villages in South Ossetia and the "buffer zone" for the purpose of forcing their residents to leave.

5. *Torture and other forms of ill-treatment*: Georgian prisoners of war as well as ethnic Georgian and South Ossetian civilians were reportedly victims of torture, degrading treatment or other forms of ill-treatment.[75]

The OTP stated that "there is a reasonable basis to believe that the war crimes of pillaging, destroying civilian property and inflicting acts of torture were committed in the context of the August 2008 armed conflict. There also is a reasonable basis to believe that the crime against humanity of forcible transfer or deportation of population was committed." At the same time, the OTP took a reserved position requiring "further evaluation of alleged unlawful attacks by all parties, including the alleged attack against Russian peacekeepers."[76]

6. EU POLICY ON INTERNATIONAL CRIMINAL JUSTICE, THE FIGHT AGAINST IMPUNITY AND THE ICC

6.1 The EU's position

The EU is playing a key role in establishing a common criminal justice space. It recognises the ICC as a mechanism of last resort which is responsible for the enforcement of justice for the victims of crimes against humanity, genocide,

---

[75] Report on Preliminary Examination Activities 2013, op. cit. note 73, paras 157-162 at 38-39.

[76] OTP Report on Preliminary Examinations, 13 December 2011, Para 97.

war crimes and aggression, as laid down by the principle of complementarity in the Rome Statute. In the 2012 Resolution on the Annual Report on Human Rights and Democracy, the EP "reiterates its strong support for ICC in the fight against impunity for the most serious crimes of international concern" and "calls on the EU and its Member States to continue their political, diplomatic, logistical and financial backing of the ICC and other international criminal tribunals, including the ad hoc international tribunals for the former Yugoslavia and Rwanda, the Special Court for Sierra Leone, the Extraordinary Chambers in the Courts of Cambodia, and the Special Tribunal for Lebanon."[77]

The EP supports "the inclusion in the EU Strategic Framework and Action Plan on Human Rights and Democracy of reference to the need to fight vigorously against impunity for serious crimes, not least through a commitment to the ICC, and the understanding that it is the primary duty of states to investigate grave international crimes, promote and contribute to strengthening the capacity of national judicial systems to investigate and prosecute these crimes".[78] It also enhanced efforts to secure full co-operation with the Court through relevant national legislation on co-operation. The EP emphasised the need to ensure that the issue of the fight against impunity is addressed more systematically in the EU's bilateral relations with the relevant countries, including by raising it in public statements, and that the EU addresses impunity more consistently at the multilateral level, for instance at the UN General Assembly and Human Rights Council.

EU institutions have clearly underlined their commitment to the principle of the 'Responsibility to Protect' (R2P), stressing the importance that the international community, including the EU, assumes responsibility through humanitarian intervention and appropriate diplomatic pressure for addressing gross human rights violations in third countries when the governments of these countries are unable or unwilling to protect their own citizens.

The EU systematically seeks the inclusion of a clause supporting the ICC in negotiating mandates and agreements with third countries. In the framework of the ENP, the Commission has included ICC clauses in APs with the following countries: Armenia, Azerbaijan, Georgia, Egypt, Lebanon, Jordan, Moldova and Ukraine.

The positive approach of the EU to recognise the ICC as an important institution to establish global criminal justice has reinforced the Court's legitimacy and potential effectiveness and sends a strong signal to the South Caucasus. The inclusion of the ICC clause in ENP APs is a positive step for the EU commitment as a successful mediator. There is a strong EU action to "condemn" instances of non-co-operation, such as invitations of individuals subject to an ICC arrest warrant and failure to arrest and surrender such individuals.

---

[77] EP Resolution of 13 December 2012 on the Annual Report on Human Rights and Democracy in the World 2011 and the European Union's policy on the matter (2012/2145(INI)), <http://www.europarl.europa.eu/sides/getDoc.do?pubRef=-//EP//TEXT+TA+P7-TA-2012-0503+0+DOC+XML+V0//EN&language=EN#def_1_6>.

[78] Ibid.

6.2 The New Partnership Perspectives: EU - Armenia

The ENP opens up new partnership perspectives for Armenia, especially in the area of economic and political co-operation.[79] Additionally, there is a "continuing strong EU commitment to support the settlement of the Nagorno-Karabakh conflict; conflict resolution and post conflict rehabilitation."[80]

The EU-Armenia co-operation further strengthened since 2009 when former Soviet republics (Armenia, Azerbaijan, Georgia, Moldova, Belarus, Ukraine) were included in the EU EaP which considers these countries separately from the other ENP regions. A new generation of AA has been negotiated with some countries, including Armenia, on an individual basis.

In priority area 7 of the APs, the EU vows to contribute to a peaceful solution of the Nagorno-Karabakh conflict by specific actions such as increasing diplomatic efforts, political support on the basis of international norms and principles, including the principle of self-determination of peoples; by intensifying the EU dialogue with the parties concerned with a view to the acceleration of the negotiations towards a political settlement, and so forth.

Co-operation on foreign and security policy is one of the main pillars of the EU, hence the EU-Armenian political dialogue includes issues on regional and international level: with the Council of Europe, OSCE and UN, and on the implementation of the European Security Strategy.

According to the EU - Armenia relations, as provided in the AP[81], Armenia should initiate the accession to the Rome Statute. The EU stated that Armenia has to:

1. make the necessary legislative and constitutional amendments for its implementation;
2. fight against international crime in accordance with international law, giving due regard to preserving the integrity of the Rome Statute.[82]

After meeting Russian President *Putin* in Moscow on 3 September 2013, Armenia's President *Sargsyan* announced his country's intention to join the Russia-led Customs Union. After this statement, European officials declared that the EU-Armenia AA, the initiation of which had been planned for November, "will not proceed with its initialling due to Armenia's new international commitments",[83] as was put in the joint Armenia-EU statement within the framework of the EU EaP

---

[79] ENPI, Armenia Country Strategy Paper 2007-2013 <http://ec.europa.eu/world/enp/pdf/country/enpi_csp_armenia_en.pdf>.

[80] Armenia Progress Report Implementation of the European Neighbourhood Policy in 2008, Brussels, 23 April 2009, SEC(2009) 511.

[81] EU/Armenia AP, 2006-2011, available at <http://eeas.europa.eu/enp/pdf/pdf/action_plans/armenia_enp_ap_final_en.pdf>.

[82] Armenia Progress Report 2010. This document reports on the progress made in the implementation of the EU-Armenia ENP AP between 1 January and 31 December 2010, at 6-7.

[83] Joint declaration of the Eastern Partnership Summit, Vilnius, 29 November 2013, 17130/13

Summit in Vilnius. They agreed on the "need to update the EU-Armenia ENP Action Plan."[84]

6.3 Russia: Lack of interest towards membership in EU and ICC

Russia does not have any interest in becoming a member of the EU although its economic co-operation with EU Member States is very important. The Westernisation of Georgia's foreign and security policies is challenging to Russia especially with regard to the "breakaway territories" - a source of disagreements in the process of conflict resolution. In addition, the connection between the Euro-Atlantic orientation of Georgian foreign and security policy and the expectations of Western support for reintegration do not support the conduct of Russian policies in the region.

However, the EU largely respects the strong Russian reservation about any change in the existing formats for peacekeeping and mediation in the "frozen conflicts" in the South Caucasus.[85] Thus, the EU's engagement in its common neighbourhood with Russia was characterised by the International Crisis Group as "working around the conflict" since 2006, i.e. not "working on the conflict".[86]

Kosovo's declaration of independence raised a lot of debate in the South Caucasus on the issues of fundamental international legal principles of self-determination, sovereignty and territorial integrity. Western governments and regional organisations that recognised Kosovo's declaration of independence argued a case of *sui generis*.[87] However, not all Member States of the EU had a common argument in favour of the case because of the fear that the Kosovo precedent would be taken into account for separatist conflicts in their own territories.[88] Indeed, the precedent had a sensitive impact on the unresolved conflicts of Georgia and on the bilateral relations between Georgia and Russia. Russia took the advantage to consider the Kosovo case as a parallel precedent for unresolved conflicts in the South Caucasus region and recognised the independence of Abkhazia and South Ossetia.

The Russian Federation is a state which is not party to the Rome Statute and its co-operation with the Court is rather vague given the fact that its former adversary, the United States, has no intention to become a party to the ICC. Hence, Russia's escape from impunity is a real challenge for the ICC, even though Russia could fall under the jurisdiction of the Court with a mandate from the UN Security Council. Considering that Russia has the right of veto in the Council, this puts in doubt the ICC efficiency to perform its tasks.

---

84 Ibid.

85 IIFFMCG, Vol 2, at 18.

86 Conflict Resolution in the South Caucasus: The EU's Role, ICG Europe Report No.173, 20 March 2006.

87 IIFFMCG Vol 2, at 2.

88 IIFFMCG Vol 2, at 26; see also: Akcakoca / Vanhauwaert / Whitman / *Wolff*, After Georgia: Conflict Resolution in the EU's Eastern Neighbourhood, European Policy Centre April 2009, at 9.

7. CONCLUSIONS

The on-going "frozen" conflicts and unresolved territorial and political disputes in the South Caucasus do not allow the proper application of post-conflict justice rehabilitation and reconciliation. The ratification of the Rome Statute seems as a guarantee for international justice; a contributor in ending impunity for the perpetrators of heinous crimes and to the prevention of such crimes.

In all the conflicts which occurred in the South Caucasus, the belligerent parties committed violations of international humanitarian law, i.e. the Geneva Conventions and other international human rights laws. The result was always human tragedy. The primary consideration and final goal of the international community should be the physical security of its population. The states are responsible to take reforms and measures in order to enhance the protection of human rights and to condemn those who breach the laws. Politics plays a critical role in mastering the will-power to go through with the process of prosecuting crimes and to bring perpetrators of alleged crimes to trial. This requires not only a common understanding and expectation among the South Caucasus, EU and ICC in the process of investigation and prosecution, but also political mobilisation of all the actors, involved in frozen conflicts, including states, not parties to the Rome Statute. Despite the complexity and uncertainty for European Integration, there is hope for the democratisation of the South Caucasus countries following the example of the Balkans: Croatia as a new EU Member State and Serbia as a candidate country to the EU.

Even though there are similarities between the South Caucasus and the Western Balkans in the transition to democracy and in the attitude towards EU integration, the co-operation with international tribunals seems to be different. This reflects upon the failure of political support to insist on co-operation with the ICC. OTP conclusions might have been drawn differently if the countries involved in the conflict would have been more forthcoming to report all the facts in their reports. Unlike Georgia, neither Armenia nor Azerbaijan is still party to the ICC. But all the conflicts in the region have the potential to escalate, thus, there is a possibility of new crimes being committed in the future. Therefore, joining the ICC would serve as a restricting factor in future possible crimes. One of the main tasks is co-ordination between the EU and international organisations in the process of further investigation and pressure towards the national governments of the South Caucasus into creating a better co-operation for enhancing access to justice to officials who committed serious crimes.

The EU underlines the importance of the EaP as a specific Eastern dimension of the ENP in order to enhance prosperity, security, democracy, rule of law, respect for human rights, good governance, sustainable development and regional co-operation throughout the South Caucasus, and it is ready to enhance efforts to support confidence building and peaceful settlements to the conflicts in the region, in close co-operation with all relevant parties especially with Armenia, Azerbaijan, Georgia and Russia. However, the lack of judicial intervention aiming to fight impunity for past human rights abuses can lead to never-ending instability, lack of transparency and denial of justice for the victims and Caucasian society-at-large. The historic argument that it would be dangerous to punish the perpetrators of human rights abuses in order to not "shame" the states and officials is quite inhuman rather than politically dangerous. Hence, no consideration was given to bring to justice those allegedly bearing responsibility for gross violation of human rights in armed conflicts.

The Fact-Finding Report and the preliminary report of the OTP concluded that it was extremely difficult to confirm and verify the truth. Nevertheless, searching for the truth is an absolute imperative for peace and unavoidable future co-existence in the Caucasus. The August war is the result of an untold truth about the wars of the 1990s, impunity for those crimes, and nearly 20 years of injustice. Ending this cycle will provide grounds for a real guarantee of peace and security not only in Georgia, but in the entire region, apart from *Realpolitik*. In this context the relationship of the EU and the South Caucasus remains a forward moving project while it seems that the ICC represents a retrospective challenge.

Full co-operation with the ICC, as well as a commitment to fair domestic war crimes trials would demonstrate the South Caucasus' maturity and commitment to fully embrace the values of the EU. Conversely, the failure to co-operate with the ICC impedes the normalisation of the relations with the other countries of the region. To maintain peace, protect human rights and prevent the recurrence of similar serious atrocities in the future, the South Caucasus countries should become parties to the ICC Statute, rely in their co-operation with the ICC on the principle of complementarity and the system of co-operation which presupposes effective implementation of the Rome Statute into national law.

Aleksandra Šaranović

RESTITUTION OF PROPERTY TO DISPLACED PERSONS IN POST-CONFLICT SITUATIONS

"Art 9 (2) AA EU-Georgia

The Parties recognize the importance of the commitment of Georgia to reconciliation and its efforts to restore its territorial integrity in pursuit of a peaceful and lasting conflict resolution, of pursuing the full implementation of the 12 August 2008 Six-Point Agreement and its subsequent implementing measures, of pursuing mutually supportive non-recognition and engagement policies, of supporting the Geneva International Discussions and of safe and dignified return of all IDPs and refugees to their habitual places of residence in line with principles of international law; and of a meaningful international field involvement, including, as appropriate, that of the EU."

1. INTRODUCTION

"Gross violations of human rights, war crimes, and mass violence have characterised modernization. Over the last two centuries, most countries inflicted violence on foreign and domestic population leading to uprooting and the mass movement of people. As many as two hundred million refugees have crossed borders in the course of domestic and international political violence. Of those, many millions were repatriated, many millions were not. Most of those who could not return remained displaced for years, at times for decades and generations."[1]

According to the information available to UN High Commissioner on Refugees, at the end of the 2010 the number of "population of concern" amounted to 33.9 million.[2] It is estimated that Georgia, Armenia and Azerbaijan have around one million of displaced persons.

Properly restitution is at the core of a solution that would help displaced persons but also overcome a part of the conflicts as well. The right to property is recognised as a human right by the international community through a number of treaties. There is a close relationship between property rights and conflicts. "Housing, land and real property issues are often origins of, or results from, conflict and are therefore inextricably linked to the achievement and consolidation of lasting peace and

---

1 *Adelman / Barkan*, No Return, No Refuge: Rites and Rights in Minority Repatriation (2011) at 3.

2 UNHCR Statistical Yearbook 2010, 10th edition (2010), available at <http://www.unhcr.org/statistics>.

prevention of future violence".[3] *Pantuliano* and *Elhawary* define four types of relationship between property and conflict: "1. grievances that trigger the conflict; 2. land and property issues that emerge during war due to the breakdown in rule of law, the policies of those in control during the conflict and, especially forced displacement; 3. property issues that arise or are exacerbated because of the poorly managed peace; 4. inequitable property relations, especially in agrarian societies, which risk causing further violence if left unresolved".[4]

As for the EU's position on property restitution, on the one hand, the issue is not covered by the *acquis*, as the competences of the EU are based on the doctrine of delegated powers as stated by Art 13 (2) TEU. In addition Art 345 TFEU states that the Treaties shall in no way prejudice the rules in Member States governing the system of property ownership. On the other hand, Art 2 TEU states that the Union is founded on the principles of liberty, democracy, respect for human rights and fundamental freedoms, and the rule of law, principles which are also common to the Member States. The EU is to respect fundamental rights, as guaranteed by the ECHR and as they result from the constitutional traditions common to the Member States, as general principles of Union law (Art 6, (2) and (3) TEU). Fundamental rights, a notion originally developed by ECJ jurisprudence as early as in 1969, have been given by means of Art 6 (1) TEU the same legal value as the Treaties. The Charter of Fundamental Human Rights contains a catalogue of basic rights and fundamental freedoms, which reflect the constitutional traditions and international obligations common to the Member States, one of the rights contained being the right to property.

"From the political criteria point of view, the EU considers property rights as part of the socio-economic rights" and "we expect a country aspiring to join the EU to pay due attention to this issue as we expect the values of the Union such as the 'respect for human rights' to be duly taken into account also in matters which belong to the sphere of national competence."[5] As from the EU point of view, property rights and therefore property restitution are regarded as human rights. The "EU Guidelines on Human Rights dialogues with third countries"[6] need to be taken into account as well. The dialogues referred to in the Guidelines include amongst others "dialogues or discussions of a rather general nature based on regional or bilateral treaties, agreements or conventions or strategic partnerships dealing systematically with the issue of human rights. These include in particular: ...and the neighbourhood policy (countries of the Caucasus in particular)".[7] The Guidelines provide that "the European Union undertakes to intensify the process of integrating human rights and de-

---

3 UN Secretary General, Report of the Secretary-General on the Protection of the Civilians in Armed Conflicts S/2007/643, 28 October 2007, para 52.

4 *Pantuliano / Elhawary,* Uncharted Territory: Land, Conflict and Humanitarian Action. Practical Action Publishing (2009) at 2.

5 Speech by Ambassador Degert, available at <www.europa.rs/en/mediji/najnovije-vesti/1064/Ambassador+Degert,+speech+on+the+Conference+on+Property+Restitution.html>.

6 Available at <http://eeas.europa.eu/human_rights/guidelines/dialogues/index_en.htm>.

7 The Council of the European Union, Guidelines on Human rights dialogues with third countries- update, 19 January 2009, Paragraph 2.

mocratisation objectives ("mainstreaming") into all aspects of its external policies. Accordingly, the EU will ensure that the issue of human rights, democracy and the rule of law will be included in all future meetings and discussions with third countries and at all levels".[8] Therefore, the EU has the legitimacy to discuss the question of property restitution in all its dialogues with third countries. Indeed, the 2011 Report on Implementation of the European Neighbourhood Policy in Georgia deals both with the question of the position of IDPs[9] and the property rights problems.[10] In the Council conclusions on the South Caucasus from 27 February 2012 it is stated that "the EU reiterates its commitment to help improve the situation of Internally Displaced Persons in Georgia and refugees from the conflicts and their unconditional right to safe and dignified return, while underlining also the need to enhance efforts to provide livelihood options and to provide conditions allowing those Internally Displaced Persons who choose to stay in Tbilisi administered territory to integrate fully into society."[11] So far the role of the EU in the South Caucasus was mostly limited to providing help in the housing solutions to IDPs which amounted to EUR 43.5 million in the period under review by the 2011 ENP report on Georgia[12] and did not cover property restitution. However, should the actual return of property take place it might be possible that the EU would play the role it played in the Balkans. Namely, in BiH the EU was involved in the restitution process through the OHR who acted as EU Special Representative as well since February 2002 and "furthermore, from 1994-1996 the EC even led the administration in the Municipality of Mostar (Arts 1 and 4 of Memorandum of Understanding) signed in Geneva on 18 March 1994) and exercised comprehensive powers of governance."[13]

As this paper focuses on UN Principles on Housing and Property Restitution for Refugees and IDPs (Pinheiro Principles) it is also important to note that the EU has not formulated its position on these principles when dealing with property restitution. Since the ECJ has referred in its jurisprudence to the relevant rights of ECHR, e.g. in the case *Regione autonoma Friuli-Venezia Giulia and ERSA*, it has stated that in determining the scope of the right to property, Art 1 of Protocol 1 to ECHR must be taken into account, it is clear that the provisions of the ECHR and their interpretation by the ECtHR fall within the notion of fundamental rights. The ECtHR in its jurisprudence on the interpretation of Art 1 of Protocol 1 to ECHR made implicit and explicit references to the Pinheiro Principles as "a relevant international document", e.g. in *Đokić v. Bosnia.* Furthermore, the Council of Europe of which

---

8 Ibid. para 3.

9 *European Commission / High Representative of the Union for Foreign Affairs and Security Policy,* Implementation of the European Neighbourhood Policy in Georgia. Progress in 2011 and Recommendations for Action Accompanying the Document 'Joint Communication to the European Parliament, the Council, the European Social and Economic Committee and the Committee of the Regions Delivering on a New European Neighbourhood Policy', SWD (2012) 114 final, 3.

10 Ibid. 7.

11 Council Conclusions on the South Caucasus 3149th Foreign Affairs Council meeting Brussels, 27 February 2012, para 23.

12 European Commission / High Representative of the Union for Foreign Affairs and Security Policy, op. cit. note 9, 6.

13 Directorate-General for Internal Policies, Private Properties Issues following the Regional Conflict in Bosnia and Herzegovina, Croatia and Kosovo, Study (2010) 42.

all Member States of the EU are members, in its Solving Property Issues of Refugees and Displaced Persons Report "calls on member states to resolve post-conflict housing, land and property rights issues of refugees and IDPs, taking into account the Pinheiro Principles, the relevant Council of Europe instruments, and Recommendation Rec(2006)6 of the Committee of Ministers."[14] Therefore, the EU will be expected to apply the Pinheiro Principles when discussing and providing help in property restitution processes.

2. POLITICAL CONDITIONS

In order for property restitution to take place it is necessary that some political prerequisites are fulfilled. As experience from BiH and other parts of the world shows, it is generally necessary to conclude some sort of peace agreement before restitution can take place. In BiH Annex VII of the Dayton Peace Agreement referred expressly to property restitution. It is important that practical issues such as property disputes are also addressed. It is also possible that the return of the displaced persons will take place even before the conclusion of a peace treaty if there is a lasting cease-fire agreement. In case of Armenia, Azerbaijan and the Nagorno-Karabakh region a cease-fire agreement exists since July 1994, but a peace agreement is yet to be agreed upon although the Minsk group presented several drafts, and conflicts on the "contact line" never ceased to happen. However, in cases such as the one involving Georgia and Abkhazia and South Ossetia, where not only the cease-fire agreements were in force and broken on several occasions but the agreements on the return of refugees and displaced persons were also broken, it is doubtful that anything less than a lasting peace agreement would encourage the return of displaced persons. It is also a good incentive for the displaced persons to return when the international community is involved in a process since it gives returnees a reassurance that the return will be properly conducted, which is especially important for the return of members of a minority group. In the case of the South Caucasus the trouble of the returnees can be described by looking at the return of Georgians to the Gali region where after the period of return in 1997 a new wave of violence took place in 1998 forcing returnees to once again leave their homes. Including provisions in a peace treaty such as those which were part of Annex VII of the Dayton Peace Agreement which laid down specific obligations of the parties in regards to the property restitution and gave the mandate to UNHCR to assist in the process sends a signal that restitution is one of the priorities.

It is necessary that the question of the return of displaced persons is also regarded as a humanitarian issue. In this way the possibility of misuse of the difficult position of displaced persons for political aims should be avoided. It is crucial that their position is not contingent on agreements such as those about the status of disputed territories. A recent case between Georgia and South Ossetia showed that any polit-

14 Parliamentary Assembly of the Council of Europe, Solving Property Issues of Refugees and Displaced Persons (Doc. 12106, 8 January 2010) para 9.

icisation of the question of the refugee return might have a counter-effect as South Ossetia refused to discuss the issue after the "Georgian-sponsored" resolution on the return of displaced persons and refugees was approved by the UN General Assembly in September 2010.[15] In the case of Nagorno-Karabakh, where the international community is strongly promoting the conclusion of a peace treaty, it should be insisted that if not the whole draft treaty is accepted then parties should agree upon the part relating to the restitution of property and return of refugees and displaced persons.

3. INTERNATIONAL NORMS

There are a number of international documents that grant refugees and displaced persons a right to return. The first recognition of this right was expressed by the UN as early as 1948 when the right was proclaimed in Art 13 (2) of the Universal Declaration of Human Rights: "Everyone has the right to leave any country, including his own, and to return to his country."[16]

The ICESCR contains the most significant articulation of the right to adequate housing. The right is found in Art 11(1). Although the ICESCR recognises the right to housing as a part of the larger right to adequate standard of living, under international human rights law, the right to adequate housing is understood as an independent or free-standing right.[17]

The ICCPR has increasingly been used to enforce housing rights, e.g. homelessness has been found to threaten the right to life (Art 4), and forced evictions have been found to contravene the right to be free from arbitrary or unlawful interference with the home (Art 17).[18] Further on, the Convention on Elimination of all Forms of Racial Discrimination expressly prohibits discrimination in the housing sector (Art 5). Other Conventions dealing with discrimination provide the same right to women, especially those in rural areas,[19] and children,[20] and to persons with disabilities.[21]

Another set of international conventions deals with the prohibition of destruction of property. That is the case with the First Geneva Convention for the Amelioration

---

15 UN General Assembly, Resolution on the Status of Internally Displaced Persons and Refugees from Abkhazia, Georgia, and the Tskhinvali region / South Ossetia, Georgia, (A/RES/63/307, of 30 September 2009).

16 UN General Assembly, Universal Declaration of Human Rights (217 A (III), 10 December 1948) Art 13 (2).

17 *Edgar / Doherty / Meer,* Access to Housing: Homelessness and Vulnerability in Europe (2002) at 17.

18 *Leckie / Huggins*, Conflict and Housing, Land and Property Rights: A Handbook on Issues, Frameworks and Solutions (2011) at 61.

19 UN General Assembly, Convention on Elimination of all Forms of Discrimination against Women (18 December 1979), United Nations, Treaty Series. Vol. 1249, pg. 13 Art. 14 (2) (h)

20 UN General Assembly, Convention on the Rights of the Child (20 November 1989), United Nations, Treaty Series, Vol 1577, 3 Art 27 (3).

21 UN General Assembly, Convention on the Rights of Persons with Disabilities, Resolution adopted by the General Assembly, (A/RES/61/10624, January 2007) Art 28.

of the Condition of the Wounded and Sick in Armed Forces in the Field (Art 50), the Second Geneva Convention for the Amelioration of the Condition of the Wounded, Sick and Shipwrecked Members of Armed Forces at Sea (Art 51), the Fourth Geneva Convention Relative to the Protection of Civilian Persons in the Time of War (Art 49, 53, 134), the Protocol Additional to the Geneva Conventions of 12 August 1949 and Relating to the Protection of Victims of International Armed Conflicts (Protocol I) (Art 69), the Protocol Additional to the Geneva Conventions of 12 August 1949 and Relating to the Protection of Victims of Non-International Armed Conflicts (Protocol II) (Art 17), the Statute of the International Tribunal for the Prosecution of Persons Responsible for Serious Violations of International Humanitarian Law Committed in the Territory of the Former Yugoslavia since 1991 (Art 2, 3, 5), the Statute of the International Tribunal for the Prosecution of Persons Responsible for Genocide and Other Serious Violations of International Humanitarian Law Committed in the Territory or Rwanda and Rwandan Citizens Responsible for Genocide and Other Such Violations Committed in the Territory of Neighbouring States, between 1 January 1994 and 31 December 1994 (Art 3, 4), and the Rome Statute for the Establishment of a Permanent International Criminal Court (Art 7, 8).

4. THE PINHEIRO PRINCIPLES

The importance of the restitution of property to refugees and IDPs has been recognised as an important issue by a number of UN bodies. The General Assembly, following the footsteps of the Commission on Human Rights and the Economic and Social Council, on 16 December 2005 during its 64th Plenary Meeting adopted the Basic Principles and Guidelines on the Right to a Remedy and Reparation for Victims of Gross Violations of International Human Rights Law and Serious Violations of International Humanitarian Law.[22] These principles state: "Restitution should, whenever possible, restore the victim to the original situation before the gross violations of international human rights law or serious violations of international humanitarian law occurred. Restitution includes, as appropriate: restoration of liberty, enjoyment of human rights, identity, family life and citizenship, return to one's place of residence, restoration of employment and return of property." The principles stand out among the international documents that recognise restitution of property as a "basic, self-standing human right"[23] and as the only effective solution to the problem of displaced persons.

---

[22] UN General Assembly, Basic Principles and Guidelines on the Right to a Remedy and Reparation for Victims of Gross Violations of International Human Rights Law and Serious Violations of International Humanitarian Law: Resolution adopted by the General Assembly, (Q/RES/60/147, 21 March 2006).

[23] *Inter-Agency*, Handbook on Housing and Property Restitution for Refugees and Displaced Persons: Implementing the 'Pinheiro Principles' (2007) 10.

However, the most important international document regarding this issue are the Principles on Housing and Property Restitution for Refugees and Displaced Persons, the so called Pinheiro Principles, which were adopted by the United Nations Sub-Commission on the Promotion and Protection of Human Rights on 15 August 2005. Adoption of this document was the final stage of a process that started with the Sub-Commission's resolution 1998/28 on Housing and Property Restitution in the context of return of refugees and IDPs. A study was conducted from 2002-2005, and finally the Special Rapporteur on Housing and Property Restitution *Paulo Sérgio Pinheiro* proposed the principles. The Principles "provide specific policy guidance regarding how to ensure the right to housing and property restitution in practice and for the implementation of restitution laws, programmes and policies, based on existing international human rights, humanitarian, refugee and national standards."[24] Although they are not legally binding as they do not represent a treaty, they represent a persuasive authority as they are based on existing treaties and national laws and were adopted by a body held responsible to all the members of the UN. Furthermore, the Principles were recognised by the ECtHR as a relevant document and were even quoted in some of the Court's decisions. The African Commission on Human and People's Rights referred to the Pinheiro Principles as "emerging principles in human rights jurisprudence" that "read together with the decisions of regional bodies such as the cited European Court decisions provide great persuasive value".[25]

Since the Principles are based on experience gathered from a number of countries that have dealt with large-scale restitution they certainly represent a document that should be taken into consideration when dealing with the restitution of the property to displaced persons in the South Caucasus.

The scope of application of the principles is rather broad. They refer to any situation where displacement occurred involuntarily giving no importance to the causes. Situations will be covered by the Principles no matter if displacement occurred because of an armed conflict, international or national, natural and man - made disasters, human rights violations etc. The fact that the Principles make no distinction between international and national conflicts is especially useful in cases where the conflict parties have a different view on the nature of the conflict. In terms of personal scope of application, the Principles use the term "refugees and displaced persons" which differs from the formulation usually used "refugees and internally displaced persons". Although the difference might seem small, this actually allows a wider protection as it covers three groups: refugees, IDPs and displaced persons who fled across national boundaries but who do not fall within the definition of refugees.[26] This is in line with the contemporary understanding that restitution is rights-based and not return-based and as it is one of the human rights it should not be limited to just some categories of displaced persons. This principle was applied

---

[24] Ibid. 11.

[25] *Williams,* The Pinheiro Principles Take a Licking (and Keep on Ticking?), 2010, available at <http://terra0nullius.wordpress.com/2010/11/18/the-pinheiro-principles-take-a-licking-and-keep-on-ticking/>.

[26] *Inter-Agency*, op. cit. note 23, 16.

by the ECtHR in the case *Đokić v. Bosnia*[27] where the applicant did not qualify as a refugee due to the fact that he had the Serbian citizenship and could not be regarded as an IDP because he fled across an international border, from BiH to Serbia, but the Court held that he should nevertheless enjoy protection. Further, for the Principles to be applicable it is necessary to have an arbitrary or unlawful deprivation of homes, lands, properties or habitual places of residence. Whether there was arbitrary or unlawful deprivation has to be determined by taking into account both national (including municipal) and international laws.

The Principles give priority to restitution over compensation. The idea behind this is that the purpose of property restitution and the reason for recognising it as an important tool in solving the problem of refugees and displaced persons is that restitution enables the return to situations which existed before the injury happened. The same approach was adopted for example in BiH which will be elaborated further on. Also, since post-conflict restitution is likely to be conducted as soon as peace is negotiated, it is expected that one or all sides might try to prevent displaced persons from returning in an attempt to preserve the situation created during the conflict. This was the case both in BiH and in Croatia. Compensation should only take place when the persons concerned express that they would prefer the compensation or when it is factually impossible to conduct the restitution. It is also clearly stated that the return or non-return of refugees shall in no circumstances play a role in influencing the right to restitution. However, some authors point out that "one of the flaws underlying all of the theoretical claims regarding the value of restitution is the possibility that restitution schemes are geared to address the concerns of Western states and as such, may render return not entirely voluntary. Just as the return of refugees to their countries of origin became a priority after the Cold War when Western nations no longer wanted to provide asylum, so too might the remedy of restitution now be in vogue to meet the needs primarily of Western nations that are not interested in providing asylum to refugees. The return of refugees and emphasis on property restitution is fuelled, at least in part, by the political and economic concerns of asylum countries."[28]

The Principles go on to promote non-discrimination in terms of the right to restitution of property, demanding that all people are given the same rights irrespective of their race, colour, sex, language, religion, political or other opinion, national or social origin, property, disability, birth or other status. Taking into account the characteristics of the wars of the late 20th century it is especially important to point out this principle as there are still intolerances between people of different racial, ethnic, national and religious origin. Prohibition of discrimination refers both to *de jure* and *de facto* discrimination which is important since the principle of non-discrimination is required under a number of international treaties which are legally binding on the countries so it is extremely unlikely that one country would adopt a law that explicitly discriminates. It is more likely that the discrimination will take place in application of the law which clearly favours the rights of one ethnic group over another.

---

[27] ECtHR, Judgment on the Merits delivered by the Chamber: *Đokić v. Bosnia and Herzegovina*, no. 6518/04 (2010) para 44.

[28] *Ballard,* Post-Conflict Property Restitution: Flawed Legal and Theoretical Foundations, Berkeley Journal of International Law 2010, 462 (487).

This was originally the case in Republic of Srpska, the Federation Bosnia-Herzegovina, Croatia, Georgia and elsewhere, where ethnic and other motivations clearly guided the content and degree of enforcement of relevant law.[29] Time-limits for restitution claims may be such that they indirectly, but intentionally, discriminate against certain groups to the benefit of another group. On the other hand, strict compliance with the non-discrimination principle should ensure that no one or no group entitled to housing and property restitution is prevented, on the basis of discrimination or inequitable treatment, from securing these rights in practice. The same *de facto* and *de jure* protection is granted to the equal treatment of men and women and boys and girls especially in regards to voluntary return in safety and dignity, legal security of tenure, property ownership, equal access to inheritance, as well as the use, control of and access to housing, land and property,[30] the joint ownership rights of both male and female heads of the household.[31]

Another important principle is granting the right to peaceful enjoyment of possessions.[32] It is very important that the text of the Principles recognised the right to peaceful enjoyment of possession rather than the right to property. In this way the right is granted to a much bigger category of people which is especially important for the displaced persons coming from ex-socialist countries where private property did not or hardly existed, and where other types of property such as social property, collective, customary or common ownership were predominant. In some socialist countries people had tenancy rights rather than ownership rights over their homes. Therefore, in case that it was the right to property that was granted and not the right to peaceful enjoyment of possession, many people would not have a chance to return to their homes of origin.

The Pinheiro Principles also include the right to free movement, a right that is granted by all relevant human rights treaties. However, it is also very closely connected to housing rights. Restitution cannot effectively take place if the freedom of movement is restricted. For example, it was the freedom of movement that allowed Georgian nationals who fled Gali region to conduct effective control over their property left behind since they were allowed to cross the river and visit their property. However, once the freedom of movement had been restricted, they lost control over their property. In the case of *Loizidou v. Turkey* before the ECHR, which involved the impossibility of return to one's property, the European Court noted that: "...the complaint is not limited to access to property but is much wider and concerns a factual situation: because of the continuous denial of access the applicant had effectively lost all control, as well as all possibilities to use, to sell, to bequeath, to mortgage, to develop and to enjoy her land....The continuous denial of access must therefore be regarded as an interference with her rights under Art 1 of Protocol No 1".[33]

---

29 *Inter-Agency*, op. cit. note 23, 33.

30 UN Sub-Commission on Promotion and Protection of Human Rights, Principles on Housing and Property Restitution for Refugees and Displaced persons, (E/CN.4/Sub.2/2005/17, 28 June 2005), Principle 4.1.

31 Ibid. Principle 4.2.

32 Ibid. Principle 7.

33 ECtHR, Judgment on the Merits delivered by the Chamber: *Loizidou v. Turkey*, No. 15318/89, 1996/VI.

The Principles also include a right to voluntary return in safety and dignity based on a free, informed, individual choice. Refugees and displaced persons should be provided with complete, objective, up-to-date, and accurate information, including on physical, material and legal safety issues in countries or places of origin.[34] This follows the practice of numerous international treaties.

In Section V, the Principles deal with ensuring restitution in practice. States are required to establish and support equitable, timely, independent, transparent and non - discriminatory procedures, institutions and mechanisms to assess and enforce housing, land and property restitution claims as well as to provide financial, human and other resources.[35] The absence of effective, impartial and accessible judicial or other effective remedies can severely compromise the restitution process. Judicial bodies play a special role in upholding the credibility and fairness of the entire restitution process. This is especially so in the case of post-conflict restitution. In Croatia, for example, the process of restitution of property was largely biased against ethnical Serbs. The Principles also invite states to ask for help of the relevant international agencies when they are not capable of conducting the process by themselves and to include restitution procedures, mechanisms and institution into peace agreements. This was done in the case of BiH and proved to be successful. It is hardly imaginable that large-scale restitution could have been successfully conducted by the local authorities on their own since the tensions between the parties were on a high level. However, some authors find that involvement of the international community in this manner "may undermine the development of democracy".[36] To be effective, these institutions must also have external support in order to meet their heavy caseloads and to overcome the many formidable challenges encountered during the restitution process. Resolving restitution claims requires the institutions concerned to have at their disposal an array of flexible remedies that can be deployed, and the equally important need for refugees to have the right to choose the remedy that is best suited for them and consistent with their rights and wishes. One challenge involved in the establishment of a national, local or international special purpose body is to ensure that its procedures are adapted to deal with a large number of property restitution and compensation cases from refugees and IDPs, who will very often have limited access to evidence to support their claims. This may require, for example, allowing for more relaxed standards of evidence than are usual before civil courts.[37]

Access to restitution procedures should be given to everybody who was deprived of his / her property. The Principles lay down a number of ways in which the procedures should be made accessible to everybody with a claim. First of all, it is required from the states not to make any preconditions that would exclude someone from the process, to make the procedure just, timely, accessible, free of charge, age and gender sensitive, to take care of the interests of children, to make it accessible to people wherever they might be; in addition it is recommend to establish a mobile

[34] UN Sub-Commission on Promotion and Protection of Human Rights, Principles (E/CN.4/Sub.2/2005/17, 28 June 2005), Principle 10.1.

[35] Ibid. Principle 12.

[36] *Ballard,* op. cit. note 28, 492.

[37] *Inter-Agency*, op. cit. note 23, 65.

unit so that it would be truly accessible to everyone and filing claims by post, proxy and in person should all be possible. These provisions are very significant in practice since many people have left their country of origin and are unable to return until their restitution claim is decided upon. It is also required that procedures are simplified as much as possible and if not, a State should make available specialist consulting services. Another requirement is that the time periods for filing the claim should be such to allow people considering their circumstances to be able to gather all the necessary document, proofs, etc. Finally no one should be persecuted or punished for making a restitution claim. Accessibility is vital in cases of post-conflict restitution where any unjust provision might exclude a number of people from filing their restitution claim.

The Principles also recognise the importance of records and documentation on property and proclaim that States should do all that is necessary to protect the records which often get destroyed during the conflicts. In Kosovo, for instance, more than half of these records disappeared. Also, any decision made in the restitution proceedings should be registered in these records.

The rights of tenants and other non-owners are also addressed. This is especially important in cases of countries with socialist tradition and in which many people would lose the rights to restitution if such provisions did not exist. In the Republic of Georgia, the legacy of discriminatory application of the 1983 Housing Code by the judiciary against Ossetians who fled their homes during the 1990-1992 has prevented large-scale return for several years. Georgian courts have routinely argued that the abandonment of an apartment by a refugee did not constitute a 'valid reason' for departure, and thus many flats belonging to Ossetians were subsequently allocated to ethnic Georgians. Similarly, in Kosovo as a result of the application of the Law on Changes and Supplements on the Limitations of Real-Estate Transactions[38] the housing and occupancy rights of the ethnic Albanian population were arbitrarily annulled and housing and property transactions were severely restricted. When housing was bought or sold between 1989-1999, this was generally carried out on an irregular basis and was never officially registered, thus complicating an already difficult restitution process. Similar processes played out in Croatia where over 30,000 occupancy rights overwhelmingly affecting Croatian Serbs were annulled.[39]

Another practically and legally important issue is that of secondary occupants, people who have taken residence in the property of displaced persons. Therefore, their rights might in some way be in conflict with the right to restitution. The secondary occupants have to be given the right to participate in the restitution process because any decision made will certainly influence their position. Furthermore, they have to be granted the right to adequate housing. That means that in case that the secondary occupants, who are themselves in most cases displaced persons, do not have an alternative housing it falls upon the State to provide it to them. However, in practice this can be used in order to slow down or even completely obstruct the return. This was the case, for instance, in Croatia where the secondary occupants

[38] Official Gazette of Republic of Srpska No 22/91, 18 April 1991.
[39] *Inter-Agency*, op. cit. note 23, 79-80.

were even given the right to refuse the alternative housing provided to them and since the returnees, especially in cases of Croatian Serbs, were not allowed to re-possess their property until the secondary occupant's status is solved, this led to obstruction of return of a number of displaced persons. So while it is undoubtedly the right of secondary occupants to have adequate housing, the inability to solve their position should not in any case influence the return.

The Principles further state that legislative measures should be taken to recognise restitution as an essential component of the rule of law. That means that a state should adopted the laws necessary to conduct the restitution and refrain from adopting any laws that might be discriminatory, or in any way obstruct the restitution. Also in case that any discriminatory law exists it should be overturned.

Even if all above conditions are met, there cannot be a successful restitution if the decisions of the relevant bodies are not enforced. Therefore, it is an obligation of any State that deals with large scale restitution to adopt an adequate enforcement system which should include designation of specific public bodies entrusted with enforcement,[40] placing a legal obligation on local and national authorities to respect, implement and enforce decisions on restitution.[41] Since, as seen in numerous countries, it is likely that return and restitution will face opposition and an escalation of violence is always possible, it is necessary to take steps to discourage any such behaviour. This can be done by imposing severe punishments on those disrupting the process and by protecting the disputed property from being looted.

Finally, if restitution is factually not possible because the property was destroyed or does not exist anymore or if the injured party has voluntarily and knowingly accepted compensation in lieu of restitution, then compensation in money or in kind should be given. The Principles take the position that the relation between restitution and compensation is not that of "either…or" but that the compensation is a subsidiary means of restorative justice. The same position was taken by the international community in restitution cases in BiH.

The Principles also recognise the importance of international involvement in restitution processes. Therefore, Principle 22 deals with the role of the international community. It proposes that the international community should promote and respect the right to restitution, and that all international bodies and organisations should respect the prohibition of forceful displacement. Also international organisations and international peace operations should work with the governments involved in restitution processes. This has proved to be very successful in many cases, such as BiH and Kosovo, where the complicated relations between the members of different ethnical groups gave no hope that the restitution could be successfully completed, but the involvement of the international community helped to a great extent in overcoming this issue. However, this position is not without criticism. *Ballard* claims that "while international support for post-conflict restitution seems benign, if not laudable, it can lead to significant international influence over domestic legal affairs. Bosnia's experience in creating and implementing its property restitution scheme illustrates that international actors can be involved in drafting, adju-

---

[40] UN Sub-Commission on Promotion and Protection of Human Rights, Principles (E/CN.4/Sub.2/2005/17, 28 June 2005), Principle 20.1.

[41] Ibid. Principle 20.2.

dicating, and enforcing local property laws. In this manner, property restitution to remedy mass forced displacement gives rise to potential law exportation."[42] On the other hand, *Moratti* claims that in the case of BiH "it was a 'Western' concept like the right to the enjoyment of possession that was reinterpreted to ensure the protection of individual rights arising from a socialist type of tenure".[43] Furthermore, he states "critiques of law and development seem ill - suited to describe a property restitution process. While law and development implies a change in the type of tenure, property restitution implies a return to the *status quo ante*. Fundamental changes in the type of tenure, as seen in BIH with the privatisation of socially owned apartments, occur only after the *status quo ante* has been restored."[44] Back on the negative side, *Ballard* points out that "the level of international support that will be available following future conflicts is not clear. For example, where dispossession has been caused primarily by a government's inability or unwillingness to maintain the rule of law throughout its territory, and the need to establish restitution is not supported by gross violations of human rights law, international agencies may lack sufficient incentive or political will to lend technical or financial assistance".[45]

5. Bosnia and Herzegovina Lessons Learned

5.1. Legal Framework of Property Restitution in BiH

In discussing large-scale restitutions of property it is necessary to mention the case of BiH which was the first time that a restitution of such scale took place following the wars of the 1990s. "Of course, every situation of displacement is unique and context-specific, such that direct comparisons are difficult. However, certain universal principles do apply; most notably, the right of refugees and of internally displaced persons to voluntary return in safety and dignity to their area of origin or to find a solution elsewhere, which for IDPs would mean integrating elsewhere in their country. The case of BiH sheds important light on what supporting realisation of these rights and resolving displacement crises requires in practice."[46] Bosnia has become the leading model for achieving post-conflict property restitution, positioning restitution as both a *per se* right and a means of promoting refugee return. In the years since the war ended, Bosnia has been held up as a model for resolving property disputes in scenarios as

---

42 *Ballard*, op. cit. note 28, 470.

43 *Moratti*, available at <http://terra0nullius.wordpress.com/2011/02/09/evictions-and-cookie-cutter-approaches-to-restitution-a-response-to-megan-j-ballard/>.

44 Ibid.

45 *Ballard*, op. cit. note 28, 494.

46 *Mooney*, Paper presented to the Conference "Conflict and Migration the Georgian-Abkhazian Case in a European Context", at 1.

disparate as Palestine and Iraq by bodies ranging from national NGOs to the recently appointed U.N. Special Rapporteur examining this topic.[47]

Restitution of property to refugees and IDPs in BiH was based on two legal sources: international norms regulating restitution on the one hand, and provisions of the General Framework Agreement on Peace in Bosnia and Herzegovina, the so - called Dayton Peace Agreement, on the other. It is clear that restitution in BiH was possible due to the Dayton Peace Agreement whose Annex VII established a number of principles relating to property restitution. However, it is also worth noting that even before the signing of the Dayton Peace Agreement several international documents regarding BiH insisted on the right of refugees and displaced persons to have their properties restored.[48] This was the case with UN resolution and the Washington Agreement of 1994 concluded between the Bosnian Croats and the Bosnian Government.[49]

Annex VII granted the following rights to the refugees and displaced persons: "the right to freely return to the homes of origin, the right to have property restored which was deprived during the hostilities and a right to compensation for any property which cannot be restored to them."[50] This is the first time that a right of return was not defined broadly as return to the country of origin as it was the practice before, but specifically as return to the home of origin. Nowadays it is widely accepted that a right to return refers to the home of origin. However, the drafters of the treaty correctly presumed that there would be an opposition to the return of displaced persons, especially in the case of minority return, so Annex VII also included a number of provisions designed to protect the returnees, a practice that should be employed in each case where there is a prolonged dispute, and especially in case of frozen disputes such as those existing in the South Caucasus. Many provisions of Annex VII appear to favour actual return over local resettlement, beginning with the statement that "the early return of refugees and displaced persons is an important objective of the settlement of the conflict in Bosnia and Herzegovina."[51] The Bosnian authorities are obliged to "accept the return of . . . persons who have left their territory"[52] and create "conditions suitable for return" by repealing discriminatory laws and preventing or punishing incitement of ethnic hostility.[53]

It was the role of the international community to persuade the parties to include Annex VII in the Peace Agreement, and subsequent documents such as Property Legislation Implementation Plan (PLIP) and Strategy Plan for South East Europe that enabled a large scale return to BiH. It is estimated that some 2 million people

---

47 *Williams*, Post-Conflict Property Restitution and Refugee Return in Bosnia and Herzegovina: Implications for International Standard-Setting and Practice, New York University Journal of International Law and Policy 2006, 442 (446)

48 Directorate-General for Internal Policies, Private Properties Issues following the Regional Conflict in Bosnia and Herzegovina, Croatia and Kosovo, Study, (2010) 71.

49 Washington Agreement signed on 18 March 1994, available at <www.usip.org/files/file/resources/collections/peace_agreements/washagree_03011994.pdf>.

50 General Framework Agreement for Peace in Bosnia and Herzegovina, 14 December 1995, Paris, available at <http://www.ohr.int/dpa/default.asp?content_id=379>.

51 Ibid. Annex VII, Art 1 (1).

52 Ibid. Annex VII, Art 1 (1).

53 Ibid. Annex VII, Art 1 (3).

have returned to their home of origin. However, the international community did not stop its involvement on passing the documents that would enable the return but took active part in the return itself. UNHCR sponsored a number of programmes some of which were support for local legal-aid centres, large-scale shelter programmes, employment creation, microcredit and community development schemes, pilot return projects, bus services, Open Cities initiatives,[54] etc.

UNHCR, OHR and a number of other institutions played a crucial role in adopting the legal framework which would enable restitution of property to take place and achieve the goals which are the general idea behind it. "The leading role in the implementation of Annex VII belongs to the UNHCR. The UNHCR was directly involved in the development of the strategy for safe return, repatriation and refugees. Particularly at the beginning of the implementation of Annex VII the UNHCR concentrated its efforts on targeted housing reconstruction and on confidence-building measures. Important tasks of the UNHCR were minority returns, returns in the Zone of Separation, effective realisation of the right to return and the right to property. In 2001 the State Commission for Refugees was established and co-chaired by the UNHCR."[55] Their part in making the appropriate legal framework has been conception, drafting and eventual adoption of the series of laws that overturned wartime laws on abandoned property. The laws that were adopted brought local law in conformity with international standards such as the Law on Cessation of Application of the Law on Abandoned Apartments (BiH), Law on Cessation of the Application of the Law on Abandoned Apartments (Republic of Srpska), Law on Cessation of Application of the Law on Temporary Abandoned Real Property Owned by the Citizens (Bosnia and Herzegovina). These laws were adopted only 3 years after Dayton, and it is clear that it was the international community's involvement that enabled their passing and established the legal framework that did not obstruct restitution. However, the case of BiH also shows how the legal provision although seemingly neutral can impede the restitution process.

5.2. Problems in the Enforcement of Property Restitution in BiH

After the signing of the Dayton Accords the authorities in BiH passed the Abandonment Laws[56] and Apartment Purchase Law[57] which in combination would have almost immediately lead to the pre-emption of the rights of pre-war holders, as the first law enabled reallocation to new occupancy rights holders and the second allowed the purchase of the apartments. The BiH Human Rights Chamber noted that the effect of the abandoned property regulations was "to

[54] International Crisis Group, Minority Return or Mass Relocation? ICG Bosnia Project, Report No 33 (1998) 15-21.

[55] Directorate-General for Internal Policies, Private Properties Issues (2010) at 68-69.

[56] Law on Abandoned Apartments, Official Gazette of Federation of Bosnia and Herzegovina No 6/92, 8/92, 16/92, 13/94, 36/94, 9/95, 33/95 and Law on the Use of Abandoned Property, Official Gazette of Republic of Srpska No 3/96.

[57] Law on Sale of Apartments with an Occupancy Right, Official Gazette of the Federation of Bosnia and Herzegovina Nos 27/97, 11/98, 22/99, 27/99, 32/01 and Law on Privatization of State-Owned Apartments, Official Gazette of the Republic of Srpska Nos 11/00, 18/01, 35/01.

reinforce the ethnic cleansing that occurred during the war."[58] Following this in 1998 the aforementioned Laws on Cessation were adopted. The influence of the international community was strengthened by the provisions of Annex IV which provided for the direct applicability of the ECHR and Bonn powers given to the OHR.[59]

The right to apartment restitution in the Federation was restricted in two ways. First, refugees and displaced persons, for the purposes of the right to return under Annex VII, were defined as those who could prove that they had left their apartment for reasons related to the conflict.[60] Failure to prove this disqualified claimants from refugee or displaced person status, excluding them from the Annex VII right to return to their apartments. This left broad discretion to the local housing authorities throughout the Federation who were quickly accused of abusing it to block restitution of apartments. Second, in the case of apartments previously declared abandoned under the Law on Abandoned Apartments, the property laws balanced the rights of any claimant against the property interests acquired by subsequent users.[61] While claimants were entitled to reinstatement of their occupancy rights, their claims to the specific apartments they occupied before the war were not automatically superior and they could be left with a right only to other unspecified apartments and the decision was once again left to the discretion of the housing authorities. The conditions were abandoned by the international community through the OHR since it was clear that they would prevent the return of a number of refugees and displaced persons. The OHR adopted provisions that cancelled all new occupancy rights to abandoned apartments *ex lege* and demoted their holders to temporary occupants[62] as well as by establishing a conclusive presumption that all occupancy right holders who left their apartments between the outbreak of hostilities and the entry into force of the property laws were refugees and displaced persons under Annex VII and, therefore, entitled to return to their homes.[63]

The procedure established in BiH was as follows: local housing authorities were given the responsibility to receive the claims, establish the relevant facts and render a decision within a 30-days period. The authorities needed first to establish whether the claimants had the right to restitution which in case of BiH was not a problem since records were mostly preserved. Then they needed to determine the status and rights of any temporary occupant. Temporary occupants without formal allocation decisions were considered illegal users and required to vacate the property within

---

58 Human Rights Chamber for Bosnia and Herzegovina, Decision on the Merits: Case No. CH/98/659: Pletilić et al. against Republika Srpska 204 (Sept. 10, 1999).

59 Peace Implementation Council Bonn Conclusions (1997) available at <http://www.ohr.int/pic/default.asp?content_id=5182>.

60 Law on Cessation of Application of the Law on Abandoned Apartments, Official Gazette of the Federation of Bosnia and Herzegovina, No 11/98, Art 3 (2).

61 Ibid. Art 3 (5).

62 The High Representative's Decision Cancelling All Permanent Occupancy Rights Issued in the Federation During and After the War in BiH and Converting Them into Temporary Occupancy Rights, 14 April 1994. available at <http://www.ohr.int/decisions/plipdec/default.asp?content_id=159>.

63 The High Representatives Decision on the Law on Amendments to the Law on Cessation of Application of the Law on Abandoned Apartments, 1 July 1999, available at <http://www.ohr.int/decisions/plipdec/default.asp?content_id=246>.

fifteen days with no right to alternative accommodation.[64] The rights of legal users in possession of allocation decisions depended on whether they had independent means of providing for their own housing needs, in accordance with criteria set out in the property laws. If so, they were considered double or multiple occupants and also given fifteen days to vacate the property with no right to alternative accommodation.[65] Temporary occupants unable to meet their own housing needs were given ninety days to vacate the property and had the right to apply to the housing authorities in the municipality where they were displaced for alternative accommodation.[66]

Upon issuance of a positive decision, an appeal did not suspend enforcement.[67] As a rule, enforcement could not proceed until the deadline to vacate the property voluntarily had expired and the claimant subsequently requested enforcement.[68] Exceptionally, the housing authorities were required to initiate enforcement proceedings *ex officio* against multiple occupants.[69]

Another measure used by Entities, but especially by the Federation, that was aimed at obstructing the minority return was that of physical return condition. Although virtually all pre-war occupancy right holders were now eligible to claim restitution of their apartments as a matter of right, the preservation of both their claim and all their subsequent rights to the apartment (including purchase in the Federation) remained contingent upon the condition of physical return. Claimants who did not actively exercise the right of return by physically re-occupying and using their apartments had thereby forfeited both the right and the apartment.[70] The terms of this requirement closely tracked the pre-conflict procedures for cancelling occupancy rights under the use requirement, specifying a nearly identical list of grounds justifying inaction and providing for cancellation through judicial proceedings. A restriction made by the OHR, the so called two-year rule, applicable only in the Federation, was envisioned to close the restitution gap between the Entities as it was believed that displaced persons were recovering their pre-war rights in the Federation while at the same time retaining their temporary holder rights on property in the Republic of Srpska. However, the rule proved to work against the minority return as their houses were primarily targeted for unannounced inspections. Furthermore, "by linking the right to restitution to the actual use of the apartment, these conditions can be assessed as discriminatory and as contradictory to the right to voluntary return."[71] Under the influence of the international community the practice of inspections was abandoned and the two-year rule followed.

The illegal practice that managed to evade the international community was that of failure to provide alternative accommodation. The primary obligation was on the local authorities. When it became clear that they were not dealing with the problem

---

64 Law on Cessation of Application of the Law on Abandoned Apartments, Official Gazette FBiH, No 11/98, Art 3 (3).
65 Ibid. Art 3 (3) 11.
66 Ibid. Art. 3 (5).
67 Ibid. Art 8 (3).
68 Ibid. Art 11 (1)-(2).
69 Ibid. Art 11 (3).
70 *Williams*, op. cit. note 47, 513.
71 Directorate-General for Internal Policies, Private Properties Issues following the Regional Conflict in Bosnia and Herzegovina, Croatia and Kosovo, Study (2010) at 74.

the international community took it upon itself to provide alternative accommodation, while the funding was supposed to be left to local authorities. However, in the end, it proved the best solution to provide the holders of this right with the lump sums necessary for finding an alternative accommodation. Once it became an express legal obligation to conduct all evictions within the legal deadlines, housing authorities managed to almost overnight find a solution to alternative accommodation.[72]

Finally, under the New Strategic Direction (NSD), an inter-agency document adopted as a result of local authorities' selective enforcement of property laws and focused on the restitution issues that proved to be most problematic in the practice, a deadline for completing the restitution process was set by December 2003.[73] This was a departure from the previous avoidance of committing to a strict date. Implementation rates rose rapidly throughout Bosnia in the wake of the NSD, and lagging municipalities and regions raced to catch up with those further ahead. The most striking progress was made in the Republic of Srpska, which overtook the Federation in August 2003. This achievement resulted from improvement in Republic of Srpska municipalities previously seen as obstructionist black holes, such as Bijeljina, which leapt from 49 percent implementation at the end of 2002 to 91 percent one year later, achieving about twice the average national rate during this time period. A number of previously hard-line Croat-controlled municipalities also experienced rapid progress during the same period. As a result, the bulk of municipalities had largely completed the PLIP, which "was conceived in October 1999 as a means of gathering the whole range of property-related activities of the different agencies into a coherent, goal-oriented strategy for securing implementation of the new laws, designed to ensure that all citizens of Bosnia and Herzegovina who were dispossessed of their property in the course of the conflict can repossess it"[74] by late 2003. The remaining laggard municipalities could not be ascribed to any single ethnic group in Bosnia.[75]

The international community now follows an exit strategy in BiH, which is highly dangerous. The responsibility for return and restitution was transferred to the national authorities of BiH. In 2004 in his 25th Report the High Representative stated that the principal targets for the transition to domestic leadership according to Annex VII have been achieved and the transfer of its Annex VII responsibilities to BiH authorities was prepared, which demanded an institutional reorganisation.[76] In September 2003 the Ministry for Human Rights and Refugees was indicated as the main policy-making and supervisory body for Annex VII issues. However, after 2003 statistics show a decline in the number of returns. The exit strategy is also

---

72 *Williams*, op. cit. note 47, 539.

73 available at <www.internal-displacement.org/8025708F004CE90B/(httpDocuments)/D6E5CEC5F9592D6E802570B700587845/$file/PLIP+12+Sep+2002.pdf>.

74 PLIP Inter-Agency Framework Document, available at <http://www.ohr.int/plip/key-doc/default.asp?content_id=5510>.

75 *Williams*, op. cit. note 47, 540-541.

76 Available at <www.ohr.int/other-doc/hr-reports/default.asp?content_id=32024>.

applied to the financing of these issues. It is very questionable whether the national institutions are able to play the same successful role in the process of returns and restitution. The Union of Associations of Refugees, Displaced Persons and Returnees calls for a more intensive involvement of the international community, estimating that the local authorities are not capable of fulfilling this commitment. This assessment is based on the practice of the several past years. Questions of competences, organisational preconditions and political will of the national authorities aside, it is evident that BiH as a state is not able to finance the return and restitution, i.e. the compensation. The national authorities will continue to depend on international financial support in terms of donations, grants or debts towards international financial institutions, the latter resulting in consequences for the national economy.[77]

Experience in BiH shows a variety of problems that may arise from the minority return and that even the policies that were envisioned to promote return can be misused for actually discouraging the return. It also shows the importance of the involvement of the international community and the variety and extent to which it must be involved in cases of complex relations between the members of different ethnic groups. In the case of BiH the constant involvement and broad range of authorities given to the international community enabled the successful completion of the restitution process. Even if in the settlement of similar disputes in other regions the international community is not given the mandate to act in the process, as seems to be likely in the case of the South Caucasus states where the international community is not united enough or does not have enough leverage on all sides, some sort of independent body that would supervise the restitution process, especially in the cases regarding the respective minorities, should be established.

6. SUMMARY

The right to restitution of property is now widely accepted as an independent human right, it has found its place in a vast number of international treaties. Although it was previously considered that restitution is linked to return, nowadays it is accepted that it is in fact a separate right and is not contingent on the return. However, the right to restitution cannot be exercised until some political conditions are met. It is first and foremost necessary that peace is established. But as seen in numerous cases peace itself is not enough as the restitution might trigger new conflicts. Restitution of the property must be agreed upon by all sides of the conflict. Furthermore, it is recommended that in settling the issue of property restitution the Pinheiro Principles are applied, if not directly then by incorporation of some of the most important principles into the legal document regarding the issue, since the practice has shown that without these basic principles restitution cannot be successfully conducted. Finally, it is useful to keep the experience from BiH in mind when regulating the restitution process, especially

[77] Directorate-General for Internal Policies, Private Properties Issues (2010) 69.

in cases of minority return as it shows the extent and possibility of obstacles that may appear in the process.

Nino Lapiashvili

CORRUPTION AND ORGANISED CRIME IN FROZEN CONFLICT AREAS: THE CASE OF GEORGIA

"Art 17 AA EU-Georgia: Fight against organized crime and corruption

The Parties shall cooperate on combating and preventing criminal and illegal activities, in particular transnational activities, organised or otherwise, such as:

(a) smuggling and trafficking in human beings as well as small arms and illicit drugs;

(b) smuggling and trafficking in goods;

(c) illegal economic and financial activities such as counterfeiting, fiscal fraud and public procurement fraud;

(d) embezzlement in projects funded by international donors;

(e) active and passive corruption, both in the private and public sector;

(f) forging documents, submitting false statements; and

(g) cyber crime.

2. The Parties shall enhance bilateral, regional and international cooperation among law enforcement bodies including developing cooperation between Europol and the relevant authorities of Georgia. The Parties are committed to implementing effectively the relevant international standards, and in particular those enshrined in the UN Convention against Transnational Organised Crime (UNTOC) of 2000 and its three Protocols, the UN Convention against Corruption of 2003 and Council of Europe relevant instruments on preventing and combating corruption."

"Art 16 AA EU-Republic of Moldova: Preventing and combating organised crime, corruption and other illegal activities

The Parties shall cooperate on preventing and combating all forms of criminal and illegal activities, organised or otherwise, including those of transnational character, such as:

(a) smuggling and trafficking in human beings;

(b) smuggling and trafficking in goods, including in small arms and illicit drugs;

(c) illegal economic and financial activities such as counterfeiting, fiscal fraud and public procurement fraud;

(d) fraud, as referred to in Title VI (Financial Assistance, and Anti-Fraud and Control

Provisions) of this Agreement, in projects funded by international donors;

(e) active and passive corruption, both in the private and public sector, including as regards the abuse of functions and influence;

(f) forging documents and submitting false statements; and

(g) cyber crime.

2. The Parties shall enhance bilateral, regional and international cooperation among law enforcement bodies including strengthening cooperation between Europol and the relevant authorities of the Republic of Moldova. The Parties are committed to implementing effectively the relevant international standards, and in particular those enshrined in the UN Convention against Transnational Organised Crime (UNTOC) of 2000 and its three Protocols, the UN Convention against Corruption of 2003 and Council of Europe relevant instruments on preventing and combating corruption."

1. INTRODUCTION

The "frozen conflict" areas of the South Caucasus are widely considered to be safe havens for criminals, and a large share of the region's trafficking in drugs, weapons and humans appears to be carried out through these territories.[1] Since very little is known about the extent of such crimes, this paper will neither deal with the actual crime phenomena nor with the EU's role in settling "frozen conflicts" as such. Rather, it is about the lessons to be learnt from the EU's approaches in South Eastern Europe towards fighting organised crime and corruption, and eventually discussing these findings with regard to the "frozen conflict" areas of Georgia. Since Georgia's "frozen conflicts" have an inherent Russian element this case study will also consider the triangle of EU - Baltic States - Russian Federation experiences. Theoretical reference is made to the finding of *Buscaglia* and *van Dijk* that "high levels of organised crime and corruption are linked to low levels of human development",[2] therefore I shall make the assumption that the reverse scenario works in the same manner. In particular, I assume that all those factors that upgrade the levels of human development in corrupted and highly criminalised societies may successfully heal corruption and organised crime.[3] It will be examined, in particular, with regard to the conditions for civilians to enjoy freedom of movement based on the EU's experience in South Eastern Europe and the Baltic States.

The Republic of Moldova offers a valuable yardstick for comparative purposes. Unlike most countries of the South Caucasus, Moldova is both a member of the Southeast European Cooperative Initiative (SECI)[4] and of the Southeast European Law Enforcement Center (SELEC).[5] It is also the place where the EU chose to launch its flagship Border Assistance Mission to Moldova and Ukraine (EUBAM). This mission does not have a mandate to "control" any part of the border; however it is tasked with targeting corruption and certain segments of organised crime. Ulti-

---

1 *Cornell / Jonsson / Nilsson / Häggström,* The Wider Black Sea Region: An Emerging Hub in European Security", Silk Road Paper, Central Asia-Caucasus Institute & Silk Road Studies Program, (2006) at 7 and 22.

2 *Buscaglia / van Dijk*, Controlling Organized Crime and Corruption in the Public Sector, Forum on Crime and Society, 2003, 3 (31).

3 This assumption will not be tested in this research but taken for granted.

4 Available at <http://www.secicenter.org/p144/Republic_of_Moldova>.

5 Available at <http://www.secicenter.org/>.

mately, there is hope on the EU's side that the "support it can offer on a technical / advisory level, to assist confidence-building measures, will… contribute meaningfully to an eventual settlement of the Dniestr conflict," - especially through facilitation of legitimate cross-border trade "including for those businesses in Transnistria that choose to register with the State Register Chamber in Chisinau."[6] The facilitation of legitimate cross-border trade as a mechanism to tackle the low levels of human development in the Transnistria region can thus be accepted as a reversed means or indirect way to achieve lower levels of corruption and organised crime within "frozen conflict" areas.

In EULEX, the EU's Rule of Law Mission for Kosovo, the EU is more seriously engaged in the fight against corruption and organised crime compared to EUBAM in Moldova and Ukraine. This is due to the fact that its capability to concentrate on the fight against corruption and organised crime is backed by the Mission's executive powers to "investigate, prosecute and adjudicate sensitive cases", but also due to the lack of the "Russian factor".[7] While in Moldova the EU's approach to tackle organised crime and corruption in Transnistria is achieved through indirect means as mentioned above, still it is to be underlined that unlike the Georgian EUMM, EUBAM is tasked with assisting Ukraine and Moldova in their fight against corruption.

What makes the case of Georgia's breakaway regions different in terms of the EU anti-crime approaches is that unlike EULEX or EUBAM, nothing is mentioned about organised crime and corruption in the EUMM mission statement for Georgia. Rather, the primary goal of EUMM is to "contribute to stabilization of the situation on the ground following the August 2008 conflict,"[8] - without making any reference to this issue as a major problem affecting Georgia's breakaway regions. The EU is merely underlining that "the mission wants to contribute to create conditions whereby civilians can cross the Administration Boundary Lines of Abkhazia and South Ossetia in both directions without fear and obstacles, thus reducing the detrimental effects of dividing lines."[9] In addition, in the EUMM mission statement it is pointed out that "EUMM is mandated to cover the whole territory of Georgia, within the country's internationally recognised borders, but the *de facto* authorities in Abkhazia and South Ossetia have so far denied access to the territories under their control."[10] The mandate of the EU Special Representative for the South Caucasus and the Crisis in Georgia and the ways of its implementation are also rather vague.[11]

---

6 Available at <http://www.eubam.org/en/quick/faqs>.

7 See *van Elsuwege*, From Soviet Republics to EU Member States. A Legal and Political Assessment of the Baltic States Accession to EU (2008).

8 Available at <http://www.eumm.eu/en/about_eumm>.

9 Ibid.

10 Ibid. See also *Rettman* stating that "Russia does not allow EU ceasefire monitors in Georgia to cross the boundary line", in "EU and Georgia to nibble at Russian occupation", available at <http://euobserver.com/foreign/120863>.

11 See Art 3 (b) of Council Decision of 25 August 2011 appointing the European Union Special Representative for the South Caucasus and the crisis in Georgia 11/518/CFSP: "…encourage the countries in the region to cooperate on regional themes of common interest, such as common security threats, the fight against terrorism, illicit trafficking and organised crime", 25 August 2011 appointing the European Union Special Representative for the South Caucasus and the Crisis in Georgia, OJ L 221 of 27 August 2011, at 5.

Therefore, when thinking in terms of organised crime and corruption in "frozen conflict" areas, the example of EUMM in Georgia shows that the EU is less powerful than it is in Moldova, and even more powerless than its presence in Kosovo. An intriguing question is what would have been the approach of the EU in the hypothetical situation that someone who poses a threat to EU security (through organised crime) and to institutional integrity (through corruption) would find guaranteed safe shelters in some breakaway regions of the EU where the local community is isolated and powerless. I believe the best approach would be to create a mechanism for free movement which would enhance and upgrade the level of development and thus increase the chances of that population to mobilise itself to struggle for better conditions, including through fighting organised crime and corruption. In order to achieve a secure neighbourhood around its borders the key idea would be to facilitate freedom of movement (or in other words to create "conditions whereby civilians can cross the Administration Boundary Lines of Abkhazia and South Ossetia in both directions without fear and obstacles"[12]). Apart from this, it also matters to see what difference EU conditionality can make in the case of Georgia.

In the next chapters I shall discuss the situation of organised crime and corruption in the two breakaway regions of Georgia - Abkhazia and Tskhinvali / South Ossetia *vis-à-vis* the rest of the territory of Georgia, as followed by the EU approaches in Georgia *vis-à-vis* South Eastern Europe; as well as the EU experience in the three Baltic states *vis-à-vis* the Russian Federation as a possible scenario to be extended to the case of Georgia.

The methodological approach of this research includes qualitative analyses and review of broadly collected primary and secondary data including academic works, reports by international organisations and research institutes, media sources, semi-structured interviews with law enforcement and other government officials as well as country studies through a comparative approach and black letter law analysis.

2. Organised crime and corruption on Georgian territory controlled by the Government of Georgia *vis-à-vis* Georgia's two breakaway regions of Abkhazia and Tskhinvali / South Ossetia

2.1. Overview

EU-Georgian relations are overshadowed by a strong Russian interest, expressed in particular through Russia's military presence in the two breakaway regions of Abkhazia and Tskhinvali / South Ossetia. Against this background it is difficult to draw parallels with South East European states or in particular with the Western Balkans. Keeping in mind the "Russian factor", it seems more natural to review the Georgian case in terms of the EU's experience in the three

---

[12] See the EUMM Mission Mandate, op. cit. note 8.

Baltic States which up to very recently were considered by the Kremlin as a sphere of its own influence. Still, the Russian Federation pushes forward an attempt to link the historically, legally and politically non-comparable case of Kosovo to Abkhazia and Tskhinvali / South Ossetia,[13] in part in order to demonstrate its own importance as a global player. In line with such an approach, the Russian Federation rushed to recognise the independence of the two breakaway regions of Georgia while Western states ignored Russian resistance towards recognition of Kosovo sovereignty.

2.2. Historical background

In any given country, the situation relating to organised crime and corruption pretty much defines the degree of democracy as well as the level of possibility to exercise personal freedom for those residing in this country. The discourse here focuses mostly on the *status quo* of contemporary Georgia, however the need to have a complete picture calls me to mention that since the Soviet break-up Georgia's transformation path towards democratic consolidation was divided into four main periods:

a) The immediate post-communist era of the democratically elected first President that was accompanied by civil war, massive chaos and a Russian-backed first round of "separatist" military conflicts with Abkhazia and Tskhinvali / South Ossetia.
b) A long stagnation marked by rampant corruption and impunity under the second President and former USSR Foreign Minister Shavardnadze.
c) The period since the 2003 Rose Revolution when Georgia succeeded to achieve impressive results in state building and democratic reforms under President Saakashvili.
d) The post-2012 October Parliamentary elections stance when Georgia as a pioneer in the region passed through the first part of the so called democracy consolidation "two turnover" test of political power–shift[14] through free and fair elections when it entered into a very painful process of "cohabitation." This very momentum was earmarked by a somehow unusual atmosphere when for the first time since Georgia declared its independence, the democratically elected billionaire Ivanishvili and his "Georgian Dream" coalition were constantly challenged by the opposition and some Western political groups suspecting him of

[13] *Cassese*, The Wolf that Ate Georgia, Civilians are Still Suffering in Georgia and it is Imperative for the World Community to Promote a Lasting Solution, 1 September 2008, available at <http://www.guardian.co.uk/commentisfree/2008/sep/01/georgia.russia1>, see also *Aleksidze*, Has the Kosovo Case Diminished the Adherence of the International Community of States to Principle of Inalienability of Territorial Integrity of States? Baltic Yearbook of International Law, 2012, 75.

[14] See *Huntington*, The Third Wave: Democratization in the Late Twentieth Century, (1991).

an attempt to steer Georgia away from its European path and bringing it back to the Russian sphere of influence.[15]

2.3. Organised crime and corruption in Georgia from the 2003 Rose Revolution up to the 2012 October Parliamentary elections period

The Government of President Saakashvili which came into power after the peaceful Rose Revolution in 2003 declared war on organised crime in each and every of its manifestations as one of the top priorities for the country. This decision resulted in the adoption of a coherent, co-ordinated and wide-ranging strategy both on legislative as well as on implementation levels. On the one hand, the national legislation was brought in line with international legal instruments and standards. Both the existing legal framework was amended (e.g. amendments were introduced to the Law on Conflicts of Interests and Corruption in Public Service and to the Law on Public Service; new proposals were launched with regard to the classification of organised criminal groups, money-laundering, corruption, terrorism, illegal circulation of drugs, illegal transfer of weapons, trafficking in persons, obstruction to justice, smuggling, victim / witness protection mechanisms, etc.). On the other hand, absolutely new legal concepts such as criminalisation of a deeply rooted Soviet phenomenon, the Mafia-style "thieves-in-law", were introduced. Besides, Georgia was among the first countries to adopt criminal liability of legal persons for a number of crimes, including corruption. Apart from this, the new tax code entered into force which harmonised Georgian law with the best international practices and the EU *aquis*.

The Government was equally successful in strengthening regional co-operation through ratification of all main international instruments aimed at combating organised crime. Impressive results were achieved soon: according to the Sub-Index on Safety and Security of the Global Prosperity Index 2012, Georgia was upgraded substantially among upper middle ranking countries where most of the EU states find their place.[16]

All these as well as subsequent efforts quickly resulted in progress which became recognized and rewarded by the international community. World rankings praised Georgia for its amazing transformation into a corruption-free society, for its lowest level of crime rates overall in Europe as well as for its huge success in contributing dynamic measures against transnational organised crime:

1. Georgia is the only ex-Soviet Union Republic that as of 2007 and up until 2013 was firmly included in the "tier 1" position of the US Department of State's annual Report on Trafficking in Persons.[17]

---

15 E.g. "EU Lawmakers Warn Georgian Premier he Risks Closing Door on Europe", Deutsche Presse Agentur, 8 March 2013.

16 Available at <http://www.prosperity.com/Subindexes-6.aspx>.

17 Available at <http://www.state.gov/j/tip/rls/tiprpt/2007/82805.htm>. It is to be noted that recently under the new "Georgian Dream" Government, Georgia has been downgraded to Tier 2 position.

2. According to the 2013 Doing Business Ranking, Georgia was upgraded to position 9 and is right among the 10 top ranking economies besides the US, Norway and the UK.[18]
3. In addition, according to the Index of Economic Freedom of Heritage Foundation, Georgia climbed to the 21st position, which is indisputably a quite significant achievement as well.[19]
4. Georgia continued its intensive co-operation with international organisations including the Group of States against Corruption (GRECO) and OECD which underlined its good performance record.
5. Georgia was selected for launching the EU Eastern Partnership / Council of Europe Joint Project on Good Governance and Fight against Corruption due to its attractive record in implementing anti-corruption policies.[20]

According to the Global Corruption Barometer Survey, undertaken by Transparency International, only 3 % of Georgians who were surveyed said that they had to pay bribes. This is one of the lowest numbers of all countries surveyed. 77 % of the respondents stated that the government was effective or extremely effective in fighting corruption.[21] Of course, there are a lot of problematic issues left. For example, Transparency International pointed out the following core problem: “The weakness of parliament and the judiciary has undermined the democratic system of checks and balances and resulted in a dominant executive branch. A number of important government agencies, including the Prosecutor’s Office and the State Audit Office, have suffered from a lack of independence from the political leadership and have been used as political tools”.[22]

Similarly, there are issues to be tackled in terms of fighting organised crime, where the main subject of criticism was the zero-tolerance policy, overcrowded prisons and cases of torture in prisons. However, the overall situation has improved since 2003. To sum up, irrespective of major problems, it has to be pointed out that during 2003-2012 Georgia has achieved tremendous positive developments in terms of fighting organised crime and corruption.

2.4. Evaluation of the situation in the fields of organised crime and corruption in Abkhazia and Tskhinvali/South Ossetia

After secessionist armed hostilities, the economies of the two breakaway regions of Abkhazia and South Ossetia collapsed. Until today, the widespread

---

18 Available at <http://www.doingbusiness.org/reports/global-reports/doing-business-2013>.

19 Available at <http://www.heritage.org/index/ranking>.

20 Available at <http://www.oecd.org/corruption/acn/GEORGIAThirdRoundMonitoringReportENG.pdf>.

21 Available at <http://www.transparency.org/whatwedo/pub/global_corruption_barometer_20091>.

22 Available at <http://www.transparency.org/news/pressrelease/20121205_transparency_international_georgia_51st_in_2012_corruption_percept>.

reliance on Russian subsidies is a means of corruption for *de facto* officials,[23] and this financial aid hardly reaches the local population.[24] Criminal groups are in charge of even the most minor economic activities.[25] Trafficking of persons, of military ammunition and even of nuclear materials[26] is a common thing along with smuggling of alcohol and fuel, kidnapping for blackmail purposes, robbery and burglary.[27] According to some surveys, by the year 2008 the separatist regions had become one the most militarised territories in the world, based on the number of different kinds of weapons per capita.[28]

Recently, the new Government of Georgia started to discuss a possible reopening of Ergneti market.[29] It is true that since 1996 when Ergneti market became functional the actual situation within the conflict zone began to improve because common business interests helped to bring people closer to each other. However, the reason for this dynamic was the trade in smuggled goods, in particular narcotics and weapons. As claimed by the Government of Georgia, this situation generated revenues for criminal groups and the separatist regime, and consequently had a negative effect on the institutional development of the Georgian state and contributed to an ongoing failure to meet the budgetary needs of the state.

In order to consolidate the integrity of Georgia's customs and economic space, the Georgian Government under President Saakashvili closed down Ergneti market, simultaneously proposing alternative solutions based on a wide-ranging plan of economic revival and development for the region.[30] This move contributed significantly to an increase in budgetary incomes. However, it provoked a series of ag-

---

[23] International Crisis Group Europe Report, Abkhazia: The Long Road to Reconciliation, N 224, 10 April, 2013, at 6-8, available at <http://www.crisisgroup.org/~/media/Files/europe/caucasus/georgia/224-abkhazia-the-long-road-to-reconciliation.pdf>.

[24] See e.g. Art 19 Survey, 2007, at 10, available at <http://www.article19.org/data/files/pdfs/publications/abkhazia-foi-report.pdf>.

[25] Interview with High Officials of Georgian Prosecution Service and the Ministry of Internal Affairs, February 2012. See also *Kukhianidze*, Organised Crime and Smuggling Through Abkhazia and South Ossetia, American University's Transnational Crime and Corruption Center (TraCCC), Georgia Office, available at <http://traccc.gmu.edu/pdfs/publications/Georgia_Publications/Kukhianidze_OC_and_Smuggling_Eng_HEUNI.pd>

[26] With regard to a possible "disappearance" of nuclear materials from the Institute of Physics and Technology of Sukhumi, see "Литвиненко могли отравить полонием-210, вывезенным из Сухуми", available at <http://www.newsru.com/arch/world/07dec2006/suhum210.html>.

[27] See National Security Concept of Georgia, available at <http://www.nsc.gov.ge/files/files/National%20Security%20Concept.pdf>, see also Kukhianidze, Kupatadze, Gotsiridze, Smuggling through Abkhazia and Tskhinvali Region of Georgia, Tbilisi, 2004, TraCCC, Georgia Office, available at <http://www.alexanderkupatadze.com/resources/Smuggling_Georgia_eng.pdf>.

[28] Analysis by The International Institute for Strategic Studies, available at <http://www.iiss.org>.

[29] Ergneti market was located in the vicinity of the occupation line between Tskhinvali / South Ossetia and the rest of Georgia, see also the scheme in Smuggling through Abkhazia and Tskhinvali Region of Georgia, Tbilisi, 2004, Kupatadze, TraCCC, Georgia Office, available at <http://www.alexanderkupatadze.com/resources/Smuggling_Georgia_eng.pdf>.

[30] State strategy on occupied territories "Engagement through Cooperation", adopted on 27 January 2010. See also "Saakashvili proposes Act of Economic Freedom", The Messenger Online, available at <http://www.messenger.com.ge/issues/1956_october_7_2009/1956_mzia.html>.

gressive actions from separatists, as well as from Russian peacekeepers and criminals because it eroded a major source of income in Tskhinvali / South Ossetia. For this reason, the current talks on the re-opening of Ergneti market should be considered in terms of historical reality that could help to promote a rational evaluation of the re-emergence of threats of organised crime and corruption in Georgia.

After the 2008 Russia-Georgia war, the EU's major policy was "engagement without recognition" which in practical terms assumes that ties are to be built with the population of the "frozen conflict" areas while continuously making it clear that the independence of Sokhumi or Tskhinvali will never be recognised. However, because this policy does not offer much possibility for the West to engage in activities without posing danger to the legal sovereignty of Georgia, the approach applied should rather be called "mainstreaming human rights". The EU and other international organisations that focus on human rights issues keep reiterating that ethnically targeted violence, looting, burning and destroying bridges, the mining of administrative borders, arbitrary detentions, constant violation of security and property rights, destruction of property, frequent punitive raids, harassment of Georgian-speaking teachers at schools and disrupting learning process, forced conscription into Abkhaz military forces, as well as forced passportisation[31] - accompanied by hindering freedom of movement and residence as well as complete isolation of ethnically Georgian local populations, - are to be halted,[32] without suggesting any effective mechanisms to solve the problem.

2.5. The „Russian element" in dealing with corruption and organised crime

It should not be forgotten that the emergence and acknowledgement of the term "occupation" alongside with "ethnic cleansing" imposed considerable political pressure on the Russian Federation. The Government of Georgia can always rely on the legal argument that the Russian Federation as the temporary administrator and occupant of the territory is obliged to preserve public order, safety and the well-being of the local populations. In addition, it is responsible for human rights protection as well as for the safe and dignified return of IDPs, for protecting the environment on these territories and for preventing nuclear proliferation, etc. - as prescribed under international standards including International Humanitarian Law (Fourth Geneva Convention)[33] and according to scholarly opinions.[34]

---

31 Op. cit. note 3.

32 *Kälin*, Report of the Representative of the UN Secretary General on the Human Rights of Internally Displaced Persons. Follow-up to the Report on the Mission to Georgia, 14 January 2009, available at <http://www.unhcr.org/refworld/topic,4565c2253e,4565c25f49d,49a55b102,0,,,GEO.html>; Letter from *Vollebaek*, OSCE High Commissioner on National Minorities, to H.E. *Stubb*, OSCE Chairman-in-Office, 27 November, 2008; Human Rights in the War-Affected Areas Following the Conflict in Georgia, OSCE, Office for Democratic Institutions and Human Rights, 27 November, 2008, see also *Hammarberg*, Commissioner for Human Rights of the Council of Europe, Report on Human Rights Issues Following the August 2008 Armed Conflict, Strasbourg, 15 May 2009.

33 Art 43 of the Hague Regulations of 1907 as well as Arts 27, 33, 32, 34, 49, 53, 59,78 of Fourth Geneva Convention, GC IV, Respecting the Laws and Customs of War on Land and its An-

On an operative level, the Russo-Georgian co-operation in matters of organised crime and corruption used to be, and still is, functioning even after the 2008 war.[35] This is due to existing international agreements signed by Georgia:

a) the CIS Convention on Legal Assistance and Relations on Civil, Matrimonial and Criminal Cases;[36]
b) the CIS Agreement on Co-operation in Combating Economic Crimes;[37]
c) the CIS Convention on Transferring of Persons Sentenced by Imprisonment for the Purpose of further Serving the Sentence.[38]

Even though Georgia left the CIS after 2008, it still remains party to all three agreements. Besides, an inter-Ministerial bilateral agreement that was signed on 21 March 1994 between the Ministry of Internal Affairs of Georgia and the Ministry of Interior of the Russian Federation is still in force and was never hindered from effective implementation.

Even after diplomatic relations had been suspended in 2008, the legal framework described above still remains a solid ground for effective co-operation between law enforcement officers on all types of crime on the territories of the signatories, except in cases when criminals managed to escape to any one of two breakaway regions of Georgia. Reportedly, in that case representatives of Georgian law enforcement organs, having strong sentiments to its own territories under occupation as well as the feeling of the so called "national pride" - would never approach their counterparts in the Russian Federation with demands to undertake or to continue the criminal proceedings in Abkhazia / Tskhinvali.[39] This policy is kept and maintained up to now, leaving no space for implementing more flexible mechanisms on the spot because it is obvious that in terms of international law any direct co-operation by the Government of Georgia with the proxy regime might mean *de facto* recognition of Abkhazian statehood.

The Georgian Government tried to establish control at least over migration flows to Abkhazia and Tskhinvali / South Ossetia by adopting the Law on Occupied Territories of 23 September 2008. Art 3 of the Law restricts free movement of foreigners to occupied regions. In particular, entering these two regions is permitted only from the Georgian territory controlled by the Government of Georgia. Crossing border checkpoints from the Russian Federation is thus criminalised. Besides, the

---

nex: Regulations concerning the Laws and Customs of War on Land. The Hague, 18 October 1907.

34 E.g. *Sassoli*, Art 43 of the Hague Regulations and Peace Operations in the Twenty-First Century, International Humanitarian Law Research Initiative, Background Paper prepared for Informal High-Level Expert Meeting on Current Challenges to International Humanitarian Law, Cambridge, June 25-27 2004.

35 Interviews with High Officials of the Georgian Prosecution Service and the Ministry of Internal Affairs of Georgia.

36 Signed in Minsk, 22 January 1993, in force for Georgia since 11 July 1996.

37 Signed in Moscow, 12 April 1996, in force for Georgia since 12 April 1996.

38 Signed in Moscow, 6 March 1998, in force for Georgia since 26 July 2002.

39 Interview with High Officials of the Georgian Prosecution Service and the Ministry of Internal Affairs, February 2012.

Law imposes a ban on all kinds of economic activity within these territories taking place without the consent of the central government in Tbilisi, as well as prohibited any real estate deals. Art 7 declared the Russian Federation responsible for any violation of international human rights norms, cultural heritage regulations and material / moral damages to foreigners that might occur on the occupied territories.

The above mentioned piece of legislation is in line with the approach of the Government of Georgia on conditions to be fulfilled if economic development is to be promoted by Tbilisi in Abkhazia. We can find the same meaning under the 1999 decision taken by the CIS Council of Heads of States on "Further Steps towards the Settlement of the Conflict in Abkhazia, Georgia" where the economic aspects were successfully interlinked with other obligations to be fulfilled, by reiterating once again that the recovery of the region's economy shall be solely linked to implementation of the organised and steady process of the return of refugees and displaced persons"[40]- that obviously will never be undertaken by separatists without permission / political will of the Russian Federation.

The Law on Occupied Territories is a strong political signal from Georgia to the rest of the world that even though Abkhazia and the South Ossetian / Tskhinvali region are under occupation, Georgian authority is to be respected and that Georgia is intending to pursue its aggressive "non-recognition policy". Actually, getting permission from Georgian authorities to enter those regions from the Georgian side is quite simple and does not take much effort, contrary to what the Venice Commission initially criticised.[41] In addition, it is a good mechanism to exercise at least a minimum of control over organised crime activities within those zones. Therefore, the recent and still ongoing talks on amending this piece of legislation should be considered very carefully in order not to damage Georgia's vital national interests.

2.6. Main concerns and challenges regarding the re-emergence of corruption and organised crime since the 2012 Parliamentary elections

This subchapter will provide a brief enumeration of challenges in the context of corruption and organised crime which are discussed in the Georgian society since the power shift in October 2012. Even though the international community along with international organisations concluded that the Parliamentary elections were held in an unprecedentedly free and fair manner, the new Government instead of consolidating democratic institutions initiated massive arrests of previous political leaders in a very short period of time which led to massive

---

40 Section 10 of the Decision taken by the Council of Heads of States of the Commonwealth of Independent States on "Further Steps towards the Settlement of the Conflict in Abkhazia, Georgia"- done at Moscow, 2 April 1999.

41 See Final opinion on the draft amendments to the law on occupied territories of 14 December 2009, adopted by the European Commission for Democracy through Law (Venice Commission) at its 81st Plenary Session, Venice 11-12 December 2009, on the basis of comments by Aurescu ,(Substitute Member, Romania), Hamilton, (Substitute Member, Ireland), Nussberger, (Substitute Member, Germany), Strasbourg, 14 December 2009, Opinion no. 552 / 2009, CDL-AD(2009)051, available at <http://www.venice.coe.int/webforms/documents/?pdf=CDL-AD%282009%29051-e>.

criticism from the West.[42] While this was being done under the veil of "restoring justice", the lack of evidence in criminal trials as well as vast procedural violations pushed the new Government into the defensive.

The amnesty[43] in which more than 16,000 prison inmates and more than 12,000 probationers were released[44] pushed the new Government to confess that this step would naturally increase the rate of crime, simultaneously preaching to the citizens of Georgia to stay patient and tolerant to the new conditions of life and to the new realities.[45]

Along with the threats of an apparent increase of organised crime in Georgia, new concerns emerged with regard to corruption. The new Georgian Government immediately fired thousands of public servants (up to 5,000 in first six months), not hiding that difference in political opinion was decisive. This process was accompanied by contracting new employees without open competitions, arguing that nepotism is a natural thing for societies like Georgia.[46] Again, conventional wisdom suggests that nepotism will increase the amount of corruption in the near future.

In another move, the new Government lifted the taboo on the issue of opening the railway between Armenia and Russia - through the breakaway region of Abkhazia via the rest of Georgian territory. This raises two issues:

On the one hand, there is the issue of who shall sign the agreement on the joint railway, whether this will be a bilateral agreement between Georgia and the Russian Federation under international law, or whether the *de facto* Abkhaz Government will be included. In addition, practical issues such as border check points and putting stamps in passports all raise the issue, whether opening the railway would lead to a *de facto* recognition of the breakaway region. It is obvious that even the very pro-Russian oriented Georgian Government will not agree to these conditions.

On the other hand, opening the railway also poses problems from an Azerbaijani perspective because it would seriously threaten the Baku-Tbilisi-Ceyhan oil pipeline and would raise concerns due to assumptions that Russia might start transporta-

---

42 See Washington Post, "Georgia's Democracy is in Peril", by Editorial Board, 31 May 2013, available at <http://articles.washingtonpost.com/2013-05-31/opinions/39653960_1_new-prime-minister-yulia-tymoshenko-ukraine>, see also Antidze, Former Georgian Prime Minister Arrested on Corruption Charges, 21 May 2013, available at <http://www.reuters.com/article/2013/05/21/us-georgia-arrest-idUSBRE94K0QA20130521>. See also Statement by *Marie Harf*, Deputy Spokesperson: In Support of Georgia's Multiparty Democracy and Euro-Atlantic Future, 12 September 2014: "The United States urges all of Georgia's pro-democracy and pro-Euro-Atlantic forces to focus on their common interests, build on recent achievements, and work together to move the country forward and address the pressing economic and regional security challenges of the day. We are concerned by the continued investigations and criminal charges against opposition figures and the risks that politicized prosecutions would pose for Georgia's democracy. The United States continues to support Georgia's democratic development, which must include respect for political pluralism and open debate", available at <http://georgia.usembassy.gov/news-events/dc2014t/harf_geo.html>.

43 Georgian Law on Amnesty, adopted on 28 December 2012 by the Parliament of Georgia, Kutaisi, N202-rs.

44 Available at <http://www.interpressnews.ge/ge/samartali/232535-amnistia-16-534-patimars-da-12-722-probacioners-sheekho.html>.

45 Prime Minister Ivanishvili in a press conference on 22 November 2012, available at <https://www.youtube.com/watch?v=jLyzJt4Y7XQ>.

46 Ibid.

tion of weapons to Armenia against Azerbaijani interests in the Nagorno-Karabakh conflict. It is not in the interest of Georgia to endanger the well-established partnership with Azerbaijan and Turkey. Still the counter-argument is that every piece of cargo which crosses the Enguri river is under the jurisdiction of Georgian authorities – so it will be up to Georgian discretion to let it pass or not.

Finally, one important point disappeared from the political agenda since October 2012: the issue of the Swiss company SGS, charged with customs monitoring of trade through trade corridors in the breakaway regions of Abkhazia and Tskhinvali / South Ossetia as part of the famous Georgia-Russia WTO deal.[47] Apparently, the new Government's declared will to restart relations with the Russian Federation does not exclude the possibility of sacrificing such an important preventive mechanism to increase the security measures in the breakaway regions of Georgia.

Overall, if the risks of re-emergence of corruption and organised crime are ignored, the danger will be increased that instead of consolidating democracy the country may end up with a "democracy's 'double'- a regime that claims to be democratic and may look like a democracy, but which is ruled like an autocracy".[48]

3. The role of EU conditionality in dealing with organised crime and corruption in the breakaway regions of Georgia

3.1 Introduction

When I refer to EU approaches in South Eastern Europe with regard to corruption and organised crime, I do not intend to discuss the root causes or the details of the degree and levels of the mentioned crimes in this region. Various surveys reveal that those states are corrupted; also they are often criticised[49] for weak government commitments to mobilise against organised crime.[50]

Considering the role of the EU, one might suggest to turn to other "similar looking" factual circumstance, e.g. the dispute between Croatia and Slovenia over territorial issues that has now been set aside for international arbitration. This fact could possibly draw lines of similarity with the Georgian case. Or alternatively, one could think of the situation in northern Mitrovica, i.e. the Serb-controlled parallel structures in Kosovo, and to try to consider EUMM *vis-à-vis* EULEX in Kosovo – reportedly, initiated due to "persistence and organised crime networks in Kosovo… at the forefront of plans to assist international supervision in the area once it achieved "supervised" independence in 2008."[51] However, against the background of histori-

---

47 Available at <http://www.civil.ge/eng/article.php?id=24158>.

48 *Krastev*, New Threats to Freedom: Democracy's Doubles, Journal of Democracy, April 2006, 52.

49 See e.g. *Lunacek*, Kosovo-Serbia: Will They Ever Come to Terms? What is the European Union's Role? in *Dzihic / Hamilton* (eds), Unfinished Business: The Western Balkans and the International Community, 2012, 149 (153).

50 *Cohen / Lampe*, Embracing Democracy in Western Balkans. From Post-conflict Struggles toward European Integration, (2011), at 147.

51 Ibid. 145.

cal, legal and political facts, a direct comparison is impossible for two reasons. Firstly, the EU does not have access to the breakaway regions of Georgia. And secondly, in the Western Balkans, neither Croatia, nor Serbia or Kosovo etc. are influenced by the so-called "Russian factor". Hence, EUMM is not equipped to address security issues on the ground.

Therefore, it would lead us to a false start if we were to draw conclusions from the EU's role in South Eastern Europe with regard to corruption and organised crime. Keeping in mind the EU conditionality approach, it is more promising to look through the prism of EU needs and interests in the two regions of the Western Balkans and the South Caucasus.

I could not agree more with *Tocci* that the "promotion of human rights, democracy, rule of law, combating international crime, contributing to international security - are among EU foreign policy objectives... yet in practice, the pursuit of narrow and short-term interests has often obstructed the EU's potential to advance those long-term goals, reflecting the very values on which the Union is founded."[52] Therefore, it is not surprising to see that the EU intensified its relations with the South Caucasus region through the ENP only after the European Security Strategy was adopted in 2003. The reasons were that "Georgia lies at the center of ... interlocking energy routes - transit hub for Azeri and Central Asian oil and gas" ...and Caspian energy was viewed as "essential to reducing Europe's dependence on Russian and Middle East supplies,"[53] therefore the ENP policy design was perfect to address energy security issues as well as unwanted spillovers of organised crime, trafficking and illegal migration into the EU. There was no reference to the issue of conflict management, and this topic rose to prominence only later on, in particular after the 2008 Russia-Georgia war.

EU membership is seen as a strong incentive for reforms which makes the EU's tasks easier to be fulfilled in the Balkans than in Georgia. There is some truth in the assumption that "...the ENP's leverage is weak owing to a missing EU membership perspective"[54] and that the "EU can be most effective as a transformative power on conflict when dealing with conflict parties and issues when political conditionality is rigorously and consistently applied."[55] However, against the background of the Georgian case this discussion must be seen in a different light.

One could argue that irrespective of the lack of a membership perspective under the ENP, the Georgian population strongly believes that one day the country is to become a full EU member.[56] Apart from this, not even a membership perspective would affect the situation of the population living in the breakaway regions of Abkhazia and Tskhinvali / South Ossetia, simply because in a non-democratic and

---

52 *Tocci*, The EU and Conflict Resolution. Promoting Peace in the Backyard, Routledge (2007), at 177-178.

53 Ibid. at 126.

54 *Sasse*, The European Neighborhood Policy and Conflict Management: A Comparison of Moldova and the Caucasus, in *Hughes* (ed), EU Conflict Management, 2010, 92 (93).

55 *Braniff*, Integrating the Balkans. Conflict Resolution and the Impact of EU Expansion, I.B. TAURIS, 2011, at 13.

56 See National Democratic Institute survey results, available at <http://www.messenger.com.ge/issues/3188_august_26_2014/3188_tea.html>.

powerless environment it is not up to people to make decisions with regard to strategic issues of foreign policy or on the fight against organised crime and corruption.

Therefore, EU conditionality works for Georgia even in its "soft" version under ENP: indirect EU leverage can possibly provide relief to people most suffering from isolation under the proxy regimes governed by organised crime and corruption in the breakaway regions of Abkhazia and Tskhinvali / South Ossetia; conditionality can thus enhance the capacity of people to self-empowerment for security reasons in the long term perspective. "Soft conditionality" has two dimensions in particular. On the one hand, there is the AA / DCFTA on the agenda, and on the other hand, one might think of the visa liberalisation perspective.[57] While it is too early to say that a deeper economic integration with the EU under the DCFTA framework will affect the populations of Georgia's breakaway regions, it is obvious that visa liberalisation might turn into something valuable giving local residents the chance to travel abroad without needing their Russian passports.

3.2. EU approaches in Georgia compared to SEE

While there is a clear suggestion from EU officials that conflict management and problems tied to conflicts including organised crime and corruption should not be interlinked with EU free movement policies,[58] there are some empirical data indicating that the prospect of free travel to the EU does create incentives towards improving the life conditions of local residents in these regions.[59] The Government of Georgia under President Saakashvili elaborated the concept of Status-Neutral-Travel-Documents (SNTDs) available for "legitimate residents of the Autonomous Republic of Abkhazia and the Tskhinvali Region who do not possess a Georgian citizen's identification"[60] – with the primary purpose of enabling the population of the occupied territories to travel abroad freely as well as to have access to social services on the territory controlled by the Government of Georgia. Even though SNTDs sometimes are mistakenly interpreted as a Georgian policy against illegal "passportisation",[61] in practice they represent a humanitarian act directed towards improvement of conditions of those populations as well as for the enhancement of people-to-people contacts.

Since 2011 nine EU Member States – Slovakia, Hungary, Bulgaria, Poland, Estonia, the Czech Republic, Romania, Latvia and Lithuania[62] - recognised SNTDs as valid documents for travelling purposes and visa application procedures in the con-

---

57 See the speech by *Füle*, fomer European Commissioner for Enlargement and Neighbourhood Policy, at the conference „Georgia's European Way", Reference: SPEECH/13/635, 12 July 2013, available at <http://europa.eu/rapid/press-release_SPEECH-13-635_en.htm>.

58 Interview with representatives of the EU Commission in 2012.

59 Interview with officials of the Georgian Ministry of Reintegration from February 2012.

60 Available at <http://www.smr.gov.ge/index.php?opt=101>.

61 According to the report of the IIFFMG "the mass conferral of Russian citizenship to Georgian nationals and the provision of passports on a massive scale on Georgian territory, including its breakaway provinces, without the consent of the Georgian Government runs against the principles of good neighbourliness and constitutes an open challenge to Georgian sovereignty and an interference in the internal affairs of Georgia." Op. cit. note 3.

62 From among non-EU member states the USA, Israel and Japan were the first to recognise, see <http://www.smr.gov.ge/index.php?opt=101>.

sular departments of their own countries. Recognition of SNTDs by "old" EU Member States could have facilitated the increase in demand of neutral travel documents even more.

Regarding the EU-Georgia Visa Facilitation Agreement[63] being in force since 1 March 2011, the EU Member States' positive gesture and pro-active steps in this direction could become a good basis for an upgraded policy on a supranational level in the future. In particular, statistical information showed that in the past the SNTDs were not very popular in the breakaway regions simply because the threat of severe punishment from *de facto* leadership and Russian soldiers were considered to outweigh the benefits.[64] However, the perspective of EU visa liberalisation apparently resulted in the local populations of Abkahzia and Tskhinvali / South Ossetia requesting more information regarding the possible benefits[65] - thus indirectly making the EU an actor in de-isolating the breakaway regions through applying its conditionality policy within the rest of non-occupied part of Georgia.

In South Eastern Europe EU conditionality focuses more on post-conflict management than on de-isolation policies. Nevertheless, some features of EU policies that affect the free movement are worth to be discussed. Here, it is to be mentioned that the EU has a mixed influence, sometimes limited (Montenegro, Croatia), sometimes direct (Kosovo, Bosnia, FYR Macedonia), on citizenship regimes in the Western Balkans. Much depends on whether citizenship legislation was imposed by the EU as a ready-made proposal, or whether sovereign governments took a careful approach in preserving fragile ethnic balances in the country, as it happened in the latter examples. The US-EU-Russian brokered Dayton Peace Agreement[66] resulted in "dual, or two-level, and politically speaking, multiethnic citizenship"… which ... "not only consolidated ethnic division and led to permanent institutional paralyses but also provoked widespread discrimination against so-called 'others', i.e. those not belonging to any of these groups or not wishing to state their ethnic background."[67]

3.3. EU approaches in the three Baltic States *vis-a-vis* the Russian Federation

When considering the experiences of the EU in the three Baltic States, it is not to be forgotten that before they joined the EU adopted the same "wait and see approach" that it also applied to Georgia. However, there is not much hope for Georgia that history will repeat itself. One should keep in mind that on the one hand, Georgia lacks an EU membership perspective, while on the other it was

---

63 Agreement between the EU and Georgia on the facilitation of the issuance of visas, OJ 2012 L 52, 34.

64 Interview with State officials, February 2012.

65 Interviews with officials of the Georgian Ministry of Justice and the Georgian Ministry of Reintegration.

66 The Dayton Peace Agreement was initialed at Wright-Patterson Air Force Base in Dayton, Ohio on 21 November 1995 and signed in Paris on 14 December 1995. The agreement is known as the Dayton Peace Accords and is available at <http://www.state.gov/www/regions/eur/bosnia/bosagree.html>.

67 *Štiks*, The European Union and Citizenship Regimes in Western Balkans, in *Dzihic / Hamilton* (eds), Unfinished Business. The Western Balkans and the International Community, 2012, 49 (53-54).

only after these three states' EU accession that opportunities for well-suggested pragmatic co-operation with Russia including on infrastructure projects (e.g. implementation of an extension of triangle Finland-Baltic States-Poland "Rail Baltica" project to Saint Petersburg) - increased proportionally. And this was largely due to the fact that Russia was left without choice rather than to start thinking of Latvia, Lithuania and Estonia as sovereign independent states. There is a wide consensus among certain circles of Georgian society that if consolidation of democracy and economic revival will turn into an irreversible process in Georgia, the country will get a chance to detach itself from the extensive influence of its Northern neighbour.

Among the outstanding political and legal problems between Russia and each of the Baltic republics are: *a)* border delimitation, *b)* integration of Russian minorities, *c)* transit of goods between the Russian exclave of Kaliningrad and mainland Russia. All of these three issues are currently on the EU-Russia strategic partnership agenda, meaning that the Baltic States' "pre-enlargement challenges have been transferred to the post-enlargement period."[68] Likewise, in order to start breaking the ice in the Russian-Georgia relationship and engaging in solving the issues related to the breakaway regions including corruption and organised crime, the decisive factor will be to embrace the momentum when Georgia's pro-democratic development path leading to full integration into EU structures will be considered irreversible from the Russian point of view. Here, the EU's involvement is considered to be very important.

There is nothing in common between Kaliningrad and Georgia's breakaway regions, perhaps except for *a)* the levels of organised crime and corruption are high all over these places, and *b)* the unfortunate perspective for Abkhazia and South Ossetia / Tskhinvali to one day become the legalised exclaves of the Russian Federation, which seems legally impossible but apparently not excluded by Moscow,[69] as may be supposed from the recent developments in Ukraine.[70] But still, when it comes to free movement of the populations living in these territories, it is interesting to review the EU stance and experience. Here it is to be underlined that it was definitely easy to deal with the transit of persons in Kaliningrad: both EU and Russia welcomed the introduction of a specific Facilitated Transit Document (FTD) and a Facilitated Rail Transit Document (FRTD) scheme[71] imposed under a Council Regulation[72] which forms part of the Schengen *acquis*[73] and enables smooth travel for the Kaliningrad population to mainland Russia.

---

[68] Ibid. 398.

[69] See „Moscow, Tskhinvali Drafting ‚Comprehensive Treaty on Integration'", 20 November 2014, available at <http://www.civil.ge/eng/article.php?id=27837>.

[70] *Somin*, The Volokh Conspiracy. Don't Forget About Russia's Invasion and Occupation of Crimea, 28 August 2014, available at <http://www.washingtonpost.com/news/volokh-conspiracy/wp/2014/08/28/Dont-forget-about-Russias-invasion-Crimea/>.

[71] Joint Statement on EU Enlargement and EU Russia Relations, Brussels, 27 April 2004.

[72] Council Regulation (EC) No 693/2003 of 14 April 2003 establishing a specific Facilitated Transit Document (FTD), a Facilitated Rail Transit Document (FRTD) and amending the Common Consular Instructions and the Common Manual.

[73] Recital 14 and 11 of Regulation 693/2003 respectively, OJ 2003 L 99, 9 and L 99,16.

The Kaliningrad compromise[74] substantially improved the conditions of Russian citizens residing and working in the Baltic states. Arranging it was relatively easy for the EU because it had a stronger leverage over the Baltic states because of their wish to become EU members. When it comes to the issue of free movement and rights of persons residing in Abkhazia and South Ossetia / Tskhinvali provinces, it is obvious that it is not Georgia, but the Russian Federation which has to compromise. Here, the interests of the EU and Russia do not coincide. Russia recognised the sovereign independence of the breakaway regions, and there is no hope that any compromise will be achieved on the Georgian-backed SNTDs. In this difficult situation the EU as an actor is taking a back seat which makes the following statement all the more true: "…it is unclear for how long the process of conflict management through closer relations with EU can provide an attractive enough framework for the key regional actors in the absence of the conditionality of a membership perspective."[75] Still, the Kaliningrad compromise could be utilised by the EU as a solid argument during the negotiations with the Russian Federation. It should be constantly reiterated that both the Georgian policy on SNTDs as well as the upcoming EU-Georgia visa-free regime should not become a pretext for punishing the local populations residing in Abkhazia and South Ossetia / Tskhinvali region, but turn into a tool of de-isolation and development.

4. CONCLUSION

As was mentioned above, unlike EUBAM in Moldova / Ukraine or EULEX in Kosovo, the EUMM mission mandate does not set the goal of fighting corruption or organised crime within the breakaway regions of Georgia. Irrespective of the fact that the security issue at the EU's outer borders stands as its top priority, the traditional method of dealing with organised crime within "safe havens" for criminals seems to be non-realistic. This is due to the lack of EUMM's access to Abkhazia and the Tskhinvali / South Ossetia regions. Still, in the Georgian case, EU conditionality could work well: both the visa facilitation mechanism and the already signed AA with Georgia could be an indirect tool to attract the disempowered and underdeveloped societies of the breakaway regions. At the same time making isolated societies stronger could enhance the opportunity for both - isolated populations and the EU - to tackle the security issues at stake. At a certain point it must also be considered that the organised crime and corruption index is substantially worse in Abkhazia / Tskhinvali provinces as compared with the rest of the territory of Georgia, [76] still the recent challenges discussed above reveal that control over organised crime by official Tbilisi might

---

[74] See "Compromise Achieved at Russia's Negotiations with EU and Lithuania on Kaliningrad Problem", 23.04.2003, available at <http://english.pravda.ru/news/russia/23-04-2003/48887-0/#.VHAnmfTF-yc>.

[75] *Sasse,* The European Neighborhood Policy and Conflict Management: A Comparison of Moldova and the Caucasus, in *Hughes* (ed.), EU Conflict Management, (2010) at 101.

[76] See sub-paragraph 2.4.

be fragile. Whatever the developments in Georgia in the near future will be, they shall not hinder the EU to apply its experience from South Eastern Europe and the three Baltic States in terms of promoting freedom of movement with the goal of integrating isolated populations while keeping in mind that the Russian Federation strives to remain the key actor in the region.

EU assistance regarding the free movement of people who are residing in the "frozen-conflict" zones will not ensure that scales of organised crime and corruption will be diminished in those regions immediately. However, it could lead to positive spillover effects, contributing to a safer neighbourhood for the EU.

Aelita Orhei and Lita Surmava

Towards Harmonisation in State Aid Law: The Case of Moldova and Georgia

"Title IV Chapter 10 AA EU-Georgia

Art 206: Subsidies

1. For the purpose of this article, a 'subsidy' is a measure which fulfils the conditions of Article 1 of the SCM Agreement irrespective whether it is granted in relation to the production of goods or the supply of services and which is specific within the meaning of Article 2 of that Agreement.

2. Each Party shall ensure transparency in the area of subsidies. To thas end, each Party shall report every two years to the other Party on the legal basis, the form, the amount or the budget and, where possible, the recipient of the subsidy granted by its government or a public body in relation to the production of goods. Such report is deemed to have been provided if the relevant information is made available by each Party on a publicly accessible website.

3. On request of a Party, the other Party shall promptly provide information and respond to questions pertaining to particular subsidies relating to the supply of services."

"Title V Chapter 10 Section 2 AA EU-Republic of Moldova

Art 339: General principles and scope

1. State aid granted by the Union or the Republic of Moldova, or through the resources of one of the Parties, in any form whatsoever, which distorts or threatens to distort competition by favouring certain undertakings or the production of certain goods and services that affects trade between the Parties, shall be incompatible with this Agreement.

2. This Chapter shall not apply to state aid related to fisheries, products covered by Annex 1 to the Agreement on Agriculture or other aids covered by the Agreement on Agriculture.

Art 340: Assessment of state aid

1. State aid shall be assessed on the basis of the criteria arising from the application of the competition rules applicable in the EU, in particular Article 107 of the Treaty on the Functioning of the European Union and interpretative instruments adopted by the EU Institutions, including the relevant jurisprudence of the Court of Justice of the European Union.

2. The obligations deriving from this Article shall apply within five years from the date of entry into force of this Agreement."

1. INTRODUCTION

Both Moldova and Georgia are similar to each other in certain aspects of their political and economic situations. This could well be the reason why their political leaders (but also the politicians of many other countries) opted for EU integration. One of the attractions of EU integration is undoubtedly gaining access to a large common market. But the demands that come with it, in particular in the field of state aid, also pose questions.

One could ask "*why*?" do countries like Georgia and Moldova need to have a state aid system like the EU does, if no membership perspective is actually promised. Promoters of reforms have to "sell" the European solutions back home in order to get the laws passed in Parliament and to preserve peoples' trust and be re-elected for a new mandate. This does not look like an easy task because one has to answer a series of stakeholders' questions related to the envisaged reforms, like: *"who will cover the expenses?"*, *"what will the benefits be?"* and *"what will the changes be?"*

In the case of state aid, the authorities who are usually granting aid (government, ministries, local authorities and companies with publicly controlled shareholding) and the market players which receive aid may be uncomfortable with introducing a monitoring system and a ban on state aid. As in Moldova, the market players are well-organised and have created a consultation body under the government. It is interesting to see what the "say" of this group will be, because on the one hand, the ban on state aid helps to create genuine competition; and on the other hand, those market players which received aid, shall abstain from receiving more aid in the future.

2. PREREQUISITES FOR MOLDOVA'S AND GEORGIA'S EU HARMONISATION CHOICE

2.1. Economy of Moldova

The Republic of Moldova's transition to a market economy was marked by a particularly prolonged and deep recession. Although growth finally re-started in the year 2000, the strength of the recovery from 2000 onwards was weaker than in other neighbouring countries. This was largely due to Moldova's high vulnerability to external shocks and adverse internal conditions. Nearly 2,000 small, medium, and large enterprises and 80 % of all housing units have been privatised based on a programme begun in March 1993. Almost all agricultural land passed from state to private ownership.

Real GDP in 2005 was still less than half of the 1989 level. This was one of the worst performances amongst the transition countries listed by the EBRD. Economic growth has also been affected by the fact that most Moldovan industry, including electricity generating plants, are located in breakaway Transnistria. The country's real GDP of USD 1,000 per capita was the lowest in Europe. Although the manufacturing sector, specialised in textiles and leather products, has been recovering,

Moldova's economy has a large agricultural sector which accounted for only almost one fifth of GDP in 2004. Agricultural and food-processing products accounted for 54 % of all exports in 2004.

Substantial emigration (close to 400,000 Moldovans were estimated to be working abroad in November 2004 - 2006) has resulted in a strong and growing influx of worker's remittances. According to official National Bank of Moldova statistics, the overall level was estimated at USD 900 million which represented close to 30 % of Moldovan GDP. Remittances are thus a key feature of economic development and social life and have contributed directly to reducing poverty. Investment is picking up and is beginning to replace remittances as the main source of growth which is an encouraging sign that the earlier model of consumption-driven growth is changing to a more sustainable one.

2.2. Economy of Georgia

Like many other post-Soviet countries, Georgia went through a period of sharp economic decline during the 1990s, with high inflation and large budget deficits due to persistent tax evasion. The situation started to change mainly after the year 2000. Georgia's macroeconomic performance and general progress with reforms in the past years have been strong. Georgia achieved significant economic growth mainly driven by large foreign capital inflows.[1] Foreign investments across different sectors of the economy have contributed to broadening the economic base. Domestic credit grew rapidly, supported by increased confidence in the banking sector and access to international financial markets, and the level of dollarisation gradually decreased. Progress with structural reforms has also been significant. The main achievements included significant improvements in the legal and regulatory framework for business creation and operations including liberalisation of the customs regime, reduction of corruption, simplification of the tax system and completion of large-scale privatisation across different sectors of the economy.

Notwithstanding significant progress, government effectiveness and regulatory quality (although in line with or slightly above the transition country average) still falls below the standards of advanced countries. Regional instability had a perceived impact on the functioning of state institutions and almost 80 % of Georgian firms in the 2008 / 2009 Business Environment and Enterprise Performance Survey (BEEPS) reported that political uncertainty is an obstacle to their operations.[2]

The financial crisis has highlighted the need to further diversify and widen the economic base. Although it has broadened significantly in recent years, growth is mainly driven by financial services and the construction sector. Developing the trade sector, by supporting exports and improving competitiveness, and promoting import substitution through domestic manufacturing, in particular in the agribusiness, are important for long-term sustainable growth. Further improvements of the business climate are necessary to boost confidence and attract more foreign invest-

1 Foreign investments of about 15 % of GDP in 2006-2007 across different sectors have contributed to consolidating the economy.

2 See <www.ebrd-beeps.com>.

ments. These include improvement in property rights, independence of the judiciary, and a further reduction in corruption.

2.3. Politics and laws in Moldova

From the 90's onwards, Moldova's legal system was reformed from a communist to a democratic one. International experts noted that legislation was quite modern (more progressive than in many prosperous countries), but only "in the books". In reality, Moldova faces corruption, and institutions are seen as still weak, due to insufficient funding and education provided to personnel. The trainings offered by many programmes lack the desired impact because institutions suffer from a high personnel fluctuation, as the jobs for the government are generally seen as low-paid.

By 2005, Moldova began to harmonise its laws with those of the EU. The law-making process has changed tremendously and so did the whole legal system. A compulsory compliance check with EU law was introduced into the legislative process. The authors of draft laws are required to present to the Centre of Harmonisation (under the Ministry of Justice) an assessment of compatibility of the proposed act with EU law. The Centre reviews the compatibility and passes the act further on to Parliament.

2.4. Politics and laws in Georgia

Georgia is committed to the principles of multiparty democracy, pluralism and market economics. There have been notable achievements on this path in recent years, including the peaceful transfer of power through a free and fair election on 1 October 2012.

The basis for this political system was established by the Rose Revolution of November 2003. The post-revolutionary Government pursued a reform programme aimed at reviving the national economy, improving living standards of the population and reducing poverty. The fight against corruption was put at the centre of the reform agenda. To continue the path of building strong democratic institutions and the rule of law the new Government announced a broad reform programme, including plans on healthcare, social protection, and employment reforms. In external relations, the Government confirmed that Georgia's pro-EU and pro-NATO aspirations remain intact. Relations with Russia have improved, and Russia has opened its markets to Georgian agricultural goods.

As for the legal environment, Georgia has implemented notable reforms in its legal system in the last years. It implemented changes to various laws dealing with the financial sector, entrepreneurial activities and tax law. In particular, the new laws have removed certain restrictions on the inflow of foreign capital and made it easier for foreign banks to enter the local market as well as facilitated integration of the financial system of Georgia into the worldwide financial system. However, the country continues to face considerable challenges in establishing legal rules and strengthening legal institutions. Although significant improvements in the legal and regulatory framework for business creation and operations have been made in recent years, including liberalisation of the customs regime and reducing corruption, insufficient understanding and respect for the rule of law do not allow for adequate and fair enforcement of laws by the judiciary.

3. WHY HARMONISE WITH EU LAW?

The less successful economic and political circumstances (mentioned in section 2.1. and 2.2.) and the desire for further economic development coupled with the attractiveness of the EU model prompted the politicians and the people of both Moldova and Georgia to look for closer relations with the EU, undertaking positive obligations of harmonisation with EU Law. The main point of attraction for both countries is the internal market - a defining element of the EU and its principal economic rationale which opens great economic perspectives for development. Art 26 (2) TFEU describes the internal market as "an area without internal frontiers in which the free movement of goods, persons, services and capital is ensured in accordance with the provisions of the Treaties", where the "free movement of goods" is at its heart and one of the principal freedoms of the EU.[3]

According to Art 3 TFEU, for the purpose of ensuring the effective functioning of the internal market, the regulation of competition is listed as an area of exclusive competence of the EU. Therefore the ban on state aid, which is implicitly an area of competition, is exclusively controlled and managed by EU institutions. The necessity of having a common competition policy within EU member states and more precisely, of having harmonised rules and standards within the EU, is dictated by the economic rationale of the internal market. A common regulatory framework is the only way to ensure the proper functioning of the internal market.

4. BASIS FOR APPROXIMATION IN MOLDOVA AND GEORGIA

4.1. Development of Moldova's and Georgia's relations with the EU

The foreign policies of both Moldova and Georgia at some point in time have been oriented towards EU integration. Both countries, in respect of their relations with the EU, have many things in common which they can share and build upon.

The relations of the EU with Georgia, as well as with Moldova, are currently based on the provisional application of the new AAs in addition to the "old" PCAs[4]

---

3 Art 28 and 29 TFEU.

4 Partnership and Cooperation Agreement between the European Communities and their Member States, on one part, and the Republic of Moldova, on the other part, signed on 28 November 1994 and entered into force on 1 July 1998, OJ 1998 L 181/3; Partnership and Cooperation Agreement between the European Communities and their Member States, on the one part, and the Republic of Georgia, on the other part, signed on 22 April 1996, and entered into force on 1 July 1999, OJ 1999 L 205/1.

which are legally still in force. The PCAs are framework agreements aimed at the development of political relations by establishing political dialogue, promoting bilateral commercial relations and development of investments, as well as by establishing economic co-operation in many other fields.

Both Georgia (since 2003) and Moldova (since 2005) are target countries of the ENP. Inclusion into the ENP was followed by APs - policy documents, adopted by the Governments of Georgia and Moldova jointly with the EU, which particularly served as roadmaps of reform to strengthen the democratic and economic situation of the countries, and therefore indicated the concrete steps for approximation.[5] Since 2008, both countries are also included in the EaP which aims at accelerating the growth of interdependence between the EU and the countries of Eastern Europe.

Recently, Georgia and Moldova within the framework of the ENP and their respective PCAs, signed AAs with the EU.[6] These AAs belong to a new type of external agreement negotiated and concluded by the EU and third countries. They are ambitious in that they go beyond the established framework of co-operation and open up a new stage in political dialogue and co-operation. The AAs, which are complemented by DCFTAs, will replace the EU-Moldova and EU-Georgia PCAs. Association Agendas replace the EU-Georgia and EU- Moldova ENP AP and will help implement the AAs through joint priorities for 2014-2016.[7]

4.2. Harmonisation with EU state aid law

4.2.1. Georgian and Moldovan PCA approximation clauses

EU integration efforts of Georgia and Moldova as regards state aid legislation have been specifically agreed in a series of agreements and political documents, including the mentioned PCAs and ENP APs. The new AAs have changed these obligations in some way. Notably, required changes including in the level of approximation required for different fields are not of the same for Moldova and Georgia.

A general provision concerning legal approximation was provided in Art 50 (1) of the PCA with Moldova, stating that the latter shall endeavour to ensure that its legislation will be gradually made compatible with that of the EU. The same ap-

---

5 The ENP AP for Moldova was adopted in 2005 <http://www.enpi-info.eu/files/interview/Moldova_May2010_ENG.pdf>, the full text is available at <http://eeas.europa.eu/enp/pdf/pdf/action_plans/moldova_enp_ap_final_en.pdf>. The ENP AP for Georgia was adopted in 2006 <http://eeas.europa.eu/delegations/georgia/documents/eu_georgia/booklet_a4_2.pdf>.

6 The AA with Moldova was signed on 27 June 2014 <http://eur-lex.europa.eu/legal-content/EN/TXT/PDF/?uri=OJ:L:2014:260:FULL&from=EN> and is provisionally applied since 1 September 2014. The AA with Georgia was signed on the same day <http://eur-lex.europa.eu/legal-content/EN/TXT/PDF/?uri=OJ:L:2014:261:FULL&from=EN>.

7 Please see the Association agenda between EU and Georgia at <http://eeas.europa.eu/delegations/georgia/documents/eap_aa/associationagenda_2014_en.pdf > and between EU and Moldova at <http://eeas.europa.eu/statements/docs/2014/140626_04_en.pdf>.

proximation clause, in a so-called "embryonic form",[8] was also provided in Art 43 (1) of the Georgian PCA. Furthermore, Art 50 (2) of the Moldovan PCA, and accordingly Art 43 (2) of the Georgian PCA, listed the areas to which the approximation clause shall extend. Among these areas were competition law, and thus state aid being part of competition policy had also to be approximated with EU law. The common approach to state aid issues was the requirement to establish a national state aid system which would be in line with the EU system, ensuring full transparency with regards to state aid.

It should be taken into account that Moldova and Georgia are not singular cases of slow harmonisation in the area of state aid. No PCA country has yet accomplished a credible attempt towards harmonisation, and state aid regulation remaines one of the most complicated and diffused spheres of approximation to EU principles for non-EU countries.

Unlike Georgia, Moldova is a member of the Central European Free Trade Agreement (hereinafter CEFTA)[9] and has assumed a similar obligation of harmonisation in the area of state aid. Art 21 of CEFTA regulates state aid, much in the manner as within the EU. CEFTA makes an express reference to the issue of assessment of unlawful practices of granting state aid on the basis of EU law principles, particularly Art 107 TFEU. The reference to Art 107 TFEU in CEFTA allows for the same broad interpretation of the scope of state aid rules as those developed in the case law of the EU courts. Moreover, under CEFTA Moldova was already required to establish a state aid regulatory authority by the end of 2010.[10] This obligation was complied with in 2012.

4.2.2. European Neighbourhood Action Plans

The ENP APs of Moldova and Georgia did not aim at replacing the existing bases of bilateral agreements (i.e. PCAs). ENP APs were built upon the PCAs and complemented them. Even though the EU generally practiced a regional approach, the ENP APs of Georgia and Moldova are partly different from one another. This is due to the fact that they have been elaborated in close cooperation with the respective Governments and take into consideration the needs of the particular country.

---

8 *Maresceau / Montaguti*, Relations between the EU and Eastern Europe: A Legal Appraisal, Common Market Law Review 1995, 1327 (1341).

9 Moldova, Albania, Bosnia and Herzegovina, Croatia, Macedonia, Montenegro, Serbia and Kosovo are CEFTA members. CEFTA objectives are to expand trade in goods and services and foster investment by means of fair, stable and predictable rules, to eliminate barriers to trade between the Parties, to provide appropriate protection of intellectual property rights in accordance with international standards and to harmonise provisions on modern trade policy issues such as competition rules and state aid. It also includes clear and effective procedures for dispute settlement.

10 See also *Schuebel* in *Stuart* (ed), State Aid Law and Policy – Approximation to EU Standards in the Republic of Moldova, International Consulting in consortium with DMI, IRZ, Nomisma, INCOM and Institute of Public Policy, Chisinau (2010) 3.

4.2.2.1. Moldovan ENP AP

The Moldova-EU ENP AP was adopted on 25 February 2005.[11] Although it is just a political document, it was of course of specific importance for the promotion of reforms with short- and medium-term priorities. Essentially, in the area of state aid, Section 37 of the ENP AP specifically declared that Moldova shall endeavour to implement state aid commitments under Art 48 / 2.2 of the PCA, by developing full transparency in the field of state aid, having as priorities:

1. to establish a binding, uniform definition of state aid which is compatible with that of the EU (either by legislation or by autonomous government act);
2. to establish full transparency as regards state aid granted in Moldova, in particular by:

(i) drawing up a complete list of aid grantors,
(ii) creating a national mechanism for centralising all information on state aid granted in Moldova, with a view to drawing up annual reports on the amounts, types and recipients of aid.

The Commission Progress Reports[12] referred to "some progress" in the sector of state aid since the national competition authority was only set up by the Government in 2007. Even so, it can easily be seen that the first Progress Report submitted in 2008 for the year 2007 was optimistic and expected speedy developments in state aid, while the subsequent reports only referred to a standstill situation. The 2011 Report noted that there was no progress at all in 2010. In 2011-2012 the Moldovan national competition authority has been active in drafting national legislation, which is now in force.

4.2.2.2 Georgian ENP AP

The ENP AP of Georgia was adopted on 14 November 2006. One of the priorities of the ENP AP was to "encourage economic development and enhance poverty reduction efforts and social cohesion, promote sustainable development including the protection of the environment, further the convergence of economic legislation and administrative practices". In the AP, convergence in the field of economic legislation practically meant approximation of legislation of Georgia to that of the EU, rather than a "common endeavour" to find a middle way as the word "convergence" would tend to suggest.[13] This presumption was

---

[11] Op. cit. note 5.

[12] European Commission staff working document accompanying the Progress Report Republic of Moldova (in 2007), Sec (2008) 399, at 11 and European Commission staff working document accompanying the Progress Report Republic of Moldova (in 2008), Sec (2009) 514/2, 13.

[13] *Hillion*, Thou shalt love thy neighbour… The European Neighborhood Policy Action Plan between the EU and Ukraine, in *Mayhew / Copsey* (eds), Just Good Friends? Ukraine, Belarus, Moldova and European Neighborhood Policy, Brighton, Sussex European Institute (2005) 17-25.

supported by Part 4 of the Georgian AP, on "General Objectives and Actions", whereas section 4.5. on "Trade-related Issues, Market and Regulatory Reforms" provided for the concrete approximation commitments listed therein. Subsection 4.5.5. "Other Key Areas" included competition policy and made the emphasis on the following points:

> Anti- trust and control of state aids policy shall:
>
> 1. ensure enforcement of the competition law, in particular by optimisation of the administrative capacity enhancing the independence of the Free Trade and Competition Agency;
> 2. converge with EU principles on competition according to Title V Art 43 and 44 of the PCA;
> 3. examine the possibility of establishing further transparency as regards state aid granted in Georgia, in particular by (i) elaborating general rules of state aid and (ii) drawing up annual reports on the amounts, types and recipients of aid.

Therefore, this part of the AP actually provided for the commitments of Georgia in the field of competition. Notably, the commitments were not limited to the institutional strengthening of the Competition Authority of Georgia, but also included the elaboration of general rules on state aid and convergence with EU principles on competition.

4.2.3. Georgian and Moldovan AA approximation clauses

4.2.3.1 AA with Georgia

Compared to the EU-Georgia PCA, the AA does not have a specific article under which Georgia accepts the obligation to harmonise its legislation with that of the EU. Different chapters are characterised by different approaches to harmonisation so that the level of approximation and the degree of specificity is different.

Rules on competition and subsidies are covered by Chapter 10 of Title IV on Trade and Trade-related Matters. The term "state aid" as such is not found in the chapter or the Treaty itself. Instead, the term "subsidy" is used. In fact, the only article relating to subsidies is Art 206 AA.[14]

Two questions come to mind when reading this provision: firstly, why is the term "subsidy" used instead of "state aid" (considering that in 2005 Georgia had introduced the term "state aid" into its legislation in order to comply with EU legislation)? And secondly, what is the degree and timeframe of approximation required in the field of "subsidies"?

With regard to the first question, a good guess would be that if the terms "state aid" and "subsidy" were to be used as synonyms, this would not raise a problem for

[14] Please see the exact wording in the introduction to this chapter.

Georgia in its internal dimension. On the international level, considering that Georgia is a member of WTO and its legislation shall also be in compliance with WTO legislation, using the WTO definition of subsidy instead of EU state aid will put Georgia even in a favourable position: Georgia would then not be obliged to strictly follow EU state aid concepts, but will refer to the WTO requirements regarding subsidies. On the other hand, WTO agreements and EU law shall not contradict each other.

With regard to the second question, it should be emphasised that a general provision stating that legislation in the field of competition or state aid shall be approximated with EU law cannot be found in the respective chapter.[15] Art 271 is more of a general nature and reads as follows:

> *"For the purposes of facilitating the assessment of the approximation, referred to in Article 416 (relates to the monitoring of approximation) of this Agreement, of Georgian law to Union law in the trade-related areas of Title IV (Trade and Trade-related Matters) of this Agreement, the Parties shall regularly, and at least once a year, discuss the progress in approximation according to the agreed timeframes provided for in Chapters 3, 4, 5, 6 and 8 of Title IV (Trade and Trade-related Matters) of this Agreement in the Association Committee in Trade configuration, as set out in Article 405(4) of this Agreement, or one of its Sub-Committees established under this Agreement"*

Although this article deals with the obligation to harmonise in the agreed timeframes, Chapter 10 (dealing with competition issues) is not covered. An analysis of other provisions on harmonisation in Chapter 5 also reveales that a direct obligation to harmonise competition law is not included in the provisions of the Chapter. This could be explained by the fact that the EU at the time of conclusion of the AA considered that competition law including state aid was already in line with EU legislation,[16] and that Georgia therefore shall be obliged to maintain its legislation which is already in compliance with EU and WTO legislation. In support of this argument, one may refer to Art 204 AA, according to which

> *„Each party shall maintain in its respective territory comprehensive competition laws, which effectively address anti-competitive agreements. Concerted practices and anti-competitive unilateral conduct of enterprises with dominant market power and which provide effective control of concentration to avoid significant impediment to effective competition and abuse of dominant position."*

The word "maintain" indicates that Parties acknowledge the fact that antitrust and merger legislations are already in place and respond effectively to WTO standards.

---

[15] Art 271 – 276 in Chapter 15 of the Title IV of the AA contain the general provisions on approximation.

[16] In fact, in March 2014 a new Law on Competition had been adopted in Georgia. On the details see below 6.2.3.

There is no similar article in respect to state aid. However, in some terms the obligation to maintain comprehensive state aid laws could be implied. Reasonably, it appears that the EU is shifting its priority from approximation of Georgia's legislation in the field of state aids to strengthening the capacity of the Competition Authority. The recently adopted DCFTA AP which covers the time period 2014 - 2017 supports this presumption. In its part on "Competition" the DCFTA AP provides for obligations to adapt the secondary legislation in the field of competition law and to strengthen the institutional capacity building of the competition authority (Competition Agency) of Georgia.

4.2.3.2 AA with Republic of Moldova

Art 339-344 of Title V Chapter 10 Section 2 of the EU-Republic of Moldova AA regulate state aid. As compared to the AA with Georgia, the term "state aid" is used (not "subsidy"), and the regulation of the country's obligations are more detailed than in the AA with Georgia. The spirit of the AA with regard to state aid takes into account the recent legislation of Moldova on state aid[17] and sectoral regulations developed by the Moldovan Competition Authority and is in line with the scope of the said legislation.

Art 339 AA states the general principle that state aid is banned,[18] providing an exception for state aid related to fisheries. Art 340 AA regulates the assessment of state aid, indicating that state aid shall be assessed in particular based on Art 107 TFEU and the interpretative instruments adopted by the EU institutions "including the relevant jurisprudence of the Court of Justice of the EU". The assessment obligations shall apply within 5 years from the date of entry into force of the AA. Art 341 deals with provisions on state aid legislation and relates to the competition authority. Moldova has to adopt or maintain, as appropriate, legislation for the control of state aid and to "establish or maintain, as appropriate, an operationally independent authority entrusted with the powers necessary for the control of state aid. This authority shall have inter alia, the powers to authorise state aid schemes and individual state aid measures, as well as the powers to order the recovery of state aid that has been unlawfully granted."

Art 342 of the Moldovan AA deals with transparency and reporting, stating that "Each Party shall ensure transparency in the area of state aid. To this end, each Party shall, as of 1 January 2016, report every two years to the other Party, following the methodology and the presentation of the EU annual survey on state aid. Such report is deemed to have been provided if the relevant information is made available by the Parties or on their behalf on a publicly accessible website."

Art 343 deals with confidentiality, meaning compliance with the limitations imposed by the requirements of professional and business secrecy when exchanging information. Art 344 is a "review clause" indicating that the parties shall keep under constant review state aid matters. Parties may refer state aid matters to the Association Committee on Trade (instituted by the Moldovan AA within the framework of

---

[17] For details on the 2013 Law on State Aid see below 6.1.3.

[18] Please see the exact wording in the introduction to this chapter.

regular meeting between representatives of the parties at ministerial level by mutual agreement). Progress in implementing the state aid rules shall be assessed every two years after entry into force of the AA.

5. EU STATE AID LAW

5.1. General framework

The EU is regulating market competition for more than 50 years. This is the reason why competition law is now a much-encompassing, detailed and developed area of law with extensive case-law, regulations and policy documents. The EU has six exclusive competences of regulation, among them competition. Harmonisation with EU law is therefore mostly about harmonisation with competition law, as this is the most relevant part of the *acquis*.

In order for a measure to qualify as "state aid", it is required that it cumulatively meets four criteria, namely: (i) it is a selective advantage; (ii) it is granted by the state or through state resources; (iii) it distorts or threatens to distort competition; and (iv) it affects trade between member states. State aid is generally prohibited, and only in well-reasoned cases it may be allowed. State aid measures shall be limited to situations in which market failures need to be corrected. Donours of state aid shall be allowed to interfere with competition in order to deal with market malfunctions only when the social aims of such measures may not be disregarded.

The aid may take any form implying a transfer of capital, non-collection of revenues or any other economic advantage such as tax exemptions, loan guarantees, reduction in social security contributions,[19] loans at preferential rates, exemptions from parafiscal levies, goods supply or service rendering at preferential prices, capital contributions, sale of lands[20] etc. The so-called "private investor principle" has been developed in European case law to differentiate a measure where the state has acted as a private investor and assumed informed decisions of making investments in order to gain mid-term or long-term benefits, from other measures, where the state acted as a sovereign power, irrespective of economic circumstances and perspectives of income.

The discretionary derogations or discretionary exemptions from the state aid prohibition are listed in Art 107 (3) TFEU, where the wording "may be considered compatible" is used, thus enabling the Commission to decide whether certain measures are compatible with the internal market. The exceptions to the general ban that are flagged by the strong wording "shall be compatible" are viewed as mandatory derogations or mandatory exceptions from the prohibition of state aid. While Art 107 (3) TFEU has been extensively interpreted by the Commission to provide a basis for tailoring measures to fit a wide range of policy objectives, Art 107 (2)

---

19 ECJ, case C-75/97 *Belgium/Commission, report 1999, Page I-03671*/ 3671, margin 23.

20 Commission Communication concerning aid elements in land sales by public authorities, OJ 1997 C 209/3.

TFEU is of a somewhat narrower use (and offers little discretion to the Commission).

It provides that the following shall be compatible with the internal market:

(a) aid having a social character, granted to individual consumers, provided that such aid is granted without discrimination related to the origin of the products concerned;

(b) aid to make good the damage caused by natural disasters or exceptional occurrences;

(c) aid granted to the economy of certain areas of the Federal Republic of Germany affected by the division of Germany, in so far as such aid is required in order to compensate for the economic disadvantages caused by that division. Five years after the entry into force of the Treaty of Lisbon, the Council, acting on a proposal from the Commission, may adopt a decision repealing this point.

When analysing aid which falls under Art 107 (2) (a) – (c) TFEU, the Commission does not have the discretion to decide whether to authorise such aid or not, it shall rather assess whether the conditions set out in Art 107 (2) TFEU are met, and if so, shall be obliged to authorise the envisaged state aid measures (mandatory derogations).

Art 107 (3) (discretionary derogations) provides that the following may be considered to be compatible with the internal market:

(a) aid to promote the economic development of areas where the standard of living is abnormally low or where there is serious underemployment, and of the regions referred to in Art 349, in view of their structural, economic and social situation;

(b) aid to promote the execution of an important project of common European interest or to remedy a serious disturbance in the economy of a Member State;

(c) aid to facilitate the development of certain economic activities or of certain economic areas, where such aid does not adversely affect trading conditions to an extent contrary to the common interest;

(d) aid to promote culture and heritage conservation where such aid does not affect trading conditions and competition in the Union to an extent that is contrary to the common interest;

(e) such other categories of aid as may be specified by decision of the Council on a proposal from the Commission.

Where regional economic development is sought, Art 107 (3) (a) and (c) TFEU allow the granting of state aid. While Art 107 para (3) (a) TFEU is of somewhat limited application due to the fact that regional development is assessed as compared to the "European" level, Art 107 para (3) (c) allows the Commission to approve aid for underdeveloped regions as compared to the "national" level. The beneficial effects of the aid must outweigh the distortions of competition. The Commission has developed guidelines[21] for examining the compatibility of national regional aid with the internal market under Art 107 (3) (a) and (c) TFEU. Criteria for granting aid include population density and unemployment level. According to the guidelines, it follows that the regional aid subject to the derogation of Art 107 (3) (c) TFEU is intended for regions which are less disadvantaged than those referred to in letter (a) of the same Article.

Art 107 (3) (b) TFEU is designed for two cases: (i) important projects of common European interest and (ii) serious disturbances in the economy of a member state. The Court underlined that the "common European interest" will be assumed if it forms part of a transnational European programme supported jointly by a number of governments of the member states or arises from concerted action taken by a number of member states to combat a common threat such as environmental pollution.[22]

The financial crisis helped to expand the case law of granting state aid based on the criterion of serious disturbance in the economy of a member state. The Commission acknowledged that the severity of the crisis justified the grant of aid on the basis of Art 107 (3) (b) TFEU and set out a coherent framework for the provision by member states of public guarantees, recapitalisation measures and impaired asset relief, whether to individual banks or as part of a national scheme. The primary rationale of the guidance in the Commission's communications is to ensure that emergency measures for reasons of financial stability guarantee a level playing-field between banks located in different member states as well as between banks who receive public support and those who do not.[23] Art 107 (3) (d) was added to the TFEU by the Maastricht Treaty in 1993.[24] It has been used as the basis for authorising aid to the film industry, as well as schemes for theatre, dance activities[25] and museums.[26]

5.2. *de minimis* aid

Regulation No 994/98/EC[27] empowered the Commission to set out in a regulation a threshold under which aid measures are deemed not to meet the criteria of Art 107 (1) TFEU and therefore do not fall under the notification procedure provided for in Art 108 (3) TFEU. This possibility of providing a threshold of minimal aid considered not to affect intra-community trade comes against the

---

21 Commission Guidelines on National Regional Aid for 2007-2013, OJ 2006 C 54/13.

22 ECJ joined cases 62/87 and 72/87 *Exécutif régional wallon and SA Glaverbel/Commission of the European Communities*, report 1988 01573, margin no 22.

23 European Commission *State Aid Scoreboard.* COM(2009) 661 final of 12 October 2009, 8.

24 Ex Art 87 (3) (d) TEC.

25 *Commission Decision*, Spain: Aid for theatre, dance, music and audiovisual activities in the Basque country, 368/2008 of 22 August 2008, OJ, 2008 C 281.

26 *Wishlade /Michie,* Pandora's Box and the Delphic Oracle: EU Cohesion Policy and State Aid Compliance *in IQ-Net Thematic Paper* (2009) *24 (2)* 19.

27 Council Regulation (EC) No 994/98 of 7 May 1998 on the application of Articles 92 and 93 of the Treaty establishing the European Community to certain categories of state aid, OJ 1998 L 142/1.

wording of the TFEU[28] and against the general line of case law developed by the ECJ. On the other hand, this approach was pragmatic because it allowed decreasing the workload of the Commission which was busy with "rubber-stamping" as such measures were clearly permissible, and set free the Commission's resources to focus on serious infringements of state aid law.

While notification is not required, the monitoring requirements are quite firm:

1. the grantor of aid shall explicitly inform the beneficiary of aid that aid is given on the basis of Commission Regulation No. 1998/2006/EC;
2. beneficiaries / recipients shall provide a declaration about other *de minimis* aid received during the past 3 years;
3. member states shall record all the information according to the *de minimis* Regulation and shall maintain such records for the next 10 years since granting the aid.

Alternatively, it should be possible to ensure that the ceiling is respected by means of a central register. It follows that if the member states are not obliged to keep a central register, compliance with the *de minimis* rule can be assured only if the beneficiary is one of good faith and declares the true and exact amount received in the past three years.

5.3. General Block Exemption Regulation

Under the General Block Exemption Regulation (hereinafter GBER)[29] more categories of state aid are added where notification is not mandatory. According to the scope of the GBER, it shall apply to the following categories of aid: (a) regional aid; (b) small and medium enterprises (hereinafter SME)[30] investment and employment aid; (c) aid for the creation of enterprises by female entrepreneurs; (d) aid for environmental protection; (e) aid for consultancy in favour of SMEs and SMEs participation in fairs; (f) aid in the form of risk capital; (g) aid for research, development and innovation; (h) training aid; (i) aid for disadvantaged or disabled workers.

---

[28] Please refer to the criteria „distorts of threatens to distort competition" and „affect trade between Member States" in Art 107 (1) TFEU.

[29] Commission Regulation (EC) No 800/08 of 6 August 2008 declaring certain categories of aid compatible with the common market in application of Articles 87 and 88 of the Treaty (General Block Exemption Regulation), OJ 2008 L 214 / 3 (14).

[30] According to Annex 1 of GBER the category of micro, small and medium-sized enterprises (SMEs) is made up of enterprises which employ fewer than 250 persons and which have an annual turnover not exceeding EUR 50 million, and/ or an annual balance sheet total not exceeding EUR 43 million. Within the SME category, a small enterprise is defined as an enterprise which employs fewer than 50 persons and whose annual turnover and / or annual balance sheet total does not exceed EUR 10 million and a micro-enterprise is defined as an enterprise which employs fewer than 10 persons and whose annual turnover and / or annual balance sheet total does not exceed EUR 2 million.

Other previously existing regulations, namely No. 68/2001, 70/2001, 2204/2002 and 1628/2006 providing block exemptions, have been replaced by the GBER for reasons of simplification.

6. Approximation to EU State Aid Law in Practice

The relevance of national state aid rules in Georgia and Moldova has increased in recent years due to developments in bilateral relations, including the fact that both countries signed AAs with the EU.

6.1. Moldova's institutional background

6.1.1. The national competition authority

The National Agency for Protection of Competition (hereinafter NCA) was instituted through the Law on Protection of Competition of 2000, but was created only in 2007 based on a decision by Parliament. The Agency was reorganised into a Competition Council with the final goal of increasing the institutional power of the NCA.

According to the Law on State Aid, the NCA's powers of investigation in state aid matters are similar to those in competition. The Law on Competition of 2012[31] is significantly tougher on market players than the old 2000 Law in matters of requesting information, initiating investigations, carrying out inspections on the premises of economic units and any other premises where relevant information may be stored.

Under the old Law of 2000, the NCA had to ask the support of police in carrying out its legal tasks, and it had limited powers to sanction market players for non-compliance with its orders to provide access to documents. Thus, the NCA's officials had to submit written requests to police and ask them to officially conclude that administrative offences were committed.[32] Under the new Law of 2012, the main tool of the NCA is the fine. Fines will be levied in cases where incomplete, inexact or misleading information are provided. The fines are relatively high, e.g. for infringing procedural rules they amount to between 0,15 % and 0,45 % of the total annual turnover, for infringing material rules fine reach up to 4 % of the total annual turnover, depending on the circumstances of the case. For delays to comply with an order or to allow an inspection, penalties of up to 5 % per day of the daily turnover will be due.

---

31 Law on Competition No 183 of 11 July 2012, published in the Official Gazette No. 193-197 of 14 September 2012, accessible (in Romanian and Russian) at the official legislation portal <http://lex.justice.md/index.php?action=view&view=doc&lang=1&id=344792>. This Law replaced the earlier Law No. 1103 of 30 June 2000 on the Protection of Competition.

32 Code on Administrative Offences No. 218 of 24 October 2008, published in the Official Gazette 3-6 of 16 January 2009 allows a multitude of public authorities to sanction administrative offences.

The NCA has co-operated with the European Commission through its Directorate General for Competition, the European Commission Delegation in Moldova, the World Bank and also with competition authorities of a number of member states by concluding co-operation agreements e.g. with Austria, Bulgaria, Romania and Hungary. Such international contacts have had beneficial implications for creating a strong state aid authority in Moldova.

6.1.2. The courts: inexperienced in what is called "state aid"

Moldovan courts usually take an active role in penalising market players which show an unlawful conduct in the market and / or infringe competition rules. Since its creation in 2007 and until 2011, the NCA brought 109 cases to court, out of which 72 cases have been finalised. Of these, 55 were ruled in favour of the NCA (76.3 %). However, the NCA has indicated[33] that its lawyers face a difficult time in convincing the judges of the sometimes revolutionary concepts introduced by the Law on State Aid into Moldovan legislation.

In the past, specialised economic courts had dealt with competition matters.[34] The judges working in such courts had typically a good knowledge of economic aspects and dealt with litigations of a commercial nature between companies, insolvency cases, intellectual property and licenses misuse cases, etc. Since March 2012 these economic courts were liquidated and commercial cases were distributed to general courts.[35] The general courts, now in charge of competition matters, are rather traditional and like to preserve some common decision-making practice. Thus, it will probably take time and effort to educate judges in the new competition law matters, including state aid, and it will be even more difficult to explain why aid given by the state is illegal given that it distorts competition and affects trade.

A central element of a realistic development strategy for state aid law and policy is the training of judges in competition law and economics and more specifically in state aid. It should be ascertained that it is impossible to enforce state aid law without proper application of substance and procedures by courts. The courts are an essential element of the institutional state aid enforcement. There is no win-win situation to have the NCA's decisions cancelled by courts - as last instances when market players know they will go bankrupt if the NCA's decision on the recovery of aid is enforced. In any case, huge efforts shall be assumed to train and retrain judges from general courts to comprehend the European approach to internal market, competition and state aid law.

Since 2002, the Competition Directorate-General of the European Commission operates a subsidies programme dedicated to the training of national judges in EU

---

33 The opinion was expressed in a meeting with the author [*Orhei*].

34 *Mateus,* IBF International Consulting in consortium with DMI, IRZ, Nomisma, Incom and Institutute of Public Policy, *"Competition Law and Policy – approximation to EU standards in the Republic of Moldova"*, Chisinau, 2009, 117.

35 Law No 29 of 06 March 2012 on the amendment of some legislative acts, published in the Official Gazette No 48 of 13 March 2012, accessible (in Romanian and Russian) at the official legislation portal <http://lex.justice.md/md/342444/>.

competition including state aid law[36] and judicial co-operation between national judges. Approximately 30 projects have now been co-financed, involving more than 3,500 national judges.[37] It would be advisable to offer to judges from third countries (at least those from specialised panels or from Supreme Courts) also the possibility of participating in some of such trainings. Additionally, the NCA shall organise trainings of communicating state aid rules to the judiciary, but also to attorneys and the staff of grantors of aid. In particular, the Commission's guidelines interpreting legal provisions for ease of understanding[38] are also a "lessons-learned" document from the EU experience. The NCA has recently actively used its soft-law making powers to improve enforcement of state aid rules where it becomes aware of deficiencies in implementing the Law on State Aid in the future.

6.1.3. The Moldovan Law on State Aid

After initial attempts to lobby a new Law on State Aid in 2008, the Law was finally drafted by the NCA with the assistance of international experts.[39] It passed Parliament in 2012[40] and entered into force in August 2013. However, this national legal act is only partially compatible with EU state aid law because the lawmakers decided to gradually introduce the state aid system and design the Law rather for the "national competition dimension" than for the "EU dimension". According to the calculations of the NCA, as from 2009 the amount of state aid given was of 1.3 billion Moldovan lei (i.e. approximately 81 million Euro).

Compared to EU law where the limitation period is 10 years, the limitation period in Moldova is 6 years. According to the Moldovan law, the *de minimis* threshold

---

36 Projects include: Italian project: " EC Competition and State Aid Law training and judicial co-operation network: Building Bridges between EC Institutions, National Judiciary and the Universities across Europe", duration: February 2011 - June 2012; German project: "Training of the Polish Judiciary on the Enforcement of EU State Aid Rules", duration: October 2010 - June 2012; Greek project: "Training of National Judges in EU Competition Law: Anticompetitive Agreements, Unilateral Conduct, Mergers, State Aid", duration: October 2010 - June 2012; German project: "Training of the Finnish and Estonian Judiciary on the Enforcement of EC State Aid Rules"; German project: "Training of the Romanian Judiciary on the Enforcement of EC State Aid Rules", duration: October 2010 - June 2012.

37 See <http://ec.europa.eu/competition/court/training.html>.

38 Please see <http://eur-lex.europa.eu/LexUriServ/LexUriServ.do?uri=OJ:C:2013:209:0001:0045:EN:PDF> as well as <http://eur-lex.europa.eu/legal-content/EN/TXT/PDF/?uri=CELEX:52004XC1001(01)&from=EN> and <http://eur-lex.europa.eu/legal-content/EN/ALL/;jsessionid=gL2TThcL7GTTrY8X1Md9TY4wJx1GPJJQqz12pQSkcVDb2VZQDFSx!-569562209?uri=CELEX:52014XC0122%2804%29>.

39 Assistance was provided in drafting secondary legislation, guidelines and rules as envisaged in the final provisions of the draft Law on State Aid through the twinning project "Support for implementation and alignment to the policy in the area of competition and State aid in the Republic of Moldova". In the area of state aid, assistance for approximation of legislation was provided by Romanian experts.

40 Law No 139 of 15 June 2012 on State Aid, published in the Official Gazette No. 166-169a of 16 August 2012. It is available online in Romanian at <http://lex.justice.md/viewdoc.php?action=view&view=doc&id=344389&lang=1>.

is 2 million lei[41] (Euro 125,000), which is comparable to the EU *de minimis* threshold of Euro 200,000. Given that the Moldovan market is much smaller than the internal market of 28 Member States, there was room to establish a smaller threshold in order to ensure that the *de minimis* rule is justified.

There is an obligation to report the granting of aid to the NCA, either by the beneficiary of the aid or by the grantor, at the latest 12 months after entry into force of the Law (i.e. by August 2014). Unreported aid is deemed illegal and shall be recovered accordingly. Illegal and misused state aid shall be recovered together with an interest of 5 % added to the base rate of the National Bank of Moldova (for the past months of 2014 - 3,5 %) for the whole period in which the aid was at the disposal of the beneficiary, until full recovery.

The Moldovan National Plan of Harmonisation with EU Law for 2012[42] envisaged that the NCA passes secondary legislation in the area of state aid: (i) on a notification procedure; (ii) on an investigation procedure and (iii) on horizontal aid (aid for SMEs; employment and training aid; aid for environmental protection, aid for research, development and innovation; and regional aid). The mentioned secondary legislation was adopted on 30 August 2013, when the NCA passed a total of 12 decisions approving rules in the area of state aid. The documents are quite detailed and lengthy, and they are all inspired by EU state aid law.

6.2. Georgia's institutional background

6.2.1. The national competition authority

Until 2014, the Free Trade and Procurement Agency (hereinafter FTPA) was the institution responsible for competition in Georgia. The FTPA had been created as a result of the merger of the Free Trade and Competition Agency[43] with the Public Procurement Agency. Following the adoption of the new Law on Competition in 2014[44] the Agency was replaced by the so-called Competition Agency (hereinafter "the Agency") which is now responsible for competition in Georgia.

Compared to similar institutions in the EU Member States, the "Law on Free Trade and Competition" of 2012 had granted the FTPA only limited institutional powers. The Law of 2014 was intended to strengthen the Agency's administrative capacity as well as to increase its powers and independence. However, it appears that the changes were not substantial enough. The main concern which had earlier been raised regarding the "Law on Free Trade and Competition" of 2012 still re-

---

41 The initial version of the draft law on state aid provided for the *de minimis* threshold of 3 million lei (close to Euro 200,000).

42 Approved by Government Decision No 962 of 19 December 2011, published in the Official Gazette No 227-232 of 23.12.2011.

43 Created by the Law No 1550 of 3 June 2005 on „Free Trade and Competition" published in Sakartvelos Sakanonmdeblo Macne (Official Gazette) No 31 on 23 July 2005.

44 Law No 2159 of 21 March 2014 „Law on Competition" published in Sakartvelos Sakanonmdeblo Macne (Official Gazette) and online <https://matsne.gov.ge/index.php?option=com_ldmssearch&view=docView&id=1659450&lang=ge>.

mains: the Agency lacks power to issue binding decisions. The procedure of granting state aid requires that a state body shall notify the Agency about the aid it intends to grant. Notification shall include information relating to the recipient of the aid, to the amount of the aid and the assessment that the aid does not seriously distort competition. After receipt of these documents the Agency shall present its conclusion on the issue, and / or issue a recommendation to the Government of Georgia which shall take a binding decision on the grant of the state aid.

With respect to investigative powers, a few positive developments can be noted. Most importantly, the power of the Agency to request information from private as well as public undertakings is strengthened: the Agency shall have the authority, in case of not providing the requested information, to impose a fine [a fee of 1, 000 to 3, 000 GEL (equivalent to 490-1, 450 EUR)] on the person infringing the rule. Compared to the Law of 2012, the Agency is now also able to start investigations on its own. According to the 2014 Law, there are three situations to be distinguished: (i) a person who has information about unauthorised state aid granted informs the Agency about the aid, (ii) an economic unit (undertaking) to whom the granted aid is of direct concern, submits a complaint to the Agency, (iii) on the Agency's own initiative.

An aspect which still signals the lack of power and independence of the Agency is that the head of the Agency is appointed (and dismissed) by the Prime Minister of Georgia. In addition, the rules referring to the general procedure for the grant aid are drafted by and approved by the Government.[45] The statute and structure (act of incorporation) of the Agency also needs to be approved by the Government of Georgia.

6.2.2. The courts

According to the 2014 Law, the court in charge of competition cases, including state aid cases, is the Tbilisi City Court. Its effectiveness and trends in the field of state aid case law are yet to be seen, as they greatly depend on the proficiency and experience of the judges in the field of competition.

6.2.3. Georgia's new Law on State Aid

In 2014 the Government of Georgia presented a draft law on "Free Trade and Competition" to Parliament. This legislative proposal was part of the reforms which were planned by the Government. When the new Law entered into force on 25 June 2014[46] all previous laws concerning competition including the Law on Free Trade and Competition were abolished.

In respect to state aid, the new Law provides for new definitions, principles and procedures for granting state aid. The definition of state aid according to the new legislation is the following:

---

[45] In the Law of 2012 the Free Trade and Competition Agency was responsible for drafting general procedures for the grant of aid.

[46] Law No 2159 of 21 March 2014 (now called „Law on Competition").

> *"State aid (subsidy) - an individual decision made in respect to an undertaking, including tax exemptions, tax reduction or their postponement, discharging (write off) of debt, restructuring, providing loans on beneficial conditions, transfer of operational assets, providing of pecuniary aid , concession and etc.*

Art 12 (1) prohibits the granting of state aid in "any form to an economic agent or specific activity which distorts competition or creates the possibility for its distortion, notwithstanding certain exemptions listed in para (2) of the present article. According to the Art 12 (2) the following types of state aid may be exempted and do not require the consent of the Agency: social support granted to individuals on the condition that it will not cause the discrimination of the relevant product / service producer / provider; state aid granted in cases of *force majeure* or natural disaster situations; aid granted for the purpose of environmental protection; aid granted for the purposes of implementation of the rights or carrying out of obligations deriving from the Georgian legislation or international agreements to which Georgia is the party; *de minimis* aid granted individually (the amount of which is to be determined by decree of the government); and aid for the implementation of the important government projects, specifically designated by a decision of the Government.

According to Art 12 (3), the following require consent of the Agency and may be exempted if they do not substantially distort competition: aid for the economic development of the specific regions in the country (regional development); aid for maintenance of culture and cultural heritage.

Overall, the provisions on state aid in the new Law have been substantially changed. Under the old Law, the scope of the exceptions on the state aid provisions, as well as the list of measures not considered as state aid, according to the definition, were very broad and thus prevented too many measures from being caught by the state aid rules. In this respect the definition as well as the exceptions in the present law can be considered as progressive.

7. WHAT WILL STATE AID RULES BRING IN THE END?

The benefits of the Moldovan and Georgian state aid laws which are now seriously aligned with EU principles, are expected to be:

a) *Fair competition.* No one can guarantee that fair competition will instantly be achieved in countries like Moldova and Georgia, however progress will be made and certain positive results will be achieved. Some of the current unfair practices will be abandoned, while other practices will be used rarely. A "level playing field" will be created due to the establishment of a neutral platform for competitors who will have to design their market strategies in a way as to gain a market sector of their own. On the other hand, this requires companies' management to think of wise solutions to resuscitate the business or run into insolvency. A genuine market would be the best judge of competitors' performances.

b) *Consumer benefits and innovation*. Where a given market is not distorted by extensive and systematic state aid, competitors will have the incentives to come up with new products and services, to work on getting the best quality for the best price. The consumers would benefit from such effects, having the right tools to distribute market shares to competitors according to their performances.

c) *Transparency*. By effectively presenting a clear picture of all state aid measures, including those which are given as allowances or exemptions, the public and the market players shall be informed on how much aid was given to a company. If an aid is given contrary to the set procedure, it shall be recovered as "illegal aid", together with the interest set by law.

d) *Budget structure*. Due to the fact that the ban on state aid will be a part of the national legal systems, it becomes clear that the structure of the budgets will also be reformed. The money which was usually given as aid for diverse beneficiaries of such aid will be used for other purposes, presumably for institution-building and sustainable growth. The section of budgetary expenses will thus be decreased or optimised, and the section of budgetary income will register additional money due to the fact that no aids in form of non-collection of revenues or waivers from paying taxes will be provided.

e) *Accountability of politics and of officials for public expenditure*. By also having changed the Law on Public Procurement, the way of selling public property (this is now largely seen as illegal due to very low prices paid to authorities for such property) and control over privatisation of companies which are still state-owned, defining of what is Services of General Economic Interest (SGEI) and making a fair calculation of expenses incurred and price to be paid by public authorities for such services.

f) *Attraction of foreign investments*. Foreign investors might be encouraged to invest in countries like Moldova and Georgia due to the fact that such investors will learn, after duly studying the market, that there are no benefits granted by government to individual firms, which could eventually distort competition. Therefore the entry and operation of firms with foreign investments will more likely increase.

g) *Poorly performing firms will be eliminated*. Fair competition will strengthen the battle for market shares between firms, and thus, the poorly performing firms will naturally be eliminated. The elimination of firms is not a good outcome *per se*, as this means that jobs will be lost and the government will not gain revenues from such firms, but the positive outcome shall be that the competitors will focus on consumers by providing goods and services "of best quality for the best price". Non-gaining of revenues by government is also a tricky argument, as the government will actually save on "non-granting of state-aids" to such poorly-performing firms on the one hand and the revenues in a larger amount will be collected from those successful firms which gained the market shares lost by the poorly performing firms, when exiting the market. The loss of jobs is a serious concern which shall be taken into account by governments when deciding whether a notified measure shall be cleared or not.

h) *Industry will become more capital intensive.* By regulating state aid, the market environment shall become more competitive and provide more incentives to firms for further development, thus leading to a higher capitalisation.

8. CONCLUSION

In the authors' view, important steps have been taken to comply with obligations listed in the PCAs concluded with Moldova and Georgia and ENP APs with both countries. Also both countries have assumed certain obligations under AAs, where Moldova probably has to do more homework in state aid than Georgia. The fact that state aid laws are not perfect and are not totally harmonised with EU state aid law, the fact that such laws allow for too many exemptions and that the *de minimis* ceilings tend to be too high (125,000 Euro in Moldova and no ceiling yet in Georgia) shall not indicate *per se* that no progress has been made.

The good part of harmonisation is that business, grantors of aid, politicians and civil society understand the need and the rationale of having uncontrolled state aid stopped. Gradually, once both countries come closer to the EU, the latter will be entitled to require that more harmonisation is achieved by the countries.

For achieving transparency, public accountability and reporting requirements, it is very helpful that state aid registers shall be created in both Georgia and Moldova. Once a system of state aid is actually being introduced in both countries and the stakeholders get acquainted with it, the legal mechanisms, ceilings of aid, procedures and other legal and / or economic issues may well be adjusted in time, so that they fit the countries' needs and that they reach the goal of harmonisation with EU law for a deeper co-operation and mutual benefits.

Sebastian Birke
Die grenzüberschreitende Besteuerung von Personengesellschaften in ausgewählten Ländern Südosteuropas
Die Lösung objektiver und subjektiver Qualifikationskonflikte bei der Beteiligung eines in der Bundesrepublik Deutschland ansässigen Gesellschafters an einer in den ausgewählten Ländern Südosteuropas ansässigen Personengesellschaft

Die steuerliche Behandlung international tätiger Personengesellschaften ist eines der schwierigsten und umstrittensten Gebiete im internationalen Steuerrecht.
Diese Arbeit geht auf die typischen Fragestellungen ein, die sich im Rahmen der Beteiligung eines inländischen Gesellschafters an einer ausländischen Personengesellschaft aus ertragssteuerlicher Sicht ergeben. Ziel dieser Arbeit ist es, die einzelnen Schritte der Entstehung der Qualifikationskonflikte bei der abkommensrechtlichen Besteuerung der Einkünfte und Verluste prägnant zu bestimmen, um somit die Verbindungen zwischen den subjektiven und objektiven Qualifikationskonflikten zu verdeutlichen.
Bd. 3, 2012, 192 S., 24,90 €, br., ISBN 978-3-643-50347-3

LIT Verlag Berlin – Münster – Wien – Zürich – London
Auslieferung Deutschland / Österreich / Schweiz: siehe Impressumsseite